Picture This!

A GUIDE TO OVER 300 ENVIRONMENTALLY, SOCIALLY, AND POLITICALLY RELEVANT FILMS AND VIDEOS

Sky Hiatt

The Noble Press, Inc.
Chicago

Printed in the United States of America

Library of Congress Cataloging-in-Publication Data

Hiatt, Sky Sinclair, 1942-
    Picture this! : a guide to over 300 environmentally, socially, and politically relevant films / by Sky Sinclair Hiatt.
        p. cm.
    ISBN 1-879360-05-5 (pbk.) : $12.95
    1. Social problems in motion pictures. 2. Motion pictures—Catalogs. 3. Motion pictures—Reviews. I. Title.
PN1995.9.S62H5 1991
016.79143'75—dc20   91-50642
                                                          CIP

Cover photographs by Archive Photos Stock Photo Library

DEDICATION

This book is dedicated to Marlon Brando—the only actor to refuse an Academy Award for political reasons. And for *Sayonara, Viva Zapata!, Young Lions, The Ugly American, Ranoi, Burn!,* and *A Dry White Season.*

Also dedicated to:

Vanessa Redgrave	Michael Murphy
Sam Waterson	Michael Douglas
Robert Redford	Oliver Stone
James Woods	Kirk Douglas
Meryl Streep	Gregory Peck
Miguel Littin	Michael Apted
Jessica Lange	John Savage
Spike Lee	Jane Fonda
Martin Sheen	Emile de Antonio
Roland Joffe	Sidney Lummet
Costa-Gavras	Sissy Spacek
Timothy Hutton	Henry Fonda
Chris Cooper	Ed Asner
Stephanie Black	Vittorio de Sica
Chris Menges	Ennio Morricone
Zakes Mokae	Haskell Wexler
Barbara Trent	James Earl Jones
Lloyd Bridges	Beau Bridges
Elizabeth Montgomery	Georges Delerue
Jeff Bridges	Robert De Niro
Christine Choy	Gillo Pontecorvo
Frederick Wiseman	Barbara Kopple
Roy Scheider	Mary McDonnell
Alan Parker	Ken Loach
Gene Hackman	Elia Kazan

And

All the other socially conscious filmmakers and creative artists who are living up to Robert Flaherty's prediction and helping, through truth in art, to change the world we live in.

And

To Shannah, Tony, and Sonny for always believing in me, no matter what.

CONTENTS

INTRODUCTION / ix

REVIEWS / 1

APPENDIX I: Listing of films / 368

APPENDIX II: Listing of films by relevant issues / 373

APPENDIX III: Listing of films by director / 380

SOURCE INDEX / 387

INTRODUCTION

"The truly great films have yet to be made. They will not be the work of the large studios, but of amateurs in the literal sense, of passionate people who will tackle something without commercial aims, and these films will be made with art and truth."

ROBERT FLAHERTY, 1926

There are three reasons for writing this book: number one, to promote the films themselves; number two, to acknowledge the enormous commitment in time, talent, and philosophy the films represent; and, number three, to pay homage to the artists who have dedicated their careers to socially relevant film work. Many of these outstanding creative talents willingly submit themselves to a lifetime without wide public recognition or formal thanks from the society and the people they ultimately represent.

While many of the titles included here are well known to American audiences. Others, equally worthy or better, remain obscure because they were banned (*Paths of Glory*), blacklisted (*Salt of the Earth*), pulled from theaters for political reasons (*Come See the Paradise*), ignored by the publicity machine (*Daniel*), crushed by the critics (*Running on Empty*), or obscured by other films (*A World Apart*).

To be banned, of course, is to die. *Paths of Glory*, one of this country's greatest antiwar films, was not even *nominated* by the Motion Picture Academy of Arts and Sciences when it was released in 1957. Leafing through a history of the Academy and its awards, one would get the impression this genuine masterpiece of social realism did not even exist.

As we approach the twenty-first century, the manipulation of film media by conservative forces continues to occur, condemning many outstanding works of art and truth to go unreleased, unscreened, unpromoted, and unrewarded.

In contrast to the controls imposed on photography and other visual arts, the censorship of film media rarely makes headlines. Many doubt that censorship exists, and fewer yet are aware of the devastating impact these pressures are having on the trend in film media to unceremoniously obey conservatively orchestrated pressures every step of the way, from script development to the theaters and into video release.

But as insidious as these controls of the production and distribution routes are, even more immobilizing is the critical press. Institutionalized and highly credible, the critics have an extremely limited tolerance for films of humane intent. Socially relevant films are often labelled "moralistic," "somber," platitudinal," and "preachy." Over and over again critics advise Hollywood to stick to entertainment and leave social issues to the less popular, less accessible, less powerful media.

Among these intolerant critics there is a call for "art for art's sake," and an enthusiasm for judging art on "technical merit" alone. In a recent issue of *American Film*, Betsy Israel speaks for hundreds when she says, "The point is that films should ultimately be judged for their dramatic and technical merits, not because they do or don't satisfy the prerequisites of a *prevailing sensibility*" (emphasis added). To Betsy's kind, praising content is "to falsely praise," and the true purpose and definition of art is to have no purpose beyond line, form, focus, and hue. I'm embarrassed for these types of critics if they can't be embarrassed for themselves.

This belligerent bourgeois travesty of the critical review process, so eager to place aesthetics ahead of ethics, has produced such "miscreations" as reviews of *Class Action* making no reference to auto industry crimes; reviews of *The Trail of the Catonsville Nine* failing to note that the film was a reenactment of *real* events; reviews of *Harry and the Hendersons* omitting words like *hunting, animal rights,* and *vegetarianism*; and reviews of *Air America* unwilling to admit CIA secret wars or secret drug sales.

The rigorous dangers of anti-ethical, anti-activist reviewing becomes clear when we try to imagine *Judgement at Nuremberg* being reviewed without reference to World War II, the Nazis, the Jews, death camps, or other "prevailing sensibilities." What a bitter kind of humor that anyone could muster enough indifference to the times to suggest that the best way to review an anti-war film is to not mention the war.

Although commodified for commerce and deflected by irresponsible coercion, art has lost none of its potential for integrity. It was created to solder the loose spiritual and cultural bonds of tribal societies, to explain the unexplainable, to protect against the unknown. The heavily coded glyphs, totems, and symbols embossed on the built environment and cultural artifacts of earlier times reflected the legacy of generations. Art will always retain this high historical potential. And critics liberated from their own evolutionary heritage will always remain as useless to society as they want their art to be.

This book in some small way wants to redress and redirect the fancifully disabling tendencies of art sterilized by technical and commercial impositions. Art needs to reassert its historical purpose. Creative, conscientious minds must be *encouraged* to analyze problems and dramatize solutions and should be rewarded for it. Critics should begin judging a film by how closely it comes to saying anything at all. What does the film do for human rights? What does it have to say about hunger and bad ozone? How many millions were spent on the film and were they just spent to make more millions?

In 1976, in *Harper's Magazine*, George W. S. Trow, not quite baffled by modernity said, "My assumption is that art exists within truth and nowhere else. . . . Decadence appears first in the ruling group . . . and it appears as the will not to remember. . . . Part of the artist's work now is to educate receivers of art who will remember and act. No one ever suggested out loud that our attempts to have a civilization be abandoned."

This book is part of that idea. It is the beginning of what I hope will be a revolution in the reviewing and awards process. The Academy Awards need to be balanced by the World Awards, which would acknowledge excellence in social realism and courageous activism in the arts. World Awards would be given in long-overdue categories: best anti-war message; most accurate minority casting; best environmental awareness; best use of traditional music; best political message; best anti-racist message; best human rights message; best feminist message; best cultural awareness. These are the themes that need to be promoted and exalted. The discrimination against social responsibility needs to be redirected to cultivate "receivers of art who will remember and act."

Picture This! uses these ideals to measure films against their own artistic ethic. Only through true analysis will the genius of responsible filmmaking evolve toward the higher levels of social excellence that Robert Flaherty predicted so many years ago.

A NOUS LA LIBERTE
(FREEDOM FOR US)

With Henri Marchand, Rolla France, Jaques Shelly, Paul Oliver, Raymond Cordy. Produced by Frank Clifford. Written and directed by Rene Clair. Cinematography by Georges Perinal. Music by Georges Auric. France. French with occasional English subtitles. Black and white. 87 minutes. 1931.

Man against machine. Guess who wins?

Two inmates sit making toy horses in the toy horse shop of the local prison. They are singing. They work on each horse until it's done. They take pride in their creations—such darling toys for unknown children. So begins Rene Clair's classic example of a long-extinct Hollywood genre, which I will call "industrial dystopia." Our two prisoners escape. Louis (Cordy) becomes a rich and powerful phonograph manufacturer. Emile (Marchand) winds up working on the phonograph factory's stupendously repetitive and monotonous production line. In the plant, a mistake is sort of like a crime, which instead of sending you to prison threatens to push you out into the streets. Emile tempts the "firing squad" more than once. But Louis and Emile meet again, and Emile sees through to the emptiness of Louis' life and understands how his factory is more like a prison than prison ever was. Together they hit the backroads to nowhere, happy in their newfound freedom. Only a few directors ever could or would do what Clair has done, and they have all died. The prison scenes are outdone only by the mansion scenes, which are outdone only by the factory scenes, which it would be very hard to outdo. Clair questioned the logic of a work ethic besieged by arc lights and monotony. "[I] wanted to fight the machine which was enslaving man instead of contributing to his happiness. . . . The film is directed against . . . work when it is uninteresting and nonindividual." He worried about the spirit stripped of pride and purpose and the fate of executives immune to human compassion. If the predominance of mechanization and the subjugation of humans to industry once worried filmmakers or anyone else, times have changed, and this type of movie has become a creative impossibility. No one speaks the language any more. It's like our species branched off in the thirties—one branch multiplied and covered the land; the other made a few movies, wrote a few books, and died out.

Also recommended: *Metropolis, Strike,* and *The Crowd.*

ABANDONED FIELDS

Directed by Nguyen Hong Sen. Vietnam. Color. Vietnamese with English titles. 90 minutes. 1979.

Lives of Vietnamese families are dominated by air attacks and sniper fire during Vietnam war.

A few dedicated American filmmakers have told stories about U.S. troop involvement in Southeast Asia. Together, these films have created a picture of war and soldiering that condemns U.S. actions and degrades the image of combat. But, no matter how many conscientious American talents gather on the plateaus of cinematic promise, their combined creative energy can never tell more than half the horror story of Vietnam and the war we fought there. From director Hong Sen comes *Abandoned Fields,* an unprecedented film about how the Vietnamese see themselves and how they see the war that threatened their independence and nearly destroyed their country. The improbably uneven balance of power pits native boat people with rifles against American helicopters peppering the Mekong Delta marshes with low level machine gun fire. They come without warning in a relentless effort to kill everything in the Delta flats. Families, who must continually adapt to life in a militarized zone, are forced to use simple evasive strategies to survive—camouflaging themselves and their small boats with leaves, breathing through reeds submerged in the shallow, tropical waterways, hiding their babies in baskets. *Abandoned Fields* establishes the visceral omnipresence of the allied force invasions. Every day, these families face the uncertainty of their own mortality. Their lives gravitate around the assaults. When the boat people gather to plan their next defensive, there are speeches on the value of freedom. For them, to fight forever is better than to be a slave. They study the teachings of Chairman Mao and have organized themselves into cells according to the revolutionary ideas of Karl Marx. The Vietnam Cong have learned to live with war. Consciousness has been conformed to it, leaving no way open for submissions, regret, or surrender. This outstanding and evocatively photographed film is as lyric as it is tragic. Even at war, the Delta is lush and inviting. In fact, this Vietnamese production was criticized for being too beautiful. The land is beautiful, the people are beautiful. Some critics implied righteousness need not be quite so idealized. But, as a strategy for american audiences, it was probably not a bad creative decision. *Abandoned Fields* is about men, women, and children trying to survive against unnatural odds in a world we continue to know very little about. Subtitles are briefly and inconsistently screened.

Also Recommended: *Storm Over Asia.*

ABOVE THE LAW

With Steven Seagal, Pam Grier, Henry Silva, Ron Dean, Daniel Faraldo, Joe V. Greco, Sharon Stone, Miguel Niño, Jack Wallace, Chelcie Ross. Produced by Steven Seagal and Andrew Davis. Directed by Andrew Davis. Screenplay by Steven Pressfield, Ronald Shusett, and Andrew Davis, based on the story by Steven Seagal and Andrew Davis. Photography by Robert Steadman. Music by David Frank. USA. English. Color. 99 minutes. 1988.

One man takes on the CIA and can't lose.

"Not one CIA agent has ever been tried, much less accused of any crime. You guys think you're above the law, well, you ain't above mine." So says Nicola Toscani (Seagal) in his "make my day" solution to covert delinquency in government. And wouldn't we all like to think that five years of martial arts training and a facility for languages suits one to open the CIA appointment book and cancel all the appointments? This pop-art CIA expose, with a plot as complex as the central nervous system, has so many people moving around in it that it is impossible to keep track of them. Some are good. Some are bad. Just keep your eyes on Seagal (which is easy enough since the camera is chained to his leg through the whole film). He's tall. He's pure. He dresses well. He has the reflexes of a ninja cyborg. How did the CIA get on his bad side? Well, he used to be one of them before he became convinced they were "fucking barbarians," which he discovers in the jungle during the Vietnam War. He drops out of the jungle but meets up with the same living lice twenty years later as a cop tracking down a drug shipment in Chicago. And he will tear their opium scam apart one human being at a time. He will save the senator who's writing the expose, but not the sanctuary priests working to save people of Guatemala, Chile, and El Salvador from U.S. covert chaos. He's amazed there are people on death row for maybe killing one or two people when 50,000 have died in Central and South America from U.S. covert action. The CIA kingpin is Zagon (Silva), the drug Dracula with a heart of C4, a serrated scalpel, and a black bag of medicinal serums. Nico is immune to knives and serums. He's also immune to reality, so the CIA lives on. Seagal wants to alert people to clandestine operations that he reportedly knows about from personal experience. He wanted to focus on the CIA, but he didn't want to have to step out of the camera shot to do it. There are some nice quotes in *Above The Law*, such as Richard Nixon quoting Abraham Lincoln: "This is a nation of laws. No one is above the law, no one is below the law, and we are going to enforce the law. . . ." And Seagal: "Whenever you have a group of individuals beyond any investigation, who can manipulate the press, the judges, members of Congress—you are always going to have those who are above the law."

Also Recommended: *Air America*.

ADVISE AND CONSENT

With Henry Fonda, Franchot Tone, Charles Laughton, Don Murray, Gene Tierney, Walter Pidgeon, Peter Lawford, Burgess Meredith, Lew Ayres, Paul Ford, George Grizzard, Inga Swenson, Will Geer, Betty White. Produced and directed by Otto Preminger. Written by Wendell Mayes, based on the novel by Allen Drury. Photography by Sam Leavitt. Music by Jerry Fielding. USA. English. Color. 140 minutes. 1962.

Political rising star is almost ruined by accusations of communist background.

Sen. Robert Leffingwell (Fonda) has just been appointed Secretary of State. He's a nice guy. He's so nice that he believes in sustaining U.S.

retaliatory power at existing levels. The idea ripples the sea of senatorial calm. Someone is pretty sure Leffingwell must be a communist, and he is hauled in front of a subcommittee to answer such questions as: is it true he does not believe in war; did he belong to communist associations while in school; is he loyal to the United States of America? To which he answers, "I don't mind admitting that I'm loyal." As the vote shifts against him, Leffingwell confesses to the President (Tone) that he attended a communist meeting in his youth out of sadly misdirected curiosity. He is sorry. He withdraws his name from consideration. The idea seems to be that it's alright to face up to the witch hunters as long as you're not a witch, but you'll lose either way. Following Leffingwell on the road to political ruin, we memorize the inner-sanctimonious rituals of the U.S. Senate. "Honorable Senator, Senator from the state of , state of, state of . . ." "Will the gentleman . . . will the gentlewoman." I wanted to add them up for you, but I lost my afternoon cool—too much pompous circumstance in the political geography. Grizzard and Fonda rise above ritual—in Grizzard's case, way above, as in he's near hysteria the whole time over the sight of a good man losing out. Laughton's triumphal overtures will have you dreaming of a recall. Walter Pidgeon wants to convince us that senators are gods after all. *Advise and Consent* has a woman senator, Betty White, and minorities—Raul DeLeon is Senator Velez and Tiki Santos is Senator Kanaho. But none of these are lead roles. There is a gay man, played by Don Murray, who winds up committing suicide when Grizzard tries to blackmail him to support Fonda's appointment—sort of a smear trade-off. Most audiences will already know that the senate doesn't like commies or gays, but it may be news to them how leaders are chosen by deceit, and how legislation is passed like a rugby ball. Or how the future of the nation, the people in it, and possibly the world depends on who wins the chamber games and beauty pageants played out on Capitol Hill.

Also Recommended: *The Front.*

AIR AMERICA

With Mel Gibson, Robert Downey, Jr., Nancy Travis, Ken Jenkins, David Marshall Grant. Produced by Daniel Melnick. Directed by Roger Spottiswoode. Screenplay by John Eskow and Richard Rush. Photography by

Roger Deakens. Music by Charles Gross. USA. English. Color. 110 minutes. 1990.

Satire about the CIA covert war in Laos and the personnel that fought it.

Four hundred flights a day carrying four tons of cargo. The largest airline in the world. Legislators out for the propaganda tour. Drugs manufactured in abandoned soft drink factories. Heroin smuggling. It's 1969. You are in a bar somewhere in Laos, in a city not found on the maps. President Richard Nixon is on the television denying U.S. combat troops are in the country as the roof collapses under bomber fire. You are surrounded by wizened, wild-sky guys boozing it up and steering by a star. The CIA has recruited plenty like you through heavily veiled, enticing want ads from Kalamazoo to L.A., which was where Downey used to be a helicopter pilot before he buzzed rush hour traffic and got fired. He was too wild for L.A.; he needed a bigger sky and the freedom to risk his life whenever he felt like it. He and Gibson are front-line flyers for "Air America"—the covert airline branch of the CIA forces waging covert war in southeast Asia. "Covert" means it's all a big, big secret, so the men aren't technically even there. So if they are shot down by enemy fire, for example, they might say, "We aren't really here, so this never happened," or "This city doesn't exist." Gibson is a Buddhist who has a monk bless his plane before every flight. He's married to an Asian woman and they have two kids. They live deep in the jungle. He speaks Vietnamese. He does not believe in war. He's in it to pull enough scams (in his case, running guns) to retire. There is no pension program in Air America. But there are daffy air crashes and emergency landings like you've never seen, no matter how many wars you've fought in. And there are startling statistics and gritty close calls. When Downey asks Gibson what's going on in his head, he answers, "I used to rate all the wars by their politics and their Saturday night, but it's just not particularly true." Downey is very good in *Air America*, as is Gibson, whose real-life father moved his family to Australia during the Vietnam era so none of his boys would have to go to war. *Air America* is sort of a trick movie. It wants to be so entertaining that no one will realize what it's about. Fortunately, it didn't work. I knew what it was about and so did a lot of other people, some of whom called it un-American and a pack of lies. A friend of a friend told me, "There was a lot of stuff in it that shouldn't have been there." Right. They could have left out the CIA and made a movie about peace on Earth. Superb, air-oriented cinematography. Strongly sympathetic to the Vietnamese. *I'd see it again.*

Also recommended: *Swimming to Cambodia.*

AKROPOLIS

With Andrej Paluchiewicz, Zygmunt Molik, Antoni Jaholkowski, Ryszard Cieslak, Zbigniew Cynkutis, Stanislaw Scierski, Rena Mirecka. Produced by Lewis Freedman. Directed by James MacTaggart. Arranged by Jerzy Grotowski based on scenes from the play by Stanislaw Wyspianski. Photography by Albert Tolley. Polish with English voice analysis. Black and white. 70 minutes. 1971.

Polish dramatic reenactment of the World War II concentration camp life.

"We want a core of reality in art . . . something that can go beyond the statistics. These are the facts—to try to be artistic is to cheapen them." *Akropolis* is art unencumbered by artifice. The pretension that pulls art into its own decay is absent from this wrenching and ritualistic performance in which the actors hammer away at their resemblance to human beings. Limp rag figures represent the ghosts of the dead, tenderly draped over clothes lines or piled into waiting carts. "Wherever I step is a grave." Death is no longer repellent. "When are you taking me?" "We are going for certain questions." From the contorted bodies of the living come strangled voices. There are mass-like refrains punctured by outbursts, the jangle of repetitive syllables, and hoarse whispering. Here, in the death camps, vanity survives. There is romance and something like families—something like a small, forbidding town. The unmelodic proclamations of fear, hate, anguish, and torment rise up from the backdrop of grim stage settings. Before they open the door to the crematoria, they remind God of His promise to save them. "Who will follow me into the fire?" One by one they crawl through the door of the black box that sits on stage like a giant coffin. "They went and only the smoke remains." The shock of life generates more odium than death in this haunting version of Wyspianski's devastating stage play. The specter of history dominates the film. The victims have no secrets. Nothing can be hidden. They are exposed and have no personal barriers. They have no alternative but to confide in the audience and share the agonies of their life inside the Third Reich.

Also recommended: *The Last Seven Months of Anne Frank.*

ALL QUIET
ON THE WESTERN FRONT

With Lew Ayres, Louis Wolheim, George "Slim" Summerville, John Wray, Russell Gleason, Ben Alexander, Scott Kolk, Walter Browne Rogers, Pat Collins, Owen Davis, Jr., Harold Goodwin, William Bakewell, Arnold Lucy. Produced by Carl Laemmle, Jr. Directed by Lewis Milestone. Written by Del Andress, Maxwell Anderson, George Abbott, and (uncredited) Lewis Milestone. Screenplay adaptation by George Abbott and Del Andrews, from the novel by Erich Maria Remarque. Photography by Arthur Edeson. Music by David Broekman. USA. English. Black and white. 140 minutes. 1930.

Young men fighting in World War I question the morality of war.

"How do they start a war?" the boy in the trenches asks. "One country offends another." "Well, then, I shouldn't be here, because I don't feel offended." Lew Ayres has been anointed by youth's innocence to witness the horrors of war. A zealous professor was the one who convinced him to enlist. After a few weeks at the front, he can't remember much of what the professor said, and every death is a bewildering tragedy. The young troops, trying to make sense of the carnage, decide the war must be doing *somebody* some good—maybe the British, maybe the generals, maybe the manufacturers. Ayres survives long enough to go back to the classroom, where the professor is still encouraging implausibly young boys to bear arms. He tells them that war is worse than their worst nightmare. "You still think it's beautiful and sweet to die for the country, don't you? Well, when it comes to dying for your country, it's better not to die at all. There are millions dying, and what good is it doing?" The class heckles him, and Ayres decides war has made him unfit for civilian life. He returns to the front and is killed while reaching over the sandbags to rescue a baby bird from the line of fire.

Also recommended: *The Grand Illusion.*

ALL THE KING'S MEN

With Broderick Crawford, Joanne Dru, John Ireland, Anne Seymor, Katherine Warren, Mercedes McCambridge, John Derek, Shepperd Strudwick. Written, produced, and directed by Robert Rossen. Based on the novel by Robert Penn Warren. Photography by Burnett Guffy. Music by Louis Gruenberg. USA. English. Black and white. 109 minutes. 1949.

Favorite son runs for public office and tries to hold out for his high ideals, but sinks under the weight of reality.

It pays to trust no one, especially working-class types who belly-flop into the governor's mansion on a save-the-world ticket. Broderick Crawford inhabits a Bermuda Triangle of skullduggery and corruption, outdoing the despotic incumbent he replaced. It's mortifying to watch. He'll build a free hospital if he has to break every law to do it. He deals, he steals, he bribes, he treatens. We like him, though; that's the funny part. You've got to like him because he's good at heart. He can tell right from wrong, which the former administration could not. But what's he doing now? It looks like one more bribe will fix everything. One more deal will close the door on corruption forever. It gets harder and harder to stand behind him. Crawford was born for this role as a man obsessed with out-shafting the system. He doesn't need a full moon to transform his entire personality. His guide is a pre-Watergate road map to political suicide, along the byways of which all his early supporters—except John Ireland, an idealistic newspaper reporter—dive for cover. *All The King's Men* is an autopsy on tactical goodness. The film earned five stars in *The Motion Picture Guide.* Some critics seem to love stories about how the good guys go wrong no matter how hard they try not to. The plot is a maze. After watching this movie, I'm pretty sure I'd never want to run for public office. The women in *All The King's Men* are nobody types. But the screenplay and photography are classic and John Ireland is just a saint.

Also recommended: *The Great McGinty.*

ALL THE PRESIDENT'S MEN

With Robert Redford, Dustin Hoffman, Martin Balsam, Stephen Collins, Jason Robards, Hal Holbrook, Jack Warden, Robert Walden, Ned Beatty, Jane Alexander, Meredith Baxter. Produced by Walter Coblenz. Directed by Alan J. Pakula. Screenplay by William Goldman, based on the book by Carl Bernstein and Bob Woodward. Photography by Gordon Willis. Music by David Shire. USA. English. Color. 138 minutes. 1976.

Two newspaper reporters uncover government corruption, leading to the downfall of the incumbent President.

All except the actual participants may need a study guide to keep up with the flash-fire of conspiracies that are going to detonate in the Oval Office and smear the all-time king of smear campaigns across the headlines of history. "They planted bugs, followed people, wrote fake letters, planted spies, stole documents, planted false press leads, investigated private lives, canceled Democratic campaign rallies, and on and on . . ." Bob Woodward (Redford), a reporter for the *Washington Post,* is covering a break-in at the Watergate complex. He hears the suspects identify themselves as: "anti-communist," "security consultant," "former CIA operative." An uptown lawyer witnessing the spectacle has "nothing to say. I have nothing to say. I am not here. I have nothing to say." Woodward and fellow reporter Carl Bernstein (Hoffman) crank out an investigation that will turn them into household words. All they want are answers to the Stonehenge-like codes suggesting names and more names. Denials are issued before accusations are made. People reverse what they have just said, if they are not too troubled to speak in the first place. The FBI, the CIA, the Justice Department, the Special Council to the President—"the list is longer than anyone can imagine. It leads everywhere." So says "Deep Throat" (Holbrook). A variety of seemingly unrelated events all have one element in common—the Committee to Re-elect the President. As the D.C. police department sits by contentedly with its line-up of suspects, criminal conspiracies rage. Woodward and Bernstein begin to merge into "Woodstein," the pair that would put Jimmy Carter into the White House. Jason Robards and Hal Holbrook give hugely applauded performances. Redford and Hoffman work like a true team (Redman?). And this film manages to transmute complex recent history into dramatic panache. At 138 minutes, the story still seems too short, and the end too sudden. We want to see Nixon's last press conference and his helicopter ride to nowhere. Instead, monster typewriter keys pound out the indictments, the verdicts, the sentences—Erlichman, Halderman, Mitchell, guilty, guilty, guilty. Critics inclined to find something wrong with *All The President's Men* cringed at the use of four-letter words, "obviously included at the insistence of some nitwit movie executive." Well, sure.

Also recommended: *Cover-Up.*

ALPHAVILLE
(LEMMY CAUTION)

With Anna Karina, Eddie Constantine, Akim Tamiroff. Produced by Andre Michelin. Written and directed by Jean-Luc Godard. Photography by Raoul Coutard. Music by Paul Misraki. France. French with English titles. Black and white. 97 minutes. 1964.

Evil computer of the future has outlawed emotion and stunted the happiness of the people of Alphaville.

"Sometimes reality is too complex for oral communication." Or visual elucidation. Godard is so committed to the incomprehensibility of the future that he wants to test our ESP quotients in the present, following P.I. Lemmy (Constantine) around the mystery beltway of Alphaville. It's not Urdu, but it won't hurt to be a legend in your own time when it comes to holding many mutually obscure clues in your head long enough to figure out what they mean. Alphaville is named after the computer, Alpha-60, that controls the city and has outlawed emotion. Emotion is out. Love, passion, anger, and fear are the new pathologies. And the laws are heavily enforced. I'm thinking that if I were a director,

I'd be intimidated by this dramatic limitation. Of course, Godard is not. He's fascinated by Lemmy and his unrepressed hostility to everything and everybody. he's risking his life throwing people against walls and trying to get facts. He's a savior. He's not afraid of Alpha-60. Maybe that's because he only has one emotion to lose—a cross between hostility and indifference. He's come to this place to be where people do things without caring and say things without feeling. Lemmy is after something, but we don't know what. The movie is a ceremony of lost-age mufflings. There are torrents of philosophizing: "The present is the form of all life." "Time is like a circle, endlessly described." "The acts of men carried over from the generations, will destroy them logically." "Minimize all unknown quantities." Heavens, yes. But maybe with more artistic distractions like great scenery, dynamic acting, special effects, appealing people, humor—just to keep us invested in the mystery plot. Forget about HAL. Alpha-60 would have shut HAL down without any help from Keir Dullea because he developed emotions you see. For me, *Alphaville* was what *2001* might look like in a plain brown wrapper.

Also recommended: *Black God, White Devil.*

ALSINO AND THE CONDOR

With Alan Esquivel, Dean Stockwell, Carmen Bunster, Alejandro Parodi, Delia Casanova. Produced by Hernan Littin. Directed by Miguel Littin. Screenplay by Littin, Isidora Aguirre and Tomas Perez Turrent, based on the children's book *Alsino* by Pedro Prado. Cinematography by Jorge Herrera and Pablo Martinez. Music by Leo Brower. Spanish with English titles. Color. 90 minutes. 1983.

Nicaraguan boy is radicalized by the fight for independence against imperialist interventionists.

Alsino and the Condor has the gratifying urge to reveal what other anti-imperialist movies find perhaps too obvious and uninvolving: there is a communion of people, culture, land, and time that were once almost sacred and are now being destroyed by the violence of advanced capital accumulation. As the condor population decreases and approaches extinction, manufacturers of modern military apparatus use its name and that of other mythic species on weapons of mass destruction sent to oppress the Third World. Alsino has never seen a condor, but he has seen the harmony of nature and family life punctured by machine gun blasts and the roar of low-flying American Condor helicopters. Dean Stockwell is the American chopper pilot flying in and out of the Nicaraguan sky. He observes, "You're a communist or you're not, fucking period. That's it." Alsino admires Stockwell and vaguely endures his bawdy, incomprehensible lectures about getting an education and getting ahead. Alsino would like to get ahead. He'd like to fly like a bird away from the atrocities he sees every day in a country under attack by U.S. saturation bombing and commodity wars, code-named "Operation Preventative Medicine." While walking through forests unchanged since creation, he witnesses mass executions—whole families killed and left floating in lakes. He climbs the highest tree he can find and tries to fly but nearly dies in the effort and now is crippled. He will soon outgrow his infatuation with American pilots and come to understand what the war is about. He will add his broken body to the guerrilla force and take on the name of the anonymous terrorist—Manuel. He is just a boy fighting free enterprise, and will probably lose. Whatever novel interpretation his way of life may have imposed on modernity will never be known.

Also recommended: *Insurreccion* and *Uprising*.

AMAZING GRACE AND CHUCK

With Gregory Peck, Joshua Zuehike, Alex English, Jamie Lee Curtis, William Peterson. Produced and written by David Field. Directed by Mike Newell. Photography by Robert Elswit. Music by Elmer Bernstein. USA. English. Color. 115 minutes. 1987.

Young boy gives up baseball for nuclear weapons disarmament.

Chuck (Zuehike) is a star Little League pitcher in the middle of a winning season. His father (Peterson) flies jets for the National Guard. Their two worlds collide when a campaigning senator shows up and takes Chuck's ball team on a tour of the missile silos buried seventy feet underground near the Guard base. The silos house Minuteman missiles, which are sixty feet long, capable of traveling 16,000 miles an hour, and carry warheads that have twenty-seven times the explosive power of the bomb dropped on Hiroshima. The ball team is dazed. Except Chuck. He wants to know why the men in the control room are wearing guns. The Senator kneels down and looks Chuck in the eye. "Imagine your Daddy worked down here, Chuckie, and we had to fire these missiles to protect ourselves, but your Daddy started thinking about you and your Mommy and he hesitated . . ." Chuck goes home and tells his mother and father he's giving up baseball until they get rid of all the nuclear weapons. "Why baseball?" "Because it's my best thing. I have to give up the best thing." Nobody believes in Chuck. His friends on the team feel cheated out of a championship. His parents are not happy. He's alone in a protest nobody understands. So it's a nice surprise when Amazing Grace (English) of the Boston Celtics shows up to visit him. He talks to Chuck about what he's doing—how hard it is to be against everyone and what it's like giving up the "best thing." "I'm going to give up basketball," he tells Chuck, until they dismantle all nuclear weapons. Now they are together, without their best things, against coaches, teams, families. Soon there is an entire community of sports heroes who have moved into the old barn Amazing is remodelling. They have all given up their best things and are converting the barn into a control center for peace. Eventually, the movement infects amateur and professional athletics all over the world. Anti-war protests rise up in country after country. The President (Peck) is pressured to stop the sports-peace movement before it can infiltrate the military. He promises Chuck that there will be negotiations. But Chuck won't play ball until the nuclear weapons are gone. There are more interviews, more promises, and more refusals until a peace plan is outlined and all the weapons are dismantled at last. The president honors Chuck, who practices for the coming season. He dedicates the first pitch to Amazing. A lot of people who saw this film were critical of it for being so implausible. But the only really outlandish aspect to this movie is the hesitancy in each individual to act on their own beliefs.

Also recommended: *Project X.*

ANGRY HARVEST

With Elisabeth Trissenaar, Wojtech Pazoniak, Armin Mueller-Stahl, Kathe Jaenicke, Hans Beerhenke, Isa Hallner. Produced by Arthur Brauner. Directed by Agniezka Holland. Screenplay by Holland and Paul Hengge based on the novel by Hermann Field and Stanislaw Mierzenski. Photography by Josef Ort-Snep. Music by Jorg Strassburger. West Germany. In German with English titles. Color. 107 minutes. 1986.

Polish farmer rescues a Jewish refugee and hides her in his basement, where a new kind of oppression takes shape.

This is one story of many stories, mostly untold, of the Jewish refugees desperately fleeing the Nazi invasions in Europe. Many who escaped concentration camps would die of starvation or exposure or be caught in the crossfire of war. Rosa (Trissenaar) has escaped from a human cargo train. A man finds her running through the woods and hides her. She begs him to leave a signal for her husband in the woods. He hangs the scarf but does not tell her what he found that morning. He wants her to understand Christianity. He wants to save her for Christ and for himself. Her seclusion and her dependence on him destroys her illusion of freedom. He cares for her even though she's Jewish. He makes love to her. She does not respond. He accuses her of finding him revolting. She tells him her father and mother and sister and brother and husband and child are dead. She only survived because she fell asleep. "I'm asleep inside. Inside, I'm frozen. If I were to wake up, I would die. I don't want to feel anything. I don't want to love or suffer. I don't have the strength. I should kill myself." Through her urging he buys an orchard from a Jewish family needing money to leave Germany. He's not uncompassionate to human suffering. But, some Jews teased him as a child. She begins to imagine he'll report her to the authorities. The uncertainty is insupportable. Alone in the basement she slits her wrists into a bucket of water and dies another victim of the war. The sight of it destroys him. Someone is knocking on the door. A man is looking for his wife who jumped off the train in the woods. He's afraid she's been found by the Nazis and killed. After the war a letter arrives from America. Rosa's husband has married the daughter of the orchard family. They are so grateful to him for his generosity. It would honor them to name their son after him.

Also recommended: *The Boat is Full.*

ANIMAL FARM

Narrated by Gordon Heath. Voices of all the animals, Maurice Denham. Produced and directed by John Halas and Joy Batchelor. Written by Lothar Wolff, Borden Mace, Philip Stapp, John Halas, Joy Batchelor, based on the book by George Orwell. Photography by S.J. Griffiths. Music by Matyas Seiber. Great Britain. Animated. English. Color. 75 minutes. 1955.

Animals oppressed by the owner of Manor Farm revolt, and change its name to Animal Farm.

A sort of *Viva Zapata!* for kids. Farmer Jones is a mercenary capitalist whose slaves are the animals he abuses, underfeeds, and overworks, until the passive laborers are transformed into radical socialist-revolutionaries. When the animals gather in the barn to talk over their resentments, an aging pig says, "Few of us will ever know the blessing of peaceful old age." Having figured out what more advanced species still ponder, they complain, "Everything we produce is taken away from us—stolen from us and sold!" They break into the food bins. They unite and drive Jones off the farm. They write new farm rules: "No animal shall kill another animal." "All animals are equal." "No animal shall ever sleep in a bed." There is equality and fair reward for all work. But Napoleon the pig moves into the farmhouse and slowly gains totalitarian control over the other animals. He begins trading with the outside world, and he and the other pigs join together to reimpose the hardships of former times. All the baby pigs wear matching pink ribbons on their coiled pink tails. The other animals are prematurely aging from overwork. When Boxer the horse is injured and can no longer carry heavy loads, Napoleon cashes him in at the glue factory. The farm is surrounded by barbed wire. Now, "All animals are equal, but some are more equal than others." Animals are killing other animals. Animals are sleeping in beds. There's nothing left of the revolution. So, once more, the animals revolt. The pigs are dethroned, along with their pack of fascist hounds. The last we see of the freedom fighters, they are lined up before the cameras, reduced in numbers and tentative about the future, a somewhat different ending than the book itself.

Also recommended: *The Road to 1984*.

THE ANIMALS FILM

With Tom Regan, Dr. Michael Fox, Peter Singer, Sandy Dennis, Roger Ulrich, Lord Houghton, Betty Payne. Narrated by Julie Christie. Produced by Victor Schonfeld and Myriam Alaux. Directed by Victor Schonfeld and Myriam Alaux. Screenplay by Victor Schonfeld. Cinematography by Kevin Keating. Great Britain/U.S. English. Color. 136 minutes. 1981.

An in-depth look at factory farming, fur trapping, animal experimentation, and slaughter houses, among other things.

The numbers soon become irrationally large. Two-hundred and fifty million chickens living in battery cages; 360,000 pigs slaughtered each day; 250 million animals shot every year in sport hunting; 85 sables dead for one fur coat; 60,000 stray animals killed every year in New York City alone. One-half of all U.S. dairy cows are permanently stanchioned. A farmer explains, "Cows walking out on pastures use up a lot of energy. This way, they don't." Veal calves are permanently stanchioned. Breeding sows are permanently stanchioned. Ten-thousand animals are confined in two buildings, creating seas of excrement. Bulls are dehorned, castrated, and branded without anesthetic. Chickens exist four to a cage in permanent semi-darkness and are pumped with vaccines and antibiotics. One man can tend 50,000 birds. When egg production declines, they are butchered for by-products, canned soups, bouillon cubes, and gravy mixes. "The complete manipulation of their life cycle stands as a model for the exploitation of all other animals." Capital-intensive farming reflects the advance of big business and the collapse of the family farm. In a world of famine and starvation, feedlot beef are fed twenty pounds of plant protein to create one pound of usable protein in the form of meat. The impact of animal-based agriculture on the environment is a global catastrophe. The impact of meat-based diet on human health is a national catastrophe. In the U.S., vegetarians outlive meat eaters by an average of seven years. Schonfeld's cameras also visit research labs. Highlighted here is a study of pain response in monkeys. Electroshocked animals are punished with additional shock if they attempt to relieve their anguish by biting on a rubber hose. This research established that animals learn not to bite the hose by reverting to psychotic behaviors and self-mutilation. The Animals Film extends to the audiences the luxury of becoming informed about what they support through their market behaviors, eating habits, recreational pastimes, and perhaps even their work. Filmmaker Victor

Schonfeld omits very little from this heartbreaking voyage into the world of animal abuse—an appalling and horrifying chronicle of the suffering of innocent animals.

Also recommended: *Harry and the Hendersons.*

ANOTHER COUNTRY

With Rupert Everett, Colin Firth, Robert Addie, Michael Jenn. Produced by Alan Marshall. Directed by Marek Kanievska. Screenplay by Julian Mitchell, based on his original play. Photograph by Peter Biziou. Music by Michael Storey. Great Britain. English. Color. 90 minutes. 1984.

Impressionable youth are sent away to be educated by the British boarding school system.

Set in the present and seen in flashbacks to the 1930s, *Another Country* discloses some secrets for keeping the world constantly at war. In the English prep school, bullies, cowards, and cheaters are turned into future leaders loyal to anything they hear repeated more than five times. Beneath the identical blazers are future Third World career colonials and the next generation of executives, politicians, generals, and mercenaries. By the time they graduate, they will know how to propagate imperialism and authoritarianism and impose their will on others. Because the boarding school is a place where bullies rise to the top, loyalty is the self. Power is the ultimate achievement. The boys have created their own class divisions, systems of domination and harshly defined categories that segregate them into dominant and oppressed groups. Superimposed on this body of student laws are the equally totalitarian and dehumanizing rules of the academy itself. Professors are adult products of the same system, programmed to perpetuate the cycle. The characters spend a lot of time talking about the taboo of homosexuality. There are lashings, humiliations, and expulsions. Tolerance is unknown. The policy is "no queers and no commies." The Marxists read radical writings under the bed covers at night. They are cynical witnesses to a complicated class system pitting young men against one another in training for a world of even harsher inequality.

The most cynical of these radicals will wind up defecting to the Soviet Union and giving an interview to a young reporter before he dies, the device that frames the story of his school days. He will try to explain how England rejected him while he was still a child. Another student, an ardent Marxist, will die fighting fascism in the Spanish Civil War. Flooded with many demoralizing insights into male social bondage and the generic innocence of childhood lost, *Another Country* exults in the sheltering brilliance of Biziou's cinematography—a beautiful film that falters somewhat thematically.

Also recommended: *Au Revoir Les Enfants*.

APOCALYPSE NOW

With Martin Sheen, Robert Duvall, Marlon Brando, Dennis Hopper, Harrison Ford, Frederic Forrest, Albert Hall, Sam Bottoms, Scott Glenn, G.D. Spradlin. Produced and directed by Francis Ford Coppola. Written by John Milius and Coppola. Photography by Vittorio Storaro. Music by Carmine and Francis Ford Coppola. USA. English. Color. 139 minutes. 1980.

War on the Mekong River in Cambodia.

In Francis Ford Coppola's *Apocalypse Now*, war is not hell. It's much, much worse. It is sight and sound and touch and speech. It's God. It's anti-god. It's muteness and blindness. It's darkness and light. The Beatles are war. Pictures of mom are war. House boats are war. White puppies are war. All is war. Because when you are in it, war is everything. Everything you see, everything you hear, everything you smell is war. Some people disagree about *Apocalypse Now*—is it a war film or an anti-war film? Those who find it exciting are war-minded people, as is anyone who doubts Coppola's intent. We know we are watching an anti-war film when a young American soldier fires off thirty-five rounds against an unarmed woman, and a distinguished officer descends so far into madness that rotting bodies and dismembered corpses decorate the pathway to his jungle sanctuary. Coppola's war is a merger of life and death, with skies full of hovering choppers, needle-nose bombers, and the rocket's red glare. Sheen excels in this role as a neo-nihilistic burn-out possessed by a nightmare. He breathes in the air of submission. "These boys are just waiting for a way to go back home," he says into the jungle, "but I've been back there and I know . . . it just doesn't exist any more." He can only go forward and never back again. He dominates every scene with his visceral indifference. His assignment is to take a crew up a river as far as the river goes. There's an officer up there, a Colonel Kurtz (Brando) who's threatening the war's good name. There are verified and unverified reports of things gone wrong—so wrong that when Sheen finds this officer, his job is to kill him. The boat slides up the river through ambushes and fog, deeper and deeper toward the place of lost souls. Here at last he finds the madness that is the cause and the result of all the other madnesses. Between living and dying, it's hard to tell the difference out here. Kurtz is being eaten away by his own insanity. The murky final scenes—shot from the last tributary of this river of psychoses—were the movie's most logical remark. Kurtz and his funereal compound of decay articulate the contagious momentum of war and the unholy alliance between Pentagon computer models and jungle combat. Having sailed to the darkness of no return, the film could not have ended any other way without swimming beyond the flow of its own discourse.

Also recommended: *In Country*.

ARSENAL
(VEFKU)

With Semyon Svashenko, A. Buchma, Mikola Nademsky. Written and directed by Alexander Dovzhenko. Photography by Danylo Demutsky. USSR. Silent with English titles. Black and white. 99 minutes. 1929.

The struggle between the bourgeoisie and the Bolsheviks in the Ukraine during World War I.

In a way, *Arsenal* is not like a movie at all. It's like thousands of priceless paintings sewn together with invisible thread. When seen in succession, the images appear to move. A mother is waiting. When the children cry, she beats them. But they still tug at her skirt and wipe away their tears, if not their sorrow. We understand it is not the children she is trying to beat down. The subtitles are poems: "There was a mother who had three sons." "There was a war." "Where is father, husband, son?" A farmer beats a skeletal horse. We understand the horse is not what he's beating, and the farmer leads the horse away. An old woman is barefoot, sowing seeds. She sinks to the ground and does not rise. Dovzhenko's people are the descendants of centuries of Tsarist domination. He contrasts these scenes of rural poverty with scenes of direct class exploitation in an urban munitions factory. Here in the turbulence of escalated war-time production, people are appendages to the apparatus of combat. But the factory will become the nexus between the callous estrangement of civil liberty and the emancipation of labor that will pull the empire down. As the horror of world war rages on the front lines and enormous casualties leave soldiers slaughtered in the trenches, the peasants at home are starving. Bolsheviks incite workers to leave their machines and enlist in a revolutionary worker's strike against the bourgeois class. The strike is a war of its own. The state-backed industrialists wage armed suppressions of workers backed only by anger. Throughout the country, the peasants and the soldiers and the workers are poised on the precipice of revolution. The leaders of the munitions strike are gunned down by Tsarist troops. Our only hero, Tymish, is shot as a deserter. Before he falls, he bares his chest to the cameras declaring, "There is something there you cannot kill." *Arsenal* is the visual and philosophic legacy of an artist of such exotic talents that, if his films hadn't been preserved as evidence, few would believe such things lie within the range of film media. Dovzhenko was more than a master of art and image; he was a realist infected with the expectation of an ideal world.

Also recommended: *Storm Over Asia*.

THE ASSISI UNDERGROUND

With Ben Cross, James Mason, Irene Papas, Maximilian Schell, Ricardo Cucciolla, Delia Boccardo, Edmond Purdom, Karl-Heinz Hackl. Produced by Menahem Golan and Yoram Globus. Directed by Alexander Ramati. Screenplay by Alexander Ramati, based on the documentary novel *The Assisi Underground*. Photography by Giuseppe Rotunno. Music by Dov Seltzer. USA. English. Color. 115 minutes. 1984.

Catholic churches in Assisi hide Jews during World War II.

It's World War II. Catholic churches in Assisi and other parts of Italy were transformed into sanctuaries for Jewish refugees. Men, women, and children are cloistered in convents that previously only nuns have entered in the past seven-hundred years. Monasteries all over Assisi are filled with Jews without identity cards who are waiting for safe passage out of Italy. Under the orders of Father Rufino (Cross), the church in Assisi orders "special" printing jobs from local printers—false identity cards for Jews who will travel to freedom as Christian pilgrims. Rufino explains to church authorities, "There are 40,000 Italian Jews—they are all our Jews. We are responsible for them." He drives the truck transporting supplies to the border and risks his life helping Jews cross the river to safety. Irene Papas is the Mother Superior, facing off the SS in their searches for "illegal residents" and army deserters. While eighty percent of European Jews were killed by Hitler's army, eighty percent of Italian Jews were saved through such efforts as are dramatized in this movie. The film is dedicated to the "compassion and the daring generosity of those . . . who made this rescue possible." Father Rufino, who won Israel's highest award, The Righteous Gentile, continued to work for the Jews until his death.

Also recommended: *Forbidden—A True Story*.

THE ATOMIC CAFE

Produced and directed by Kevin Rafferty, Pierce Rafferty, and Jayne Loader. Music coordinated by Rick Eaker. USA. English. Black and white and color. 92 minutes. 1982.

History of the promotion and acceptance of the atomic age.

This film is made up entirely of archival footage produced by the United States government to promote acceptance of the bomb and to generate distrust of the Soviet Union. You might think nobody could be gullible enough to believe the hokum our government put to film, but we still have warheads aimed at every major city to prove the success of this government propaganda campaign. Filmmakers Rafferty, Rafferty, and Loader have edited this footage into a kind of billboard flashback that teaches you a lot about how the people around you got to be the way they are. It shows you what our government is capable of, such as Troop Test Smokey. Agreeably compliant Army privates who participated in this "atomic maneuver" at Camp Desert Rock proudly identify themselves for the camera. Each man is supplied with a "film badge" that will alert the wearer if he receives a *lethal* dose of radiation. These men, who would not begin to suffer and die from cancer for another thirty years, are advised by superior officers that they have nothing to worry about because, "If you get enough radiation to really get sick, you'll probably be killed by the blast anyway"—the perfect consolation. First we see Hiroshima and Nagasaki melted into gray rubble. Then we hear the mushroom cloud after-effect of atomic bomb blasts described as one of the "most beautiful sights ever seen by man." Even the religious leaders in this film are behind the bomb all the way. One chaplain reassures the troops that "the fireball in the heavens is a wonderful sight to behold." Another advises civilians that anyone forced to retreat to their fallout shelter in time of war should take adequate "protection" with them to ward off needy passers by. We see Paul Tibbits, the pilot of the *Enola Gay*, talking about the day he dropped the bomb. We see the Castle Bravo Test and the Trinity Test. We see the Bikini Islanders shipped off their island paradise and watch it detonated to ruin and contaminated forever by nuclear fallout. We see pigs loaded in to the blast zone to determine the effects of fire and fallout on living things. We watch their scarred and deformed, but still conscious bodies thrown into a transport vehicle after the blast. All the songs in the film are pro-bomb mutations of Woody Guthrie-sounding tunes. The lyrics revolve around loving the bomb, selling the American way of life, and hating the com-yoon-ists. Nixon is on hand, sunk into gawky silence by Nikita Khrushchev, who he has just accused of "not knowing everything." "Well, if I don't know everything," Khrushchev responds, "you know nothing at all about socialism, except to fear it." There are scenes of other social phenomena of the 1950s, such as news clips of the Rosenbergs prior to their executions in 1953. *The Atomic Cafe* helps you understand how powerful film has been in shaping American values, fears, and prejudices. It documents the casualness of human and animal sacrifice to war consciousness while dramatizing the mind-numbing destructive capacity of nuclear weapons. *The Atomic Café* was privately funded, of course, by groups such as The Pioneer Fund, The Evergreen Fund, The Institute for World Order, and The Film Fund.

Also recommended: *The Day After Trinity*.

AU REVOIR LES ENFANTS
(GOODBYE CHILDREN)

Gasparde Manesse, Raphael Fejto, Stanislas Carre de Malberg, Francine Racette. Written, directed, and produced by Louis Malle. Cinematography by Renato Berta. Music by Franz Schubert and Camille Saint-Saens. France. In French with titles. 103 minutes. 1987.

A Jewish boy is sent to a Catholic academy to escape the Nazis in World War II.

The visual eloquence with which Malle tells this story of children in the infatuation of innocence in war amplifies the specter of Nazism haunting Jews throughout Europe in World War II. Raphael Fejto casts a shadow of vulnerability as the Jewish boy hidden in the cloister of a Catholic academy. He is the Renaissance ideal of the purity of youth. As the train pulls away from the station and his mother's face fades into the crowd, Raphael's sense of trust envelops him. He's going to enter a sanctuary—a haven from Hitler and the war. The moss-covered stone walls of the academy create a refuge into which evil cannot enter. He has become "Jean Bonnet" and wears the dark blue cape and dark blue suit of Christianity. The boys walk through the churchyards in harmonious uniformity. Outside, there is a war. Malle moves soldiers into the edges of the frames. Does the boy understand? Does he know he will never see his mother again? Does he know he was seen praying in the night? The Nazis are searching the convents and private schools. They know Jean Kipplestein has been given the benediction of the fathers. Taken from real events in the childhood of Louis Malle, *Au Revoir Les Enfants* recreates in the academy a hierarchy of social classes where misfits (another kind of victim) graduate into SS uniforms, accepted by the Third Reich. Social indifference creates societal failure, and inadequacies of culture make hate possible and war inevitable. Malle's film is a compassionate testimony against war as a thing denying even children the ultimate civil right. The Gestapo arrests Raphael in the name of racial purity. He is part of the solution. In his backward look, the temper of war becomes agonizingly clear. Malle illustrates the cold tyrannies of genocide using only the intimation of violence. His unmenacing world is an island in a sea that is inundating sanity. *Au Revoir Les Enfants* is an artistic and philosophic achievement caressingly crafted by Malle and cinematographer Renato Berta.

Also recommended: *Border Street.*

THE AUTOBIOGRAPHY OF MISS JANE PITTMAN

With Cicely Tyson, Michael Murphy, Rod Perry, Joel Fluellen, Eric Brown, Josephine Premice, Thalmus Rasulala, Collin Wilcox-Horne, Beatrice Winde, Richard Dysart, Valeria O'Dell, Woodrow Chambliss, Sidney Arroyo, Ted Airhart. Produced by Robert W. Christiansen and Rick Rosenburg. Directed by John Korty. Screenplay by Tracy Keenan Wynn, based on the novel by Ernest J. Gaines. Photography by James Crabe. Music by Fred Karlin. USA. English. Color 109 minutes. 1973.

An elderly black woman looks back on her life from slavery to civil rights.

No, it's not Mama Africa. It's Mama Americana and the embosomed memories of her 109 years of human antiquity. She unloads it all onto Michael Murphy from a rocker on the porch, and you can probably tell already that it won nine Emmies on American T.V. Her name is Miss Jane, and it's her birthday. The young people want her to go into town with them and to drink from the white man's fountain in the name of civil rights. "Your very presence will bring forth the multitudes." But she stays right where she is, telling her life story to investigative reporter Murphy. What was it like "back then," he wants to know? She was a young girl when the slaves were freed, and she wanted to go to Ohio but only made it as far as the "Great Missasip" because she didn't have a nickel for the ferry. She lived out her life on the wrong side of the river, watching close personal relatives be killed by white people and white horses. "Reconstruction never really worked," she gasps. Murphy is spellbound. She quotes Frederick Douglass, "We are one. We have worn a heavy yolk." Sometime around the Spanish-American War, her adopted son began saying, "I'm a Black American and I'm proud." "We were always looking for a leader," says Miss Jane, as news of JFK and the Reverend King come over Murphy's car radio. Murphy has to say good-bye—he's scheduled to cover John Glenn's earth orbit shot though he'd rather stay and listen to how Miss Jane can walk "a-a-a-ll the way d-o-o-own to da ribber," when she's in the mood. Right now she's in the mood to join the young people in the park after all. And the multitudes do sort of gather. *The Autobiography of Miss Jane Pittman* is almost too uncharismatic to help us tolerate the leanly doctored story line and the obviously stumped Tyson waging war on old age. Only small children will be surprised to learn that there used to be slaves and that now there aren't.

Also recommended: *The Learning Tree.*

THE BATTLE OF ALGIERS

With Jean Martin, Yacef Saadi, Brahim Haggiag, Tommaso Neri, Samia Kerbash, Fawzia el Kader, Michele Kerbash, Mohamed Ben Kassen, Ugo Paletti. Produced by Antonio Musu and Yacef Saadi. Directed by Gillo Pontecorvo. Screenplay by Franco Solinas and Gillo Pontecorvo, based on an original story by Franco Solinas and Gillo Pontecorvo. Cinematography by Marcello Gatti. Music by Ennio Morricone and Gillo Pontecorvo. Italy. French and Algerian with English titles. Black and white. 120 minutes. 1966.

Algerian freedom fighters struggle to overcome French colonial rule.

Included in the imperial holdings of France's colonial realm of the 1950s was the formerly sovereign nation of Algeria, North Africa. Held under totalitarian control, the Algerian people would resist French occupation and eventually free themselves of foreign domination. The people's struggle is electrifyingly dramatized here by Gillo Pontecorvo in one of the greatest revolutionary films ever made. *The Motion Picture Guide* describes the *Battle of Algiers* as a "primer for guerrilla warfare and patently communist in every sense," and labels Pontecorvo a revolutionary Marxist/Maoist. Well, if it was "a primer for guerrilla warfare," it was also a primer on defeating both organized terrorism and urban guerrilla strategies. The French imported paratroopers and specialized counter-revolutionary forces who understood the communist revolutionary cell organizational technique. A methodical destruction of the cells advanced one person at a time. Using a wall chart as a guide, counter-revolutionary forces captured Algerian resistance fighters and tortured them into revealing the names of other cell members. One by one, the cell members were arrested and tortured until only the leaders remained free. They were tracked down and forced to surrender or die. When the last cell was broken, the rebellion collapsed. All of this was supported by the usual military tactics. Barbed wire surrounded the Kasbah in Algiers, and free movement through the country was restricted. French foot soldiers patrolled the streets, and Algerians suspected of participating in the revolution were shot on sight. Pontecorvo took the trouble to reveal French counter-revolutionaries as normal people simply doing a job they were hired to do. This is typical of Pontecorvo. He sees both sides as victims of different forces that perhaps neither side really understands. Independence came to Algeria in July 1962. In 1966 *The Battle of Algiers* stood as one of the world's most virulently anti-imperialist films. As a testament to Pontecorvo and perhaps as a commentary on contemporary filmmaking, it remains so twenty-five years later.

Also recommended: *Burn*.

BERKELEY IN THE 60's

Produced and directed by Mark Kitchell. Written by Stephen Most, Mark Kitchell, and Susan Griffin. Photography by Stephen Lighthill. Narrated by Susan Griffin. USA. English. Black and white and color. 117 minutes. 1990.

The rise of radicalism and the counterculture at the University of California at Berkeley.

It was May 1960. Students protesting HUAC suppression of political freedoms are hosed out of a local courthouse by fire hoses. For many of these Berkeley students, this first confrontation with police catalyzed their fear into a determination regarding everything that came after. Banning together to protest a restriction of student literature, groups from across the political spectrum surrounded and immobilized police vehicles called in to make arrests. The crowd swelled to six thousand, igniting a spontaneous open forum of three-minute speeches that would last for the next thirty-two hours. From this, the scope of student protests spread to challenge every abuse of authority it encountered for the next ten years. Students demonstrated for fairness in hiring, political liberty, free speech, free press, and of course, an end to the war in Vietnam. As the U.S. is being devastated in the war, the students at home are blocking troop trains and closing down the Oakland army terminal and military induction center, while incoming buses of recruits are protected by riot squad deployments. Governor Ronald Reagan condemned "the mess at Berkeley" and the "so-called free speech advocates." Radicals, dropouts, intellectuals, misfits—all were attracted to Berkeley by the university's tremendous notoriety. Organizers began to see that whatever was happening was bigger than Berkeley. It was the birth of the "counterculture." As radicals took over campuses across the country, civil rights conflicts erupted in every major city, and war protests escalated, J. Edgar Hoover suggested he might not be able to "insure domestic security." As riots raged, Stokely Carmichael warned the military to "keep your filthy white hands off our beautiful black children." President Lyndon Johnson refused a second term in office. The Black Panthers armed themselves by selling copies of Mao Tse-Tung's "little red book." The women's liberation movement brought equal rights for women to national attention. The line from the Gil-Scott Heron song describes the times: "The revolution will not be televised, the revolution will be live." Survivors of the era remember the feeling of living in phenomenal times. There was an exhilarating atmosphere of dynamic resistance. But the entire strategy of direct action was running up against its own limitations. There was little philosophic depth to the sweeping but superficial changes. And the government was getting better at controlling the protests. When a student demonstration was gassed at People's Park, it signaled the end. This film is a spectacular trip through a period in American history when the energy for change promised to rise up and make the world right. Audiences will wonder where all the idealism came from, and where it is today.

Also recommended: *Underground.*

THE BEST MAN

With Henry Fonda, Cliff Robertson, Edie Adams, Lee Tracy, Margaret Leighton, Shelly Berman, Gene Raymond, Kevin McCarthy, Ann Sothern, John Henry Faulk, Richard Arlen, and Howard K. Smith and Mahalia Jackson as themselves. Produced by Lawrence Turman and Stuart Millar. Directed by Franklin Schaffner. Screenplay by Gore Vidal, based on his play. Photography by Haskell Wexler. Music by Mort Lindsey. USA. English. Black and white. 103 minutes. 1964.

Presidential candidate is ruined by opponent's smear campaign.

In 1964, *The Best Man* could have been called an expose of the democratic process. These days there is nothing left to expose, and *The Best Man* comes off as an air raid siren gone off on the wrong side of the moon. Reality passed this movie by, much as the *The National Enquirer* passed by stone tablets. Fonda plays William "Nice Guy" Russell, contender for the presidential nomination of an unnamed political party. Cliff Robertson is his scheming opponent, who will reveal Fonda's psychotherapy records to the delegates on the floor of the convention center before the second ballot. What Fonda needs is a means to prevent him from doing that, like evidence of Robertson's homosexual encounters—which he actually has, but refuses to use. The convention floor is populated by extraneous middle men and smooth-talking politicos axing careers while blowing smoke rings. They all want Fonda to ruin Robertson. But *The Best Man* is about the importance of integrity among those seeking higher public office. Fonda and the reptilian Robertson face off behind the scenes trying to out-bluff one another. In the end, Fonda is too principled to be president of the United States. His wife loves him for it, and everyone else is beyond shock. Talent abounds in the minor roles. Shelly Berman peaks as the other half of Robertson's homosexual liaison.

Also recommended: *Advise and Consent* and *Tanner 88*.

BETRAYED

With Debra Winger, Tom Berenger, John Heard, Betsy Blair, John
Mahoney, Ted Levin, Maria Valdez, Brian Bosak. Produced by Irwin
Winkler. Directed by Constantin Costa-Gavras. Screenplay by Joe
Eszterhas. Photography by Patrick Blossier. Music by Bill Conti. USA. En-
glish. Color. 123 minutes. 1989.

Undercover agent infiltrates white supremacist group in Nebraska.

Debra Winger is the FBI agent assigned to infiltrate the Zionist Occupation Government (ZOG) in Nebraska where ZOG command control is
suspected of organizing a white supremacist overthrow of the United
States. The plan includes establishing a racist nation patterned after
apartheid in South Africa. The FBI has evidence of a national communications network linking white supremacist organizations across the
country. The ZOGs have just machine-gunned a Chicago talk show
host. Winger's assignment is to get to know Gary Simmons (Berenger)
and find evidence implicating him in the murder in Chicago or con-
necting him with ZOG command. The trouble with Berenger is that
he's a very nice guy. He lives in the country in a beautiful old farm
house with wood floors and big windows and poster beds. He's got two
kids, Rachel and Joey (Valdez and Bosak). Then Berenger invites
Winger on an afternoon hunting trip with his buddies. The hunters have
a black man in the back of a truck; they throw him into the woods,
track him down, and kill him. From here, Winger's undercover assignment leads to paramilitary maneuvers and survival camps where
women and children are indoctrinated into the terrorist consciousness
of intolerance and race hate. The families are banded together by a
genuine belief in their obligation to protect the U.S. from domination
by blacks, Jews, homosexuals, and Arabs. Children grow up believing
they have been asked by God to help establish a racially pure world.
Winger is horrified to hear five-year-old Rachel tell her, "We *have* to
get rid of them, Katie." Winger discovers there is a computer network
linking the survivalists and monitoring the buildup for war. There are
shipments of weapons and large sums of money. Using undercover
leads, the FBI wedges a legal window of opportunity into the ZOG
commandos, and Winger works on a plan to save the kids from their
own prejudice. Like a lot of films that seem too shocking to be true,
Betrayed irked critics rankled by such alarmism in film media. Unfortu-

nately, it was classified as box-office dogma and left to drift out of sight and out of mind.

Also recommended: *Mississippi Burning.*

THE BICYCLE THIEF

With Lambert Maggiorani, Enzo Staiola, Lianella Carell. Produced and directed by Vitorrio De Sica. Screenplay by Cesare Zavattini, based on the novel by Luigi Bartolini. Photography by Carlo Montouri. Music by Allesandro Cigognini. Italy. Black and white. In Italian with English titles. 87 minutes. 1948.

A day laborer, employed for the first time in two years, loses the bicycle he needs for his job.

In De Sica's quest to "deromanticize the cinema," he plagues audiences with the rare inhumanities that the poorest of the poor must suffer for the screen. Antonio is our savior of economic sabotage, sparring with the anonymity of his poverty. He has no gift left to give except his honest appetite to prove he can survive. His smile redeems his unconditional sincerity, and we see his folly amplified by an anemic, misplaced dream. De Sica's invitation to witness this man's personal, public devaluation is the final humiliation of his fragile faith. His wife rips the bed sheets off the beds and sells them to buy the bicycle he needs for the new job. But the Zavattini screenplay plots with thieves to steal the bike before Antonio can make it through one day of full employment. He quickly organizes friends who, along with his young son Bruno, join him in an ambitious and methodical search for the bicycle and the thief. The point is never to lose hope. They circulate from bike shop to bike shop. Stolen bikes are disassembled, repainted, and sold to shops a piece at a time. The open-air stalls are lined with heavy racks of tires, tubes, and frames, and tabletops crowded with bells and pumps of every description. Outside, the city streets are pressed full of men on bikes. The police refuse to help them find one bike among the millions. Antonio is unwavering. He is a working man with rights and expectations. He demands that the establishment stand behind him. He accuses people as is his right as a member of the accusing class. One by one, his friends desert the search. He is subject to denunciations. The locomotion of his integrity falters. The thief, when they find him, denies everything. In the end, Bruno and Antonio are left alone, walking the streets. It's unthinkable to go home without the bike. At rush hour, the flood of cyclers intensifies. In the final scenes, the bicyclists have given way to men on foot, walking home from the day's work. Antonio and Bruno are absorbed by the crowds of faceless laborers, their backs to the camera, shoulder to shoulder, filling the screen with a river of human monotony. Montouri's lens weighs heavy on them, and we see that the supply of the working poor and their supply of tragic stories could fill all the stages in this society.

Also recommended: *Umberto D.*

BLACK AND WHITE IN COLOR
(LA VICTORIE EN CHANTANT)

With Jacques Dufilho, Jean Carmet, Claude Leros, Jacques Spiesser, Dora Doll, Dieter Schidor. Produced by Arthur Cohn, Jacques Perrin, Georgio Silvagni. Directed by Jean-Jacques Annaud. Photography by Claude Agostine and Nanamoudou Magasouba. Music by Pierre Bachelet. France and Ivory Coast. In French with English titles. Color. 100 minutes. 1976.

The French colonialists in Africa reduce the natives to slaves, soldiers and file clerks.

Some of Africa's most astonishing traditional architecture graces the backgrounds of this sagacious and beautiful film by Jean-Jacques Annaud. *Black and White in Color* is filmed at the warm end of the spectrum—dusty yellows, ochre, beige, red. So what? Well, when you see how Magasouba and Agostine have used light, color, space, and shadow to make a good story a thousand times better you'll really appreciate their artistry. But I rave on. Africa was colonized by, among others, the French and the Germans. In this movie, these colonials are now comfortably ensconced on the continent, waited on by abundant nonunionized labor. The natives cook their meals, wash their clothes, and dig their graves. So naturally, when France and Germany go to war, it is the natives who fight it for them in Africa. A cast of true characters acts out this satire of French colonialists bumbling away the lives and traditions of the blacks, while picnicking under broad acacia trees. Owing to a serious recruitment blunder on the part of the French, the Germans have rounded up most of the available natives for the war. The French are forced to rope men and lead them by the necks to the training grounds to learn words like "gun," "bayonet," and "bullets." They are dressed alike and sent off to fight for France. A variety of black African types inhabit the sets—monolingual, bilingual, trilingual, colonial secretaries, tribal chiefs, army aides, farmers. One black beauty moves in with the French geographer, Herbert Fresnoy (Spiesser), shocking people for whom there is always plenty to be shocked about. Fresnoy has the job of saving his French countrymen from themselves—crass, moronic racists who have yet to fall back on the use of diplomacy. The war ends and bagpipes announce that England now owns that part of Africa to which the Germans heretofore laid claim. An English attache arrives speaking neither French nor German, but a kind of English that will sound to English speakers like a flower might sound if it could sing.

Also recommended: *Chocolat.*

BLACK FURY

With Paul Muni, Karen Morely, William Gargan, Barton MacClane, John Qualen, J. Carroll Naish, Vince Barnett. Produced by Robert Lord. Directed by Michael Curtiz. Written by Abem Finkel and Carl Erickson, based on the play *Bohunk* by Harry Irving and the story "Jan Volkanik" by M.A. Musmanno. Photography by Byron Haskin. USA. English. Black and white. 95 minutes. 1935.

A labor dispute in the Pittsburgh coal mines.

Panned as being too brutal, dreary, realistic, and more powerful than anything the Soviets ever dreamed up, *Black Fury* would actually give Eisenstein a heart murmur if he ever saw it, even if it was banned by the state of Pennsylvania for dumping so hard on coal town. There *is* coal company corruption and an unsafe work environment. There is a well-shot sequence of families evicted from coal-town housing. There is Paul Muni, who did a lot of relevant film work during his time and was equally overshadowed in each one. Here, he's insurgent miner Joe Radek, standing stiff as statuary in front of the labor force. When the workers disagree about the strike, Joe locks himself in the mine shaft to stop the "dead work" and the loading. Luckily there's a phone down there so Muni can communicate with the audience in a side-saddle accent, which was the way the Pennsylvania Dutch were supposed to have talked and which is typical of Muni's reverence for things that could ruin a film. When they win the strike, his brief victory speech, "Glad we win," comes out, "Glod ve vin." The story is that he took weeks to learn to talk this way making me think the title of the play would have been a more appropriate choice for the title of the movie.

Also recommended: *How Green Was My Valley.*

BLACK GOD, WHITE DEVIL
(DEUS E O DIABLO NA TERRA DO SOL)

With Yona Magalhaes, Geraldo del Rey, Lidio Silva, Mauricio De Valle, Othon Bastos. Produced by Luiz Augusto Mendes. Written and directed by Glauber Rocha. Cinematography by Valdemar Lima. Music by Bach and Villa Lobos. Songs by Sergio Ricardo. Brazil. In Portuguese with English titles. Black and white. 120 minutes. 1986.

Preacher and his wife join forces with revolutionary rebel leader.

Don't expect a revolution from Manuel (del Rey), or his wife, Rosa (Magalhaes), who give up their adoration of the charismatic religious prophet Sebastiao to join forces with the revolutionary guerrilla leader, Corisco. They seem to be his only followers, and in the end, promise to travel throughout Brazil telling people what he has taught them, no matter how long it may take. Director Rocha has a new and very personal film style which most critics have praised for its "folk art" qualities. Rocha has said, "The first mandate of the Third World is to smash the inferiority complex by creating a new artistic style based on Brazil's heritage." I admire Rocha's interest in reversing the debilitating trends engendered by cultural imperialism in the third world. Unfortunately, he's done such a good job of speaking about Brazil to Brazilians that other audiences may find no familiar narrative toeholds to sustain their interest in *Black God, White Devil*. The protracted, tensionless episodes may strike some as calm and others as boring. Funding restraints were perhaps to blame for technical lapses, such as English subtitles that do not always stay on the screen long enough to read, do not always match up with the person speaking, and are sometimes missing altogether. I didn't like the way all human physical movements slowed down in a crisis. I didn't like the way Rosa and Manuel screamed when they weren't mumbling and I didn't like being bewildered by the plot and the dialogue and almost everything in between.

Also recommended: *Bye Bye Brazil*.

BLACK LIKE ME

With James Whitmore, Roscoe Lee Browne, Al Freeman Jr., Will Geer, Sorrel Booke, Lenka Peterson. Produced by Julius Tannenbaum. Screenplay by Gerda Lerner and Carl Lerner, from the book and diaries by John Howard Griffin. Photography by Victor Lukens and Henry Mueller III. Music by Peter Kupferman. USA. English. Black and white. 105 minutes. 1964.

White reporter disguises himself as a black man to investigate racism in the U.S. south.

Black Like Me is the true story of John Howard Griffin (called John Finley Horton in the movie) a writer and civil rights supporter who darkened his skin artificially in order to discover what it was like to be a black man in the south. Halfway through a three-month experiment, he is disillusioned and embittered. He meets humiliations, rejections, and cruelties he never imagined. He has become a helpless and terrified witness to the disintegration of his own identity. His pride is stripped away and replaced with "prejudice, like a poison." He's a stranger to himself, unable to sustain professional objectivity. Everywhere he goes he's a threat to white superiority. Mothers grab their children away from him. Employers are "weeding you guys out." Park benches occupied by whites are off limits. If he steps over the color bar in the former Confederacy, he learns that "down here, you guys are completely off the record." Even white "liberals" are unable to conceal their unconscious bigotry. As his identity decays, his personality transforms. Once outgoing, he becomes suspicious, wary, and sullen, retreating into defensiveness and hostility. The screenplay, taken from Griffin's own journals, tells a grim story of hate in the eyes of strangers. When he fails to control his anger, blacks console him. In the last days of his experiment, he confesses his identity to a black family, which rejects him—not for living a lie, but for being white. *Black Like Me* is one long revelation—try not to let the musical score derail all of the sensitive moments. Ironically, it was Griffin's use of skin-darkening chemicals that was responsible for his premature death.

Also recommended: *Gentleman's Agreement*.

THE BLUM AFFAIR
(AFFAIRE BLUM)

With Kurt Erhardt, Gisela Trowe, Paul Bildt, Gerard Blenert, Clause Becker, Hans Cristian Blech. Produced by Herbert Uhlich. Directed by Erich Engel. Written by R. A. Stemmle. Photography by Friedl Behn Grund and Karl Plintzer. Music by Herbert Trantow. German Democratic Republic. German with titles. Black and white. 100 minutes. 1948.

Prejudice drives an innocent man to jail.

Dr. Blum (Becker) is a prominent Jewish industrialist. One of his former employees has disappeared and is presumed murdered. Under questioning, the real murderer, Gabler (Erhardt), fans everyone's anti-Semitism by fabricating a web of monstrous accusations indicting Blum, whose innocence becomes increasingly impossible to visualize. Blum is arrested and becomes the target of malicious prejudice. His wife receives hate mail. A swastika is painted on their home. When the body of the dead man is discovered in his basement, Gabler fashions more lies, pawning himself off as a victim of Blum's blackmail. When Blum testifies, under oath, that he is being framed, court magistrates threaten to prosecute him for insulting a German court. "I *am* German," he responds, "Justice is not German, it's international." Elaborate rationalizations challenge his question as to a possible motive for the crime. Police department detectives ignore Mrs. Blum's petitions for an investigation, and it is only through the intervention of an independent investigator that the truth is proven and Blum exonerated. He is released from prison and rejoins his wife. She comforts him explaining, "You are home again. This is a free state. This is Germany." The year is 1928.

Also recommended: *Judge Horton and the Scottsboro Boys.*

THE BOAT IS FULL
(DAS BOOT IST VOLL)

With Tina Engel, Hans Diehl, Martin Walz, Curt Bois, Gerd David, Renate Steiger, Mathias Gnaedinger. Produced by Limbo Film. Written and directed by Markus Imhoff. Cinematography by Hans Liechti. No music. Switzerland, Austria/West Germany. German dubbed into English. Color. 101 minutes. 1981.

The plight of Jews seeking refuge in Switzerland from the Nazi invasion of Europe.

By July 1942 there were 8,300 refugees in Switzerland. The doors were closed; the boat was full. Ten thousand Jews who tried to cross the border after the quotas were filled were turned back to the concentration camps and gas chambers of the Third Reich—unless they could qualify as exceptions to the refugee limit. Families with children under the age of six and deserters from Hitler's army were excepted. Suddenly the young French orphan has a mother, grandfather, and sister who don't speak French. The Nazi deserter traveling with them is his new father. Another wears a Nazi uniform to bolster the illusion that he's a deserter. They are discovered hiding in the shed of a couple who feed them and grow protective of them. These stowaways on the ark of Swiss sanctuary register the semi-quavers of a social whim that has no bearing, to be sure, on the reality of war, but rather on the scrupulous minutiae of town meetings and the problematic finality of immigration law. The Swiss do not see themselves as weapons of Hitler's war; they are worn out with refugees and so ignore the significance of barring them. The refugees understand that history is killing them by degrees. They have walked out on the thin ice of the neutral zones and it is cracking underneath them. The citizens of this small Swiss town, far from the death camps and massacres, do not understand what their decisions will mean. Imhoof's screenplay dwells on this notion. In this film, the Nazi deserters stay. The rest cannot find seats on the boat of neutral Switzerland, and will instead fall back into the war. With a transcendent cast and rarified dubbing, *The Boat is Full* is technically as superb as it can be. This film substantiates the notion that "neutrality" is a semantic and historic illusion.

Also recommended: *The Last Seven Months of Anne Frank.*

BORDER STREET

With Maria Broniewska, Mieczyslawa Cwiklinska, Jerzy Lescynski, Jurek Zlotnicki, Jerzy Pichelski, R. Vrohota, E. Kruk, Wladyslaw Godik, J. Muclinger, Wladyslaw Walter. Narration and introduction by Quentin Reynolds. Produced by Film Polski. Directed by Alesander Ford. Screenplay by Ludwik Starski, Jan Fethke, Alesander Ford. Photography by Jaroslaw Tuzar. Music by Roman Palester. Poland. Polish with English titles. Black and white. 110 minutes. 1948.

Inside and outside the Warsaw ghetto, Jews fight for survival in World War II.

As the circus of war advances, all definitions of human social expectations advance beside it. The enemy is not only the unseen pilots and executors of combat, but also those neighbors who sell out to the Nazis for a deferred place in the party line. War pushes social dissolution ahead of it. Prejudice is fanned into fever. Generous spirits stand up for the innocents. Righteousness burns back the fires of fascism. In 1939, many citizens of Warsaw refused to accept the awful potential for war and destruction represented by the Nazi threat. Ford and Tuza work in filial harmony, stoking their artistic outrage with some kind of clairvoyant courage. The drama falls uniquely to the surviving children. They are the final hosts for resistance. When asked by an adult, "What will you fight with?" a child responds, "With our fists." Typhus and famine rage behind the wall closing off the ghetto. Children raid the outside for food and ammunition to feed a resistance that grows into revolution. Now they are saving others from a ghetto inferno torched by Nazi command. Archival clips reveal the terror of the enormous blaze reducing city blocks to ash. The last children we see are David (Zlotnicki) and Jadzia (Broniewska) disappearing into the wreckage that was the ghetto. Famed war correspondent Quentin Reynolds narrates, "The barriers that separate man from man will continue to be torn down." Somehow, director Ford has managed to put ruinous terror on the same screen with the unretouched hope that is youth. These children are their own personal archetypes. They turn into heroes the way mist turns into storm clouds. A wonderful cast is surrounded by Roman Palester's immensely effective musical score.

Also recommended: *Au Revoir Les Enfants.*

BORN ON THE FOURTH OF JULY

With Tom Cruise, Willem Dafoe, Frank Whaley, Caroline Kava, Kyra Sedgwick, Raymond J. Berry, and Abbie Hoffman. Produced by A. Kitman Ho and Oliver Stone. Directed by Oliver Stone. Screenplay By Ron Kovics and Oliver Stone from the book by Ron Kovics. Photography by Robert Richardson. Music by John Williams. USA. English. Color. 145 minutes. 1989.

A young man joins the Marines to fight in Vietnam and discovers the deceit of U.S. aggression in Southeast Asia.

In an interview after this film's release, Ron Kovics, upon whose experiences the film is based, was asked how he felt about his service in Vietnam. "I felt cheated, lied to, misled, deceived. . . . I felt I was drowning in a sea of lies and a whirlpool of injustice." Would the movie make a difference? "Movies should not merely entertain; movies have a responsibility to portray the truth so effectively that those . . . who watch it . . . are not the same again. . . . We have very important work to do, all of us, to strive to tell the truth in our writing, in our painting, in our filmmaking, in our everyday utterances, in our everyday interactions, so that these awful things can never happen again and so that we can have peace." But, as Kovics sat in his wheelchair in the aisle next to Tom Cruise at the Academy Awards ceremonies, best picture, best actor, and best director awards went elsewhere. For Hollywood in 1990, America is still hard to see. *Born on the Fourth of July* is the story of Ron Kovics—student, soldier, hero, victim, patriot, radical activist, author. He listened to Kennedy when he said, "Ask not what your country can do for you," went to Southeast Asia to save democracy, and came back crippled in body and mind. "I would give everything, Timmie, everything I've got, everything I believe, all my values, just to have my body back again, just to be whole. But I'm never going to be whole again." He's not that much different from the thousands of vets he will join in the streets chanting, "One, two, three, four, we don't want your fucking war." Perhaps they all feel they are "drowning in a sea of lies and a whirlpool of injustice." They disrupt the Republican national convention, and Kovics is beaten by riot police who possibly also heard Kennedy say, "Ask not what your country can do for you." Oliver Stone's film not only portrays the truth, it is a monolithic accusation of American international aggression and a masterwork of genuine social realism that perhaps will ensure that "these awful things . . . never happen again and . . . we can have peace."

Also recommended: *Hearts and Minds* and *In Country*.

BOUND FOR GLORY

With David Carradine, Ronny Cox, Melinda Dillon, John Lehne, Randy Quaid, Ji-Tu Cumbuka, Gail Strickland. Produced by Robert F. Blumofe and Harold Leventhal. Directed by Hal Ashby. Written by Robert Getchell, from the autobiography of Woody Guthrie. Photography by Haskell Wexler. Musical score by Leonard Rosenman. USA. English. Color. 147 minutes. 1976.

Depression-era folk singer Woody Guthrie fights for the worker.

This wonderfully resolved biography of the legendary American folk singer Woody Guthrie tenderly invokes the spirit of gentle hope he sang about with a soft charisma that defined his style. David Carradine is Guthrie, the drifter who used his talent to speak out for the working class during a time of violent social upheaval. The Depression drove many workers away from their homes and off the land. Guthrie himself was on the road, hunting for work and witnessing the collapse of free enterprise. He started to work with unions, and he started writing music, and he put everything he saw into his songs. They were just so simple and so beautiful and so honest that they define the era and they define the worker's plight. When he began to sing about human rights, Guthrie was pressured by radio stations, fired from jobs, threatened, and asked to delete union songs from his shows. He routinely declined artistic compromise and suffered tremendous personal hardship when times were hard. The most inspired quality of the film is its untroubled promotion of activism for everybody—the idea that change comes from the idea for change, power from the idea of power. The simple formula for change that he marched for and sang about permeate the lyrics of his songs. His music inspires people to imagine that they have the courage to work for a better world. The cameras move nimbly around the Depression-era civil tragedy, revealing both the horror and the hope of those times. Carradine is simply ideal in the role. There could have been more emphasis on the activism and revolutionary qualities that Guthrie came to epitomize, and the music that make him a timeless folk hero.

Also recommended: *A Vision Shared.*

BREAKER MORANT

With Rod Mullinar, Edward Woodward, Jack Thompson, Bryan Brown, Charles Tingwell, Terence Donovan, John Waters, Lewis Fitzgerald. Produced by Matthew Carroll. Directed by Bruce Beresford. Screenplay by Jonathan Hardy, David Stevens, and Beresford. Based on the play by Kenneth Ross. Photography by Don McApline. Music by Phil Cunneen. Australia. English and Afrikaans. Color. 103 minutes. 1980.

The court-martial of three men accused of murdering POWs during the Boer War in South Africa.

A group of Boers surrender under a white flag and are then shot. A Boer POW has been murdered. A German priest is dead in his buggy. From the vast dictionary of war atrocities, these are singled out as crimes. "Field consciousness": what do the words mean? Breaker Morant could tell you how 5,000 years of evolution can cease to register in five seconds. He and two of his men are being court-martialed. Lord Kitchener's aide calls it a "sideshow of the war." Their lawyer denies nothing: "Soldiers at war should not be judged by civilian rules even though they may commit acts, which when calmly viewed afterwards, could only be seen as unchristian and brutal." It's not an unfamiliar idea. "War changes men's nature. The barbarities of war are seldom committed by abnormal men. They are acts committed by normal men under abnormal conditions." As each witness testifies, the battleground comes silently to life. The charade of truth shadows the operatives in a battle to the death over South Africa's diamonds and gold. They are alone on the Transvaal plateau to reinterpret life. Doubts, hesitation, innocence, and trust are impediments. Acts of conscience now are complicated by automatic weapons. Thousands of women and children are starving in British-run concentration camps. Prisoners of war are expendable. Did Lord Kitchener give a verbal order to shoot all prisoners? He refuses to testify. The three are sacrificial, and nothing can save them. Breaker Morant, speaking on his own behalf, says, "It is customary during war to kill as many of the enemy as possible." The defense summarizes: "If all the men in war who committed reprisals were to be charged and tried, court-martials like this one would be in permanent session, wouldn't they?" The accused are career pawns of the colonial guard. They are found guilty and sentenced to die. One of these sentences is committed to life in prison. Morant and one other are shot in kitchen chairs on the open veld, torched by the fire of the African sunrise.

Also recommended: *Gallipoli.*

BREAKING WITH OLD IDEAS

With Guo Chen-Ch'ing, Wang Su-ya, Chang Cheng, Hsu Chan, Li Shi-Chang, Hsiang Hung, Chen Ying, and Ko Ts'un-Chuang. Directed by Li Wen Hua. China. In Chinese with English titles. Color. 126 minutes. 1975.

A post-revolutionary Chinese university copes with the proletarian modifications in higher education.

Chinese social realism is almost outlandish enough to classify as a separate medium. *Breaking With Old Ideas* is a classic of the genre. It's flashy. It's conspicuous. It's animated by primary colors pushing a straightforward Maoist campaign in the public interest. The people's propaganda—I love it. We are in the mountains at the Sungshan branch of the Communist Labor College. The revolutionary idea is called egalitarianism. The new Maoist director, Principal Lung, wants to open classes to the peasants, who could help build new buildings, plant crops, and make the school more self-sufficient and less dependent on the state. His redesigned curriculum will include theory and more practical programs, like developing plant breeds and making harvests more efficient to avert famine. He wants to teach cooperation, communist consciousness, and opposition to Confucianism and bourgeois ideas. There is emphasis on women's liberation, the equality of all peoples, and the importance of individual contributions to society, "from each according to his ability." He explains that the rationale for schools in the People's Republic is to improve the quality of life for all Chinese. Trouble comes from the resident professors who oppose Principal Lung and undermine his programs, but eventually come to understand they were wrong to cling to their elitist ways. They will embrace the Marxist/Maoist teachings and become enthusiastic supporters of Lung's programs, and willingly work side-by-side with peasant students who never tire of working, studying, singing, and planning for a better future for China. Everyone understands the true meaning of human social groupings—cooperation toward scientific socialism. I could watch this stuff all day long and into the night.

Also recommended: *Abandoned Fields*.

BROKEN ARROW

With James Stewart, Jeff Chandler, Debra Paget, Basil Ruysdael, Will Geer, Joyce MacKenzie, Iron Eyes Cody, Jay Silverheels, Arthur Hunnicutt, Raymond Bramley. Produced by Julian Blaustein. Directed by Delmer Davis. Photography by Ernest Palmer. Music by Alfred Newman. USA. English. Color. 93 minutes. 1950.

Cochise, the Indians, and Jimmy Stewart solve the Indian problem.

Broken Arrow calls itself "The first major Hollywood movie to renounce time-worn cliches and . . . portray Indians as full-blooded human beings." Well, they only missed it by twenty-five years, which is not far off considering that barely one movie per decade is made on the subject. "This is the story of a land . . . and a people . . . and a man, whose name was . . ." Jimmy Stewart. Well, alright, Cochise—Jeff Chandler—a man of earth energies making the point that renegade whites played an important role in American Indian problems. It was not just the Bureau of Indian Affairs and the cavalry and the United States government. (And the prospectors and the railroads and the trappers.) Jimmy Stewart used to be in the Union army and is tired of the fighting. "Cochise didn't start this war. A snooty lieutenant fresh out of the east started it." "I'm sick of all this killing, and who asked us out here in the first place?" "Our people have done you a great wrong." He's an emissary of peace and reconciliation. One of the film's choice lines is delivered to General Howard, who has been quoting out of the Bible. It says, "All are God's children." Jimmy asks, "Suppose their skins aren't white, are they still God's children?" posing a vigorous recollection of traditional people all over the world, massacred and enslaved in the name of faith. It's a movie of uneven courage. Here's *Broken Arrow* turning Indians back into human beings, but not one real Indian among them was good enough for Jimmy. He marries Debra Paget—an Indian princess dressed like a Lakota Sioux saying of Stewart, "With him I do not tremble." Paget is the phoniest imitation Indian of all time, and the whole romance is about as potable as sea water. She's a "white, painted lady" alright. The nicest thing about *Broken Arrow* is that there are four-hundred Apaches in it. The worse thing is that Paget isn't one of them. Stewart is amiable and seems sincere, but if somebody calls him an "Indian lover," dive for cover.

Also recommended: *Indian Agent*, *Vanishing Americans*, and *Cheyenne Autumn*.

BUFFALO BILL AND THE INDIANS OR SITTING BULL'S LESSON IN HISTORY

With Paul Newman, Burt Lancaster, Geraldine Chaplin, Denver Pyle, John Considine, Frank Kaquitts, Shelly Duvall, Harvey Keitel, Kevin Mc-Carthy, Mike Kaplan, Joel Grey, residents of the Stony Indian Reservation. Produced and directed by Robert Altman. Screenplay by Alan Rudolph and Robert Altman. Based on the play *Indians* by Arthur Kopit. Cinematography by Paul Lohmann. Music by Richard Baskin. USA. English. Color. 120 or 137 minutes. 1976.

Robert Altman takes on the American West.

It's definitely inimitable. Every hypocrisy, flaky notion, uncontrollably overblown lie, and genre-pathic stereotype known to the American western is set up here to be shot down by Altman, with the help of Buffalo Bill (Neuman) and his crafty band of klutzes. Like most people, Bill has a "better sense of history than history ever did." He understands the tremendous advantage inherent in the United States—first we conquer them, then we capitalize on them. The Indians—through no fault of their own—were misfits of the historic process. Buffalo Bill Cody made a show that gave the Indians a reason to be famous. There are fur-chapped, double-breasted, brass-buttoned marching bands, precision riding, Annie Oakley (Chaplin), and lots of custom brocade buckskin. And there are accidents. He's got real Indians playing themselves because "We are in the authentic business." It's a blockbuster lineup. But attendance is down. They need something for the center ring. So Sitting Bull (Kaquitts) is released from prison for a season promotional. It's not good that he turns out to be homely and short and speaks only through a seven-foot-tall intuitive interpreter—Mr. Hausley (Denver Pyle). And he wants a new show added to the Wild West lineup—something about the massacres of Indian women and children by the U.S. cavalry. Bill wishes he'd never heard of Bull. Annie Oakley is packing to leave. Ned Buntline (Lancaster) realizes that no one but Buffalo Bill Cody could make such tremendous profits by "telling a pack of lies as though they were the truth." At the end of the season, Sitting Bull is returned to captivity, and is shot trying to escape (actually, while trying to resist being returned to prison). Buffalo Bill, however, has a clear conscience: "God meant for me to be white, and it ain't easy. I've got people with no lives living through me."

Also recommended: *Little Big Man*.

BURN!
(QUEIMADA)

With Marlon Brando, Evaristo Marquez, Renato Salvatori, Norman Hill, Tom Lyons, Wanani. Produced by Alberto Grimaldi. Directed by Gillo Pontecorvo. Written by Franco Solinas and Giorgio Arlorio from a story by Pontecorvo, Solinas, and Arlorio. Photography by Marcello Gatti. Music by Ennio Morricone. France/Italy. English. Color. 112 minutes. 1970.

Slaves are freed into wage-labor bondage by Marlon Brando.

Burn! opens on an island in the Antilles, during the slavery era. To this island Sir William Walker (Brando) is sent in the service of the British government to urge a revolt among the slaves and to establish a puppet government cooperative to British merchant bosses. This he does. The slaves are freed. Ten years later, Sir William is interrupted in the middle of a perpetual drunk to answer another call to the same island. What he finds this time is something like slavery, only different. It's the Greater Antilles Sugar Company. They hire, abuse, underpay, and fire. Slavery—only different. The islanders are threatening revolt. They want control over their lives. Brando's job is to crush such ideas. He doesn't really believe in the sugar company, but he's being paid to do a job and justifies it all by saying, "I'm not quite sure what I'm doing here. I'm not sure why I'm doing what I'm doing. Perhaps its only for the pleasure of it or maybe it's because I don't know how to do anything else. Perhaps

I've nothing else to do. But I do know that whatever I do, I try to do it well and see it clearly through to the end." Maybe only Brando can breathe a fever into such shapeless passages of murk. He plots against the native workers—a counter-revolutionary on the payroll of Greater Antilles Sugar. His job is to provide the audience with an understanding of the cyclical nature of oppression in a capitalist environment. It seems that sugar shares are in great shape and the government of the island is manipulated by entrepreneurs who have gotten stupendously rich off the labor power of others. In his role as turncoat/revolutionary/corporate mercenary, Brando waxes philosophic, spouting such lines as "So often we have to realize that our judgments and our interpretations and even our hopes may have been wrong—wrong, that's all." And, "When one builds to make profit, sometimes it's necessary to destroy. Yes, I think it's inevitable." To Jose, the leader of the native uprising, he says, "It is inevitable that somebody has to lose. It's inevitable that it would be you, otherwise how could I have won?" Jose responds, "Fire does not destroy everything. Even after a fire, there will be one blade of grass." Blades of grass do not stop the sugar corporation or the tyranny of economic despotism. The Antilles are lost to advanced profits worked out by indigenous wage slaves. The English have sugar for their morning tea. It's a harsh and hopeless world. Brando became interested in working with Pontecorvo after seeing *Battle of Algiers*. He wanted to make a "strong political film." *Burn!* is the product of that collaboration. It summarizes the evolution of economic oppression in a way that even the president of General Motors could understand.

Also recommended: *The Ugly American*.

BYE BYE BRAZIL

With Jose Wilker, Zaira Zambelli, Betty Faria, Fabio Junior, Principe Nabor. Produced by Lucy Barreto. Written and directed by Carlos Diegues. Photography by Lauro Escorel. Music by Chico Buarque, Roberto Menescal, and Dominguinhos. Brazil. Portuguese with English titles. Color. 110 minutes. 1980.

A story about a performing gypsy theater in the new Brazil.

Diegues' unanesthetized gypsy heroes are the new-age poor—rootless, shifting populations of immediate gratification cults and freakish social relationships living without a past. They are the gaudy, soulless marionettes of progress, perfecting their marketability. There will be neon lighting and tinsel fringe added to the traveling sideshow, along with music struggling toward melodiousness. The villages they visit are monochromes of decay. Each boom town is more exotically seedy and balkanized than the one before. The people on the streets clutching colas wave their arms at the benediction of wealth waiting beyond the last outpost. The schizophrenia of development is commodifying everything in its path. The caravan of rootless gypsies travels down roadways newly carved from the fragile arborescence of Amazonia. The rain forest lies in ruins. The red earth is ripped open as far as the eye can see. Tradition is squandered, and the lush equatorial tropics are converted to wasteland. The whole process plagiarizes the concussion of urbanization and deforestation worldwide. The cascade of decomposition is graphically pondered by Diegues' raw production values, inflaming the euphoria of change. A brilliant film about a world out of control.

Also recommended: *Pixote.*

CAMILA

With Hector Alterio, Susu Pecoraro, Elena Tasisto, Hector Pellegrini, Mona Maris, Carlos Munoz, Imanol Arias. Produced by Angel Baldo, Hector Gallardo, and Edecio Imbert. Directed by Maria Luisa Bemberg. Written by Maria Luisa Bemberg, Beda Docampo Feijoo, and Juan Stagnaro. Photography by Fernando Arribas. Music by Luis Maria Serra. Argentina. Spanish dubbed into English. Color. 105 minutes. 1984.

The true story of two people executed for falling in love.

Camila lived in 1847 in Buenos Aires, where she met and fell in love with Ladislao—a man sensitive to the poverty, political repression, and future of Argentina. He's also the parish priest. Camila has been raised an independent thinker. She enters the confessional to confess her love. It is Ladislao who passes over her at the sacrament. But he will give in to his feelings and her urgings and leave Buenos Aires with her to start a new life as a fugitive from dictatorial law. The governor orders "these two miserable offensive disgraces be apprehended and jailed." Camila's father disowns her and despises her. Their act is "unprecedented, unheard of in our motherland." They have new names and identities, but the church finds them. They are arrested and executed, for the crime of sacrilege is punishable by death. Ladislao is shot. Camila is pregnant, but she is also executed by firing squad. They are buried in the same coffin. The film pities them and cocoons them in the serene beauty and pureness of nature and the simplicity of sunlight. Camila and Ladislao are immersed in it and enveloped by it. They lose their lives trying to approach it.

Also recommended: *Country Lovers/City Lovers*.

CANNIBAL TOURS

Produced, directed, and photographed by Dennis O'Rourke. Music by W.A. Mozart. Australia. English, German, and Maori with English titles. Color. 77 minutes. 1987.

Tourist reaction to Papua New Guinea aborigines. Aborigine reaction to European tourists.

In New Guinea, as tour boats ease up to the docks, laden with an international clientele contemplating cholesterol and calories and intellectualizing about the native's "vegetative existence," former cannibals arrange hand-carved icons on straw mats, sweep the ancient temples, and wait. Yes, they still climb trees for food and cut them down to build their homes. But the experts agree they are satisfied. They do not seem unhappy. When the natives first saw pale-skinned people, they thought they were their ancestors come back from the dead. Now they know the difference, but still they say, "Look, the dead have returned." For two dollars they guide Europeans through the "spirit house." They sit expectantly beside the items they make for sale. One world traveler has long been interested in "primitive art" and is saddened to see the natives "deviating from that for the tourists." Others note the use of the baroque curves on the masks of ancient design and wonder if they should buy them to hang over their mantels. They bargain down the

prices on the works of art. They know how much native crafts are selling for on five continents. The local tour companies have established a
hierarchy of prices to keep their clients happy. If you don't like the first
price, you can hold out for the second price—30 percent lower. There's
even a third price. The natives complain to the filmmakers that there is
no second price for them when they buy shoes for their children, or
food, or parts for their trucks. Former warriors pose for photographs.
None of them understands why the tourists in their bush fatigues and
tight skirts want pictures of them and pictures of the spirit house. But
the tourists understand the natives completely. "I don't think they understand money. We must help them...educate them...stimulate
them to behave differently and have different aspirations... The problem is apathy and indolence...living in a world completely overwhelmed by nature." In O'Rourke's treatise on sanctimonious cultur-
alism, time has stopped and we meet world-class travelers who would
fight the colonial wars all over again if they could. Paternalism lives
and indigenous societies once overwhelmed by nature are now being
overwhelmed by commerce.

Also recommended: *The Last Tasmanian.*

CHAPAYEV
(TSCHAPAJEV)

With Boris Babochkin, Boris Blinov, Leonoid Kmit, Varvara Myasnikova,
Stephan Shkurat, Illarion Pevtsov, Georgy Vasiliev. Produced and
adapted for the screen by Sergei Vasiliev and Georgy Vasiliev, based on
the writings of D.A. Furmanov and A.N. Furmanova. Photography by Alexander Sigayev and Alexander Ksenofontov. Music by Gavril Popov.
USSR. Russian with titles. Black and white. 99 minutes. 1934.

**A clash between the communists and "White Russian" armies in
which the values of communism are recognized by villagers.**

Chapayev was Vladimir Ilyich Lenin's favorite film, in case you ever
wondered what he did for fun. It takes place during the civil war of
1919. Chapayev is the leader of the village "volunteers" who are con-

fused about which side they're on and so keep misplacing their rifles at the bottom of the river. They know all about the White army, whose soldiers steal from the farmers and whose officers rule from replicas of Roman temples—they are the beneficiaries of class difference. The Red army commissar explains to Chapayev that his army is different. "The peasants and the workers are the people for whose freedom we are fighting." The working class is elevated to the highest social status. "The common person can do anything. . . . They can be generals, doctors, anything." Women are extended equality and the right to dismantle and rebuild machine guns to use against the Whites. Gradually, the villagers stop dropping their weapons into the river and join wholeheartedly in the struggle for the people's union. Lenin wasn't the only one who liked this film. *Chapayev* was shown around the clock when it was released in the USSR in 1934. People camped in the streets to hold their place in line. The film employs few of the cinemagraphic innovations of the early Russian filmmakers, stressing instead the philosophical awakening of the worker to the power of the proletarian unity and revolution.

Also recommended: *Arsenal.*

CHEYENNE AUTUMN

With Richard Widmark, Carrol Baker, Karl Malden, Doloris del Rio, John Carradine, Patrick Wayne, James Stewart, Ricardo Montalban, Edward G. Robinson, Gilbert Roland, Sal Mineo, Victor Jory. Produced by Bernard Smith. Directed by John Ford. Screenplay by James R. Webb, based on the novel by Mari Sandoz. Photography by William Colthier. Music by Alex North. USA. English. Color. 159 minutes. 1964.

The suffering of the Cheyenne Indians in 1887.

The Cheyenne have been so thoroughly domesticated (make that demoralized) by the U.S. cavalry that they wrap themselves in grey blankets and die quietly of measles, smallpox, malaria, and starvation on a reservation where death has claimed three-fourths of their population. But they are still willing to stand in rows all day long in the Oklahoma sun waiting for government officials who never show up. The dedicated

Quaker schoolteacher, Carrol Baker, is on their side but can't get anybody in authority to listen. When the Bureau of Indian Affairs refuses to investigate their hardships, the Cheyenne, with Baker among them, set out on a 1,500 mile-long walk to their homelands in "Yellowstone country." The Indians become colder, hungrier, and more desperate than before. They are attacked by the cavalry and shot at by ranchers. They starve and freeze, but they keep going. Winter sets in, and there is a divergence of opinion on the whole idea of dying to keep from dying. The group splits. One group gives itself up to Fort Robinson, where they suffer more deprivation and injury, including an order to march back to the reservation on foot in winter time. This convinces them to join the rest of their tribe in the Dakotas, which is much reduced in number. However, they are living free and in their own homeland. *Cheyenne Autumn* is a litany of the white man's cruelty, indifference, and hate toward native Americans. Of course, there is a savior: Captain Thomas Archer (Widmark), who marvels with us at the lunacy of life. He's baffled by racism and exhausts himself trying to hold back the destructive force of the military. He is extremely engaging as a man tormented by suffering he is powerless to prevent. Carrol Baker is very good as the Quaker schoolteacher. What a shame her dresses are so tight that she can't talk above a monotone. Don't we wish the casting department had found some real Indians for the lead roles? (Roland is Dull Knife, Montalban is Little Wolf, etc.) If they tried to cast white people in a film about black history, there would be riots. I saw the restored "Road Show" version of the film, which includes a long Wyatt Earp (Stewart) episode that is about as relevant to the plot as a moon probe. Seek out the "unrestored" version. I didn't like the music either. John Ford shot many of his films in Monument Valley, so find a wide screen.

Also recommended: *Indian Agent.*

THE CHINA SYNDROME

With Jane Fonda, Jack Lemmon, Scott Brady, Michael Douglas, James Hampton, Peter Donat, Wilford Brimley, Richard Herd, Daniel Valdez, Stan Bohrman. Produced by Michael Douglas. Directed by James Bridges. Written by Mike Gray, T.S. Cook, and James Bridges. Photography by James Crabe. USA. English. Color. 122 minutes. 1979.

A nuclear power plant malfunction threatens workers and local residents.

The idea of this movie is that a nuclear power plant could burn a hole all the way to China if things went just the right way. For instance, if a needle on the temperature gauge was stuck, control room personnel could throw on enough coal to melt down the containment walls without even knowing what they were doing. If, in addition to a stuck needle, there were other technical miscalculations or structural defects in the plant, just imagine a bigger hole. Jack Lemmon is trying to warn the public about doctored x-rays, lethal radiation leaks, and personnel errors at his plant. Reporter Fonda and photographer Douglas are trying to get his story on the air. It's them against the corporation, the bureaucracy, the law, and plant employees who don't want to lose their jobs even if it does mean softening their genetic codes. The China Syndrome was a curiously timely film. Nuclear power promoters claimed that no parallels could be drawn from the virtual simultaneousness of the release of the film and the accident at the Three Mile Island nuclear plant on the Susquehanna River in Pennsylvania, which was the worst nuclear accident in U.S. history, mirroring the fictional event in many ways. To anti-nuke activists, the movie and the accident were proof that atomic fission was a bad idea. The general public began to lose interest in plutonium-based energy systems and the apogee of the age was passed on by. It was a powerful moment for art. The China Syndrome is extraordinarily amplifying entertainment. It would be indulgent to ask for a better cast. Producer Douglas insisted on having no musical score in the name of nuclear reality. The Motion Picture Guide called The China Syndrome a "blatantly political movie." What they mean is that if there are ten tons of RAD waste being generated out of unsafe plants every day, that's none of Hollywood's business. Stan Bohrman—a T.V. anchorman and reporter in this movie and in real life—went on to cover the Three Mile Island story in his real-life job.

Also recommended: Silkwood.

CHOCOLAT

With Giulia Boschi, Isaach de Bankolé, Mireille Perrier, Francois Cluzet, Cécile Ducasse. Directed by Claire Denis. Written by Denis and Jean-Pol Fargeau, based on Denis' childhood recollections. Photography by Robert Alazraki. Music by Abudullah Ibrahim. France. French with English titles. Color. 105 minutes. 1988.

Unresolved tensions of French colonial life in Africa.

There is a saying, "He who drinks of Africa will drink again." What it means is that Africa will consume you if it can, because it is an avaricious and seductive land. Colonialists were drawn to its exotic places. In this film, they do nothing that is not stylish, seductive, sanguine, prohibited, uncompressed, perhaps steamy, perhaps shielded from the sun, perhaps caught in a soft dry wind. They live with knowledge of invisible turbulence. They tempt the continent and dare the dark-skinned Africans to allow them to survive. It is a circus of tensions and sensual adventure. There are three-hundred years of high-strung social estrangements. And the handsome but overly trusting French area representative will leave his even handsomer wife alone at their open veranda home on the wide side of nowhere. She waits there alone with her daughter and a compound full of native men and women, and visitors who drop by to make bewildering statements about racial mixing. There are stranded urbanites waiting for airplane parts and a young European man who will sleep on a mat in the compound with the blacks, presuming to know their thoughts. And the servant and protector Protee (Bankolé) who will pull her off her knees, forcing her to see that the skin she wanted to touch is black. The child (Ducasse) registers everything as being the same; she has no way to fathom how or why minor events transform their world, while crowds and spectacles leave everything unchanged. She sees things that bring her back to Africa as an adult. Watching the film, we are remembering her life. Wherever she is, she watches from the shadows in the background, out of the way, out of the picture's frame. She watches Africa while we watch her. We aren't sure what she's looking at, but we do know what she's not looking at. *Chocolat* presents layer upon layer of things unspoken about things too honest to be mere art.

Also recommended: *Black and White In Color*.

THE CITADEL

With James Donald, Anne Blythe, Hugh Griffith, Lloyd Bockner, Larry Gates. Adapted for television by Dave Wasserman. Directed by Paul Bogart. From the novel by A. J. Cronin. USA. English. Black and White. 110 minutes.

An idealistic doctor sets out to serve the poor and gets derailed into a lucrative private practice.

The chronic problems associated with medicine for profit are all too conspicuously detailed here. Competitive economics sabotages health care, thus dealing the working classes an early death. The Welsh miners in this surprisingly watchable film suffer from silicosis and tuberculosis. Dr. Andrew Manson would like to serve the health needs of these people. He worships Hippocrates, but there's no money and no supplies. It's just hopeless, and the plush offices of an uptown medical group are tempting him away from the coal mines. The idle rich invent the ailments. The doctors invent the treatments. They prefer hypochondria over Hippocrates. It's lucrative, prestigious, and practically effortless work. You'd have to be part saint to walk away from such a calling. So, Dr. Manson forgets his humanitarian goals. He doesn't even want to talk about the poor and their unpopular occupational diseases. He settles into his wealthy complacency, but fate will bring him back to his senses. A friend and former patient from the mines has a daughter suffering from t.b. Manson looks into her eyes and sees the truth again. He takes her to a biologist who has developed a new, controversial treatment. She is cured. For participating in a "nonmedical" procedure, Manson loses his license to practice medicine. From the witness box, he condemns doctors, society, and public service law. He leaves medicine to work with the biologist, giving the revolutionary treatment to anyone who needs it. He's on his true course again, acting out for us the dilemmas of ethics and health. Campy performances all around. You want to be in this film just to buck the system and win.

Also recommended: *Doktor Judym*.

CIVILIZATION

With Howard Hickman, Enid Markey, Lola May, Herschel Mayall, George Fischer, J. Frank Burke, Charles K. French. Produced by Thomas Ince. Directed by Raymond B. West and Reginald Barker. Screenplay by C. Gardner Sullivan. Photographed by Irvin Willat, et al. Music by Victor Schertzinger. USA. Silent with English titles. Black and white. 102 minutes. 1916.

The whole wide world is saved by goodness.

It's the Teutonic kingdom of Wredpyd. There is a war in progress with enough corporate industrial enthusiasm behind it, with so many thousands of dollars to be made by so many thousands of people (especially the fat ranks of the military), and so few peace advocates speaking out against it, that it could well go on forever. The fact that people are dying is the only thing that distinguishes the event of war from a major oil strike or any other general economic bonanza. Business is booming. But it's an awful slaughter on both sides, and given the severity, *Civilization* suggests that the only thing that can stop it is a visit from Christ in the body of the dead Count Ferdinand. Ferdinand/Christ pleads with the King to sue for peace, which the King does. The divine interdiction, works and closing scenes are of Christ releasing a dove to the heavens, a symbol of the potential for good up there. If this film is too religious for some, it will be too much of a towering bore to others, overstepping as it does all sense of its own thematic proportions. It's a little vacuous from the start and simply swells and swells until it collapses in a celestial vapor. If the idea of peace had been more important to the filmmakers than the idea of out-hulking the latest hulking epic, maybe they could have produced something that integrated the divine visit in some palatable and inspirational way. After all, a personal visit from the son of God is not a bad idea; it couldn't hurt. But it doesn't work this time for a dozen complicated reasons, one of which is that the industries are still there concentrating capital and subduing the land after God goes back to heaven. They started the war in the first place, and they are still there somewhere off-stage wringing twelve hours of hard labor out of their low-paid help. Anyway, my dictionary says the Teutons died out before the time of Christ. Well, *Civilization* is an anti-war film. It's just a little on the impractical side, too impersonal, and probably one of the greatest technical flops of all time.

Also recommended: *All Quiet on the Western Front.*

CLASS ACTION

With Gene Hackman, Mary Elizabeth Mastrantonio, Colin Friels, Joanna Merlin, Larry Fishburne, Matt Clark, Donald Moffat, Jan Rubes. Produced by Ted Field, Scott Kroopf, Robert W. Cort. Directed by Michael Apted. Screenplay by Carolyn Shelby, Christopher Ames, Samantha Shad. Photography by Conrad L. Hall. Music by James Horner. USA. English. Color. 109 minutes. 1990.

Gene Hackman represents the people killed or maimed in the Argo Meridian.

Quite a few critics who saw this film got so excited about the thing going on between father and daughter they failed to notice the auto company or the exploded cars or the disfigured and dead victims. I'm just the reverse. I never forget an exploded car and I'm glad director Michael Apted doesn't either. Margaret Tucker Ward (Mastrantonio) was raised by parents who knew what People's Park was and who the Rosenbergs were. As a child she was lugged along to rallies and marches, but now she's a lawyer for a predatory law firm representing the interests of Argo Motors. They chose Mary Elizabeth to try the class action suit against her own Dad (Hackman). He's gathering evidence on behalf of those killed and injured while driving in a model called the Argo Meridian. Mary has strayed inward from the radical fringe. She doesn't even like her Dad anymore: "The only thing you cared about the huddled masses was standing on their bending backs." (In order to get his picture on the cover of *Time*). He can't believe his ears: "Doesn't she care that people are getting blown up?" He is saddened to see his only child working for corporate "vermin," especially when Argo unloads truckloads of useless paperwork on his doorstep. How will he find the misfiled, missing, or destroyed report of the former Argo employee, Mr. Pavel, who knew the Meridian could explode if rear-ended while the left-turn signal was on? Yes, the report was submitted a decade ago. Argo (read Ford) read it, but noticed it was cheaper to let people die than fix the car. While Hackman worries that the "fascist Reagan judges" will throw his case out of court, Mary uncovers the truth about Argo, her law firm, her slithering boyfriend, and the meaning of life. She's supposed to impale all of Dad's clients on the witness stand. Instead she sets up Argo for a class action victory, and the victims of auto company negligence win landslide claims. Visible through the aura of Gene Hackman's radiant performance is the obvious resemblance of the film to the history of the Ford Pinto. Goose bumps will crawl as knowledgeable theater-goers hear Argo statistics lifted almost directly from Ford's infamous interdepartmental memo tabulating the costs of death versus design modifications. In both the real case and the Argo case, it is cheaper to let people die. In Ford's case, a lot cheaper—until the lawsuits forced recall. Father and daughter know each other at last. And let's hope at least a few members of the audience and a few critics will know what this tremendously important movie is all about.

Also recommended: *Tucker.*

THE COCA-COLA KID

With Eric Roberts, Greta Scacchi, Bill Kerr, Rebecca Smart, Max Gillies, Kris McQuade, Colleen Clifford, Tim Finn, Chris Haywood. Produced by David Roe. Directed by Dusan Makavejev. Screenplay by Frank Moorhouse, based on his stories "The American Baby" and "The Electrical Experience." Photography by Dean Semler. Music by William Motzing. Songs by Tim Finn. Art direction, Anni Browning. Australia. English. Color. 94 minutes. 1985.

Ambitious Coca-cola marketing whiz arrives in Australia to expand Coke markets.

The Coca-Cola Corporation neither authorized nor approved of this fictional expose of monopoly marketing strategies in Australia. Which is why it's in this book. Eric Roberts is Ace, the marketing oracle who styles his sales campaigns after CIA takeovers. He's a bottom line zealot—a kind of profit wizard whose master's thesis was titled "Money is God's Music." His job is to sell more Coke and delete waste, such as that caused by a kid making unnecessary copies of her face on the copy machine, and the secretary discovered hiding in a beverage cooler. He also must delete the arid zone on the marketing map—Anderson Valley, where carbonated beverages are made by T. George McDowell. Fleets of Coca-Cola trucks flood the McDowell zone with Santa-ettes in red and white mini-suits passing out samples of the Real Thing to the "Sounds of Australia" ("Ain't gonna go where there's no Coca-cola-a-a-a . . .") The Santas and the songs don't work on T. George or his customers. They don't even work on Roberts, who accidentally drinks some Anderson Valley soda and loves it but still must expunge it. McDowell cannot win. He makes a counter offer—the creation of a new brand called "McCoke"—a sad gesture. Then Terry, the secretary fired for hiding in the cooler (Scacchi), falls in love with Roberts, and her daughter, the copier abuser, falls for him too and brings him flowers. The Ad-master is beginning to crack. He's very confused. The corporate headquarters are in a faraway place, and he's so alone. When T. George detonates his bottling plant, they all lose the will to fight. Roberts gives in to love and moves in with Terry in a roof-top apartment, Coke-free and poor but stung by novel emotions. Eric Roberts is a special talent and this film is a powder keg going off under First-World capitalists, naming corporate names. It's a victory for director Dusan Makavejev—a victory over the epidemic of corporate intimidation of the arts. The song, "The Sounds of Australia" should have pulled down an Oscar, but it couldn't happen, because Coca-Cola doesn't own the copyright and The Academy of Motion Picture Arts and Sciences offends big business only in its bad dreams.

Also recommended: *Head Office.*

COME SEE THE PARADISE

With Dennis Quaid, Tamlyn Tomita, Sab Shimono, Shizuko Hoshi, Stan Egi. Produced by Robert F. Colesberry. Written and directed by Alan Parker. Photography by Michael Seresin. Music by Randy Edelman. USA. English and Japanese with English titles. Color. 120 minutes. 1990.

Irish union organizer falls in love with Japanese-American woman during World War II.

During World War II, first-generation Japanese (issei) were denied citizenship by law. Second-generation Japanese (Nise) were citizens, but were denied the right to own property or marry outside their race. Promoted as a "touching romance," *Come See The Paradise* is more like a book of knowledge about one of the more outrageous civil rights abuses in recent U.S. history. After the Empire of Japan attacked the U.S. Naval base at Pearl Harbor in World War II, America plunged into an anti-Japanese hysteria of civil injustice, including mass arrests and the internment of millions of Japanese-Americans in detention camps dreamt up by J. Edgar Hoover as a national security measure. Executive order #9066 gave the Japanese six days to sell out their homes and businesses and submit to legislated racism. In the forced internment, they left behind everything they couldn't carry. Ruthless opportunists—always waiting in the woodwork of war—underbid each other on the Japanese-Americans' family treasures. Dennis Quaid is a union organizer who marries a nisei (Tomita) and suffers his own civil persecutions. On parole for labor activities, he is drafted under the War Powers Act and separated from his family, who are stuck in the camps. After the gates lock behind them, his wife's family must take loyalty oaths, which force people who have first been denied American citizenship then to deny allegiance to Japan. If they signed, they could then be sent to fight against their own country. This convoluted interpretation of justice resulted in both issei and nisei who refused to sign the oath being traded to Japan for U.S. prisoners of war. Families living in prison camps had stars hanging in the windows of their stark rooms—one star for each child killed fighting for the U.S. By the time the U.S. Supreme Court rules the camps unconstitutional, Tomita's father is dead. One brother is traded to Japan. Another is killed in battle. The internment of Japanese citizens and residents was conceived and executed in a mood of nationalistic mania. The film itself, cataloging this horrendous transgression against innocent people, was released just a few weeks prior to U.S. declaration of war against Iraq. When the bombing started the film was pulled, and *Come See the Paradise* had to settle for small audiences at local art theaters. A lot of people will never see this wonderful, insightful film—another casualty of war. The audience I sat with was predominantly Japanese-American. I don't know which was more moving, the film up on the screen or the Japanese crying behind me.

Also recommended: *Eat a Bowl of Tea.*

THE CONFORMIST

With Jean-Louis Trintignant, Stefania Sandrelli, Dominique Sanda, Pierre Clementi, Gastoni Moschin, Enzo Tarascio, Jose Quaglio, Yvonne Sanson. Produced by Maurizio Lodi-Fe. Directed by Bernardo Bertolucci.

Written by Bertolucci based on the novel *The Conformist* by Alberto Moravia. Photography by Vittorio Storaro. Music by Georges Delerue. Italy. Italian dubbed into English. Color. 108 minutes. 1970.

Life and death of a hit man who guns down anti-fascists because he wants to fit in.

Marcello Clerici (Trintignant) had an oddly decadent childhood, surrounded by luxury, servants, a mother who mainlined morphine supplied by her Japanese chauffeur/lover, and a father who tortured people for the fascist government and wound up in a mental hospital. At the age of thirteen, Marcello killed a chauffeur for whom he felt a homosexual attraction. Now he's an adult yearning for a normal life. He wants to "feel" normal. For this reason he marries a bourgeois blonde, joins the fascists under Mussolini, and hires out to hunt down subversives. "I want to construct my normalcy," says Clerici. At confession he pleads, "I want to confess today for the sins I will commit tomorrow." Tomorrow's assignment is to kill a professor and former friend, Dr. Quadri (Tarascio). In order to conform to the Mussolini regime, he will kill a man he studied under and still admires. As he plots the assassination, his bourgeois wife lives her bourgeois life of white fox fur and dinner parties. Part of Marcello's assassination technique is to visit the professor and meet his friends. This saps his enthusiasm—not his enthusiasm to conform, but his enthusiasm for killing Quadri, especially after he discovers that the professor and his friends know he's a counterrevolutionary. Quadri's wife, Anna (Sanda), says, "Don't think we didn't know . . . you're a fascist, you're lower than a worm, you revolt me, you disgust me, you're a spy." The professor tells him he could change. But Marcello can't change, he can only cease to do anything. All he wants is to fit in. Other henchmen are called to kill the Quadris. Marcello is forced to watch, helpless, from a nearby car. Then Mussolini resigns, but Marcello has burned his bridges at both ends. He discovers that the chauffeur he thought he'd killed is alive, celebrating the fall of fascism. His whole life has been a cruel mistake. He was never as odd as he thought. He was never a killer. He's dizzy at the vagaries of life. And we are dizzy at the vagaries of film.

Also recommended: *The Pedestrian.*

COUNTRY

With Sam Sheppard, Jessica Lange, Wilford Brimley, Matt Clark, Theresa Graham, Levi L. Knebel, Sandra Seacat, Jim Haynie. Produced by William D. Wittliff, Jessica Lange, and William Beaudine, Jr. Directed by Richard Pearce. Written by William D. Wittliff. Photography by David M. Walsh and Roger Shearman. Music by Charles Gross. USA. English. Color. 105 minutes. 1984.

Farm family tries to save its farm amidst crashing crop prices and mortgage call-ins.

By 1984, when this film was made, 40 percent of outstanding farm loans in the U.S. were delinquent. The inevitable build-up of agribusiness empires, many of which sunk deep roots during the Depression, now had the power to underbid, undersell, destroy, or buy out any farm or farmland worth the trouble in the U.S. Many of the family farms survived the shakedown of the Depression era only to be strangled out in the decades to come by corporate food monopolies, with an assist from the farm policies of the Carter and Reagan administrations. Sam Sheppard and Jessica Lange own a farm in Iowa that's been in the family for a hundred years. They know farming; their friends are farmers. But, one by one their friends' mortgages are foreclosed and they have thirty days to come up with a mortgage payment before the farm goes on the block. Lange spends the night going over the books so that when Sam wakes up in the morning, she can tell him, "I've just figured out why we are going broke. We're losing 75 cents on every bushel of corn we produce." Sheppard, never one to overact, stares at her with the light draining from his eyes. He begins to drink and becomes violent toward his family, because losing a farm is not like losing a gas station. When you're a farmer, it's your home, your work, and your history. There are animals and buildings and land you grew up on. Your whole world is going and nothing will ever be the same for you again. In *Country*, farm after farm goes on the auction block. Organized bidding blockades will not stop it. Human tragedy will not stop it. Nothing will stop it because it's the free enterprise system. *Country* shows an average farm fold with the family still trapped inside, because that's the way it happens. It's a very personalized look at the cool escalation of capital and the loss of power and independence that it leaves behind. Sheppard and Lange, a couple in real life, play crumbling marriage partners with a measured, reckless authenticity.

Also Recommended: *The River.*

COUNTRY LOVERS, CITY LOVERS

With Ryno Hatting, Nomse Nene, Brian O'Shaugnessy, Joe Stewardson, Denise Newman, Rachel Frey. Produced by Christopher Davies. *Country Lovers* directed by Manie van Rensburg. Screenplay by Nadine Gordimer. Photography by Tai Krige. Music by Art Heatlie. *City Lovers* directed by Barney Simon. Screenplay by Barney Simon, from the story by Nadine Gordimer. Photographed by Paul Hambides. Music by John Oakely-Smith. South Africa and England. English. Color. 120 minutes. 1982.

A dramatization of two stories: the first an interracial romance in the city; the second, an interracial romance in the country.

"The English gave away Rhodesia, but South Africa is still a civilized country—a white man's country with an Afrikaans government." South Africa abounds in cruelties of forced separation, social estrangement, lost love, broken families, criminal prosecution, humiliation, and lives shattered weakly against the Immorality Act of 1957. The cost of implementing and enforcing monstrous intrusions into the civil rights of South African citizens is a cost apartheid supporters have always been willing to pay. Before the bureaucracy of petty apartheid began to crumble in the late 1970s, blacks, orientals, coloreds, Indians, and whites grew up memorizing the *legal* taboos of the exclusionary fraternization laws. In *City Lovers,* a visiting geologist who is inexperienced in apartheid falls in love with a young colored woman whom he convinces to move in with him and pose as his cleaning lady. Intolerant neighbors report them, and she is found hiding in the closet while he phones for legal aid. He leaves the country, never knowing how she was examined like an animal for signs of criminal sexual behavior. In *Country Lovers,* a young Afrikaans man is attracted to an African woman. They are too young to understand what it means to be in violation of immorality codes. They will repeal all their promises and their integrity for the magistrates of the apartheid court. These two stories reveal just a small part of the toll in human unhappiness South Africa has demanded from its people who are denied the experience of harmonious, egalitarian social existence. Author Nadine Gordimer is a visionary talent. Her stories are of ordinary people living unordinary lives. She explores how ordinary people submit to tyranny and how their lives are destroyed. Although the Immorality Act of 1957 remains on the statute books, the Mixed Marriages Act was repealed in the 1980s. *Country Lovers, City Lovers* was filmed on location in South Africa.

Also recommended: *Master Harold and the Boys.*

COVERUP: BEHIND THE IRAN-CONTRA AFFAIR

Narrated by Elizabeth Montgomery. Produced by Barbara Trent, Gary Meyer, David Kasper. Directed by Barbara Trent. Written by Eve Goldberg. Photographed by Gary Meyer. Music by Richard Elliott. USA. English. Color. 72 minutes. 1988.

Documentary testimony to Reagan-Bush corruption during the 1980 campaign and in the White House.

In *Coverup*, former presidential campaign aide Barbara Honegger testifies that Reagan and his staff conspired with the Iranians prior to the presidential elections of 1980 to delay the release of the American hostages as a campaign ploy, in exchange for which Reagan-Bush would make available to Iran, after Reagan's election to the presidency, "...all the arms they would ever need in the war against Iraq." According to Honegger, payments to Iran began early in 1981 and with them began the "Ultimate Covert Operation." The deal was set in October of 1980 by George Bush, who went to Paris to make offers that would effectively stall the release of the hostages until after the November election. According to Trent, Honegger, Daniel Sheehan of the Cristic Institute, Peter Dale Scott, John Stockwell, and others, this treachery against the American people was the bedrock of a towering deceit in an administration corrupt enough to defy the U.S. Constitution, divest laws of their meaning, and throw into jeopardy the welfare of millions of innocent people all over the world. They dismantled ethical gains made by President Jimmy Carter, who during his term in office had fired over 800 corrupt CIA personnel. Reagan-Bush extended lethal privilege to the CIA, supporting them and benefiting from intense covert drug trafficking, worldwide illegal weapons sales, assassinations, and military interventions on behalf of U.S. multinationals. The trial of

Oliver North was a well-planned diversion to keep the public focused on the Iran-Contra connection and to camouflage the drug connections that would have lead to impeachment. Secret "executive sessions" were set aside to answer questions about drug trafficking and cocaine smuggling raised in open court. Also channeled to executive session were questions related to North's "Readiness Exercise 1984" (Rex, 84), a plan to suspend the U.S. Constitution in case of a national emergency. Drug trafficking is traced back to Vietnam and the illegal secret war in Cambodia funded by opium sales. "Gargantuan amounts of money" were generated in narcotics and weapons trading—the major world money makers. *Coverup* is so incriminating of the Reagan-Bush administration that when the Cristic Institute offered Michael Dukakis the film to use in his 1988 bid for the presidency, he refused, saying the evidence was so outrageous that it would shake his public credibility.

Also Recommended: *The Hidden Agenda.*

THE CROWD

With James Murray, Eleanor Boardman, Bert Roach, Estelle Clark. Directed by King Vidor. Screenplay by King Vidor and John V.A. Weaver. Photography by Henry Sharp. USA. Silent with titles. Black and white. 104 minutes. 1928.

Poverty pulls down all the hopes and dreams of John and Mary.

Something has happened since King Vidor made *The Crowd*. Industry has concentrated capital, dominated the political process, bought and sold Third-World countries, defamed human rights, and dehumanized the work place, and everyone else has forgotten it ever happened because it's just the law of life. It's progress. Creative artists of the free world don't even see it anymore, so how can they paint pictures or make movies about the monotony, regimentation, and alienation? It doesn't sell; there's no place for it in the "entertainment" industry. Because of this, *The Crowd* is a priceless antique—sort of an autographed edition of the story of John, born on the 4th of July to parents who believed the billboards in the land of social mobility and material promise. But bad times lead John to desk number 10a in a gridlock of identity redundancy. He's a worker conspicuous of his replaceability. He will marry, have two children, and live in a cottage. He wins $500 in the lottery, still unaware there is no margin for error in the worker idyll. When his son dies in a car accident, his grief saps his strength, and he is fired from the grid. His marriage fails. He hires out as a sandwich-board man like the one his parents ridiculed when they still held him in the protective circle of their adoration. His wife forgives him and they celebrate their reunion at a vaudeville show where they can feel happy, at least for the moment. The people beside them feel it, too. Row after row of faces reflect back the overly artificial light. There are so many faces in the huge theater that from a distance they look exactly like larvae squirming toward a future they lack the capacity to foretell in a world they lack the power to understand. They are incubators for working-class dehumanization in one of the most brilliant and most terrifying scenes in film media—a view of valueless humanity existing by reflex to random stimuli. Each half of the reproductive pair occupies space in the worker catacombs, subsisting to pollinate increased productive capacity. To history, they are faceless, memorable only in the aggregate. They have accepted every social belittlement. Populations of the present differ from them only in the magnitude of their self-deception.

Also Recommended: *A Nous la Liberte.*

CRY FREEDOM

With Denzel Washington, Kevin Kline, Penelope Wilton, Zakes Mokae, Josette Simon, John Thaw, Sophie Mgcina. Produced by Richard Attenborough, Norman Spencer, and John Briley. Directed by Richard Attenborough. Screenplay by John Briley, based on the books *Biko* and *Asking for Trouble* by Donald Woods. Photography by Ronnie Taylor. Music by George Fenton and Jonas Gwangwa. USA. English. Color. 157 minutes. 1987.

Black consciousness leader in South Africa is detained and killed by police.

Not surprisingly, many reviewers were critical of Denzel Washington's brief screen time in a movie billed as the story of the character he played: Bantu Stephen Biko, the South African black consciousness leader who died in police custody in 1977. But while blacks have suffered the full force of apartheid brutality in South Africa, it would be unfair to Donald Woods to deny him screen time in this film, since the story of the two social activists follows the format of his book from which the screenplay depends. If Wood's eventual escape is too adventurous for what has gone before, it was his expatriation that allowed the book to be published and the movie to be made. And perhaps more white South Africans should follow his lead and leave the country. (Even a liberal white is counted in the population tallies by the ruling minority.) After its release, Woods followed *Cry Freedom* around the world, answering questions about the film and South Africa, and he is only one of many expatriates who are still working, in their own way, to end apartheid. More than ten years after his escape, he was able to bring his former maid, Evalina (Mgcina), to England, where she stood amazed to see white women washing their own stoops and sweeping the sidewalks. That Denzel Washington is so appealing on the screen and definitely captures Biko's charming charismatic personality makes it tempting to demand more of him. Biko's screen time is well laid out and audiences learn so much about white suppression and barbarities that the after-image is one of wholeness and depth. Of the many insights tucked into this film is a background on Afrikaaner consciousness ("We arrived in 1652. We didn't colonize this country, we built it. Do you think we are going to give it all up?") and insight into Afrikaaner police tactics couched within the protective custody of corrupt magistrates and ministers of the law. Through Biko *Cry Freedom* says something other films in this elite genre don't get around to—that most of the violence and death whites inflict on blacks is the starvation in the homelands and in the relocation camps and the imprisonment of true leaders who could help gain equal rights for South Africa's black majority. Biko and Woods' first interviews on the screen and in real life centered on themes of black consciousness, which liberal newspaper editor Donald Woods (Kline) believed would build a wall of race hate in South Africa. Biko explained that the biggest stumbling block to majority rule was the national black inferiority complex of people who judged their humanity and their "blackness" against the wealth and power of white culture. Here, at least, the film could have followed the book more closely and included passages such as "It isn't a negative, hating thing. It's a positive black self-confidence thing involving no hatred of anyone, not even the Nats (Nationals). . . . We want to work to establish a country in which all men are free . . . white as well as black." Woods readily understood Biko's theories and began to promote them in his editorials. He hired two black reporters to cover the native news. His activism led to his eventual banning under the Internal Securities Act, as well as attacks on and threats to his family. After Biko's death, Woods pushed for an inquest and was able to acquire and release to the world press posthumous photos of Biko which proved how terribly he had been beaten before he died. Closing scenes are of the black children's school boycott that Biko had helped organize and a list of the names of the dozens of black activists who had died in police custody in South Africa. "Suicide by hanging" and "no explanation" were the most commonly documented causes of these detention deaths. *Cry Freedom* is a film that informs without pontificating. It is full of gifted performances by Washington, Kline, Wilton, and Mokae, although perhaps it does not quite make it clear that Donald Woods considered Stephen Biko, "the greatest man I ever had the privilege to know."

Also recommended: *A World Apart.*

DANCES WITH WOLVES

With Kevin Costner, Mary McDonnell, Graham Greene, Rodney Grant, Tantoo Cardinal, Fred Red Crow Westerman, Maury Chaykin, and Teddy and Buck as Two Socks, the wolf. Produced and directed by Kevin Costner. Photography by Dean Semler. Music by John Barry. Screenplay by Michael Blaked, from the simultaneous book by Michael Blaked. USA. Color. English and Lakota with titles. 160 minutes. 1990.

U.S. Army lieutenant meets the Sioux and rejects white culture.

It's 1863. The U.S. Civil War has loomed to a raging lull. Our hero, Lt. Dunbar (Costner), lies on the amputation table in a frontline surgical tent. It looks bad, but when the doctors take a breath from their grisly work, Costner grits his teeth, pulls his boots on over his messed-up foot, and rides off into enemy fire hoping a rebel bullet will end his pain. He's an incredibly easy target, but mere bullets cannot touch him. He does not die, and he does not lose his foot because the general is so impressed with what he's just seen that he sends for his private surgeon to save the guy. The general also gives him a nice horse, Cisco, *and* the appointment of his dreams to the "farthest frontier." Dunbar treks to the run-down, deserted outpost on the edge of Indian territory. The subhuman war groupies he meets along the way help deify the Sioux, who will enter like craft marvels built of buckskin, fringe, and feathers. At the frontier outpost, uncouth agonies of the Civil War are washed away by hushed prairie expanses and the Dakota hills—sacred lands of the Sioux nation. The first Indians we see, though, are the marauding Pawnee, who drive five or six arrows into the departing buckboard driver but still leave him twitching. Not only are they bad, they are a bad aim. The Sioux, on the other hand, are mythic. The camera dwells on delicate red-skinned hands parting the prairie grasses. Costner's gradual acquaintanceship and identification with the Sioux is what this movie is all about. If Costner fancies himself a hero whom only the Indians can make more heroic, *Dances With Wolves* salvages enough dignity and heraldic calm for everyone. It's a doorway to another time. Costner becomes a lieutenant without guile, touched by innocence wherever he should find it. He becomes Dances with Wolves. He learns Lakota and practices the fire dance in melancholy clumsiness alone after dark at the post. Costner's love interest, played skillfully here by Mary McDonnell, layers the thematic tension of the film. Her fidelity to Indian traditions and culture mirrors his own nascent fascination. That Dances with Wolves *and* Stands With Fist (McDonnell) are both white poetically accentuates the rejection of the commercial, genocidal white culture. In *Dances With Wolves*, progress is *not* our most important product and modernity is the flaw in human history. Those who complained the Indians were "just like us" ought to take a few trips around the D.C. beltway, and whoever should find any tradition or ancestral heritage there or any widespread sense of purpose or love of the land will know they have fallen into a carbon-monoxide trance. Of course, the gimmick is that they *are* just like us. They eat, they sleep, they love, they dance. It's not a defect in the script; it's more like a revelation. Like most films, *Dances With Wolves* is pretty easy to follow. There's never more than one thing happening in each scene, making Costner's narration mostly just a lull in a three-hour screenplay. As an actor under his own direction, he's endearing in this role that is emblematic of a craving for permanence and community and a freedom to love nature and know the land. Most critics appreciated real Indians Greene, Grant, and Westerman cast in lead roles. Others wanted only Lakotas. Many resented the violence directed toward animals. All applauded the use of the Lakota language—a victory for cultural integrity in the arts. Indian critics are tired of having their oppressors telling their story, no matter how they do it. For the critical record, in the film's final scene, Costner does not leave the Indians "to their fate"; he leaves to decoy cavalry retaliation against an AWOL lieutenant. Barry's score is sadly soggy. But fabulous buffalo stampedes and Semler's cinematography simply stun the senses.

Also recommended: *Never Cry Wolf.*

DANIEL

With Timothy Hutton, Amanda Plummer, Mandy Patinkin, Ed Asner, Ellen Barkin, Joseph Leon, Lindsay Crouse, Ilan M. Mitchell-Smith. Produced by Burtt Harris. Directed by Sidney Lumet. Screenplay by E.L. Doctorow, based on his novel *The Book of Daniel.* Photography by Andrzei Bartkowiak. Music by Bob James. Songs by Paul Robeson. USA. English. Color. 130 minutes. 1983.

The story of Daniel and Susan, whose parents were executed for espionage in the 1950s in the U.S.

After Julius and Ethel Rosenberg were arrested and accused of transmitting a sketch of the A-bomb implosion lens to a Soviet agent, they were tried and executed in the electric chair by the United States government. Whether they were guilty or ought to have received the death penalty is not the focus of this film. It is to be noted, however, that Klaus Fuchs, who transmitted virtual catalogs of atomic bomb secrets to the Soviets during World War II, served eight years in a British prison for his crime. *Daniel* is about the "Isaacson's" surviving children. Daniel (Hutton) and his sister Susan (Plummer) are now adults, coping with the tragic phenomenon of their lives. Susan is a dedicated activist tormented by her novel position in history. As her mental health deteriorates and she confesses, "I've forgotten what you are supposed to expect from life," the long-cynical Daniel (Hutton) begins to reconstruct his radicalism. He interviews people about his parents' case. "[They] were party members." "In those days, before the Sputnik, we downgraded Soviet technology. If they had a bomb, it was *our* bomb—we had to blame . . . someone." "Falsified evidences." "Classified stuff." "It's never been proven any secrets were stolen." The young Daniel grew up familiar with Marxian theory. To his father a box of Wheaties was a convenient breakfast exhibit. "They are lying. That's what advertising is—lying. He sells his name and his picture to the cereal company for money. But he's a worker. . . . And the fact that he plays baseball makes him no different . . . than a man who works in the factory and do you know why?" "Because he doesn't own the team." "And there are Negro players who can't play and do you know why" "Jim Crow." "No matter how good they are." The young Daniel, played with precocious aloofness by Mitchell-Smith, ratifies the futility of placing trust in the nation state. "How will they kill you, Mommy?" "Well, darling, it's something called electrocution, and it's very painless. How's school?" "Fine, I'm going to be a lawyer, so I can get you free." Their father raves, "We are the ideal family." At rallies, the children are passed over the heads of crowds chanting for their parents' freedom. The ardent tension of the narrative pays punitive tribute to a society divided by political and economic ideal.

Also recommended: *Katherine*.

THE DAY AFTER

With John Lithgow, Jason Robards, Doug Scott, John Gullum, Bibi Besch, Vori Lethin, Steve Guttenberg, Amy Madigan, Jeff East, Calvin Jung, Lin McCarthy, Clayton Day, Georgeann Johnson. Produced by Robert A. Papazian. Directed by Nicholas Meyer. Written by Edward Hume. Photography by Cayne Rescher. Original score by David Raksin. USA. English. Color. 126 minutes. 1984.

The people of Kansas are hit by nuclear missiles.

You'll like the way this film opens inside a nimbus cloud in the blue sky over the Kansas grain fields. It is surely an ideal panorama, symbolizing a host of pious, priceless visions fundamental to American gothic utopian ideals. But by 1984, time has caught up to Americana. The Oscar Control Mission Launch Site is twenty miles east of Kansas City, and there are 150 Minuteman missile silos strung out halfway down the state of Missouri. If Kansas used to be on the road to nowhere, "there is no nowhere anymore." The Minutemen rise without warning into the prairie sky. Over barnyards, grocery stores, laundry on the line, and

people who feel nothing at the sight. They are still standing in the
checkout aisles as the returning Soviet warheads explode and the malignant sunrise vaporizes wheat fields and converts buildings into the
howling debris of civilization. Men, women, and children are incinerated. All living things are incinerated. Forests are sunk into ash. And
now it's the day after—shortages of shelter, food, water, power, hospitals, doctors, medical supplies. A gray snow is falling—the remnants of
the world. Survivors move about like phantoms. Underground garages
are mortuaries for the living dead. Nuclear war is war, plus epidemic,
catastrophic, unnatural disaster, collapse of technology, collapse of
culture—trauma of the master race. Deterrence has delivered humankind to the furies of proliferation. There is radiation poisoning. Those
who can walk roam in packs. They are nauseous, weak, dizzy and disoriented. Their hair is coming out. Their skin burns with ulcers. Farmers
worry, "If we dispose of all the contaminated topsoil, what will be left
to farm?" Churches are the new junkyards. Everything you touch and
everything you see and everything you eat is infected with decay. They
say it's not the end. And they are right. The end is yet to come. The filmmakers have appended a reading list to the credits, including: *Nuclear
Madness*, by Helen Caldicott; *On Thermo Nuclear War*, by Herman
Kahl; and *The Fate of the Earth*, by Jonathan Schell.

Also recommended: *Threads*.

THE DAY AFTER TRINITY

Directed and produced by Jon Else. Written by Jon Else, David Peoples,
and Janet Peoples. Music by Martin Bresnick. Photography by Tom
McDonough, et al. Narrated by Paul Frees. USA. English. Color and
black and white. 88 minutes. 1980.

Story of the building and detonation of the first atomic weapons.

Imagine a town in New York with several subdivisions: metallurgy, or-
dinance, chemistry, theoretical physics, experimental physics, bomb
physics, and explosives. Imagine 6,000 people secretly gathered together in this town in the desert with dance bands, scout troops, ball
teams, and a radio station with no call letters. Imagine J. Robert Oppen-

heimer ruling over a secret A-bomb city—Los Alamos, New Mexico—the most expensive science project in the history of the world. Ten pounds of plutonium alone cost one billion dollars. Here they build the bomb that will kill 100,000 people in nine seconds in Hiroshima and 80,000 more in Nagasaki in World War II. Oppenheimer's dazzling comprehension of nuclear theory overrides his radical, bohemian reputation, and he wins top security clearance to build the bomb. He's a Jew anxious about Hitler's rise to power and spread of fascism in Europe. Believing the bomb will save western civilization, he agrees to coordinate the U.S. effort. The A-bomb is meant for the Third Reich. But, when fascism falls, few at Los Alamos suggest they stop work on "the gadget." *The Day After Trinity* reveals the development of the bomb as an intellectual game that nobody wanted to stop playing. It was *the* puzzle that they could not put down until all the pieces fit together. The potential destructive capacity of the new weapon was an abstraction, even to Oppenheimer and certainly to those whose job it was to find a place to use it after Hitler's defeat. When the first nuclear weapon was detonated at La Jornada Del Muerte in Trinity, New Mexico, many of these physicists and chemists were horrified as the mushroom cloud rose up bright enough to be seen from Mars. Their comments captured forty years later retain the disillusionment and despair of that day. "When you've sold your soul to the devil, there's no going back on it." "I thought I would vomit," said one scientist remembering the "overpowering vision of it," dwarfing the surrounding mountains. "What have we done, what have we done?" The question remains unanswered. "I don't know any part of history where it would be proper to use one of those very powerful bombs." Oppenheimer recalled a line from the Bhagavad-Gita, "I have become Death, the destroyer of worlds." The game was over. The puzzle was solved. Oppenheimer began a campaign to initiate international control of nuclear weapons. He believed the bomb should never be used. "Our only hope in future safety must lie in a collaboration based on confidence and good faith with the other peoples of the world." His dream of stopping the arms race before it could begin was never realized. The Americans had just lost 50,000 men at Okinawa. They had the bomb and the "perfect" excuse to use it. The military was advised not to plan air strikes on Hiroshima or Nagasaki so that the effects of the new weapon could be assessed on virgin targets. On a clear August morning in 1945, with office workers at their desks and the city at peak population density, the bomb was dropped. Oppenheimer never forgave himself. "Physicists have known sin, and this is a knowledge which they cannot lose." The world became a testing ground for a Faustian arsenal of bombs. The first test of an H-bomb—1,000 times more powerful than the A-bomb—vaporized an entire island in the Pacific. To the scientists, the bombs "... created an illusion of illimitable power ... for people to see what they can do with their minds." Oppenheimer's opposition to the development of the hydrogen bomb during the height of Senator McCarthy's HUAC rein in 1953 lead to the reversal of Oppenheimer's top security clearance. He was accused of treason and never worked in nuclear energy again. When, in the 1960s, he was asked what he thought of President Johnson's efforts to halt the spread of nuclear weapons, he lit his pipe before answering, "It's twenty years too late," he says, at last. "It should have been done the after Trinity."

Also Recommended: *The Decision to Drop the Bomb.*

DEAD END

With Humphrey Bogart, Marjorie Main, Sylvia Sidney, Joel McCrea, Clair Trevor, Wendy Barrie, Billy Halop, the Dead End Kids. Produced by Samuel Goldwyn. Directed by William Wyler. Screenplay by Lillian Hellman, based on the play by Sidney Kingsley. Photography by Gregg Toland. Music by Alfred Newman. USA. English. Black and white. 92 minutes. 1937.

A successful crook returns to the old neighborhood to see how little things have changed.

Dead End is a high-camp caper along the waterfront where the superrich and the hoodlum youth are clashing. There is Humphrey Bogart. There is Sylvia Sidney. There is Joel McCrea. There is Marjorie Main as Bogie's unresponsive mother. Few film moments match Marjorie the Magnificent pulling herself up the tenement stairwell, despising Bogie with every step. She carries the heartache of the ages up those stairs with her. She doesn't want him or any of his kind. Bogart is the black sheep Mafioso, back home on the waterfront to show off his new suit, see his mom, and let everybody know crime does pay. He's pretty stealthy the way he goes about it, too, lurking around corners with his two thug friends. He used to be a street urchin himself, just like the former Dead End Kids/future Bowery Boys who are out to kill us with their dastardly boyish deeds. The rich kid who lives near the docks despises them, and the trouble with *Dead End* is that we sort of despise them, too. They are MGM's robotic Pinocchios, dicing dialogue and practicing for the forthcoming long years of bullshot delivery as the Bowery Boys. That's the way it used to be for kids in Hollywood, and Hellman's script just lets it happen.

Also recommended: *Wild Boys on the Road.*

DEAR AMERICA: LETTERS HOME FROM VIETNAM

With letters read by Sean Penn, Elizabeth McGovern, Willem Dafoe, Martin Sheen, Tom Berenger, Ellen Burstyn, Richard Chaves, Josh Cruze, T. Kenneth Campbell, Robert DeNiro, Kevin Dillon, Matt Dillon, John Heard, Fred Hirz, Eric Roberts, Tim Quill, Raphael Sbarge, Tico Wells, Robin Williams, Brian Dennehy, Robert Downey, Jr., Michael J. Fox, Harvey Keitel, Judd Nelson, Ray Robertson, John Savage, Tucker Smallwood, Jim Tracy, Kathleen Turner, Randy Quaid, Mark Harmon, Roger Steffens. Directed by Bill Couturie. Screenplay by Richard Dewhurst and Bill Couturie, from the book *Dear America: Letters Home From Vietnam*, edited by Bernard Edelman. Photography by Bill Couturie and Thomas Bird. USA. English. Color and black and white. 84 minutes. 1987.

"This film is about young men in war. It is their own story, told in their own words—words they wrote home in letters from Vietnam. Every scene ever shown in the film is real, nothing has been reenacted."

"I feel like I'm at the bottom of a great sewer." "The guns don't bother me. I can't hear them anymore. I'm hollow. I'm a shell." For men living in their own nightmare, letters home are the only way out. "The frightening thing about it is that it is so very easy to kill. There's no remorse. Not even regret. You kill because that little son of a bitch is trying to kill you and you desperately want to live." One boy lies sobbing on the jungle floor. Others sit nearby, emptied of feeling, rotely arranging their gear. "I went through the Purple Heart ritual. It left me sicker than I was before and with a medal I never wanted anyway." The film supplies running totals of the American combat figures and death counts. The first 3,500 combat troops were sent in March 1965. By December 1966, 385,300 U.S. troops were on hand in Southeast Asia. By December 1967, 16,021 had died there. "This war is all wrong." "It's not that I can't understand *this* war, it's that I can't understand war period." There are home movies taken on R&R—broadly smiling faces not quite masking the fear. And there is combat footage recapturing the shock of the war. "Why don't your hearts cry out and shed a tear for the 40,000 brave men who have given their lives. We are not pleading for your praise. All we are asking for is for our great nation to support us and help us end the war." The Kent State killings are reported by Chet Huntley. And John Lennon is singing, "Give peace a chance." In the winter of 1973, homecoming POWs return to the states, and, finally, the U.S. is out of the war. But the war is not out of the U.S. Mothers bring letters to The Wall—personal messages to names carved in marble, trying to push love through the curtain of death to men who died alone and afraid.

Also recommended: *Apocalypse Now*.

THE DECISION TO DROP THE BOMB

Written and produced by Fred Freed. Directed by Len Giovanitti and Fred Freed. Narrated by John Rich. USA. English. Black and white. 82 minutes. 1965.

History of the development and detonation of the first atomic weapons.

In Oak Ridge, Tennessee, a government facility is using twice as much energy as the entire city of Memphis. The power-guzzler is the secret manufacturing site of uranium 235. As Japan issues surrender signals to the U.S.S.R., and one million Japanese roam homeless from U.S. fire-bombing, and General Curtis LeMay brags, "We are sending the Japs back to the caves," U.S. bomb enthusiasts scuttle to project huge potential American combat losses in a war they pronounce will continue to the fall of 1946. By July 1945, Japan is in ashes. High-level testimonies surface questioning the use of the A-bomb "as the war was ending." Among those who agree to the bombing, some question using it without warning. Others oppose using the weapons on civilian targets. Many suggest that a demonstration blast alone might end the war. Secretary of War Stimson says, "Failure to use the weapon *in all its fury* . . . would make it difficult for the world to understand what it was facing." Petitions are gathered and ignored. On Friday the 13th, one billion dollars worth of plutonium is delivered in a small warm container to Los Alamos, New Mexico. The first nuclear weapon test turns the desert sand to glass and sinks the earth nine feet below ground zero. Franklin Delano Roosevelt is dead. Truman has been in office only three months. Handed a twenty-four page summary of the atom bomb project he complains, "I don't like to read long reports." The decision to drop the bombs that killed 180,000 people was the by-product of an almost complete lack of consensus about the development of the bomb—where, when, or whether to drop the bomb, how to promote or pay for the bomb, and the long-term application or bomb diplomacy on the international scene. Enthusiastic consensus comes only from the military. Acquiescence to anti-Japanese hysteria, intellectual curiosity about the bomb's power, and the irresistible allure of imperial potential overwhelm moral and ethical considerations. Concerning the murder of hundreds of thousands of noncombatants, opponents remember, "we were operating in a climate of opinion in which it was almost taken for granted a tremendous destruction of civilians lives, civilian dwellings, houses and of cities." All decisions concerning the use of the bomb were carried on in a vacuum of practical understanding—no one had ever *seen* an atomic bomb blast. Few, if any, comprehended its power. Some did not even believe the "rumors" of radiation. The Trinity test was scheduled only weeks before the Hiroshima and Nagasaki drops. As the 509th composition group polish their B-29s in the Utah desert, General Grove and Secretary Stimson agree that Kyoto is too beautiful to bomb. Hiroshima is substituted because it is large enough that "the effects of the bomb will be able to run out." On August 6, 1945, the *Enola Gay* dropped the bomb that killed 100,000 people in nine seconds. Truman is at sea on the *U.S.S. Augustus*. Secretary Stimson turns to the camera, "Death," he says, "is an inevitable part of every order the wartime leader gives."

Also recommended: *The Day After Trinity, The Atomic Cafe, The Day After, Threads, When the Wind Blows,* and *Children of Nagasaki.*

DIARY OF A COUNTRY PRIEST
(JOURNAL D'UN CURE DE CAMPAGNE)

With Claude Laydu, Jean Riveyre, Marie-monique Arkell, Nicole Lad-
miral, Armand Guibert, Jean Danet, Antoine Balpetre, Nicole Maurey,
Yevette Etievant. Produced by Leon Carre. Directed by Robert Bresson.
Screenplay by Robert Bresson, based on the novel by Georges Bernanos.
Photography by Leonce-Henry Burel. Music by Jean-Jacques Grunewald.
France. French with English titles. Black and white. 120 minutes. 1951.

**Young priest accepts his new post and endures the cruelties and
unkindness of parish residents.**

The country priest is a survivor of original sin consumed with innocence and love. He is unable to respond to the scorn and intolerance
that pour off the screen in somber waves. In his diary he writes, "I
would have given anything this morning for one human word of
compassion—of tenderness." At times he is the only sign of moral life in
a world smothered in deceit. He survives on bread and wine. He is
primitive purity willing to transform anguish into love. He works and
prays for an altruistic world. But his humanity is too obvious. Children
tease him. The vicar berates him for lacking practical sense, "Your
great schemes hold no water." When he tries to move discord toward
resolution and forgiveness, he is isolated by an undisguisable crusade.
"Behind me there was nothing, in front of me a wall, a black wall." All
around him he feels sadnesses and wounds he is powerless to heal. "I
know nothing about people, I never shall know anything." *Diary of a
Country Priest* emotes sensuous energy and the visual philosophies of
human intellect. Beneath the surfaces are consuming fires of loneliness
and desperation. Burel's cinematography is a bathysphere of visual
currents—emerald shadows engulfing sentience like a sea. Somewhere
on the ocean floor ripples are rising through the darkness into tides.
Nothing he can do can calm the tempest that only he can feel and see.
"It was as though all the time I could hear from her lips other words
than she had spoken . . . Our hidden thoughts poison the air." As forces
mass against him, he seeks one small success to prove the value of his
existence and the legitimacy of the priesthood. The vicar's lectures are
intolerable. "Your pet idea is to be loved . . . and to create order, create
order all day long." Torment fills his diary pages, "There is an extraor-

dinary force piling up inside, life will not be enough to spell it." He is an emissary and a victim of the desperation of life.

Also recommended: *Jesus of Montreal.*

THE DIARY OF ANNE FRANK

With Millie Perkins, Joseph Schidkraut, Ed Wynn, Shelly Winters, Rich ard Beymer, Gusti Huber, Lou Jacobi, Diane Baker. Produced and directed by George Stevens. Photography by William Mellor. Music by Alfred Newman. Screenplay by Francis Goodrich and Albert Hackeet, from their play based on the novel *Anne Frank: Diary of a Young Girl.* USA. English. Black and white. 151 minutes. 1959.

Experience of Jews trying to hide from the Nazis during World War II.

When Anne Frank started a diary soon after moving to a third-floor attic in Holland to evade the Nazis, she wrote, "Who will ever be interested in what a thirteen-year-old girl has to say?" It was a great act of faith for a father to give his daughter a diary as they withdrew into hiding from the scourge of fascism in Europe. He and his family and five other people lived in an attic in Holland from September 1942 until June 1944. Only a few months before liberation armies moved through, as they listened to the news of troop movements on their small radio, Anne writes, "I may be back in school by fall." Instead, she was in a concentration camp, where she and her sister and her mother died of malnutrition and disease in 1945. In her diary are details of life in Holland before the attic. "Things went well for us until the war came and the German occupation. Then things got pretty bad for the Jews." As the Nazis stormed across Europe, Jews were gradually denied legal access to the by-products of civilization. "You could not do this and you could not do that. You had to wear a yellow star. I had to turn in my bike. I couldn't go to a Dutch school. I couldn't go to the movies or ride in an automobile or on a streetcar or a million other things." As the months wore on in hiding, bitter arguments were fought over scarce food supplies. There were constant tensions and petty cruelties. Much of the footage caters to the drama of teenage infatuation and troubles with a pet cat one boy has brought with him. The picture of Anne yearning toward an adulthood we know she will be denied is a tormenting sight, especially as she fancied herself living "a sort of adventure." To Anne, the world was going through a "phase." "I really believe," she wrote, "in spite of everything that people are really good at heart." The historic significance of this film, great as it may be, cannot save it from dramatic lapses. The fugitives could be almost any people in any attic with any war crashing away outside. High notes on the violin only make matters worse. It did win eight Academy Awards, but is still much too long and has aged poorly since 1959.

Also recommended: *The Last Seven Months of Anne Frank*.

DINGAKA

With Juliet Prowse, Ken Gampu, Stanley Baker. Produced, written, and directed by Jamie Uys. Photography by Manie Botha and Judex C. Vijoen. Music by Bertha Egnos, Eddie Domingo, and Basil Gray. South Africa. English. Color. 96 minutes. 1965.

Traditional native law runs up against civilized jurisprudence in South Africa.

Lawyer Tom (Baker) can't even get his wife pregnant because he's so organically cynical about life. It wasn't always this way though. He started out full of humanitarian ideals and was going to save the underprivileged and do good work. Now he's so burnt out on pro bono that all he cares about is big Rand returns on his court cases. Juliet Prowse is his wife. Ever since he got this way, she's been losing touch. When his one legal aid case for the year turns out to be defending a tribal native new to Johannesburg who is accused of attempted murder, Baker calls the aid offices to complain that Mtuku (Gamba) is a waste of council assignment. Mtuku's entire defense consists of confessing that he *did* try to kill Masaba and that he'll try even harder if they'll just find him "not guilty" and set him free. How typical of natives from the bush. They'll be strapping him into the electric chair any time. But as Baker gets to know Mtuku, he begins to believe that Mtuku is justified in tracking down Masaba, the man he alleges killed his daughter. If Masaba is guilty, Mtuku was operating within legitimate tribal law when he got snared by the South African legal system. This early film reveals Uys' infatuation with the native peoples of South Africa and their traditional tribal cultures. He navigates apartheid's tight censorship codes and works around racial intolerance to communicate his philosophies. In *Dingaka*, exposure to black culture can cure whites of practically everything that's wrong with them. When Stan and Julie clean out the camper to follow Mtuku to his tribal homelands, they discover she is pregnant at last. They help expose Quehaba, the tribal witch doctor, as a fake, who is responsible for everything and who is later executed according to tribal law. They admire the natives' closeness to nature and the communal and traditional values whites have long since lost. Typical of Uys, *Dingaka* has a strong anti-urban message—when the city dwellers arrive in the homelands, they are restored by the balm of the open veld. Of course, Uys is a controversial figure because he holds South African citizenship. His films are carried by video shops and included in catalogs that cunningly omit country of origin. No one seems quite sure that he's not a clever propagandist whose real message is that blacks and whites do better *apart* under their own sets of laws. Maybe he's just a government pawn illustrating how it could work that way if the world only knew. Compliance to Quehaba's death is surely an open toleration of the death penalty. Some native sequences are unflattering, but so are scenes of urban and social life in Johannesburg. His films seem to be about human beings of different cultures getting along somehow. If this is apartheid propaganda, it's subtle enough to defeat the purpose.

Also recommended: *Four Days of the Masai.*

DISTANT THUNDER
(ASHANTI SANKET)

With Soumitra Chatterji, Babita, Sandhya Roy, Gobinda Chakravarty, Romesh Mukerji. Directed by Satyajit Ray. Screenplay by Satyajit Ray, based on the novel by Bibhuti Bhusan Bannerji. Cinematography by Sowmender Roy. Music by Satyajit Ray. India. In Hindi with English titles. Color. 110 minutes. 1974.

World War II brings the "man-made famine of 1943" to India, causing the deaths of five million people.

Director Ray's drama focuses not so much on the actual starvation, of which we see almost nothing at all, but on the sociological responses to shortage and want and general atrophy of public understanding about the origins of the torments of the modern world. The deepening crisis of inflation and food shortage is a fatal lapse in the incomprehensible architecture of history, confronted with which the peasants of Bengal possess only the power to submit. "Our king is fighting the Germans and Japan." "The Japanese have taken Burma." "The Japanese have taken Singapore." "The government takes the rice for the army." They are so far removed from the machinations of their own catastrophe of survival that the starving villagers still marvel at fighter bombers thundering overhead and wonder at the miracle of flight. If Ray's intention was to show us the effects of war on people to whom the war has no meaning, he succeeds. If his intent was to dramatize the magnitude and severity of these effects, he falls far short. *Distant Thunder* is a visually sensuous intrusion into the subcontinent of India, scored with exotic music echoing village intrigues. But the starvation of five million people passes fairly unrecorded. The beautiful wife and her Brahmin husband, on whom Ray chooses to focus, never really seem hungry. They have no children, and their troubles are superficial compared to the plight of the peasants. There are black-and-white news flashbacks of famine victims. But we see it all from a great distance and feel a little like the Indians themselves must have felt wondering about things too far away to comprehend.

Also recommended: *Home and the World.*

DO THE RIGHT THING

With Spike Lee, Ossie Davis, John Turturro, Richard Edson, Danny Aiello, Sam Jackson, Paul Benjamin, Robin Harris, Frankie Faison, Ruby Dee, Giancarlo Esposito, Bill Nunn, Rosie Perez, Joie Lee, Roger Guenveur Smith, John Savage. Produced by Spike Lee and Monty Ross. Written and directed by Spike Lee. Photography by Ernest Dickerson. Musical score by Bill Lee. USA. English. Color. 120 minutes. 1989.

Blacks and whites clash in the inner-city.

The only thing critics agreed on about this movie was that it was a very hot day with no air conditioning when they did the filming. After that, depending on which review you read, it's tragic, socially real, volatile, shockingly irresponsible, loyalist, muddled, ambivalent, personalized, apocalyptic, a cultural event with Hawaiian colors and a huge, gigantic theme. In addition, according to the *National Review*, it's not a good movie because it was not "fair to all sides." As a beacon in the fog to refute this last point, we should realize that 80 percent of everything that appears on America's screens is written by white men. Spike Lee may be a naive insurrectionary and a "middle-class, armchair revolutionary" on an ego trip, or maybe life *is* a lot like it is at Sal's Famous—doomed to be torched—Pizzeria. It's an ordinary, jazz aerobic, Air-Jordan, twenty "D" cell battery "fight the power" day in Bed-Stuy. And if it's insurrectionary for Esposito to organize a boycott of the pizza place because he's tired of looking at Frank Sinatra's face on Sal's wall of Italian fame, then the idea of community has lost all its meaning, which it probably has. Lee has a compulsion toward casting acrobats, and his movie is a little bit like three rings without the big top. For a while, you are having such a good time and there are so many fine performances that you forget there ever was a Montgomery, Alabama. But you will be reminded. The geometric resolution, high-color values, and stream of consciousness direction are setup for a face-off of two-hundred years of social alienation. In *Do the Right Thing*, resentments are multi-generational, and they are cumulative, and today, it's the hottest day of the year and there are no photos of Malcolm X at Sal's. Everyone knows there's a baseball bat under the counter, and after Sal uses it to destroy Radio Raheem's music machine, we know that it's just not going to work out no matter who won the Civil War, and the yuppie, the old drunk, the single mother, the Japanese grocers, the deaf mute, the Hispanics, and Mr. Senor Love Daddy are all going to be caught up in it. When Nunn is killed by the white police, Mookie throws a trash can through the front of the pizzeria, and the riot begins. To put it in Lee's own words, "the days of silence have come to an end."

Also recommended: *Jungle Fever*.

DO-DES'-KA-DEN

With Yoshitaka Zushi, Kin Sugai, Toshiyuki Tonomura, Yuko Kusonoki, Michio Hino, Shinsuke Minami, Junzaburo Ban. Directed by Akira Kurosawa. Screenplay by Akira Kurosawa, Shinobu Hashimoto, and Hideo Oguni, based on the novel by Shugoro Yamamoto. Photography by Takao Saito and Yasumichi Fukuzawa. Music by Toru Takemitsu. Japan. Japanese with English titles. Color. 139 minutes. 1976.

People living in the city dump struggle to survive.

Kurosawa's *Do-Des'-Ka-Den* is part judgment against the social order and part surreal nightmare inhabited by the dump dwellers of Japan. They are mindless, tormented souls shut up in windowless huts. They are women disconnected from love. They are businessmen. They clear roadways through the rubble and build ramshackle homes. To make a living, they cook, they beg, they sell things, they steal. One father sends his son out to pick up day-old food from restaurants. Kurosawa conjures up certified optical daydreams that the poor will see one last time before they die of food poisoning in the back seat of the junk car they've been living in. The stress of survival foments physiological disorder, mental disorder, cruelties, violence, and even aberrant niceness. One charming gentleman is plagued by a compulsion to be helpful. When a prowler breaks into his house, he advises him to take all his money and come back for more. "I'll save up for you. . . . And next time, just come in through the door instead of the window." Later, he offers to take over a tantrum a young man is having. "You must be tired, waving that heavy stick around for so long." These are the garbage people. Capitalism's social castaways. Even children will die alone in this decayed suburb across the bridgeway from free enterprise.

Also recommended: *Fires on the Plain.*

DR. STRANGELOVE: OR HOW I STOPPED WORRYING AND LEARNED TO LOVE THE BOMB

With George C. Scott, Sterling Hayden, Keenan Wynn, Peter Sellers, Slim Pickens, Peter Bull, James Earl Jones, Tracy Reed, Jack Creley, Frank Berry, Shane Rimmer, Paul Tamarin, Gordon Tanner, Robert O'Neil, Alexi Sadesky. Produced and directed by Stanley Kubrick. Screenplay by Stanley Kubrick, Peter George, and Terry Southern, based on the novel *Red Alert* by Peter George. Photography by Melvin Pike. Music by Laurie Johnson. USA. English. Black and white. 102 minutes. 1964.

Flub-up in the military chain of command sends the world to the brink of World War III.

"It is the stated position of the U.S. Air Force that their safeguards would prevent the occurrence of such events as are depicted in this film. Furthermore, it should be noted that none of the characters portrayed in this film represent any person living or dead." So no one like General Jack Ripper (Sterling Hayden) works for the U.S. military? Hayden is the paranoid delusionary who has decided it's a good day for the ultimate demolition derby. He has locked himself in his office at Burbleson Air Force Base with the British attache (Peter Sellers) and has issued a missile launch command to airborne bombers that are on their way to blowing the land of the Bolsheviks off the map. He has caught on to their fluoridation schemes. Fluoride and armed attack—they go together. Sellers listens to Hayden's theories while noticing that the entire bomb wing is twenty minutes from its target. Sellers will have to issue the recall code himself. But the doors are locked, the keys are gone, and the phone is out. When word of the imminent diplomatic and global catastrophe reaches the President (also Sellers), he marvels, "I thought I was the only person with the authority to O.K. a nuclear attack." George C. Scott explains that he's right and that Hayden has "probably exceeded his authority" but that emergency war "Plan R" did allow lower-echelon commanders the power to retaliate after a sneak attack. He's a genuine genetic genius of war strategy talk. "All planes fly continuously at their fail-safe points, such that, once the 'go code' is received, they are more or less beyond their fail-safe, they do not require a second order to carry out their mission, *and* we cannot recall them without the three-letter codes which we do not have." The President and his staff can only stare at him over the ten-ton marble table of the war room. "In fifteen minutes, the Russian radar will detect our planes and they will then go absolutely ape-shit and strike back with everything they've got, and we will suffer virtual annihilation." Burbleson is the birthplace of socialized mass destruction. The military gravy train has paid off, and this radioactive screenplay relays decade of unheard protest into the bushes outside Hayden's office, where machine gun fire is trying feebly to save America from its appointment in Samarra. *Dr. Strangelove* is satire distilled into a tactical attack on the mad bombers of the Pentagon. It's a virtuoso aria, wild with hysterical comic relief about the novel notions of advanced war dementia. It's also entertaining, except for that part where the U.S. government took the trouble to claim it could never happen.

Also recommended: *War Games.*

A DRY WHITE SEASON

With Marlon Brando, Donald Sutherland, Susan Sarandon, John Kani, Jurgen Prochnow, Zakes Mokae, Janet Suzman, Thoko Ntshinga, Winston Ntshona, Susannah Harker. Produced by Paula Weinstein. Directed by Euzhan Palcy. Screenplay by Euzhan Palcy and Colin Welland, based on the book by Andre Brink. Photography by Kelvin Pike and Pierre-William Glenn. Music by Dave Grusin. English. Color. 107 minutes. 1989.

White South African newspaper editor wakes up to the reality of racist oppression.

Donald Sutherland is a white, liberal newspaper editor who discovers there is police brutality in South Africa. This ignites him, not to oppose the system, but to indict police officers responsible for the deaths of his gardener. In his passion for justice, he alienates his apartheid-supporting wife (a serpent being played by Janet Suzman, niece of the former Formal Opposition party leader, Helen Suzman) and his racially pure daughter. He and his son are on the verge of discovering the source of all evil. They walk to the edge, but no further. We see the violent manifestations of hate, but nothing of the monstrous campaign to disenfranchise native peoples from the land. We see nothing of the relocation programs that create virtual graveyards and thousands left homeless and hungry in the open veld. No explanation follows the forced removal of the gardener's widow from her residence. We don't know where she goes or why she has to leave. The movie also fails to make a clear connection between the Afrikaans language and apartheid and does not explain that those forced to learn it instead of English would be unable to communicate with anyone outside South Africa. In place of explanations, the film hammers home the sadistic retaliation of the South African police to the student protest. The spectacle of violence justifiably devastated American audiences. Too bad there were so few clues about what the horror of violence covers up. Marlon Brando is a living legend in his sliver of a role. Sarandon never successfully overcomes the handicap of having no real function, and Sutherland is the last puppy you adopted at the pound.

Also recommended: *A World Apart, Cry Freedom, Master Harold and the Boys*, and *Come Back Africa*.

EAT A BOWL OF TEA

With Cora Miao, Victor Wong, Eric Tsang Chi Wai, Hui Fun, Wu Ming Yu, Lau Siu Ming, Russell Wong. Produced by Tom Sternberg. Directed by Wayne Wang. Screenplay by Judith Rascoe, from the novel by Louis Chu. Photographed by Amir Mokri. Music by Mark Adler. USA. English and Chinese with English titles. Color. 104 minutes. 1989.

Cultures clash as the youngest member of a Chinese-American community goes to China and brings back a bride.

For sixty years prior to World War II, America's exclusionary immigration laws prohibited Chinese women from immigrating to the U.S. Other laws prohibited Chinese men from marrying American women. Still more laws prevented Chinese men (or women) from qualifying for U.S. citizenship. The Chinatowns, filled with aging populations of single men, were dying out. After World War II, all these exclusionary laws were rescinded. It became possible for a man to go to China for a bride and to return with her to the States. *Eat a Bowl of Tea* follows the gentle, naive, good-looking Ben Loy (Wong) on such a journey. He brings his bride back to America, submitting 4,000 years of Chinese tradition to the American tradition demolition machine. He introduces her to the Wang family association. They love her—the first woman. They love them both—the first couple. But what they will love even more is the first baby. A baby Wang would signify regeneration of the American Wang family association, the rebirth of the Chinatowns, and the new future awaiting all Chinese-Americans. The newlyweds become Wang property. Everything they do is Wang news. The pressure hampers Ben Loy's ability to enjoy sex. It hampers his ability to perform sex. He wants to make everyone happy but he just can't concentrate anymore. Rumors, gossip, scandal, and disgrace preoccupy him. The Wang men are obsessed. They have waited too long, and the traditions have waited, too. Under the weight of such great expectations, Ben Loy's life falls apart. His wife gets pregnant, but not with his baby. Amidst the blizzard of Wang family recriminations, Ben loses his job, moves away, moves back, finds a new job, forgives his wife, loves the baby, and has a new baby (his own). He just can't hold a grudge, especially since it was all his fault. He lacks the will to oppose. No one in *Eat a Bowl of Tea* ever does quite what audiences will expect them to do in this slightly loony, slightly flambe film about Chinese cultural regeneration in the new world.

Also recommended: *The Great Wall.*

84 CHARLIE MOPIC

With Jonathan Emerson, Jason Tomlins, Christopher Burgard, Nicholas Cascone, Russ Thurman, Glenn Moshower, Richard Brooks, Byron Thames. Produced by Michael Nolin and Jill Griffith. Written and directed by Patrick Duncan. Photography by Alan Caso. Music by Donovan. USA. English. Color. 85 minutes. 1989.

84 Charlie is the company. "Mopic" is the motion picture set in Vietnam in 1969.

A cameraman (Thames) follows 84 Charlie through the Vietnam jungle, filming details of infantry life and recording mottos and slogans that some of the bigger-name war films left out. Like, "Mercenaries kill for money, sadists kill for fun, paratroopers kill for both." "We are the sanest killers the Army's got." "Here's my weapon, here's my gun. With this I kill gooks, with this I have fun." And so on. They curse and confess and reload and clown around. Maybe most of the men would just as soon not be at war, but for the commanding officer, it is de rigueur. "Wars don't come along very often. It's the chance of a lifetime for a career officer. Combat duty is the foundation of a successful career." What he's saying is, no war, no nothing. The reenactments are moved along by low-key dialogue between the soldiers as they work their way through the underbrush. There is severe treatment of the "gooks" and a grisly stabbing of a POW. Eventually, they are struck by enemy fire. On the front line, the dead are snapped into tarps with their dog tags taped in their mouth. The tarps are strung on bamboo poles and carried back to base. The men react very differently to war. Some appear to enjoy it. Others appear irrational. One foot soldier says, "I'm not saying all gooks look the same. I'm just saying they all look like someone I shot . . . like ghosts." There is no story line to *84 Charlie Mopic*, but it is not a documentary either. If it seems antiseptic, that's because filmmaker Patrick Duncan did the best he could having very little money and filming the whole thing in the hills around L.A.

Also recommended: *Dear America: Letters Home from Vietnam*.

EL NORTE

With Zaide Silvia Gutierrez, David Villalpando, Ernesto Gomez Cruz, Alicia Del Lago, Mike Gomez, Trinidad Silva. Produced by Anna Thomas. Directed by Gregory Nava. Written by Gregory Nava and Anna Thomas. Photography by James Glennon. Music by Gustav Mahler, Samuel Barber, Giuseppe Verdi, The Folklorists, Emil Richards, Linda O'Brien, Melecio Martinez. USA. English and Spanish with English titles. Color. 139 minutes. 1984.

Destitute laborers from South America enter California illegally, hoping to find a better life.

El Norte traces the split personality of the ever-contagious, evercashable capitalism and because of this is considered a milestone classic of social realism, impetuously reunifying, as it does, the twin diablos of the free market. After being backed to the wall by capitalist entrepreneur landowners in Guatemala, where indigenous campesinos who speak out for change risk imprisonment or death, Rosa and Enrique raise enough money to pay for passage to the U. S. In this case, the two young people have been fleeced into believing the U.S. has something to offer the poor besides poverty. For a couple hundred dollars, they will be allowed to endanger their lives, risk arrest, and brave rat-infested drainage tunnels to arrive at the smog-congested capistrano of L.A.—El Norte, where agrarian reform has been excised from the national vocabulary and the "power corrupts" axiom reinvents itself better every year. It's pretty discouraging to watch Rosa (Gutierrez) and Enrique (Villalpando) being transformed from Guatamalan refugees from advanced capitalism to peons of the northern branch of the same system. Here they will find something more brutal and dehumanizing, invisibly enshrouded, as it is, in myth. In L.A., the employment office for undocumented workers is a wide place on a dirt road where any prospective employer pulling up in his expensive car could be an immigration officer. But this is what you paid your money for, so hold your hands high—maybe you can be king for a day below the minimum wage. Rosa becomes a domestic drone in mansionland. Brother and sister will be pulled apart like families are in downwardly mobile, industrialized cities. When it turns out that Rosa has typhus from the sewer rat attack, Enrique can't make it to the hospital. She dies alone in a ward bed. The next day, there are more men than usual raising their strong arms at passing motorists, hollering "Choose me, choose me!" Neo-colonial or non-colonial—ultimately the only difference is the nakedness of the "naked self-interest" and the callousness of the "callous cash payment." Resplendent cinematography throughout, and a superior performance by the serpent-eyed Trinidad Silva.

Also recommended: *Burn!*.

THE EMERALD FOREST

Powers Booth, Meg Foster, Charley Boorman, Dira Paes, Rui Polonah, William Rodriquez. Produced and directed by John Boorman. Screenplay by Rospo Pallenberg. Photography by Phillipe Rousselot. Music by Junior Homrich and Brian Gascoigne. USA. In English and Tupi, with English titles. Color. 113 minutes. 1984.

American boy is kidnapped by Amazon Indians.

John Markam (Booth) has moved to the Amazon to oversee the construction of a dam for the Amazco Corporation. On an outing with his family to the production sight, his son, Tommy, walks into the rainforest. They find an arrow, but Tommy is gone. Ten years go by. The dam has grown like a colossal tombstone. Booth is organizing one of his annual trips down the river to search for his son. On this trip, he loses his boat and his crew and is trapped in the river rapids. He fights for his life against the Fierce People, when he turns and sees another Indian behind him near a waterfall. He raises his gun. The Indian raises an arrow. But something makes them both hesitate. As the falls thunder around them and the spray drenches their bodies, they both say something. Tommy (Boorman) thinks he is seeing his dream "Daddé," a vision of his night-time imagination. Booth is seeing Tomme, one of the Invisible People who used to be his son. To the Indians, the edge of the forest is the edge of the world: it separates them from the land of the dead. Tomme thinks his dream "Daddé" should stay with them in the forest. When Booth tells him that he's from another world, he can only answer, "But, Daddé, that was a long time ago." He feels sorry for his "other father" who found what he was looking for but still is not happy. When Booth asks Wanadi, Tomme's new father, why he took his son so long ago, he answers, "Tomme smiled at me, and even though he was not one of the Termite People, I could not send him back into the land of the dead." Theirs is the innocence of the eons. But, Tomme's world is threatened by the machines and the slums and the fringe businesses that followed his real father into the forest. As he accepts his son's new life, Booth also accepts his own responsibility for the devastation caused by the dam. When he explains to Tomme that the dam will bring more white people who will destroy everything, Tomme promises to pray to the rain frogs to stop the dam. "But the dam is very, very big, Tomme." "Then I will pray very, very hard." John Boorman lugged a production crew and truckloads of equipment where no equipment had gone before to film on location in the Amazon basin. According to Boorman, the weather pattern in Belen was "a daily torrential downpour." There was enough humidity, heat, and rain to rust platinum and turn scripts back into wood pulp. The rain forest was intimidating. "A man twenty feet away is swallowed up by it." The exhaustion and fa-

tigue on the actors' faces is often real. Powers Booth nearly drowned in
one sequence where Charley Boorman is supposed to be helping him
cross the river. Charley's cries for help were interpreted as part of the
action. The Invisible People are the heroes in *The Emerald Forest*. And
there is much romanticizing of the Indian people, who Boorman found
to be living lives of grace, harmony, ritual, and spirituality which he unashamedly admired and emulated. As the Amazon Indians wear barely
any clothing, the cast and crew began every day with nude aerobic exercises. Released with native language dialogue, *The Emerald Forest*
became the first feature ever made for U.S. markets in a principal language other than English. A note to those reviewers who called the
movie a "metaphor for our insensitivity to nature"—there was nothing
metaphorical about it.

Also recommended: *Raoni*.

THE END OF ST. PETERSBURG

With A. P. Chistiakov, Vera Baranovskaya, Ivan Chuvelev, Sergei
Komarov, V. Obolensky. Produced by Mezhrabpom-Russ. Directed by
Vsevolod Pudovkin. Scenario by Natan Zarkhi. Photography by Anatoli
Golovnya. Music by Herbert Stothart. USSR. Silent with English titles.
Black and white. 115 minutes. 1927.

**Peasants fight in the Russian revolution that brought the fall of
the last Tsar.**

To Pudovkin, history was a system of granite barriers that were mountain ranges, blocking human social evolution in on every side. The only
thing that could move them was the spark of individual will and courage, at the slightest touch of which the granite would resolve into the
mists of dissolution. His unswayable belief in the transcendent potential of human will was born directly from the testaments of Marx and
Engels, for whom the peasants and the workers held all hope of earthly
utopia. On the eve of the Russian Revolution, a destitute peasant, Ivan
(Chuvelev), walks into St. Petersburg to discover a poverty more demoralizing than the farmland ever offered. People live in cell-like cellars,
slaves to the capitalist class in a city of stunning wealth—huge cranes

and steaming factories beyond belief, built by the workers to keep the workers poor. The city's munitions plant has received unconditional government contracts—the Tsar needs weapons to fight peasant revolutionaries. The stock market is a frenzy. Fortunes can be made off the bent backs of the lower classes and their futile struggles for freedom. To meet production deadlines, workers are driven beyond endurance—they call it "slavery for a cellar and potatoes." Strike organizers wonder how they can succeed. "Within a week, we'll die of hunger." As the workloads intensify, the strike begins and erupts into violence. Scabs in rags are trucked in, desperate for work. Ivan takes the money the union busters offer him to lead them to the organizers. He watches as everyone is arrested, even his cousin, to whom he went for help. The woman they leave behind reviles him, and he's alone in the city. The strikes have become riots and the war has begun. The crusade deforms the countrysides. Trenches go on for miles. Flames light up the horizon. Bodies lie bloated in riverbeds. Pudovkin lifts heroes up out of the mire. There is a pure impulse there that will pull down the Romanov empire and put a people's union in its place. Peasant soldiers gather in the city. They are roasting potatoes over campfires in the bitterest cold. Ivan is there in the uniform of the guard. The woman is there cradling his head in her arms. They sit on the marble steps leading to the magnificence of the Winter Palace. St. Petersburg becomes Leningrad.

Also recommended: *Strike*.

ENEMY MINE

With Dennis Quaid, Louis Gosset, Jr., Brion James, Bumper Robinson. Produced by Stanley O'Toole. Directed by Wolfgang Petersen. Screenplay by Edward Khmara, based on the story by Barry Longyear. Photography by Tony Imi. Music by Maurice Jarre. USA. Color. English and "Drak" with titles. 108 minutes. 1985.

Two life forms, alien to each other, bridge the gap between species and cultures.

It's the future. There is peace on Earth, but not in space, where the non-human alien Draks are at war with humans about anything left worth fighting for. They are claiming squatters' rights to some of the richest star systems in the galaxy. Willis V. Davidge (Quaid) crashes his spaceship into a granite planet unpopulated except for a lone Drak (Louis Gosset, Jr.). He will subdue the marsh man or vice versa. But the planet is home to spectacular electrical storms, asteroid showers, sand-pit monsters, and other camping perils. He needs the Drak, and the Drak needs him. They entertain each other. They chisel away at the days by building shelters that fall apart and by learning each other's language. What does Drak language sound like? Picture a pipe organ sinking into quicksand. It's not easy for either of them. But eventually "Jerry" learns enough English to observe, "Your Mickey Mouse," gurgle, gurgle, "is just one big stupid" gurgle, "dope." Quaid learns to read from the Drak "Talmut," a small book Gosset wears on a chain around his neck. One of the messages is "Extend love to the enemy so that love might unite them." In their dialogues about the never-ending war, Quaid learns that the Draks have been hunted ruthlessly for slave labor to mine the galaxy's valuable minerals. Quaid becomes a serious sponge, soaking up facts of Drak culture. When a Drak baby, Zammis, shows up from a very strange place, Quaid takes care of him, plays with him, teaches him baseball, and protects him from dangers. He and Zammis tumble through savage canyons of the lonely planet. They chase each other across bluish plains. In the film's most touching scene, Willis tries to explain to Zammis why they don't look the same. "Draks have three fingers," he says, holding their hands together and thinking how it will be clear enough one day, "and humans have five." When Quaid is injured trying to save Zammis from slavers, he is picked up by an Earth ship, pronounced dead, *looks* dead, and is moving along a conveyor belt to space burial when life grabs him back. None of the humans can figure out why Davidge would be wearing a Drak Talmut, speaking Drak language and raving about a Drak child. He's just a Drak-lover who has been too long on tour. Closing scenes are of the multiple-mooned Drak home planet at the grand gathering of the Holy Council held to hear the recitation of the lineage of Zammis—with Willis J. Davidge proudly standing in for Joriba Shigan.

Also recommended: *Harry and the Hendersons.*

EXECUTIVE ACTION

With Will Geer, Burt Lancaster, Robert Ryan, Gilbert Green, Paul Carr, Ed Lauter, John Anderson, Colby Chester. Produced by Edward Lewis. Directed by David Miller. Screenplay by Dalton Trumbo, based on a novel by Mark Lane and Donald Freed. Photography by Robert Steadman. Music by Randy Edelman. USA. English. Color. 91 minutes. 1973.

Who really killed President Kennedy: Lee Harvey Oswald or a conspiracy of right-wing members of the military industrial complex?

Does it pay to analyze the motives of filmmakers? Why would anyone *want* to make a film about a conspiracy behind the assassination of a popular president or even to write a book about it? Unless they had a good reason. For example, did President Lyndon Johnson give a three-hour interview, segments of which were classified because they suggested that Oswald was innocent? Dalton "arrested-by-HUAC" Trumbo's screenplay hints that the CIA disapproved of the way Kennedy littered their inter-office mail with pink slips after the Bay of Pigs. Overlooking that, there was the nuclear test ban treaty. And he was examining the Constitution with an electron-scanning microscope. Plus, he made remarks about bringing troops home from Southeast Asia for Christmas. I'm willing to imagine the CIA would take this personally. So, for me, it's not hard to envision a group of well-dressed gunmen out in the desert aiming their high-powered rifles at garden vegetables (sorry, wrong movie) or aiming at wax dummies sitting in open limousines. Watching *Executive Action* was the first time I remembered seeing news footage of Oswald denying he had killed anyone. "I didn't kill anybody. . . . I emphatically deny these charges." What I do remember is that he was some kind of defector to the Soviet Union who married a Russian citizen who could barely speak English. The drawback to believing Kennedy was killed by the CIA is that you then have to suspect that Oswald was murdered, too. And if he was murdered, so was Jack Ruby. And perhaps there was something unusual about the way eighteen other witnesses died in the next three years, since the odds of that random occurrence were approximately 100,000 trillion to one. Anyway, here are Burt Lancaster, Robert Ryan, Will Geer (also HUACed), and some other fine actors relaxing in comfortable chairs and running the world into the ground. How were they to know that Oswald adored Kennedy and was excited about the coming civil rights updates? (No, that's not in the movie; that's in an interview of Marie Oswald on American television in 1991.)

Also recommended: Oliver Stone's movie on Kennedy due out at the end of 1992.

THE EXILES

Produced by Richard Kaplan and Lou Potter. Directed by Richard Kaplan. Written by Lou Potter. Narrated by Sabine Thompson. Music by Arther Cunningham. English. Black and white and color. 116 minutes. 1989.

Cultural impact of Jewish exiles to America during World War II.

"We are the last ones. Question us. We are authentic. We carry the file with the arrest warrants of our friends like a vendor's tray. Research institutes bid for the laundry tickets of the missing. Museums preserve the catch words of our agony under glass. We are the last ones. Question us." By 1936, intellectualism in Germany was in chaos. Hundreds of intellectual leaders were black-listed, banned, or killed. "It felt like the end of the world." "Goering gave the impression of a raving madman." "They hated the intellectuals." Immigrants escaping fascism were artists, architects, designers, actors and directors, musicians, Freudian psychologists, philosophers, writers, promoters, and theoretical physicists. For the U.S., it was a transfusion of genius and controversy for the arts, sciences, and philosophies of the times. The exiles were overwhelmed by the new world. "One felt he had landed on the moon." They had to change to survive. They changed America in the process. They started a School of Exiles in New York City where they could continue their work. The school offered jobs to Jews needing U.S. work visas. Very few Jews were appointed to positions in Ivy League colleges. The U.S. refused to accept large numbers of refugees because there was a quota system. In addition, there was the recent Depression, and many felt immigrants took jobs away from Americans. As a controversy stormed, Jewish physicists were working with the Americans to build an atomic bomb to stop Hitler. When the bomb was used on Japan instead, many who worked to build it were overcome with guilt. "I have no hope of clearing my conscience. Nothing we can do will save our souls." They were shocked by Enrico Fermi's indifference: "I have been put on this Earth to make certain discoveries. What the politicians and governments do with them neither interests me nor concerns me." The bomb the exiles helped build killed 100,000 in Hiroshima and 80,000 in Nagasaki and established America as the uncontested world power. But it did not stop persecution of the Jews. When the McCarthy era began, many war immigrants came under suspicion. "Anti-fascism, liberalism, communism"—it was hard for HUAC to tell them apart. Radical thinkers were forced to emigrate again to avoid oppression. To them, McCarthy was like Hitler with a different face. Bertolt Brecht went back to Germany, as did Fritz Lang and many others. But this reversal of the immigration tides could not undo what had been done to the sciences and the visual and performing arts. The U.S. took the gift of their talents and used them to dominate the world with no apology.

Also recommended: *Metropolis*.

FAHRENHEIT 451

With Oskar Werner, Julie Christie, Anton Diffring, Jeremy Spenser, Bee Duffell, Anne Bell, Cyril Cusack. Produced by Lewis M. Allen. Directed by Francois Truffaut. Written by Francois Truffaut, David Rudkin, Helen Scott, and Jean-Louis Richard, from the book by Ray Bradbury. Photography by Nicolas Roeg. Music by Bernard Herrmann. France. English. Color. 112 minutes. 1966.

Government book eradicator succumbs to the passion of reading.

Montag (Oskar Werner) is a fireman. He does not put fires out. He starts them. The fuel for these fires is books, which combust at a temperature of fahrenheit 451. Books cause dissension and unhappiness. They fuel revolution. "Books disturb people." Montag is the perfect fireman. When his superior (Cusack) asks him what he does on his days off, he answers, "I mow the lawn, Sir." "And if the law forbids it?" "I just watch it grow, Sir." He burns books, and he never questions why. He's trusting like a child. When his neighbor, Clarissa (Christie), asks if he reads the books before he burns them, his face shadows the tabula rasa of his soul. Read them? The idea is just a thorn in the side of a cloud. The blackening titles were never meant to be read. Soon, he has a dozen volumes. He reads at night, slowly sounding out the unfamiliar words. "The Personal History of...David Copperfield...by Charles Dickens...London, Chapman and Hall Limited & Humphrey, Milford...Chapter 1, I Am Born." He burns them by day and reads at night. But today the Fire Department has discovered a library in the attic of an old house. Montag walks through the treasury of forbidden volumes—thousands of books crowded into narrow aisles. Cusack walks in front of Montag, sweeping whole shelves to the floor in disgust. He derides the great names and great titles. Novels, philosophies, diaries, intimate memoirs, biographies, autobiographies, row after row falling open. The fire crew throws them over the railing to the floor below and sprays the pages with gasoline. The woman (Duffell) who owns these books stands in the center of the growing pile, refusing to leave. In her hand is a box of matches. She ignites the fire that will consume her. They cannot part her from her books. The pages burn as her face glows in the pain and ecstasy of martyrdom. "I can't be a fireman any more," Montag tells Clarissa. She says there is a sanctuary beyond the city where the "book people" live. Before Montag can follow her out along the river, he will witness one last burning. When the fire truck arrives, he throws the books out of the cupboards in disgust. "Burn them," he says, "burn them to ashes, then burn the ashes." Huge pages fill the screen. Words of wisdom and genius disappear into the appetite of flame. Montag runs to the river and along the riverbanks where voices repeat the passage of Tolstoy, Shelley, Dante, Mark Twain, Dostoyevsky, Bradbury (*The Martian Chronicles*), and Thoreau. Where the "bookpeople" live, each person "becomes a book. They commit the books to memory, so there is nothing to burn. The title is their name. When their lives near an end, the books pass themselves on to children, who will pass themselves on before they die. Recitations of timeless classics rise in a murmur through the trees. Montag has brought the stories of Edgar Allan Poe. If this town along the river were a real place, *Fahrenheit 451* would be one of the timeless classics recited there. The film version of the book, under the direction of Francois Truffaut, is an ageless vision of the love of truth and the power of intellectual freedom.

Also recommended: *Soylent Green.*

FAIL SAFE

With Henry Fonda, Dan O'Herlihy, Walter Matthau, Frank Overton, Edward Binns, Fritz Weaver, Larry Hagman, William Hansen, Russell Hardie, Russell Collins, Dom DeLuise. Produced by Max E. Youngstein. Directed by Sidney Lumet. Written by Walter Bernstein, based on the novel by Eugene Burdick and Harvey Wheeler. Photography by Gerald Hirschfeld. USA. English. Black and white. 111 minutes. 1964.

**Military technology gone astray under the presidency
of Henry Fonda.**

The fail-safe point is a line on the map beyond which bombers cannot advance "without direct orders from a designated authority." The whole appeal of fail-safe is its irreversibility. Once the order is given, no one can scramble up your radio waves with fake peace orders. In *Fail Safe*, a squadron of Strategic Air Command bombers loaded with nuclear weapons is flying toward the Soviet Union following incorrect mission activation orders. They will not turn back. One even shuts his radio off to save himself the hassle. He's not to be blamed—this is the fail-safe rule. Meanwhile, President Henry Fonda has locked himself and his Russian translator (Hagman) into a concrete root cellar in D.C. From there, he talks with his war advisors on one phone and the Soviet Union on the other. When an attempt to overtake and destroy the bombers fails, Fonda orders the military to release information to the Russians making it possible for them to target the U.S. bombers with Soviet missiles. Every decision Fonda makes sends the war cabinet—gathered in the war room—into battles of their own. They are divided on the idea of war, ". . . now that we have the *upper hand."* "I'd rather have an American culture survive than a Russian one." "Who would survive?" "There won't be any survivors, that's the beauty of it." "In a nuclear war, everyone loses." The Soviets hit all the planes but one. Fonda must face the inevitability of American bombs dropping on Moscow. He is the President of our daydreams—tolerant, humanistic, rational, persevering, always certain what to do next, able to make tough decisions, never doubting a solution exists whatever the solution might be. The choices are limited. He orders a U.S. bomber to target New York City. He advises Soviet leaders that when the bomb hits Moscow, one of identical destructive power will hit the U.S. And he hangs up the phone. The tears in his eyes are not only for the loss of life about to take place, but for his wife whom he put on a plane to New York that morning before he answered the call from the War Department. Startling freeze frames of the streets of New York foretell the horror to come.

Also recommended: *Seven Days in May.*

THE FALCON AND THE SNOWMAN

With Timothy Hutton, Sean Penn, Pat Hingle, David Suchet, Joyce Van Patten, Richard Dysart, Lori Singer, Dorian Harewood, Mady Kaplan. Produced by Gabriel Katzka and John Schlesinger. Directed by John Schlesinger. Screenplay by Steve Zaillian, from the book of the same name by Robert Lindsey. Photography by Allen Daviau. Music by Pat Metheny and Lyle Mays. USA. English. Color. 131 minutes. 1985.

The true story of Christopher Boyce and Daulton Lee—two California boys who sold military secrets to the USSR.

When Julius and Ethel Rosenberg were executed in 1953 for allegedly transmitting to the Soviets a single sheet of paper upon which was a rough sketch of the implosion lens of the atomic bomb, there was an international outcry on their behalf to reverse the death penalty. This film helps us understand why. *The Falcon and the Snowman* is the story of two young American spies who, over a period of many months, made available to Soviet agents thousands of classified documents, many of them highly sensitive. For this transgression, they were tried and sentenced to life (for Lee) and forty years (for Boyce) in federal prison. This film tells their story (which they actually survived to tell themselves). They were no more disillusioned than a lot of young people in the protest-riddled '70s. The incident that would isolate them in history was Boyce's placement (through his father's intercession) in the Black Vault of the local aerospace defense plant. The "Vault" was the top-secret code room at RTX. High-level intelligence information came in on the telexes around the clock. Buried in the daily deluge were reports of third-world coups, manipulation of governments in developed countries such as Australia, RTX subcontracting for the CIA, and other actions. Boyce (Hutton) fails to see *any* justification for these violations of national ethics and decides to test the lax security standards at RTX. Instead of feeding documents into the shredder, he feeds them into his briefcase and takes them home. No one questions him. No one searches him. No one suspects him. Once outside, he entertains the possibility of deflecting American hegemony. For Boyce, weakening the U.S. is a way to help stem the spread of injustice. Following the book perhaps too closely, the film now absorbs itself with the mechanisms of data transmission. Boyce and his friend and minor drug-lord Daulton Lee (Penn) conspire to deliver documents to the Soviets in Mexico. While working toward later charges of espionage and treason, Hutton lives an otherwise normal life. But Lee's self-absorbed, belligerent personality leads to his arrest, which leads to Hutton's, who confesses everything. Lee is found guilty and sentenced to life in prison. Boyce gets forty years in federal prison. After the trial, a reporter asked him why he didn't manifest his revolutionary ideas in a more acceptable way. "It wouldn't have made any difference," he answered, "I freely chose my response to this absurd world. If given the opportunity, I would be even more vigorous."

Also recommended: *Daniel*.

FIRES ON THE PLAIN
(NOBI)

With Eiji Funakoshe, Osamu Takisawa, Mickey Curtis. Produced by Masaichi Nagata. Directed by Kon Ichikawa. Screenplay by Natto Wado, based on the novel by Shohei Ooka. Photography by Setsuo Kobayashi. Music by Yasushi Akutagawa. Japan. Japanese with English titles. Black and white. 105 minutes. 1959.

War at its worst.

Kon Ichikawa, the anti-war mastermind, has indulged his deepest distastes in this voyage of trashed-out war zombies relentlessly slogging through the underbrush. Our "hero," Tamura, along with various other war-ravaged, starved, and depraved fighting men, is heading for a muster point inconveniently located behind enemy lines in New Guinea during World War II. Everyone he meets is desperate and dehumanized by war. Tamura travels alone hoping for some sign of hope and truth, but instead he finds one desperate group of soldiers after another. Most of the men moving toward the muster point are killed, either by the Americans or by their fellow Japanese soldiers. They have no supplies, no support, and no leaders. Eventually we begin to hear about cannibalism. Then we suspect cannibalism. Then we witness cannibalism. Then we witness self-cannibalism. And the horror goes on. Tamura is despondent, watching people who will stop at nothing to survive. He throws his gun away and walks toward an encampment with his hands over his head. He is killed, of course, and that's the end of the movie. If there are any of the other Japanese soldiers left alive, we get the impression that they would be better off dead. No one escapes from Ichikawa's utterly consuming war. The star Eiji Funakoshe does a splendid job of playing the dazed victim of combat stress. He creates a character who seems both like a child and like a madman. He walks toward the last encampment with his hands over his head, saying, "I just want to see people leading normal lives." By then, of course, we all do. The photography is flawless and artful throughout, although this is not what will stick in your mind.

Also recommended: *Harp of Burma.*

FORBIDDEN: A TRUE STORY

With Jacqueline Bisset, Jurgen Prochnow, Irene Worth, Peter Vaughan, Robert Dietl. Produced by Mark Forstater. Directed by Anthony Page. Teleplay by Leonard Gross, based on his book *The Last Jews in Berlin.* Photography by Wolfgang Treu. USA. English. Color. 114 minutes. 1984.

A wealthy woman hides Jews in Nazi Germany in World War II.

There aren't too many films about the persecution of the Jews during World War II that have less than a tragic ending. In this film the very privileged Countess (Bisset) is using her social status to hide Jews during the Nazi occupation of Europe. Before the war, the Jewish population of Berlin was 30,000. By 1943, there are fewer than 4,000 Jews left living in the city. The Nuremberg Laws are in place, forbidding Aryans from marrying or having intimate relations with Jews. The barometer of hate is so finely tuned that one risks arrest even talking to Jews on the street. Jews are not allowed to own radios, telephones, fur, silk, or other luxuries. Hitler's laws have legalized immoral interdicts of racial supremacy. In this climate of oppression, Fritz (Prochnow) and the Countess fall in love. He tells her, "I try not to confuse the Nazis with the German people." While Jewish friends and associates are sent to labor camps and arrested for anti-Nazi sentiments, Bisset hides Fritz in her apartment and spends her days helping others escape Berlin or find safe havens in the city. When she discovers that she's pregnant, a non-Jewish friend must sign on as the baby's father. Her entire life is a facade—an invention of unquavering lies. She is dedicated to the resistance under the pretense of bourgeois obligation. When Hitler orders the last Jews to be deported to Poland or to concentration camps, she tries to convince Fritz to escape Berlin on a train taking Jews to safety. He refuses. He would rather die than leave her alone in Berlin. Bisset distinguishes herself in this stylistically genteel film about the ordinary courage of ordinary people facing down fascism in the racist state.

Also recommended: *The Boat Is Full.*

FORBIDDEN GAMES
(JEUX INTERDITS)

With Brigitte Fossey, Georges Poujouly, Lucien Hubert, Suzanne Courtal, Jacques Marin, Laurence Badie, Andre Wasley, Amedee, Denise Perronne, Louis Sainteve. Produced by Robert Dorfman. Directed by Rene Clement. Screenplay by Jean Aurenche, Pierre Bost, and Rene Clement, based on the story by Francois Boyer. Photography by Robert Juillard and Jacques M. Robin. Music by Narciso Yepes. France. French with English titles. Black and white. 85 minutes. 1952.

Children's games morbidly mimic World War II war consciousness.

A young girl walks with her family down a road in France during World War II. Hundreds, perhaps thousands, of refugees are on the same road, fleeing Paris. As enemy planes approach, Paulette's puppy jumps from her arms and runs ahead. She runs after him. Her mother calls out and follows her daughter, and her father runs after them both. As the mother's hand touches Paulette's shoulder, enemy bomber fire bites into the crowd of bodies pressed to the ground for protection. When the planes are gone, Paulette turns to see her mother and father dead where they fell. The puppy is also dead. Along the road, many bodies remain motionless as others rise from among them and continue on. Paulette lifts the dog and carries his limp body off among the column of surviving refugees. So begins Rene Clement's strange film of life made strange by war. Paulette will live with a farming family and learn the rituals associated with death and the magic of the symbols of the church. When one of the farmers dies, it is Paulette who says, "May God welcome him into paradise." The children use the myths in the burial of the puppy. The eerie vacuity of ritual encompasses them. The ritual is neutral to death and indifferent to war. Perhaps life requires death to remind the living of their own mortality. Paulette and her young friend succumb to the allure of ceremony. They create their own hidden cemetery, decorating the graves of small animals with stolen artifacts of the church. Hitler's war has generated this fascination for death. The children play their morbid games as the adults play at war. Life and death subsist on each other. Clement's film is a pastoral allegory of submission to evil. It reflects the documented behavior of real children during the war when popular childhood games were grave-digging, sentry duty, and interrogation. It's the same on the farms. The tender psychologies of the young are deformed to accept and perpetuate the diseases of violence. This is the way the seeds are transferred through the generations.

Also recommended: *Border Street.*

FOUR DAYS OF THE MASAI

Produced and directed by Jean-Claude Luyat and Jean-Noel Levaton. Written by Milton Hoffman. Music by Rosemary Fishel. Narrated by Michael Tolan. USA. English. Color. 120 minutes. 1980.

**Filmmakers take their cameras into a Masai village in Kenya to
record the people and their traditions.**

There are 200,000 Masai living along the Great Rift Valley in Kenya
and Tanzania. They are the protected tribes of the Masai, the living legacy of thousands of years of uninterrupted tribal evolution. Their society is one without leaders or classist division. Perhaps for this reason
time, for them, is an illusion. Social hierarchies are formed around age
groups that are distinguished by an extraordinary life-long intensity of
brotherhood and sisterhood. Young boys who herd together will be
warriors together and elders together. Young girls will one day gather as
women to build the dung and thatch dwellings that look like giant
loaves of bread on the Serengeti Plains. As they pass through life together, they move upward into the tribe. Elders retire into homage and
reverence. "If you are Masai, life is good when you are old." Elders are
the storehouses of tribal knowledge and spirit revelation, shepherding
the Masai toward a future rooted in the past. To these herders, the Earth
is sacred—they cannot dig in the Earth or plant crops. God is Ungai, the
unknown. They are herders whose cattle saved them from colonial invaders. Other tribes were forced off their homelands into cities to work
to pay the British head tax. The Masai had their cattle to sell. They
never gave up their culture. They never gave up their lands. Nor do
they seek to extend these lands or dominate their neighbors. They do
not covet or envy. Clashes with neighboring clans may result in ritual-
ized battles fought with women and children yodeling in the background. When an elder walks between the battling tribes holding out
his arm for peace, the tribes gather in an immense ceremonial circle in
the veld, and each person will greet every other person in a gothic reception line of intertribal animation. Even one hand pulled away trig-
gers a breakdown of peace. The cameras recorded the tensions and the
enticing wisdom of these people as well as native surgeries, Masai art,
dance, and the astonishing spiritual harmony of one of the world's most
beautiful people living within a corona of unbroken cultural unity ex-
tending as far back as memory can measure. Superior, uncredited camera work throughout.

Also recommended: *Raoni.*

FRINGE DWELLERS

With Kristina Nehm, Justine Saunders, Kylie Belling, Ernie Dingo, Bob Maza, Denis Walker. Produced by Sue Milliken. Directed by Bruce Beresford. Screenplay by Bruce Beresford and Rhoisin Beresford, from the novel by Nene Gare. Photography by Don McAlpine. Music by George Dreyfus. Australia. English. Color. 96 minutes. 1986.

An Australian Aboriginal girl resists and rejects her traditional heritage.

Among the remnants of traditionalism, the Australian Aborigines, basking in the outback, are as belligerent as any of the rest of the world's endangered peoples. The tribes have endured centuries of colonialist oppression. But it's not always invaders from the dominant culture that threaten them. Trilby Comeaway (Nehm) stands in the cluster of village shacks, and what does she see? There are men drinking themselves drunk against tree trunks at noon. There are caverns of car bodies rusting into ruin. There is junk and debris. There are wild-haired children and thin animals. Whatever sociologic logic ordained such a remedial world, it is for Trilby a cultural relic deteriorating from within. She wants her family to move to a project house in town and to assimilate there. Perhaps part of her problem is how she looks. She's very pretty— too pretty to live in a hut in the dried-out wasteland and to die there in the midst of meaningless tradition and family and friends. Her family moves to town, but their oddly painted home is soon crowded with relatives. Her parents forget to save for the rent. They forget to work to make the money to save for the rent. Back in the country, Trilby will carry her discontent far enough to possibly kill her own baby (it dies off-screen as she's entering a fit), freeing her to reject her people for a new life in a faraway town. *Fringe Dwellers* is an insider's look at the pressures undermining family life and culture among Australia's indigenous people. It succeeds so well that we like everyone in this film except Trilby, who caves in to materialism and monocultural myopia. The fact that she had such caucasian features seems to imply that the filmmakers had a few doubts themselves about the pivotal point of the story line, which I gathered was that we don't all have to be white. Weak casting for some of the principal characters (including Trilby) strains the cadence of this mission of cultural mercy.

Also recommended: *The Last Wave.*

THE FRONT

With Woody Allen, Zero Mostel, Herschel Bernardi, Michael Murphy, Andrea Marcovicci, Marvin Lichterman, Remak Ramsey. Produced and directed by Martin Ritt. Written by Walter Bernstein. Photography by Michael Chapman. Music by Dave Grusin. U.S.A. English. Color. 95 minutes. 1976.

Woody Allen works as a "front" for blacklisted screenwriters during HUAC's Hollywood heyday.

Imagine you're Michael Murphy playing Alfred Miller, a radical screenwriter who suddenly can't sell a script anywhere in Senator Joe's U.S.A. What would you do? Murphy hunts up his old pal Howard Prince (Allen) and talks to him about it. Sitting in the dive where Allen tends bar, Murphy explains, "I can't work anymore Howard." "What! Writer's block? What, you're not sick are you?" "No, I'm not sick, I'm blacklisted." "But, but, you feel O.K.?" "I feel terrible." I love Michael Murphy. He's so earnest. He talks Allen into wearing tweed and pretending to be the person who writes all his (Murphy's) scripts. He gets $100 for every story he sells to the ravenous directors who are starving for material since so many members of the screenwriter's guild are going to jail for un-American thoughts. Soon Allen is submitting screenplays for four blacklisted writers. He's a sensation. He's gifted and he has no history of political involvements. He's a prolific, smooth-talking, apolitical wonder. A rewrite? Well, sure just allow me to lower the script out a window to a waiting cab and get right back to you. The press is three deep for interviews. He's on the circuit. So, it's time to tail him through an average day as a national security precaution. When an average day turns out to be breakfast, lunch and dinner with communist screenwriters, Wood is invited to appear before a special Un-American Activities showdown. Humor in *The Front* is used to clarify what a comedy the Constitution can be—unable to guarantee freedom in the land of the free. The supporting cast includes formerly blacklisted talents Mostel, Ritt, and Bernstein. Blacklisting ruined thousands of careers. Many talents disappeared from the screen credits overnight and were never heard of again. Some left the country. At least one committed suicide. *The Front* saves us from the *Advise and Consent* syndrome where all ends well because nobody was communist after all. These writers are allowed to use the "C" word, and we are spared the spectacle of watching former radicals undergo philosophic cave-ins or repent mis-directed ideals of youth.

Also recommended: *Hollywood on Trial.*

FULL METAL JACKET

With Matthew Modine, Adam Baldwin, Lee Ermey, Dorian Harewood, Arless Howard, Kevyn Major Howard, Vincent D'Onofrio, Ed O'Ross. Produced and directed by Stanley Kubrick. Written by Stanley Kubrick, Michael Kerr, and Gustav Hasford, based on the novel, *The Short Timers* by Gustav Hasford. Cinematography by Douglas Milsome. Music by Abigail Mead. USA. English. Color. 118 minutes. 1987.

Boot camp followed by the front lines of Vietnam for U.S. Marines.

A full metal jacket is a type of shell casing that keeps bullets intact as they enter the body. You would know this if you'd ever been a Marine. Marines pray the Rifle Prayer, "This is my rifle, there are many like it, but this one is mine. My rifle is my best friend. It is my life. I must master it as I master my life. Without me, my rifle is useless; without my rifle, I am useless." They canonize great murderers of our time: Charles Whitman hit human targets at 400 yards from a bell tower; Lee Harvey Oswald killed President Kennedy at 250 feet—both were former marines. There are slogans, "Your rifle is only a tool. It is your heart that kills." Basic training is intentionally brutal and demoralizing. In *Full Metal Jacket*, Gunnery Sergeant Hartman is a drill sergeant in real life. It's not clear why he would want to play a man who drives recruits to suicide. As the boys become more dehumanized, parade ground drills become more precise. They are progressing. Soon they will be promoted to the real thing. "Goodbye Sweetheart, hello Vietnam." Surviving recruits are followed around in the war zone. There is a lot of overly calm face-to-face charlas with the camera lens. This is because two of the young men from boot camp are now working for *The Stars And Stripes*. One is a cameraman. The other writes the stories. Their job is to track down photo opportunities, check out "unusual" combat veterans or combat situations, and submit inspirational stories for publication. They have not been completely dehumanized. They submit articles about war crimes and atrocities. They lack respect for military ways, and they are punished. It is not clear if they will live or die. *Full Metal Jacket* is a film about the two halves of war—you could not have one half without the other. If either of these halves seems unreasonably alienating, it is important to remember, "The Marine Corps does not want robots, it want killers."

Also recommended: *Dear America: Letters Home from Vietnam.*

GALLIPOLI

With Mel Gibson, Mark Lee, Bill Hunter, Bill Kerr, Charles Yunupingu, Heath Harris, Ron Graham, Harold Hopkins. Produced by Robert Stigwood and Patricia Lovell. Directed by Peter Weir. Screenplay by David Williams, based on the story by Peter Weir. Photography by Russell Boyd. Music by Brian May. Australia. English. Color. 111 minutes. 1981.

Young men from Australia volunteer to fight for the British in the Battle of Gallipoli in World War I.

Somewhere in the outback of western Australia, young men are growing up with an intense freedom of spirit, measuring themselves against elemental things and against each other, testing the limits of physical perfection. Youth has distilled in them ideal qualities. The youthful competitions test them: they are in training for their lives. These Australian boys go to war singing, "If England needs a hand, well, here it is," and they take their sharp instincts with them to the trenches. They polish the brass and oil the weapons of war. They are invulnerable, but they are issued no ammunition. The allies are fighting to take Constantinople from the Turks. What England needs in the Battle of Gallipoli are decoys. The Anzacs are sent to meet an incoming force of Turkish infantry machine-gun fire. Some are shot as they crawl out of the trenches. Some fall five feet from the trenches, others at ten. They die on top each other, rank upon rank. The commanding officer calls it cold-blooded murder. To advance is to die. Wedding rings, medals, and photos are left behind. The trench divides the universe: on one side, a peaceful and sunlit plain; on the other, corpses already in decay. Mel

Gibson is Frank Dune, the runner. He is pulled to run the trench maze between the command post and the field. The next unit up is his own. His lungs are shrieking for air as he races with the new orders before they go marching into the graveyard of war. In this single campaign, 241,000 British combat troops lost their lives. Of the 60,000 Australians sent in, 24,000 were killed. Peter Weir has shadowed this sacrifice through the entire film. Every action confirms it. Every promise anticipates it. The young men are pulled up to it by their innocence and joy of life. The musical score aligns them along death's parallel. A *New York Times* reviewer called *Gallipoli* "prettier than any war film has ever been." That's because it's not a war film; it's an anti-war film. The beauty of the film is the beauty of life, which war takes away and death denies.

Also recommended: *Born on the Fourth of July.*

GANDHI

With Ben Kingsley, John Gielgud, Roshan Seth, Rohini Hattagandy, Geraldine James, Edward Fox, Trevor Howard, John Mills, Ian Charleson, Saeed Jaffrey, Martin Sheen, Athol Fugard, Alyque Padamsee, Amrish Puri, Candice Bergen, Daniel Day Lewis. Produced and directed by Richard Attenborough. Written by John Briley. Photography by Billy Williams and Ronnie Taylor. Music by George Fenton and Ravi Shankar. United Kingdom. English. Color. 188 minutes. 1982.

The story of the Indian human rights activist, Mahatma Gandhi.

Gandhi is not so much a movie as it is a cinematic guide for peaceful, practical revolutionaries. The secret to harmonious social existence appears as a collage of logical motives, the aptitude for which everyone is infected with from birth. If the Mahatma's actions seem mundane, that's because they are. It's not meant as an epic. It's meant to convey the routines of passive revolution so that audiences will understand how one person could do what he did. He was not a god. He was a man, who would tell the Viceroy of India, "It's time that you left." Gandhi started as a lawyer burning pass cards in South Africa, where he learned to resist compromising the common ideal. He realized that it's the daily concessions that collide into war and poverty and illegal dominion. For all its superlative technical excellence, *Gandhi* has only one very simple, very urgent, very misinterpreted message—the singular, first-person pronoun of historic incident. I can change the world. I can stand up for justice. I can respond to the imperfections of civilization. I can speak out for human rights. Gandhi promoted the theory of passive resistance and practical action to all forms of oppression, even violence. In the struggle to free the subcontinent from British colonial rule, he tells the people to burn all British cloth. He learns to weave and wears his own homespun. He undermines colonial economics further by leading a campaign to make salt from the sea. He calls for strikes and fasts for unity and peace. This film is so unified, pressureless, and tonal that time seems to stop, and 188 minutes later, Gandhi's funeral pyre burns almost gloriously. Nehru, superbly interpreted by Roshan Seth, is abandoned to history. And the rest of us are abandoned to conscience. Gandhi was shot down by an assassin on January 1, 1948. Archival scenes of the funeral procession are astonishing evidence of the national reverence in which he was held during his life. The Academy of Motion Picture Arts and Sciences extended generous homage to this film—far away and safe enough to celebrate.

Also recommended: *King—From Montgomery to Memphis*.

GENERATIONS
(POKOLENIE)

With Janus Paluszkiewicz, Tadeusz Lomnicki, Zbigniew Cybulski, Urszula Modrzynska, Tadeusz Jancar, Ryszand Kotas, Roman Polanski. Produced by Film Polski. Directed by Andrzej Wajda. Screenplay by Bohdan Czesko, based on his novel. Photography by Jerzy Lipman. Music by Anrzej Markowski. Poland. In Polish with English titles. Black and white. 92 minutes. 1954.

Communist youth brigade fights fascism in World War II Poland.

Maybe Andrzej Wajda is not a genius, but he's a lot like one. His memories of World War II are poised between myth, the potency of art, and malice toward tyranny. When the Nazis hang people in the public square, Wajda pulls the horror of it from the crowd, voiceless as effigies. The young people who die for freedom leave behind aging parents who have to beg for a living. *Generations* refuses to battle itself with the eccentricities of reality. Caught between Jerzy Lipman's intensely divided earth and sky are lessons in capital accumulations. "You work at the wood-shop, you make a door. The boss sells the door for forty-eight dollars. He pays you six. The more you work, the richer he gets." This makes so much sense to Bartek (Lomnicki) that he joins the communist party's fighting youth league, led by the beautiful Dorota (Modrzynska), who presses him into rebel cadence. "I'm a communist." "You're not a communist, you're a coward. If you were a communist, you'd fight." They rescue people from sewers. They run for their lives up endless Hitchcockian stairwells—up toward the dizzy suspense between life and death. They sink into slabby shadows and are edged out by a phosphorescing sun. It's a world of long-receding store fronts met by infinity along buckled and tormented roadways. People are formed from light and dark. They speak and sink under the weight of fate. In the end, there are four men, one woman, a bicycle, and a telephone pole. They are ready to conquer and consume, as soon as they can emerge from the rock face they seem born of. For those who care about such things, a young Roman Polanski speaks a few lines in his role as one of the fighting youth.

Also recommended: *Men of Iron* and *Men of Steel*.

GENTLEMEN'S AGREEMENT

With Gregory Peck, Dorothy McGuire, John Garfield, Celeste Holm, Anne Revere, June Havoc, Albert Dekker, Jane Wyatt, Dean Stockwell, Sam Jaffe. Produced by Darryl F. Zanuck. Directed by Elia Kazan. Written by Moss Hart, based on the novel by Laura Z. Hobson. Photographed by Arthur Miller. Music by Alfred Newman. USA. English. Black and white. 118 minutes. 1947.

A magazine writer poses as a Jew to get first-hand experience on anti-Semitism for a series of articles.

You've heard of blacks passing for white (*Pinky*). You've heard of whites passing for black (*Black Like Me*). Well now you can hear about a gentile writer (Peck) passing for a Jew with an inner voice and an inner vengeance against anti-Semitism. From an irrepressible Moss Hart (love the name) script and probably the purest reduction of prejudice drawn out in any Hollywood movie before or since, Peck ingratiates himself so deeply into his charitable charade that his own fiance (McGuire) approaches critical mass about it. After all, they are planning a big wedding and who's even going to show up if she can't tell anybody he's not *really* Jewish? And where will they have the reception, and who will cater? She's near tears that he can't consider the seriousness of his surely worthy but immoderate experiment. No, she's not anti-Semitic, which is hardly the point. We kind of want Peck to give up on McGuire, but the gyroscopic Moss Hart resolve wants more than anything to surmount these precipitous bourgeois battlements and inoculate all he finds therein against the disease of passive racism. After bad locker-room experiences, poor restaurant service, and face-offs with crude hotel clerks, Peck patiently explains to McGuire that acquiescence to bigotry is also bigotry. When his son (Stockwell) tells him that he's been harassed at school because they think he is a Jew, Peck is stunned to hear McGuire assure him that he is no such thing. Even though the film is black and white, Peck's face seems to pale. He takes the boy aside to explain that being a gentile is not the thing to be thankful for. Everyone has the right to their own beliefs and to persecute someone on religious grounds is wrong—he can be thankful he knows that. McGuire continues to accuse him of being naive and going perplexingly overboard. He continues to explain his philosophies until she finally understands what it means to bend to hate in any form—until she sees herself doing it and is ashamed by it. This film was astonishingly controversial when it was released. Apart from the obvious reasons, many of the Jews in Hollywood preferred that filmmakers didn't "stir it up." Zanuck persevered. *Gentlemen's Agreement* is the beautiful, award-winning, superbly resilient result.

Also recommended: *Black Like Me*.

THE GODS MUST BE CRAZY

With Marius Weyers, Louw Verwey, Sandra Prinsloo, Xao Ar Xi. Narrated by Paddy O'Byrne. Written, produced, and directed by Jamie Uys. Photography by Buster Reynolds, Robert Lewis, and Jamie Uys. Music by Johnny Boshoff. South Africa. English and Click language. Color. 109 minutes. 1984.

Quintuple cultural bypass surgery.

The "Little People" of the Kalahari Desert in Botswana are the most contented people in the world. They have no crime, no punishment, no laws, no leaders, no judges, no juries. They are happy primitive people, with a culture unchanged for a thousand years. They are perfectly attuned to desert life. They know little of the modern world, and the modern world knows little of them. Sandra Prinsloo is an inner-city teacher in Johannesburg, six hundred miles away. She has just quit her job for a new position in a rural school in the veld. Two-thousand miles to the northwest trouble's brewing in an unnamed country. Rebel forces jump into their jeeps and speed southward in clouds of dust. Somewhere in between, a shy research scientist studies animal droppings and is happy in his work. A Coke bottle dropped into the Kalahari from a passing plane will bring these people together. Nixau is trying to return the bottle to the gods that lost it when he meets the biologist and helps save Prinsloo and her students from Marxist revolutionaries. The biologist and the teacher fall in love. Nixau throws the Coke bottle off a cliff, and we all learn something about how diverse cultures interact. South African filmmaker Uys has made this surprisingly engaging comedy about life in subequatorial Africa in spite of the fact that critics all over the world thought he should have made a film against apartheid. Well, so should everybody. But they don't. In his films, Uys has always promoted traditional cultures as more attuned to nature and more nurturing to the human spirit. His films speak to racial understanding, cooperation, and the integrity of rural living. His cities are dehumanizing, commercial war zones on the map. For me, it wasn't a complete waste of an hour-and-a-half to learn something about the natives, something about the allure of Africa, and something about the oddity of life.

Also recommended: *Eat a Bowl of Tea.*

GOOD FIGHT

With the volunteers of the Abraham Lincoln Brigade. Narrated by Studs Terkel, with Colleen Dewhurst. Produced and directed by Noel Buckner, Mary Dore, and Sam Sills. Photography by Stephen Lighthill, Peter Rosen, Joe Zilagliano, and Renner Wunderlich. Music by Wendy Blackstone and Bernardo Palmobo. USA. English and German with English titles. Color and black and white. 98 minutes. 1983.

American volunteers recall their participation in the Spanish Civil War.

As the Great Depression roars across the U.S., radical and union movements emerge, and the far right rises up to oppose them. Membership grows in the German-American Bund, The Silver Shirts, and the KKK. Abroad, fascism is spreading through Europe and Asia. But in Spain, a democratically elected government institutes land reforms, builds 8,000 village schools, and extends the vote to women. It's an enticing sign of freedom. But, aided by Hitler and Mussolini, fascist Francisco Franco declares war on the Spanish Republic. Within a week, 300,000 are dead. As the peasants of Spain fight for independence, twenty-seven countries sign a nonintervention pact. President Roosevelt commits the U.S. to "complete impartiality," promising to "scrupulously refrain from any intervention in the *Spanish problem.*" The U.S. prohibits all travel to Spain. By 1936, Madrid is on the brink of collapse, and those sympathetic to Spain begin aid campaigns. Communists in the U.S. recruit combat volunteers through word of mouth and newspaper ads disguised as job offers. Men and women, black and white, sign up to fight for Spain. "I thought, I'm not going to sit down and just let this happen. I'm going out to help, even if it is my life. It's my world, too. And I'm a nurse." "It seemed like the natural thing to do. I knew what oppression was." Risking loss of citizenship, brigade volunteers fly to France and cross the Pyrenees on foot to reach Spain. Ahead of them are volunteers from fifty-two other countries. The Abraham Lincoln Brigade is the youngest, most inexperienced brigade in the force of 40,000 international volunteers. One black man remembers, "It was the first time in my life I was treated as a man. I hated to leave." "I forgot I was black," says a Brigade nurse, "Until I came back to America." The Abraham Lincoln Brigade suffers enormous combat losses. Of the 3,200 who fight, seventy percent are dead or missing by 1939. Ernest Hemingway canonizes them: "Those who have died have already achieved immortality." Paul Robeson, Helen Keller, Albert Einstein, Carl Sandburg, and others support the volunteer corps. But the USSR is the only country supplying guns and other support to the troops, and it isn't enough. By 1939, Franco's fascist army has defeated the Spanish Republic. Brigade survivors are honored by the fallen democracy, "You are history. You are legion. You are the heroic example of democracy, solidarity, and universality. We shall not forget you." Forty years later, volunteers recall how they felt leaving Spain. "The pain of that loss, it never quite leaves you." "It takes on the characteristics of a metaphor for the human condition." "I've never regretted losing my arm, because I gained so much more." "We lost." "But we won the war against fascism...on V.E. Day." After millions of additional lives were lost in World War II, fascism fell. After the Spanish Civil War, many Brigade members were labelled "premature anti-fascists" and hounded by the FBI. Some were called before HUAC. "We were wiped out of the unions. Every job, the FBI would hound you until you were fired." "For ten years it was hard." "You're a revolutionary, you must expect all this type of stuff. It's not always gonna be like that. . . . That's why we have to keep fighting. To give up would be the worst form of cowardice." "I've done something to help the people. That's what I'm here for . . . that's what we're all here for."

Also recommended: *You Got To Move.*

GORILLAS IN THE MIST

With Sigourney Weaver, John Omirah Miluwi, Bryan Brown, Julie Harris, Iain Cuthbertson, Waigwa Wachira. Produced by Arnold Glimcher, Terence Clegg, Robert Nixon, and Judy Kessler. Directed by Michael Apted. Screenplay by Anna Hamilton Phelan, based on the story by Harold T.P. Hayes. Cinematography by John Seale and Alan Root. Music by Maurice Jarre. USA. English. Color. 129 minutes. 1988.

Famed primate ethnologist Dian Fossey studies gorillas in Rwanda.

When Joy Adamson was killed in Kenya in 1980, her death would soon seem like the beginning of a curse that would kill Dian Fossey five years later in Rwanda and take George Adamson's life in Kora, Kenya, in 1989. The three well-known figures in African wildlife conservation all shared the same obsession with increasing our understanding of primates. Fossey was so committed to winning Louis Leakey's appointment to primate research in Zaire that she underwent an elective appendectomy after he commented that anyone serious about African research would have the useless organ removed. Her initial six-month assignment would last the rest of her life. She never gave up her research. After fleeing civil war in Zaire, she set up the Karisoke research station in Ruhengeri, Rwanda, which grew into a settlement of eight cabins and included the first trained anti-poaching force in Rwandan history. She was a devoted, disheveled protectress of the animals she gave her life to save. In the film, Fossey (Weaver) and her assistant Sembagare (Miluwi) track down the timid primates, and Weaver resigns herself to the submissive posturing and gesturing that will win her acceptance by the mountain troop. She exhilarates in the euphoria of inter-species communication and understanding. But, as driven as Weaver is in this role, she can't compare to the real-life Fossey. As evidenced in the actual *National Geographic* footage, Fossey was not merely happy when Digit touched her open palm in the common primate greeting gesture— she was moved beyond emotion to the depths of her capacity to feel. Her very soul seemed submerged by this rare and exotic happening. Weaver, certainly a wonderful actress, is often enough satisfied to let iron resolve stand in for the personal psychic identity Fossey felt for Africa's mountain gorillas. So much so that we are caught off-guard and retroactively moved to see that she has been buried beside Digit in the misty Rwandian highlands and that Miluwe has united their eternal souls by joining the stones that surround their graves. Apted, who was evidently as moved by Miss Fossey's life as were millions of others, has achieved something quite extraordinary with this film. The only falsity is the ecstatic overture that rises as the final credits roll. The implication is of a planet rehabilitated and a species saved. A dirge would have been a more appropriate finale as the struggle to save the animals promises never to be won. Miluwi gives a priceless performance, and Seale's cinematography is not to be outdone.

Also recommended: *The Emerald Forest.*

GRAPES OF WRATH

With Henry Fonda, Jane Darwell, Charley Grapewin, Dorris Bowdon, John Carradine, Russell Simpson, O.Z. Whitehead, John Qualen, Eddie Quillan, Zeffie Tilbury. Produced by Darryl Zanuck. Directed by John Ford. Screenplay by Nunnally Johnson, based on the book by John Steinbeck. Photography by Gregg Toland. Music by Alfred Newman. USA. English. Black and white. 129 minutes. 1940.

Story of displaced American farm families during the Great Depression of the 1930s.

They were sharecroppers, many generations of whom had lived on the land. "We were born on it, we worked it and we died on it. That's what makes it ours, not some piece of paper." But bulldozers razed the buildings just the same on behalf of the "Shawnee Land and Cattle Company." During the Depression, millions of farmers were plunged into poverty by forces beyond their control. Corporations moved in, assuming ownership of vast tracks of repossessed, foreclosed properties at Depression prices. Ford and Toland fill the screen with lean vistas and caravans of ancient vehicles overloaded with homeless nomads and their belongings, heading westward, following the jobs and rumors of jobs. These vistas have a drifting, methodic momentum. There are camps full of itinerant workers. There are poor people gathered everywhere. And still *The Grapes of Wrath* fails to communicate to audiences the turbulent upheaval and the magnitude of the exodus of those times. There are no stark vistas of the Midwest consumed in drought or the common road to nowhere filled with common people. No montage of Hoovervilles. The film focuses on Henry Fonda and his homeless family, which has been brutalized by poverty. They pray for a miracle in the lush, fruited valleys of California, where the faded handbills advertise jobs. As they drive across the country, they live in tents and bury loved ones by the side of the road, but the jobs and the dreams never come. Although the Fonda family is lucky enough to find a government camp to live in, there are few social safety nets and no compassion for the poor. Organized labor wages unsung battles for workers' rights. Union membership escalates and brings with it violent efforts to beat it out of existence. Corporate mercenaries terrorize defenseless, desperate job seekers. Local police take orders from landowners and assault, kill, and jail union leaders. Union men talk about alternative economic systems. The word "reds" surfaces, encouraging some reviewers to claim this film was "almost a cry for socialism." *The Grapes of Wrath* captures capitalism at a historic pinnacle—deploying formerly independent labor into the wage corral and concentrating the land, the money, and the power into agricultural monopolies. Fonda's "I'll be there" speech is a moody evocation of human resolve in the darkest of times.

Also recommended: *The Little Foxes.*

THE GREAT DICTATOR

With Charles Chaplin, Paulette Goddard, Reginald Gardener, Emma Dunn, Jack Oakie, Billy Gilbert, Maurice Moscovich. Written, produced, and directed by Charles Chaplin. Photography by Roland Totheroh and Karl Struss. Music by Meredith Wilson. USA. English. Black and white. 127 minutes. 1940.

Major mix-up between ruthless dictator and kind-hearted barber that could save the world.

Charlie Chaplin could not resist being funny. He saw humor everywhere. Hitler was funny. The persecution of the Jews was a tragedy but was not without comic potential. Even the concentration camps were funny. The time is post-war and the place is Tomania in a veteran's hospital where Chaplin has signed in for long-term therapy for a war injury. He's shut away from the world, so how is he supposed to know that the dictator, Hynkel (his exact look-alike), has come to power? Hynkel's storm troopers terrorize towns full of innocent people while Chaplin recuperates in the ivory sanctum. After his discharge, he opens a barber shop, teams up with Paulette Goddard, and gradually learns the truth of Herr Hynkel's world. Hynkel (also played by Chaplin) is not a sick, murdering racist so much as a pampered child whose speeches are improved in translation—a self-absorbed klutz who can't tell why he does what he does. *The Great Dictator* is peppered with slapstick, vaudevillian episodes and clever sight gags that help stretch the film to 127 minutes. The climactic switcheroo of identities is postponed until the last fifteen minutes. Chaplin, the barber, speaks out for Chaplin, the zealot, "I don't want to be emperor. I want to help everyone, if possible: Jews, gentiles, black man, white man. We all want to help one another. Hu-

man beings are like that. We don't want to hate and despise one another. Life can be free and beautiful, but we have lost the way. Greed
has poisoned men's souls. We think too much, we feel too little. The
hate of dictators will pass, and the power they took from the people will
return to the people. Soldiers, don't fight for slavery, fight for liberty. In
the name of democracy, let's all unite. Let's all fight to do away with
national barriers, to do away with greed, hate, intolerance." Millions
cheer through the miracle of archival clips. Paulette Goddard rises from
where she has fallen on the Earth. He speaks to her directly about a new
world, where the soul of humanity will be given wings to fly into a rainbow, into the light of hope, into the glorious future that belongs "to you
and to me and to all of us."

Also recommended: *Underground.*

THE GREAT McGINTY

With Brian Donlevy, Akim Tamiroff, William Demarest, Allyn Joslyn,
Louis Jean Heydt, Muriel Angelus, Harry Rosenthal, Libby Taylor. Produced by Paul Jones. Written and directed by Preston Sturges. Photography by William C. Mellor. Music by Frederick Hollander. Great Britain.
English. Black and white. 81 minutes. 1940.

Story of a man who has a chance to make the world a better place, but loses out.

"This is the story of two men who meet in a banana republic." Well,
they meet, but you will wait in vain for the story of the second guy. This
is the story of McGinty (Donlevy). The other guy sits on a barstool all
night, listening to McGinty fill him in on his "twist of fate" in life. He
was nothing but a nervy hood when he lucked into being a candidate
for alderman in a fixed election, went on to become mayor, and rode
the gravy train all the way to the governor's mansion. He got things he
never dreamed of, but he didn't get them fair and square. This didn't
bother him. He was happy and an example to his kind. But the wife he
married as a campaign edge is turning his head. He's falling for her, and
she thinks he should give up graft and start thinking about the poor and
downtrodden. Why not clean up the tenements instead of building

roads that aren't needed? He's the governor. He can do good. When he looks into her blue eyes, he cares as much as she does about the needy. He cancels the swollen highway budget and, in exchange, the graft lords destroy his career overnight. He doesn't even get twenty-four hours to do good. He's ruined, and he leaves it all behind and winds up in a bar in a banana republic, telling a long story to two people on bar stools who don't know whether they should believe him or not. The moral is that McGinty did okay as long as he dealt from the bottom, but honest dealing ruined him. Donlevy is a doll and will win you over.

Also recommended: *All the King's Men.*

THE GREAT WALL

With Peter Wang, Sharon Iwai, Kelvin Han Lee, Li QuinQin, Wang Xiao, Hu Xiaoguang, Shen Guanglan. Produced by Shirley Sun. Directed by Peter Wang. Written by Peter Wang and Shirley Sun. Photography by Peter Stein and Robert Primes. Music by David Liang. USA. In Mandarin and English with English titles. Color. 103 minutes. 1985.

Chinese-American family goes to China to discover you can't go home again.

There are a lot of people in the world who are living out of their element. Leo Fang (Wang) is one of them. He doesn't match the majority phenotype. He has lived in America for thirty years. He has an American home, an electric blanket, a Chinese-American wife, and a Chinese-American son, Paul (Han Lee), who dates American girls and thinks, "All Chinese parents are racists. Why do we have to do everything the Chinese way anyway? It gets you nowhere. This is America." Leo will be passed over for a promotion, quit his job, and take his nucleus of a family to China, where people speak Chinese and do things the Chinese way. He will show his wife and son how Chinese he is and show his brother how American he is, and he will feel at home for the first time in thirty years. But not in this movie. In *The Great Wall*, the Fangs are atypical wherever they go. His wife and son are curiosities—Chinese people who can't speak Chinese. They are like jelly beans lost in a fortune cookie factory. This movie is so adorably loaded with intricate, overlapping values, mores, and customs that you need to take a seeing eye dog with you to the theater if you hope to catch them all. The actors are buoyant decoys in a nostalgic undertow. Electrical gifts fizz out from improper voltage. They're confused about Calvin Klein. And antiquities now nag from t-shirts, "Put the Great Wall on your chest." Han Lee is the ideal, full-blooded misfit, harmlessly happy, shrugging his big American shoulders about everything except being aced out at the ping pong championships. "I hate losing. I hate it so much." He's willing to alarm his cousin with the news that it's an invasion of privacy for her mother to read her mail before she gets it. The film is vivid with marginal gems. Of special note: "The Gettysburg Address" like it's never been addressed before. Paul thinks the Americans and the Chinese are a lot alike—back in the U.S., he tells Linda, "People in America think I'm too Chinese, and people in China think I'm too American. What do you think about that?" The curse of the shifting gene pool.

Also recommended: *Eat a Bowl of Tea.*

GREED

With ZaSu Pitts, Gibson Gowland, Jean Hersholt, Dale Fuller, Tempe Piggot, Chester Conklin, Sylvia Ashton. Produced and directed by Erich Von Stroheim. Screenplay by Erich Von Stroheim, June Mathis (uncredited), based on the novel *McTeague* by Frank Norris. Photography by Ben F. Reynolds, William Daniels, and Ernest Schoedsack (uncredited). USA. Silent. Black and white. 133 minutes. 1925.

**A story of how money transforms people and destroys
their lives.**

Slashed from forty-two reels (nearly nine hours) to twenty-four reels and then to eighteen and to ten this film is still not short. Evidently Von Stroheim was set upon by some kind of equatorial truth bug (the Norris novel) and wanted to leave little left over for the archangels to say about greed. By now, many seriously appalling subplots have been excised, but what remains *is* a wholesale, greed-soaked saga about ZaSu

Pitts and Gibson Gowland falling in love. Gibson proposes and ZaSu accepts, but they do not live very long or very happily ever after, although they might have if $5,000 in gold hadn't fallen into ZaSu's lap off a lucky lottery ticket. But their troubles really start long before this, long before they wed, long before they meet, in fact several geologic ages before the onset of organic evolution when the Earth first bled purified precious metals out into its veins. By the time ZaSu cracks, the curse has already wasted a few people down deep in mine shafts dredged through rock-beds by men without souls. Murder taints every gram of gold dust measured onto surveyor's scales. Now ZaSu, the triumphant letch, trembles not from desire but from, well, greed. There's no point in chronicling the litany of tragic transformations that follow. The cosmic cracker barrel runs empty for these two, and their hearts no longer intertwine. Pitts, the precocious pixie-elf woman, is now a bull whip, leaving blood welts across Gowland's immortally wounded soul. When he is discovered to be practicing dentistry without a license, she invites him to move into the street to survive. It's a fine reward for a fine man ruined by his darling, darling bride. He will kill her and take the gold and wind up baking away on Death Valley's desert plateaus. He and another guy will die fighting for the gold, which will long outlast their fossil remains. *Greed* will burn your brain with its beauty. It struck a strong chord in audiences when it came out so very long ago, but Von Stroheim's cyclopic epic jousts at windmills and never the wind itself.

Also recommended: *Strike*.

GUESS WHO'S COMING TO DINNER?

With Katherine Hepburn, Spencer Tracy, Katherine Houghton, Sidney Poitier, Cecil Kellaway, Beah Richards, Roy E. Glenn, Sr., Isabelle Sanford, Virginia Christine. Produced and directed by Stanley Kramer. Written by William Rose. Photography by Sam Leavitt. Music by Frank De Vol. U.S.A. English. Color. 108 minutes. 1967.

White daughter brings black fiance home to meet her parents.

For those who think *Guess Who's Coming to Dinner?* is a social relic, my guess is that it won't become part of the fossil record until nobody is surprised by who's coming to dinner. Maybe Poitier *is* a little too perfect for mere mortality and blessed with twit parents, and maybe Isabelle Sanford is sawing herself off a limb, and maybe they flash F.D.R. one time too many and drink a lot and eat meat. Still, she brought him home and things happen because of that that are interesting to watch. Hepburn, for one, speaking to a soon-to-be ex-employee as she pushes her into her car and shuts the door: "I want you to get straight back to the gallery—start your motor. When you get there, go into the office and make out a check for $5,000, because you deserve it. Then take the check for $5,000 and get permanently lost, because I feel we are not the kind of people you can afford to be associated with." Maybe you had to be there. When Daddy Spencer Tracy opposes the marriage (for their own good), Hepburn is a ghost of Christmas past. "We made her, Matt. We said that those who thought white people were superior were wrong. We didn't say, don't fall in love with one. . . . I've never seen her quite so happy. . . . I have to be happy for her." Joanna (Houghton) is simply airborne: "He thinks that the fact that he's a negro and I'm not creates a serious problem." "Does he?" Does Hepburn have all the good lines in this movie or am I under hypnosis? "No, I'm not going to faint, but I will sit down just the same." Cecil Kellaway is darling as Monsignor Mike advising Tracy. "You're off balance. You don't know what you're doing. You've gone back on yourself." When Poitier's father sails in on a storm cloud to prevent the union, Poitier loses his preternatural cool, ". . . not until your whole generation has lain down and died will the dead weight of you be off our backs." Tracy gives in finally (and anticlimactically) deciding, "You can ignore the blind hatreds and stupid fears, or you can say, 'screw all those people.'" This was Tracy's last film, and he knew it. His health was so precarious that both he and Hepburn offered their salaries as collateral to win him the part. If he died before filming was complete, they would get nothing. It meant a lot to them, at least, to make this film.

Also recommended: *The Story of a Three Day Pass.*

GUILTY BY SUSPICION

With Robert DeNiro, Chris Cooper, Annette Bening, Martin Scorcese, George Wendt, Sam Wanamaker, Patricia Wettig, Ben Piazza, Luke Edwards. Produced by Arnon Milchan. Written and directed by Irwin Winkler. Photography by Michael Ballhaus. Music by James Newton Howard. USA. English. Color. 105 minutes. 1990.

The Hollywood film community is harassed by The House Un-American Activities Committee (HUAC).

In 1947, HUAC invaded Hollywood hunting for communists and communist sympathizers; anyone in favor of peace or opposed to war, the bomb, and weapons in general; or anyone who may have handed a sandwich to someone who was. You don't want to be an informant? "Real Americans have demonstrated their loyalty." Life in the movies has become "a little startling and ambiguous." Studio lawyers want director David Merrill (DeNiro) to submit to HUAC to get his name cleared. "Cleared of what?" He's not ready to become a HUAC protozoa even if they have already sent ten men to jail. "Do you want to be next?" "I went to a couple of meetings ten or twelve years ago, that's it." Some film professionals are leaving the country to be able to carry on with their lives. Martin Scorcese is leaving. "I'm a communist, David. I was a communist twenty years ago. I'm a communist now." "I didn't hear that." "It's not my country anymore." He's been subpoenaed, so he's going to London and HUAC can just take a dive off the home planet. Left behind, Merrill discovers his credentials were written in disappearing ink, and the FBI is ruining his new career as a film equipment repairperson in New York City. He's lost everything except his ex-wife (Bening), who falls in love with him all over again now that he's sleeping on her couch and is one day away from the bread line. In the news, Julius and Ethel Rosenberg are on death row. Charged with espionage in 1953, they will be executed by the red scare of the century. Sympathy for their children is countered by the media, "What little suffering the boys might endure is a small price to pay for national security." DeNiro believes there is a disease spreading. Everyone does not agree. "There are a lot of people in this country smarter than you, David, who think that the committee is a good thing . . . a good thing." DeNiro gets an offer he can't refuse and submits himself to a HUAC crossfire of accusations—blazing bonfires of reporters, cameras, a snake-pit of microphones and sweaty-faced accusers, and emotional torment curling up the marble columns. "The Federation of Atomic Scientists...wants the elimination of the bomb, period." "The Hollywood Peace Forum cries for peace every chance they get." "I'm going to charge you with contempt of Congress." "In whose homes were the meetings held?" "Communist filth." "I want to know their names." "Here she is at the Ban the Bomb bash." We aren't sure which one is supposed to be Senator Joe. There's a lot of Draconian oratory coming over the bench—none of it as odious as McCarthy actually could be. *Guilty by Suspicion* fills in a lot of missing pieces about HUAC havoc. The stories dramatized here should be taken to imply hundreds like them are untold. Extraordinary performances by DeNiro, Bening, and Cooper (as a true sell-out) and tightly strung fencing in scene after scene by writer-director Winkler.

Also recommended: *Hollywood on Trial.*

HANDMAID'S TALE

With Aidan Quinn, Elizabeth McGovern, Robert Duvall, Faye Dunaway, Natasha Richardson, Victoria Tennant. Produced by Daniel Wilson. Directed by Volkor Schlondorff. Screenplay by Harold Pintor, based on the novel by Margaret Atwood. Photography by Igor Luther. Music by Ryuichi Sakamoto. USA. English. Color. 109 minutes. 1990.

Future women forced to live as vessels for men.

In the Republic of Gilead, things have gone terribly wrong. Toxins have caused mass sterility in women. The few that bear young—only one in a hundred—are herded into former livestock warehouses and preached to by willing taskmasters. It is the mandatory reproductive age, and it has its own vocabulary. "You are the lucky ones. You are going to serve God and country. I pronounce you handmaids." Shall we pray? "I pledge allegiance to the Bible....O God, make me fruitful." They sleep on folding cots in blue, down sleeping bags. They wear riveted I.D. bands. They whisper their names after lights out. They sing old Christian hymns. New lyrics glorify fertility. Nuns are executed for refusing to produce. Lesbians are guilty of gender treachery." The thing to hope for is an appointment to a family wanting a child. With such an appointment, you go to the family and have a mock marriage ceremony so the husband (Robert Duvall) can rape you without sin. If you have a baby, they will take it as their own. Another infertile couple has your older daughter and only a victory for the people will get her back. Duvall might want to play Scrabble to get to know you. He may have read your file. "You're a librarian." "Was." Others used to be lawyers and executives. Now they are vessels. Outside the warehouse compound there is resistance. The world is a battle zone. It's hard to say who's winning. There are guerrilla forces in the mountains. The city below is in flames from May Day terrorist strikes. *The Handmaid's Tale*, taken faithfully from the pages of Atwood's novel, dramatizes forced reproduction, which is a fairly well-delineated issue. The problems of forced separation from birth parents may be much less understood and seem only improbably and dimly possible to some viewers. But in the real world, families are torn apart by adoption, early death from hunger and disease, forced work exile such as exists in South Africa, day care in the U.S., schools, and divorce. In the present century, the breakdown of the family qualifies as a social disaster. But it is invisible and even glorified in films where destitute parents give their babies to wealthy families for a *good* life. Nothing could be more pertinent to the lives of ordinary people than that they begin to recognize and oppose forces that pull such unnatural sacrifices from the poor.

Also recommended: *A Question of Silence.*

HANUSSEN

With Klaus Maria Brandauer, Erland Josephson, Ildiko Bensagi, Walter Schmidinger, Karoly Eperjes, Grazyna Szapolowask, Colette Pilz-Warren, Adrianna Biedrzynska. Produced by Artur Brauner and Laszlo Babarczy. Directed by Istvan Szabo. Screenplay by Istvan Szabo and Peter Dobai. Photography by Lajos Koltai. Music by Gyorgy Vukan. Hungary/Germany. In Hungarian and German with English titles. Color. 117 minutes. 1989.

A man with clairvoyant powers predicts Hitler's rise and fall.

Klaus Schneider (Brandauer) kneels behind his rifle sights, murmuring the Lord's prayer as birds somewhere are singing. The night is gone, and the sky burns broad and bland and blue. He kneels in a long line of men who are also murmuring in prayer. Soon most of them will lie dead. Rifle fire and cannon fire break the promise of the day. Klaus Schneider receives a head wound but survives. While recuperating, he develops the capacity to read other people's thoughts and see the future. After a long rehabilitative hospital stay, he pursues a stage career and becomes a minor sensation. He changes his name to Eric Jan Hanussen. Brandauer is perfect in this part—a mordant madman degenerating into premonition and unable to divest himself from his fascination with prophecy. He isn't obsessed so much as unwilling to calm the voices and the visions he apprehends. While still mortal, he has come upon the gateway to all knowledge. When he begins to foresee the rise of Hitler and fascism, the limelights dim. When he predicts that Hitler will be the next chancellor of Germany, he is no longer a messiah but rather a pariah, forecasting the menace of history. "What I see is not necessarily what I want." The man is a standing metaphor for spectral treachery gone unrecognized and the irresistible, international denial to face fascism in time to stop it. As he predicted the Third Reich, there was still opportunity to prevent the genocide of the Jews, the fall of Spain to Franco, and the loss of hundreds of thousands of combat lives. Hanussen loses his career predicting Hitler's rise. He loses his life predicting his fall. When he sees the Reichstag going up in flames, he is marked by the Nazi death squad. "I see flames rising. The Reichstag will burn." The headline is censored, and Hanussen is walked to the woods and executed while murmuring the Lord's prayer. No birds sing. This film is an extremely captivating and foreboding work of social realism. Based on real events, it's invidiously germane and contains some of the most artful and imaginative photography of all time. Brandauer towers.

Also recommended: *Mephisto*.

THE HARDER THEY COME

With Jimmy Cliff, Janet Bartley, Carl Bradshaw, Ras Daniel Hartman, Bobby Charlton, Basil Keane. Produced and directed by Perry Henzell.

Screenplay by Perry Henzell and Trevor D. Rhone. Cinematography by Peter Jassop and David McDonald. Music by Jimmy Cliff, Desmond Dekker, and The Slickers. Jamaica. English with English titles. Color. 93 minutes. 1973.

A young Jamaican man goes to Kingston to discover the true meaning of capitalism.

Ivan Martin (Cliff) is a lot like the real Jimmy Cliff and a little bit like Rhygin—a legendary Jamaican outlaw of the 1950s. He's a nice guy, sort of a cross between Robin Hood and Attila the Hun. He *will* make compromises to survive, but the houses of the Zodiac cannot be denied. After failing at everything and becoming a household pest to local police, he goes, on the advice of friends, down to the local recording studio to make a record. The Kingston recording companies are geniuses of low overhead. The greatest talent of the reggae generations could walk through their doors and they's still only get a flat twenty dollars for each single they cut. If the record fills bank vaults worldwide, it won't help the destitute singers who made it happen. They have to sign off for the twenty dollars just to get in the door, which is still better than no money at all, and most of the records are duds anyway. The production company owns all rights to all songs. Audiences can grind their teeth as Jimmy Cliff sings some of the most haunting reggae overtures of all time just to be hustled back on the street, wondering how he'll survive until Tuesday. Of course, Jimmy's teeth are grinding, too. So much so that he becomes an armed vigilante rebel, sold on the idea of taking a few people down with him if he has to go. As he racks up a list of warrants and his name works its way up the "wanted" register, his song works its way to number one. He's an indigent outlaw, hearing himself sing from passing cars and restaurant loud speakers. The final countdown is on a beautiful Jamaican beach—the ocean behind, the law in front. As the palm trees sway and the music plays, Jimmy Cliff meets the fusillade of the Kingston light infantry police, busy keeping the world fit to live in.

Also recommended: *Burn!*

HARLAN COUNTY, USA

Produced and directed by Barbara Kopple. Photography by Hart Perry, Kevin Keating, Phil Parmet, and Flip McCarthy. Music by Hazel Dickens, Merle Travis, and others. USA. English. 103 minutes. 1973.

Documentary of striking coal miners in Kentucky in 1973.

In east Kentucky mining towns, coal companies value a mule more than a human being. "We had to buy that mule," they told the miners. "Don't let a rock fall on that mule." And the miners said, "What about me? What about the rocks falling on me?" In these Kentucky coal towns, the Duke Mining Company and the Eastover Mining Company control the city and everyone in it, including the courts and the sheriff's office. All the powers are tied to the coal company. Even the priest tries to talk the miners into backing off and giving up. When members of the local UMW strike, the women stand in the picket lines too and watch the full force of the "law" come down on them. "We've been shot at, dynamited, threatened." They are beaten and gunned down in the roads. "If I get shot, they can't shoot the union out of me. . . . Just give me a gun, because I'd rather be dead than know there are scabs down there." They work in the mines for forty years to qualify for a pension. If they have black lung, they'd better be sure they are sick enough for full disability before they quit. "My daddy worked in the mine. We never saw him. He worked all his life 'til he was too old to work. Then they kicked him out to die." "One man dies every day to provide the energy we all use." Strikers are ordered not to blockade the trucks bringing in the scabs. They are ordered not to *use* the word "scab." They are ordered not to carry sticks, weapons, or anything resembling a weapon. They work in the mine if they want to work at all because the "company keeps other industry out of coal country so they will have a monopoly on the labor." Miners from all over the U.S. join the Kentucky picket lines. They know from experience that they can only depend on each other. The system doesn't care about the miners. "I learned what happened when you took a position against the capitalists." Democracy does not guarantee them either the right to organize or the right to a fair share of the wealth their labor generates. *Harlan County, USA* is considered one of the greatest human rights films ever made, proving that "company towns" did not die out in the coal wars of the 1920s and have not died out yet. In 1989, striking miners in Virginia wore battle fatigues to fight for their rights against the state-backed Pittson Coal

Company. They were sold out by the government the same way miners have been sold out for a hundred years.

Also recommended: *You Got To Move.*

HARP OF BURMA
(BIRUMA NO TATEGOTO)

With Shoji Yasui, Yunosuke Ito, Tanie Kitabayashi, Tatsuya Mihashi, Rentaro Mikuni. Produced by Masayuki Takaqi. Directed by Kon Ichikawa. Screenplay by Natto Wada, from the novel by Michio Takeyama. Cinematography by Minoru Yokoyama. Music by Akira Ifukube. Japan. In English and Japanese with titles. Black and white. 116 minutes. 1956.

Japanese soldier exchanges his uniform for the robes of a Burmese monk.

It's hard to believe that the director of the savagely dismal *Fires on the Plain* could have created this melodic refrain to the mystical power of all that is good. From an inspired script by Natto Wada, *Harp of Burma* unfolds its intricate story of a Japanese soldier who moves so far from war-mindedness that he becomes a Buddhist monk dedicated to burying the war dead left rotting across the blood-red fields of Burma. Opening scenes are set in a Burmese village at sundown. A company of Japanese soldiers is resting there when a British unit stops in the woods nearby. Under cover of darkness, the Japanese camouflage an ammunition wagon, singing as they do to convince the British that they're farmers from the village. Back inside, they wait for the attack. Instead of gunfire, the voices of the British soldiers drift out of the darkness, singing the never-more haunting, "No Place Like Home." The melody holds the Japanese in silence, until Mizushima picks up his harp and begins sounding out the chords. Lured by something none of them can name, the Japanese men one-by-one join their voices to the British voices in the night. Disneyesque it is not. It is artistic alchemy, rarely conceptualized and unlikely to be duplicated. The war, they learn in the morning, is over. Mizushima will be sent out from prison camp to convince isolated Japanese units to give up fighting. On his way back, he meets a priest who tells him, "In Burma, the bones of many foreigners remain unburied." Mizushima never returns to the POW camp but begins burying the dead wherever he finds them. In this poetic cry for international peace and understanding, the music and cathedral domes of Burma and sensuous turns in the drama envelop the film in an aura of metaphysical elegance. *The Harp of Burma* laces together scenes of the war weary, the lull of Buddhist temples, decaying bodies, and angelic music with the myths, dreams, and nightmares of legends of war. Mizushima has taken the vows and now wears monk's robes as he continues to work. In a last attempt to communicate before being shipped home, his unit trains a parrot to fly to him with the message, "Mizushima, come back with us, to Japan." His own bird flies to them with the answer, "There are too many dead all over Burma. I can't leave their bones scattered." Transcendent cinematography embellishes every frame of this classic of Japan's anti-war film heritage.

Also recommended: *Gallipoli.*

HARRY AND THE HENDERSONS

With John Lithgow, Joshua Rudoy, Don Ameche, David Suschet, Margaret Langrick, Melinda Dillon, M. Emmet Walsh, Lanie Kazan, Kevin Peter Hall. Produced by Richard Vane and William Dear. Directed by William Dear. Written by William Dear, William Martin, and Ezra Rappaport. Photography by Alan Daviau. Music by Bruce Broughton. USA. English. Color. 111 minutes. 1987.

The Henderson family discovers Bigfoot and rediscovers life.

Harry and the Hendersons is an anti-hunting, anti-fur, anti-meat, anti-speciesist, anti-materialist film in which typical American audiences can watch a typical American family turn into human beings. How does it happen? Well, they go camping. They argue the whole time. They pack everything into the station wagon and are on their way home along a winding, blinding forest road when they hit something—something big. And it looks dead. It's so big and hairy and dead that it could be the mythical "Bigfoot." Dreaming of book rights and world fame, they tie it to the car-top carrier and keep going. When they get home, they discover they were right, it is Bigfoot. But they were wrong, he's not dead. He's alive, hungry, and too heavy for the furniture. And he's having a burial ceremony for Grandma's ermine stole and Dad's eight-point buck trophy in the flower garden. He's harmless, trusting, gullible, and good with the dog. And he learn tricks. "Harry" (Hall) is a sheep in wolf's clothing. He believes in the harmony of living things, and he's in for a lot of disappointments. He has lived out in the backwoods for a long time (well, forever), so how's he supposed to know why people are screaming and trying to kill him? The Hendersons overcome their fear and greed and spend the rest to the movie trying to save him from hunters and riot police while living up to his very high expectations. They quit serving meat at meals. They quit wearing fur. They quit hunting. George (Lithgow) gives up his job at his Dad's sport hunting store. They have all fallen for Harry and his charming ways. He's a doll—a child at heart who screams a pathetic scream when he opens the door to the closet where George has hidden the rest of his hunting trophies. Harry's afraid of his own shadow, but not afraid of trusting that people will turn toward kindness in the end. *Harry and the Hendersons* is the creation of a talented collaboration of filmmakers. Lithgow tempts us to believe in Harry the way he does and the whole idea of intraspecies bonding. Melinda Dillon is Dillonesque. Alan Daviau's cinematography is part comic strip, part over the rainbow. It's not a movie for the hard at heart. Or, maybe, it is.

Also recommended: *Enemy Mine.*

HEAD OFFICE

With Judge Rhinehold, Rick Moranis, Danny DeVito, Eddie Albert, Jane Seymour, Lori-nan Engler, Richard Masur, Don Novello, Merritt Butrick, George Coe. Produced by Debra Hill. Written and directed by Ken Finkleman. Photography by Gerald Hirschfeld. Music by James Newton. U2SA. English. Color. 90 minutes. 1986.

Satire of corporate commercial sin and the cost to the community and its people.

"Do you think there's something wrong with the world when a company like ours produces women's hair removal cream *and* nuclear warheads?" Judge Rhinehold's senator Dad has just bought him a toehold in Inc., Inc., and he is so new to it all that he doesn't really know what he's saying. He's surrounded by self-possessed, self-absorbed, bottom-line corporate clones who think the only thing wrong with the world is that it doesn't have enough advertising space per column inch. Rhinehold, who will blunder his way to the vice-president's floor incapable of comprehending how he got there, is in customer complaints at the moment. That's where he first hears about plant closures in Allenville that will result in the elimination of 25,000 jobs and probably destroy the town. The beautiful spokesperson (Seymour) wants Inc., Inc. to let workers buy the plant. Rhinehold thinks she's a genius even if she despises him for being an Inc. plebe living off the labor power of others. Eddie Albert is the president of Inc., Inc. He orders fighter planes and has been accused of choreographing third-world coups to stabilize business interests, which he neither confirms nor denies, but does say, "The Marxists are denying third-world people the right to eat Mr. Chicken. When that right is compromised, it undermines everything this country stands for. . . . We are protecting the entire concept of internationally franchised chicken." Rhinehold thinks "America's a democracy—not some goddamned fried chicken chain." *Head Office* is such a blistering, acidic, sarcastic, sneering, scornful, contemptuous satire on *big* business that you will wonder how they got any big business to pay for it, distribute it, or show it at their conglomerate neighborhood theaters. I presume they figured the American public would just laugh it up and forget it. Predicting reactions like that is how they got so big. Rick Moranis is a wild man. Rhinehold goes where angels fear to tread. Albert is devious to the end. "The third world is the last frontier. The corporation that controls the third world in the 21st century controls the world." You saw it at the movies.

Also recommended: *The Coca-Cola Kid.*

THE HEART IS A LONELY HUNTER

With Alan Arkin, Laurinda Barrett, Stacy Keach, Jr., Johnny Popwell, Chuck McCann, Biff McGuire, Sondra Locke, Percy Rodriguez, Cicely Tyson, Jackie Marlowe. Produced by Thomas C. Ryan and Marc Merson. Directed by Robert Ellis Miller. Screenplay by Joel Freeman from the novel by Carson McCullers. Photography by James Wong Howe. Music by David Grusin. USA. English. Black and white. 124 minutes. 1968.

Deaf man tries and fails to win acceptance in a small town.

Beneath the grand and petty intolerances in any society, a ubiquitous network of indolence thrives. Overt prejudice survives unconscious of the filial inheritance owed to casual insensitivity. Trapped in this world between honest hate and open friendship, millions live unknown to us and unknown to each other. Alan Arkin lives in this world on an inferior plateau of social isolation. Nothing he can do leads him out. "I am a deaf mute," says the card and black doctors will treat white patients, fathers and daughters will give up old grudges, and a young girl will see the beauty of life. A man's faith will be restored. Children will share their secrets. Arkin has the ability to remedy things in the world of sound. He helps others see themselves as he can see them. But his own world is sealed away from audible reality. No one imagines he has dreams and terrible despair. He's alone in a very quiet world where others are happy not to intrude. No one knows why he came to this town. They haven't presumed to ask. They don't know his close friend has died. They don't know what it's like to be an impersonal repository for their sound. They don't know where he got the gun. They liked him even though they never said so. They are shocked and saddened he would kill himself when so many thought so highly of him. It's just the senseless death of a kind man. Alan Arkin is a magician of lenient expression and small gestures in this film, diagnosing a widespread and untreatable disease that is fatal only to those uninfected by it. The gift of speech and sound is a generalized handicap. Arkin reveals the grief of his solitary life and the dry ice of his execution by those too absorbed to give anything back to the children of a lesser god.

Also recommended: *24 Eyes*.

HEARTS AND MINDS

With Clark Clifford, Harry Truman, John Foster Dulles, Dwight Eisen-
hower, John F. Kennedy, Lyndon Johnson, Richard Nixon, William Ful-
bright, J. Edgar Hoover, Joe McCarthy; Gen. William Westmoreland;
Daniel Ellsberg, Corporal Stan Holder, Lt. Robert Fuller, Capt. Randy
Floyd, and others. Produced and directed by Peter Davis. USA. English.
Black and white and color. 112 minutes. 1974.

**Vietnam through the eyes of those who planned and executed
the war.**

"Truman lied from 1950 on on the nature and purpose of the French involvement. Eisenhower lied about the reason for and the nature of our
involvement. Kennedy lied about our own combat involvement. Johnson lied and lied and lied, about the plans for bombing and the nature
of the buildup in north Vietnam. Nixon lied about the bombing in Laos
and the reason for the invasion of Cambodia. The American public was
lied to year after year." According to Daniel Ellsberg, America wasn't
fighting on the wrong side in the Vietnam war, "We *were* the wrong
side." In this extraordinary documentary, interviews with anti-war activists are cut with flashbacks of the war and the speeches and lies that
allowed it to happen. "We must fight," Johnson said. "Victory will depend on the hearts and the minds of the people who live out there."
Captain Randy Floyd was a bomber pilot. "I was a technician. I was a
good pilot. It's very exciting. You never see the people. You never hear
the screams." A former prisoner of war visits schools explaining to children the satisfaction of dropping bombs that all land in the right place.
Unlike Floyd, he still has not seen the people or heard the screams.
When a young boy asks how he felt when the U.S. pulled out, he answers, "Real good. We wanted to win, so when we knew that we had
won, we felt great." Senator Joe McCarthy breathes dragon-like over a
microphone, "If we lose Indochina, we'll lose the Pacific. We'll be an
island in a communist sea." Whole commercial scenarios are laid out—
marketing strategies for the third world, soft-drink companies, Mekong
Ford, and other Mekong conglomerates feel a lot safer with each combat victory. And Captain Randy Floyd now wonders what he would do
if someone dropped napalm on his two little girls. Veterans talk quietly
of war crimes they witnessed. Some prisoners were thrown out of helicopters. One female P.O.W. describes how she was treated by the U.S.
military guards. "They said, if we were innocent, they would beat us

until we were guilty." A Vietnamese man lies on the ground while U.S. soldiers take turns kicking him in the stomach. In interviews with veterans, the camera pulls back revealing wheelchairs and artificial limbs. *Hearts and Minds* condemns a war that killed 58,000 American servicemen and women, almost destroyed Vietnam, and left war survivors on both sides of the world plunged into pain and guilt. It's a desolating spectacle of the destructive capacity of advanced capital accumulation and the ultimate price of economic imperialism.

Also recommended: *Vietnam: In the Year of the Pig.*

HEROES FOR SALE

With Loretta Young, Robert Barrat, Richard Barthelmess, Aline Mac-Mahon, Gordon Wescott, Berton Churchill. Directed by William Wellman. Screenplay by Robert Lord and Wilson Mizner. Photography by James Van Trees. USA. English. Black and white. Eight reels. 1933.

World War I veteran returns from the war to watch his luck turn bad.

Heroes for Sale. Lovely title. The hero they are talking about is Tom, who goes off to win the war but is wounded, put in a hospital, and becomes addicted to morphine. The truth is that he was left to die by a guy who took the credit for Tom's heroism, got a medal, and went home in a cloud of glory. Only Tom knows the way it really was. He gets a job at the bank, and it seems he's going to have a new life, but his morphine habit ruins it all. He's fired and sent to the sanatorium for a cure. The thing about Tom is that he doesn't take stuff like this the wrong way. He gets the cure, moves to Chicago, gets a job in a laundry, and meets a Marxist. He also meets and marries Loretta Young, and they have a baby boy. He and the Marxist invent an improved laundry machine, which they sell with the stipulation that it not be used to throw workers out of jobs. They almost get rich, and the Marxist turns into a money-hungry druid, spitting on the memory of egalitarianism. There is a good chance for the movie to end here as it's winding into its own script tornado. But new owners of the laundry use the apparatus to eliminate three-fourths of the workers. There's a riot. Tom is trying to *stop* the riot when the police come along and he gets five years hard labor for being a so-called Red. While he's off splitting granite boulders with a tire iron, the invention that put him in jail earns him $53,000. Back out, he gives the whole check to the local soup kitchen because the Depression is on and he won't take money that belonged to the workers in the first place. Tommy, Jr., glows with pride, looking at the plaque honoring his Dad's donation. Pinch me, I'm thinking. But now Tom moves out of town, because once a red, always a red, and the Feds are on to him. He hops a freight train and starts up a conversation with some hoboes about how rosy the future looks for America—yes, America, where the government sends you to war, gives you a drug habit, leaves you for broke, arrests you for something that you didn't do and that shouldn't be illegal even if you did it, and hounds you out of town and away from your wife and kid forever. Wow, what a place.

Also recommended: *Wild Boys on the Road.*

HIDDEN AGENDA

With Frances McDormand, Brian Cox, Mai Zetterling, Brad Dourif, John Benfield, Berard Block. Produced by Eric Fellner. Directed by Ken Loach. Written by Jim Allen. Photography by Clive Tickner. Original music by Stewart Copeland. United Kingdom. English. Color. 106 minutes. 1990.

The CIA and British conservative politicians conspire to permanently destabilize the British labor government and put the conservative party in power.

Hidden Agenda ignited critical tumult and shouting matches when it aired at the Cannes Film festival in 1990. This is not particularly surprising since four of director Loach's documentary works have been banned in Great Britain as "too controversial." Nowadays, these bannings are accomplished "legally" via legislation restricting telecast of anything issuing from the political arm of the IRA. The story line of this new film is based on "very strong evidence" (testimonies of former British intelligence agents and military officers) of a conspiracy of corruption posing the CIA and the British conservative party against the electoral integrity of Great Britain and against the IRA. The film opens in Belfast at a press conference given by a team of American civil liberties investigators. They have been talking to Irish Republicans who have suffered in the fight to restore "the entire ownership of Ireland" to the "people of Ireland." The investigators are answering questions and offering proof of British army violence, including evidence of "shoot to kill" orders directed at the IRA. Before filming, Loach sent this team of actors (McDormand, Dourif, Zetterling, Block) to Ireland—land of British paratrooper occupation and political graffiti on every open wall—to talk to people who had been "beaten or tortured" while under arrest. This could be why the four lend such intense, natural credibility to their roles. The news conference marks the end of formal investigations, but the testimony will not be silenced. Following new leads will take the life of one investigator and leave McDormand tracking down CIA-backed corruption on her own in the violent world of the imperialist war against Northern Ireland. She is a frail link to the truth of a vast underground offensive of civil abuse, smear campaigns, threats, and assassinations of which Margaret Thatcher was the principal political beneficiary. McDormand will witness every form of human rights violation only to be told, "You will shake the state if you . . . make people insecure about government . . . the abuse of power allows us to enjoy freedom." Closing scenes suggest that she may not survive long enough to pass on the incriminating "tapes" to others. It could turn out to be news to some Americans that the conservative shift in international politics is not limited to third-world outposts. For others, this film only confirms the rumor that the CIA services heavy capital investments wherever they are to be found. Loach's film is a courageous effort to illuminate the darkest secrets of the free enterprise system.

Also recommended: *Coverup: Behind the Iran-Contra Affair.*

HIGH HOPES

Lesley Manville, Edna Dore, Philip Jackson, Ruth Sheen, Heather Tobias, Philip Davis. Produced by Simon Channing-Williams, Victor Glynn, and Tom Donald. Written and directed by Mike Leigh. Cinematography by Roger Pratt. Music by Andrew Dixon. United Kingdom. English. Color. 98 minutes. 1989.

A peek into the private lives of the working-class British.

This film has three problems. First, there's no plot whatsoever; you need a slide rule to decipher the twists in the story line. Second, it's pretty dull. Third, it's often garishly overacted. High Hopes wants to think of itself as innovatively Marxist, and we are expected to get some hunches about how hopeless things have gotten since we've drifted into Thatcherdom. It's a morose look at what competitive economics has done to the world and the people in it who have bypassed the promise human civilization once held out. The rich are phony, perverted, insensitive, or insane. The poor don't mind their poverty. They have a refined sense of the subtleties of cockney humor, dress like thugs, and slave away making other people rich because they'd rather be exploited than exploit others. The characters, with all their off-the-wall airtight palaver, might as well be on separate mountain tops for all the mortar they contribute to the crumbling brickwork of the drama. All the characters lack appeal, even the ones we are supposed to like. And each has the depth and individuality of a cut-out. The actors are so thrilled to be in front of the camera saying immortal things that you begin to believe it's their fault. You wish they'd run out of film. But "deviser and director" Mike Leigh believes improvisation is more like real life than 'normal' movie-making techniques. Other filmmakers may appreciate this flare for ingenuity, but to me, the lack of plot and tension, pattern and point is just unelectrifying. It was as though the director and the sound man and the cinematographer were all in cahoots to strip the film of enduring satisfaction. The score, like everything else, soars deafeningly out of control when you are least in the mood for it. About the cinematography, the less said the better; it's not that kind of movie. Pratt never thinks, "What can I do that's new and different since I'm the one holding the camera?" He just expects innovative things to trip and fall into the shot, and his job is to be there when it does. The visit to Marx's grave was nice. But in this movie, anticipated cleverness never materializes. Just like the overly obvious shots of radical posters and memorabilia in the hero's flat, it's not that newsworthy to discover that Marx said, "Workers of the world unite." This film is laced with inaccuracies of Marx's theories. In one scene, a friend describes her plan to open a stand and sell handmade jewelry. She's accused of being a capitalist, while any cursory reading of Marx reveals that a capitalist is one who acquires wealth from the labor power of *others*. Another (almost universally) perpetuated inaccuracy is that Marx thought it was a sin to have nice things—that nice things themselves would drive you into some sort of dizzy, schizopathic limbo. More accurately, his dream was to create a society in which everyone enjoyed the material comforts and rewards of social labor. The fact that our hero and his Olive Oyl girlfriend are rolling joints with sly, toothy grins every chance they get is also wearing. This is the only way these caricatures can oppose the "system." *High Hopes* is supposed to be a comedy, and some will be amused, but not those who view the decay of social value, quality of life, and revolutionary philosophy as tragic rather than comic. You've heard of social realism—*High Hopes* invents "anti-social realism."

Also recommended: *Underground*.

HIMATSURI

With Kinya Kitaoji, Kiowako Taichi, Ryota Nakamoto. Directed by Mitsuo Yanagimachi. Written by Kenji Nakagami. Photography by Masaki Tamura. Music by Toru Takemitsu. Japan. Japanese with English titles. Color. 120 minutes. 1985.

The mountain people of Japan cope with the moods of forest goddesses as they react to intrusion.

Watching this film is not unlike breathing in a vacuum. I'm betting that a few people will be fighting for air ten or fifteen minutes into this film. The dim outlines of the narrative make it necessary to rely completely on one of your extra senses, and while this is not a bad thing, it is worth knowing so you can check to see if there's an iron lung in the lobby before you get comfortable. Then, since you've come this far, just compose yourself. It's only a movie: populated by icons, forest moods, and men in jeans, who have been bred on the blood of unseen wounds, couched in crypticness, and set upon by superstition and rumors of superstition. They are surrounded by moaning winds, people moving in random patterns toward instinctual destinations, fish dying strangely, accusatory remarks, distant echoes, bitterness, undefined hates, allegory, dogs attacking boars in pens, nonlinear conversations, blue-green hues, tidal pools, entrepreneurial quandaries, precarious small families, houses on stilts, purposeful belittlement, and lots and lots of other stuff meant to slow the beating of your slowly beating heart. *Himatsuri,* I'm told is based on actual events. So is the red shift of receding galaxies.

Also recommended: *Black God, White Devil.*

HIROSHIMA MON AMOUR

With Emmanuelle Riva and Eiji Okada. Produced by Samy Halfon. Directed by Alain Resnais. Screenplay by Marguerite Duras. Photography by Sacha Vierny and Michio Takahashi. Music by Giovanni Fusco and Georges Delerue. France/Japan. In French with titles. Black and white. 90 minutes. 1959.

French woman and Japanese man meet and fall in love in the aftermath of World War II.

"It was the end of the war, and the beginning of a new fear, followed by indifference, and fear of indifference." *Hiroshima Mon Amour* is Alain Resnais' masterpiece specializing in the confusing use of the personal pronoun. Resnais was asked to make a film about the atomic bomb drops in Hiroshima and Nagasaki during World War II. Too bad he chose to be so obscure that some people are still wondering what they missed. Thanks for the amorphous metaphor, Alain. There are whole books of aerial philosophic terms set aside just for talking about this movie. I'm not saying that's bad, I'm just saying be sure you take that book with you to the theater (or at least the Cliff Notes). The first fifteen minutes need no study guide: 10,000 degree heat—equal to the heat of the sun; 100,000 people killed in nine seconds; 80,000 more wounded; another 80,000 dead three days later in Nagasaki; masses of molten bottle caps hardened into stone; mounds of human hair pulled off the heads of the dead; babies born to radiated mothers. The scenes need no translation. Now, on to the romance between the enigma people—Him and Her. They are in love. But, there are things over which they have no control that are pushing them apart. There is a monumental moodiness about them. There are resolutions made and broken. It's impossible to know their pain. Him and Her. Who are they? They are Nevers, France and Hiroshima, Japan. It's a message of universal tolerance and understanding, or universal intolerance and misunderstanding. Resnais has tried to personalize the impersonal, impersonalize the personal. The film is immersed in abstraction, except for the part about the protest march. Huge banners ask the question: If one atom bomb is equal to 20,000 ordinary bombs, and one hydrogen bomb is equal to 2,500 atom bombs, how destructive are the 4,000 hydrogen warheads now stockpiled? (As of 1960.) It lacks the power to shock, coming at a point in the drama where anything comprehensible is good news. I guess Resnais wanted an anti-bomb film that would not age. He succeeded. *Hiroshima Mon Amour* will be just as beautifully bewildering to the future as it was to the past.

Also recommended: *MacArthur's Children*.

HOLLYWOOD ON TRIAL

Produced by James Gutman. Directed by David Helpern, Jr. Screenplay by Annie Reisman. Narrated by John Huston. USA. English. Color. 90 minutes. 1976.

House Un-American Activities Committee attack on the Hollywood Screenwriter's Guild.

Hollywood on Trial is a condensation of HUAC's "entomological" investigations of the film community during the 1950s. HUAC is tracking down the "ideological termites" and subversive germs of Hollywood, and many celebrities are helping them do it. Adolph Menjou and Walt Disney are friendly HUAC witnesses. Gary Cooper says, "I haven't read Karl Marx. I don't know the basis of communism, but what I've heard, I don't like it, because it's not on the level." Ronald Reagan—concerned for the ruined careers and lost screen credits of fellow creative artists— composes a list of things that anyone can do to save themselves. Top on the list—just go to the FBI and HUAC and tell them you're not a communist. Hubert Humphrey promotes the idea of emergency detention camps to contain all radicals in times of national uncertainty and doubt. This fits in nicely with J. Edgar Hoover's interest in a quarantine of "an evil and malignant way of life." *Hollywood on Trial* takes a historic perspective on the HUAC fiasco, which grew out of larger fiascos such as the drought and economic depression in the U.S. and the rise of fascism in Nazi-occupied Europe. Many concerned people sought alternatives. Socialism, communism, and labor unions all rose up and were battered down. It was the labor union movement in the creative guilds that drew HUAC fire. The Motion Picture Alliance for Preservation of American Ideals was a HUAC-inspired organization created to drown out the commies and fink on fellow artists. The Hollywood Ten came under suspicion. They were all members of the Screenwriter's Guild, and most were also members of the Communist Party of America. They were called to testify about their subversive philosophies and behaviors. All ten refused to cooperate. All were found in contempt of court. All were sentenced to jail terms and imprisoned. They sold their homes, said goodbye to their careers, served their time, and went on with their very changed lives. Dalton Trumbo, one of the ten, later remarked, "It was a completely just verdict. I had a contempt for that Congress, as I have had for several since." Some recanted and were forgiven; others left the country. Others worked for years to reestablish their artistic credentials and career standing. But it wasn't just these ten who were affected by HUAC's investigations. Hundreds of artists in Hollywood were blacklisted and never heard of again. Careers were destroyed overnight. Concerned about the box office, the motion picture industry was careful not to release a film subject to public boycott. The "legal Department" x-rayed all resumes and contracts. Not a few screenwriters hired "fronts" to pose as authors of their material. For three consecutive years during the HUAC heyday, the Motion Picture Academy of Arts and Sciences unknowingly awarded Oscars to the screenplays of blacklisted writers. As late as 1975, blacklisting anxiety still stalked Hollywood as grown children of blacklisted artists encountered residual prejudices and hiring slights. Today, an unwritten "list" prevents outspoken performers and technical staff from being considered for jobs in the industry.

Also recommended: *Guilty by Suspicion*.

THE HOLLYWOOD SHUFFLE

With Robert Townsend, Keenen Ivory Wayans, Starletta Dupois, Helen Martin, Jimmy Woodard, John Witherspoon, Paul Mooney, Kim Wayans, Marc Figueroa, Robert Shafer, Roy Fegan, Lisa Mende, Dom Jack Irrera,

Anne-Marie Johnson, Sena Ayn Black, Ludie Washington, Craigus R. Johnson. Produced and directed by Robert Townsend. Screenplay by Robert Townsend and Keenen Ivory Wayans. Photography by Peter Deming. Music by Patrice Rushen and Udi Harpaz. USA. English. Color. 81 minutes. 1987.

A black man struggles with his acting career in Hollywood, California.

So, you wanna be in pictures. There will be problems. Especially if you're black. Bobbie (Townsend) is a black actor, auditioning and occasionally getting call-backs. He even lands a role as a Buckwheat look-alike detective who whines, jives, bugs his eyes out, and does anything else they want him to do because it's the chance of a lifetime. But his subconscious is warning him that his grandmother is soon going to be writing a book called *Bobbie Dearest*. And his friends are going to be saying, "Bobbie Taylor is a Tom. His mama was a Tom, his daddy was a Tom, his uncle was a Tom. They eat Tom turkeys on Thanksgiving." Is it a bad dream or is he a sellout waiting to be found out? "The NAACP is picketing *my* film!?" "We believe black actors should not accept such roles. They can never play the Rambos until they stop playing the Sambos." Rambo! That's the guy in leather screaming, "I have to kill more than thirty-eight people, I'm the star." Well, if white actors are merchandised, black actors are homogenized. "What we're looking for is an Eddie Murphy type. We want Murphy-like, Murphyesque, Murphonic...." "Can you film more black?" Forget the sun block, casting directors are hunting for butlers, slaves, dope dealers, pimps, muggers, punks, rapists, perverts, murderers, and the lost tribes. They will be happy to teach you these roles at the "Black Acting School." Stepinfetchit is still a student there, learning how to be a freed slave, "I don't know why we's leaving the Massah's house." Oh, Bobbie, snap out of it, you're having another subconscious voice experience. Just keep rehearsing those lines because you've quit your job at Winky Dinky Dog and the years are passing you by. "But, this is not the kind of acting I wanted to do." Fine, so maybe they're hiring at the post office. "Get him off the set." Townsend ran out of money trying to finish this film on whether it's better to play a slave or to be one. He was desperate enough to put on a UCLA t-shirt and show up at the student supply shop with a fresh credit card asking for 10,000 feet of film. They rang up the sale, the card was maxed, and now he's a star.

Also recommended: *Do the Right Thing*.

THE HOME AND THE WORLD

With Victor Bannerjee, Soumitra Chatterjee, Swatilekha Chatterjee. Director by Satyajit Ray. Written by Soumitra Chatterjee, Victor Banerjee, and Swatilekha Chatterjee, from the novel by Rabindranath Tagore. Photography by Soumandu Roy. Music by Satyajit Ray. India. Bengali with English titles. Color. 140 minutes. 1984.

An Indian couple encounter revolution and suffer the perils of change.

Around the turn of the last century, high-caste women in India were prisoners of matrimonial bondage, obliged never to leave their husband's home after the wedding day. They also lived by the law of purdah—the prohibition against talking to any man other than their husband. Nikhil and his wife Bimala live in those times. Nikhil is progressive. He and an old college roommate, Sandip, pledge to ignore purdah and work for change in India. Sandip is a professional revolutionary, organizing a boycott in Bengal against foreign goods. When Nikhil introduces Sandip to Bimala, she joins the revolutionary movement. The once sheltered, indulged housewife is now an active participant in the fight for freedom, ashamed of the European clothing and ornaments she wears. When Nikhil declines to join the boycott, explaining that the people on his land are too poor to discard all foreign goods, Bimala turns from him and falls in love with Sandip. She's been given independence and wants to dedicate her life to helping win emancipation for others. But as the revolution advances, she notices that Sandip does not give up foreign goods or make any true sacrifice for the revolution. Ultimately, he gives nothing and is a charlatan reveling in the glory of notoriety. During the rioting and violence the boycotts generate in the area, Nikhil is killed. Now a widow in compulsory white robes, Bimala realizes that she loved him all along. She's learned a lesson from all this and so has the audience: give a woman her freedom and she'll cheat on you and get you killed while she's off chasing after daydreams the way women always do. A charming foray into the folly of womanhood and revolution.

Also recommended: *Distant Thunder.*

HOME OF THE BRAVE

With James Edwards, Frank Lovejoy, Jr., Douglas Dick, Lloyd Bridges, Jeff
Corey, Steve Brodie. Produced by Stanley Kramer. Directed by Mark
Robson. Screenplay by Carl Foreman, based on the play by Arthur
Laurents. Photography by Robert De Grasse. Music by Dimitri Tiomkin.
USA. English. Black and white. 86 minutes. 1949.

A black man encounters racism in the U.S. Army.

The eccentric thing about this film is the way the two men drawn together in the beginning will be counterpoised in the end on opposite
sides of a curiously unpredictable crisis. When Moss (Edwards) shows
up at the Army Special Scout unit as the new technical aide, we imagine his old pal from high school (Bridges) is going to run defense for him
against the barracks' racists until the movie ends. Instead, they set out
to prove that nothing is that simple in the world of race relations. When
the men go into the jungle to map for projected military tactics, Bridges
is killed by sniper fire. He and Moss were in the middle of an argument
when the shots hit. The intense relief he experiences when Bridges falls
overwhelms Moss with guilt and psychosomatic paralysis. Hysterical
shock causes him to lose the use of his legs. In therapy, the staff psy-
chologist (Corey) has to convince Moss that he was not relieved Bridges
was dead, but rather that he himself was alive—a common combat response to a field casualty. Eventually, Moss believes Corey, forgives
himself for the momentary indifference to the death of a friend, and re-
gains the use of his legs. The open-minded men in the unit rally to him
and quiet the racists. No trumpet solos, just a lesson in human weakness and strength couched in low-budget panache. Star James Edwards,
appearing in this drama about open-mindedness, would lose out in the
real world of the Hollywood blacklist. Called before the House Un-
American Activities Committee to answer questions about his political
philosophies, he refused to cooperate and his career as an actor was
over.

Also recommended: *Story of a Three Day Pass.*

THE HORSE

With Genco Erkal, Harum Yesilyurt, Ayberk Colok. Directed by Ali Ozgenturk. Photography by Kenan Ormanlar. Music by Okay Temiz. Turkey. In Turkish with English titles. Color. 116 minutes. 1983.

A Turkish father struggles to get his son an education.

In Turkey, they jail filmmakers for presuming to acknowledge that poverty has been institutionalized by plutocrats who understand the threat
of economic mobility. Filmmaker Ali Ozgenturk was sent to prison by
the Turkish government for making this film that reveals a few modest
truths about the laws that keep the poor poor. His talent as a filmmaker
draws him to actors (Erkal and Yesilyurt) who can articulate innocence
and confirm the disabling allure of hope. No hazard of fate can deter
Erkal's petition for an education for his son. Only death will silence his
appeal. He has promised to buy his son a horse if he will agree to go to
school. They move from the farmlands to the city streets. Here their precious savings are lost when Erkal's vegetable cart is confiscated by police in a raid of the produce stands. It's illegal to vend without a license,
which the poor cannot possibly afford. The cart was his only way to
earn money for tuition fees. Education demands forfeiture. The only
free school is a charity association for orphans. Faced with the con-
founding obstructions to his obsession, Erkal begins to presume the
state would save his son if he were dead. When the boy leaves the city
after Erkal commits suicide, we realize that Erkal could never have kept
his promise to buy a horse even if a school had materialized and that
the whole drama has been based on a futility inherent from the beginning. Erkal never understood that poverty was a legacy from above, sus-
tained by the tragedy of class.

Also recommended: *The Bicycle Thief.*

HOTEL TERMINUS: THE LIFE AND TIMES OF KLAUS BARBIE

Produced and directed by Marcel Ophuls. Cinematography by Michael Davis, Reuben Aaronson, Wilhelm Rosing, Pierre Boffety, Lionel LeGros, Daniel Chabert, and Paul Gonon. France/USA. In French, German, English, and Spanish with titles. Black and white and color. 267 minutes. 1988.

The life, career, and arrest of Nazi war criminal Klaus Barbie.

Edited down from 8,000 minutes (130 hours), *Hotel Terminus* tracks Klaus Barbie's career as a war criminal and a fugitive from justice following World War II. Survivors of his tortures describe him as indiscriminately cruel to men, women, and children, taking special pleasure in forcing mothers to watch their children's sufferings. Stories of atrocities are cut with interviews on the streets. Some have never heard the name. Others think forty years is a long time. Some wonder about cameramen who are out to sensationalize the past. Former U.S. and French military personnel talk about Barbie's employment by U.S. government intelligence during the war. The Americans and Barbie had at least one thing in common—they both hated the communists. Barbie's recruitment is comfortably justified by former U.S. intelligence agents. They liked him so much that they aided his escape from Europe to South America after the war. Not only Barbie, but other Nazi SS and Gestapo personnel won wide support in their effort to evade arrest on war-crimes charges. The awesome scope of *Hotel Terminus* expands its implications from country to country and continent to continent, interviewing participants in an international network of espionage, corruption, and the deceit of democratically-elected governments around the world. The Nazis and the CIA and the drug lords and the gun runners are all playing the same game and using the same rules. Barbie leads the good life in Peru and Bolivia, associating with heads of state as easily as hit men. For forty years, he manages to elude detection. His arrest for war crimes comes from a betrayal by a businessman from whom Barbie stole the equivalent of 500,000 German Marks. Barbie was well-known in the village where he lived. One man's shop was burned to the ground when he denied service to Barbie and his wife. Others remember him as friendly and well-liked. There are clips of Barbie looking very composed after his arrest. Much time is spent questioning the integrity of Barbie's lawyer. His daughter and daughter-in-law talk about the gentle family man. *Hotel Terminus* is a horrifying indictment of world order defeated by forces owing no allegiance or alliance to any ethical standard.

Also recommended: *Coverup: Behind the Iran-Contra Affair.*

HOW GREEN WAS MY VALLEY

With Walter Pidgeon, Maureen O'Hara, Anna Lee, John Loder, Donald Crisp, Sara Allgood, Barry Fitzgerald, Patric Knowles, Morton Lowry, Arthur Shields, Ann Todd, Fredric Worlock, Richard Fraser, Rys Williams, Roddy McDowall. Produced by Darryl F. Zanuck. Directed by John Ford. Screenplay by Philip Dunne, based on the novel by Richard Llewellyn. Photography by Arthur Miller. Music by Alfred Newman. USA. English. Black and white. 118 minutes. 1941.

A coal mining family crumbles under the crush of "The Company."

The sunlit cottages of coal town, populated by imitation miners living in a parody of poverty, convinced Welsh nationals to diagnose this film as suffering from flamboyant idealization of Welsh mining life in an era that was actually genuinely miserable. To sum up critical opinion issued at the film's release, "It is not *The Grapes of Wrath.*" The "high production values" and "perfection of cinematic narrative" work only to make it "prettified, unconvincing" and "phony." John Ford, short on "first-hand knowledge of the subject," borrowed the Llewellyn novel and used it as a springboard into virtuoso whitewash of conventional Hollywood proportions. In *How Green Was My Valley*, workers and their families are handsome, happy people, eating at trestle tables heavy with ten course meals three times a day, every day of the year. Maureen O'Hara is the center of the large family, which is slowly crumbling as the boys leave home one by one to find their fortunes outside Wales. Those who remain must go down into the mines to work in the coal company's structurally unsafe tunnels. There's at least one serious cave-in, maybe more. Loved ones risk their lives saving others trapped below. Families are split on whether unions rescue the working masses from slavery or are merely pointless "socialist nonsense." The strike, when it comes, lasts five-and-a-half months. It's a degenerating disarray of nature's wonders and the dismal crash of homelife for the miners. Amongst the other challenges the cast must survive are divorces, illegitimate babies, people falling into freezing rivers, the 29th Psalm, family feuds, and lots and lots of communal singing. The orchestra is anchored somewhere off the coast of Monterey. Maybe you could call it Ford's Folly. Even though it flops as an example of social realism and is much like a Hallmark greeting card of coal mine films, you can still see that Ford wanted to do good, and he hired a superb cast to do it and iced the whole thing with the "high production values." This, plus the wonderfully talented Roddy McDowall, saves the film.

Also recommended: *The North Star.*

H-2 WORKER

Directed by Stephanie Black. Cinematography by Maryse Alberti. English. Color. 70 minutes. 1990.

**Workers imported from Jamaica suffer loss of civil rights
and breach of contract while working for U.S. sugar companies
in Florida.**

The United States Sugar Corporation imports 10,000 workers a year from Jamaica to cut the cane in south Florida fields. There are 400,000 acres of sugar cane down there, which cuts into 4.8 million tons. The processed cane fills railroad cars to the horizon and beyond. Workers are flown in every six months and are bused from the airport directly to residential stockades that are surrounded by cane fields on all sides. They are not allowed to leave this camp for more than twenty-four hours at a time. Visitors are restricted. Workers are hired for $5.02 an hour, but they are paid by the row. On a bad day, they may make as little as $1.30 an hour. If they do too well, they will learn "there wasn't enough sugar in the cane." Room and board are deducted. Transportation is deducted. Sick days are deducted. The injury rate is high. Fingers and toes are lost in the field. Choppers work all day with machetes cutting crop-dusted cane. For Alberti's clandestine cameras the workers talk about their exploitation in subdued voices. They don't know how to explain the lack of money to families back home. The workers are fed rice that is delivered to them in the fields; they eat standing up. They are in the fields to cut cane—as much as a ton an hour. Rice is just not enough. They buy overpriced food at the company store. For some, it is impossible to buy shoes and other items from the lists their families sent with them. An old-timer remembers what it was like in 1943 when workers were chained to the beds at night. Chains are the only thing missing in the modern corporate slave trade. Sugar company executives boast from their lounge chairs, "It's good for us; it's good for them." Company families are among the richest in Miami County. At the annual sugar festival, bosses celebrate the tremendous wealth of the sugar business. Plump, overdressed babies are pushed toward the cameras. The U.S. government subsidizes sugar production so U.S. corporations can beat the prices of third-world producers. A big part of the subsidy is the H-2 worker status and the Department of Labor's blindness to contract fraud. When 350 Jamaican workers refuse to work the fields unless they are paid the contracted $5.02 an hour, they're rounded up in the night by riot police and dogs. With barely enough time to gather their few belongings, the terrified men are bused to the airport and flown back to Kingston. A government blacklist will prevent them from ever working in the U.S. again. Closing shots are of a Jamaican farmer dreaming of his chance to make the trip to America. "I hear it's really nice up there," he says.

Also recommended: *Matewan* and *The Wave*.

HUNGRY FOR PROFIT

Written and produced by Robert Richter. Cinematography by Burleigh Wartes, Terry Hopkins, and Robert Achs. USA. English. Color. 85 minutes. 1989.

Impact of monopoly agribusiness on third-world hunger.

The fashion that caught on in *The Grapes of Wrath* never did go out of style. After the dust settled and the Hoovervilles dispersed, the family farms kept right on failing. In current times, heavily industrialized agri-

business goliaths range worldwide for lands to appropriate into mono-
culture. When traditional peoples cannot be displaced by bulldozers
alone, the marginal economics of third-world countries are destabilized by imported staple foodstuffs priced to bankrupt small farms and
drive families into the streets. By now, this carnage of capital acquisition boasts businesses that orbit their own spy satellites—optical scan-
ners in the sky—observing the agrarian Earth. Competitor crop failure
means profits and possible land acquisition for ever-expanding conglomerates. The "Green Revolution" has become a revolution of corporate hegemony generating more efficient food production and more
efficient starvation, along with public confusion and indifference to
both. Widespread disenfranchisement from the land seems beyond the
intellectual tolerance of the general public and beyond the control of
democratic ideals or legislative constraint. *Hungry for Profit* predicts a
balkanized future of expanding corporate profits and expanding subur-
ban slums filled with the landless poor. The dust bowl of the 1930s was
only a mild version of the pandemic tirade of economic polarity trans-
forming our planet into an industrialized slave state dominated by
mega-businesses backed by the banks. Richter's film follows this catastrophe into eight third-world countries, interviewing executives and
peasants alike to determine why half a billion people now go to bed
hungry every night. The answer comes from the boardrooms where
"starvation" is just a crude way of saying, "no effective demand."
Dole, Del Monte, and Gulf & Western are profiled in their tropical fruit
and sugar campaigns. Richter could as easily have included indicting
profiles on hundreds of transnationals fighting over the cheapest land
and the cheapest labor left on Earth. When former cloud forests and
rain forests are grazed bare and deserts begin stretching beyond their
borders, multinationals just leave the people and land behind and
move on to greener pastures in a continuing cycle of economic and environmental devastation.

Also recommended: *H-2 Worker.*

I WILL FIGHT NO MORE FOREVER

With James Whitmore, Sam Elliot, Ned Romero, John Kauffman, Emilio Delgado, and members of the Nez Perce, Cherokee, Wappo, Blackfoot, Cocopa, Apache, and Winnebago Indian tribes. Produced by Stan Margulies. Directed by Richard Heffron. Written by Jeb Rosebrook and Theodore Strauss. Photography by Jorge Stahl. Music by Gerald Fried. USA. English. Color. 109 minutes. 1975.

Chief Joseph and the Nez Perces on their long march to escape the reservation.

By 1877, the American Indian had become "an exile in his own land." One of the few tribes still free was the Nez Perces under Chief Joseph (Heinmot Tooyalaket) in Washington State. When Joseph meets with General Oliver Otis Howard (Whitmore) to plead for protection from the attacks of local ranchers, Howard gives the Nez Perces four days to relocate to a reservation. (History gave them thirty.) Joseph tries to decline. "We do not want to be white men: we want to be ourselves." Reservation Indians "are not white, not Indian, not anything." The Nez Perces set out toward the northeast, the mountains, and Canada. The rest of the film follows Joseph's campaign for freedom and Howard's campaign to prevent it. Through the mountains, many Indians die of exposure and cavalry attack. We are to believe there was growing public alarm to save the Indians and censure Howard's legally authorized pursuit. Howard denies the compassionate entreaties of his troops, thus encouraging dissension within the ranks. He is a man of principal caught in the clash of bad times. One of his own lieutenants is ready to walk. "When I joined the army, I didn't think I'd be fighting old men, women and children. . . . I keep telling myself there's a good reason for what we're doing, and I'm following orders. . . . from my government. But, I still can't sleep at night. . . . When Joseph's men are scattered dead on the plains, you will have done your job. . . . The Indians were here first." (Lt. Woods did leave the army and spent the rest of his life a champion of human rights.) In the final scenes, Indians and cavalry meet in the wilderness to swear allegiance to peace. The movie ends. The music soars. A trailer tells us that Joseph would be "respected and admired, but he never could go home again." Indeed, he went to Fort Leavenworth and was confined as a prisoner of war. He and his people were eventually moved to a reservation in Washington. Joseph died there in 1904, reportedly of a broken heart. ". . . You might as well expect the rivers to run backwards as that any man who was born free should be contented when penned up and denied liberty."

Also recommended: *Broken Arrow*.

IMITATION OF LIFE

With Lana Turner, John Gavin, Sandra Dee, Dan O'Herlihy, Susan Kohner, Robert Aldo, Juanita Moore, Karen Dicker, Mahalia Jackson, Troy Donahue. Produced by Ross Hunter. Directed by Douglas Sirk. Written by Eleanore Griffin and Allan Scott, based on the novel by Fanny Hurst. Photography by Russell Metty. Music by Frank Skinner. English. Color. 125 minutes. 1959.

The story of two mothers, one black, one white, and their two daughters, who are both white.

The star of this flamboyantly gracious film is supposed to be the lavish Lana Turner and her lavish life. She's just a blonde, creamy-complected zephyr whose feet no longer touch the ground. She's risen to shimmer as a star on the silver screen. She's a paragon of the cinema, terribly rich and still beautiful. She's lost her true love (Gavin) to reach such elevations. But the only really interesting thing about *Imitation of Life* is not Lana Turner, but Lana Turner's maid's daughter—Sara Jane (Kohner). Sara Jane is a black girl with a white girl's skin. Not only does she have to grow up in the same house with Turner and Sandra Dee, she has to look in the mirror every day at the phenomena of her own appearance. Some invisible part of her anatomy has power over her. She finds it intolerable. She finds it incomprehensible. If her mother visits her at school, it is only to discover that Sara is passing for white. As a teen, she dates white boys who beat her when they learn the truth. Her mother tries to console her, but Sara Jane is not to be consoled. "I don't want to have to come through back doors or feel lower than other people." After graduation, she moves to another city. Wherever she goes, her mother visits and destroys the charade of her life. Their relationship cannot withstand the stress of Sara's light skin. So, on her last visit, her mother introduces herself to Sara Jane's friends as her former nanny. Now Sara can have the life she always wanted. A few months later, her mother dies. Knowing that her fears of discovery are over forever, Sara plunges into guilt. At last she is free to love her mother unconditionally and collapses on the funeral hearse, begging forgiveness. Although the issues of color and race are not the principal theme in *Imitation of Life*, it is the mother's death that signals the movie's end. For Sara, the world of Sandra Dee and Lana Turner is attainable at last, although—as she has had ample time to notice—it is no guarantee of happiness.

Also recommended: *Pinky*.

IN COUNTRY

With Bruce Willis, Emily Lloyd, Joan Allen, Kevin Anderson, John Terry, Dan Jenkins, Stephan Tobolowsky, Richard Hamilton, Judith Ivy, Peggy Rea. Produced by Norman Jewison and Richard Roth. Directed by Norman Jewison. Screenplay by Frank Pierson and Cynthia Cidre, based on the novel by Bobbie Anne Mason. Photography by Russell Boyd. Music by James Horner. USA. English. Color. 120 minutes. 1989.

Vietnam vets recover from war-shock trauma with the help of Bruce Willis' niece.

"In country" means "in Vietnam." Men who used to be there are now back home in Mayberg, Kentucky, losing the war every day. Bruce Willis is the burned-out vet. Emily Lloyd is his niece, who feels sorry for all the returned vets her Uncle Emmett hangs out with. Why don't any of them have girlfriends or normal lives? Through her, we come to know that an excavation is impossible because what she wants to find just doesn't exist any more. She can only study the remains to fathom the missing parts. Willis lives in the moment. The rest is just a void. He may be suffering after-effects of Agent Orange poisoning. He's burning himself up just making it through the days. This is what all the vets have in common. They fear recrimination more than they crave esteem. "This is a Bronze Star." "What's it for?" "Bravery, I guess." "And this is a Purple Heart." Willis talks about Agent Orange and trees full of white birds rising up from the bombs and friends left to die in the swamps. "After a while you just don't care any more. After a while you just quit feeling. . . . There's something wrong with me," he confesses to Lloyd, "Like a hole in my heart." The film moves the vets through the days like nomads in a world of imperishables. And it does this so affectionately that audiences may begin to acknowledge themselves extensions of the drama—absentee extras holding certain subtle opinions about a war that is still being fought, because "Mayberg" is just another name for every town in the U.S.A. *In Country* reaffirms the waste in human life and human potential that the war took while giving nothing in return. Closing scenes are of the Vietnam Veterans Memorial, which is filled with 58,000 names of those who died in Vietnam. Bruce Willis was chosen to play Emmett because he agreed to read for the part. He generates something remarkable. Casting went to England to find Lloyd's innocence, which is outdone only by the delicate innocence of the war veterans. *In Country* does not comment on the rightness or wrongness of the Vietnam intervention. It just tells a story. In exchange for acceptance, patriotism, and trust, much destruction was delivered to American servicemen and women. It's a movie about the salvages of war and the eternal wariness of the human debris. It is aimless, uncharismatic, and deeply moving.

Also recommended: *Dear America: Letters Home From Vietnam.*

IN THE KING OF PRUSSIA

With Daniel Berrigan, Philip Berrigan, Molly Rush, Carl Kabat, Dean Hammer, Elmer Maas, John Schuchardt, Anne Montgomery, (the Plowshares Eight) and Martin Sheen. Written, produced and directed by Emile de Antonio, from the trial transcripts. Photography by Judy Irola. Songs sung by Jackson Browne and Graham Nash. USA. English. Color. 92 minutes. 1983.

Anti-war protesters are arrested and tried for trespassing on a nuclear weapons plant and damaging nose cones.

In 1981, the Plowshares Eight occupied the General Electric plant in King of Prussia, Pennsylvania, as a protest against the Mark 12A first-strike warheads produced at GE's Re-entry Systems Division. They entered the plant, located the missile "mid-sections" that carry the warheads, and, using hammers brought along for the purpose, beat ceremoniously on the polished metal, symbolically turning swords into plowshares. (From the biblical admonition: "They shall beat their swords into plowshares... neither shall they learn war any more.") They poured vials of their own blood on secret documents. For this, and for restraining the night guard to prevent him from phoning for help, they were arrested and charged with criminal trespass, criminal mischief, burglary, conspiracy, assault, and kidnapping. Trial testimony revealed that neither the workers at the GE plant nor the citizens of King of Prussia knew that the Re-Entry Systems Division was a nuclear warhead production sight. The Mark 12A is a 335-kiloton nuclear device—thirty times more powerful than the one dropped on Hiroshima in 1945. When questioned about using a hammer to destroy private property, Daniel Berrigan refers to the Mark 12A as "anti-property" and warheads as the "hammers of the world." The judge (Sheen), clearly wishing he'd gone to veterinary school, moves, "the harmonic convergence is not relevant," "there will be no humming from the spectators," "I don't want a speech. No speeches, no speeches, no speeches." This film is half court reenactments and half clips of actual mayhem outside the courthouse during the trial. There is police harassment in every kind of weather, and the Plowshares Eight and others burn money, indictments, and draft cards. After the trial, a member of the jury confesses that they deliberated to acquit the Eight, but the judge's instructions and the fact that all eight confessed to charges allowed no alternative to a guilty verdict. Four of the men, including the Berrigan brothers, are sentenced to three to ten years. Other sentences range from one-and-a-half to five years. About prison life: "I hate the degradation and the humiliation. . . . My stomach turns over. . . . I don't do particularly well in jail." Three of the defendants are priests; one of the women is a Catholic nun.

Also recommended: *The Trial of the Catonsville Nine.*

INDIAN AGENT

With Tim Holt, Noah Beery, Jr., Richard Martin, Nan Leslie, Harry Woods. Produced by Herman Schlom. Directed by Lesley Selander. Screenplay by Norman Houston. Photography by J. Roy Hunt. Music by C. Bakaleinikoff. USA. English. Black and white. 63 minutes. 1948.

Bureau of Indian Affairs agent rips off Indian food shipments and lives to regret it.

Noah Beery is Chief Red Fox, who can only stand and watch as the local representatives of the Bureau of Indian Affairs (BIA) smuggle Indian food shipments off to miners in North Dakota. He does send out scouting parties to find snakes or lizards or anythng else to eat. But still everyone is hungry. One mother in particular is so desperate that she leaves her baby at the home of two local ranchers (Tim Holt and Richard Martin) who, unmarried as they are, manage to take care of the foundling and even grow to love her. They try to find out who the parents are, refusing to turn the baby over to the Indian agent who comes to claim it. They want to find the mother and talk to her about why she gave her little girl away. When she confesses that she left the baby with them so she'd have enough to eat, they begin an investigation of the BIA. They pressure the publisher of the local newspaper to write a story about conditions on the reservation. While greed, corruption, and prejudice surround the Indians like the sea surrounds a fish, Holt and Martin have come from another ocean. They are affable, open, and seem to care about the human race. They love the baby and believe justice and fair play is for everyone. Through their intervention, the food shipments are restored and the conditions on the reservation improve. Turquoise gets her baby back, and the newspaper prints the story. I like this film even if the Indians are helpless and dependent. Maybe they could have solved all their problems without Holt and Martin, but then we wouldn't have been able to compare these two to the bigots of the BIA. It's a warm and rewatchable film that was made when westerns were popular and only two or three of them ever told the truth about anything. If they had hired real Indians, maybe the war dances would have been an asset rather than the low point in the film.

Also recommended: *Vanishing Americans.*

THE INHERITORS

With Wolfgang Gaser, Roger Schauer, Ottwald John, Helmit Kahn, Kurt Jaggberg, Evelyn Faber, Gerhard Swoboda, Michael Janisch, Nikolas Vogel. Produced and directed by Walter Bannert. Written by Erich Richter and Walter Bannert. Cinematography by Hanus Polak. Music by Gustav Mahler. Austria. In German with English titles. Color. 89 minutes. 1984.

Young boys in postwar Germany join the youth branch of a neo-Nazi organization.

Producer/director/writer Bannert is trying to help us understand what attracts young people to extremist organizations. Although he doesn't very successfully reveal why anyone would be attracted to this particular group, it's clear that the disintegration of the nuclear family has become an alluvial jackpot for white supremacists and race hate. Recruitment ploys offer alienated, weak-willed, strong-willed, unhappy young people a haven of security and the illusion of self-importance. Members are valued protectors of the white race and white society. Once indoctrinated into and dependent on the organization, the true goals are revealed—violent repression of minorities for a future white state. By this time, new members are apt to rationalize moral inconsistencies to sustain their new identity. The main club activities of these saviors of racial purity are wearing black leather, assaulting anyone for any reason, and watching others have sex. The youth group is lead by a man campaigning for public office on the race purity ticket. It was sad watching potentially appealing actors stuck in these degrading roles. It could be that even playing a Nazi is a bad idea for some kids. I didn't like the overly pointless and sleazy sex scenes, including scenes of rape and forced oral sex. Due, perhaps, to the broad stereotypecasting, I didn't find the story line convincing. And I'm not sure the point is made to any constructive end.

Also recommended: *Betrayed.*

INTOLERANCE

With Lillian Gish, Mae Marsh, Robert Harron, Miriam Cooper, Constance Talmadge, Alfred Page, Elmer Clifton, Margery Wilson, Eugene Pallette, Fred Turner. Written, produced, and directed by D. W. Griffith. Photography by G. W. Bitzer and Karl Brown. USA. Silent with titles. Black and white. 14 reels. 1916.

Four different types of intolerance dramatized in four different historical eras.

D. W. Griffith was a filmic imperialist—a ruler of kingdoms, a leader of thousands. Buyer and seller of humanity. Source of all light. Source of all salaries. We must recognize him before we can recognize the intolerances. He has set them into four historic eras—each crushed against the other in sets hammered together by the working class as an affront to the working class. What you are apt to remember most is droves of high-strung miniature people trapped in ten-ton cardboard sets. In a way, Griffith generates more intolerance than he manages to assuage while posing the question—what is bigger than a space-station but still anchored to the back lot? The most successful segment is the one sandwiched between ancient Gothams revealing how poverty turns ordinary people into criminals and outcasts. Our contemporary couple loses almost everything. They are split apart and their infant daughter placed with a wealthy family. They never do get her back and only catch glimpses of her now and then through the shrubberies surrounding the mansion. They have no chance of escaping their poverty. Our hearts break to see the child living in luxury while the adults are renounced by society and allowed to fail. We regret modern filmmakers find so little time on their creative agendas to do anything more than glorify the breakdown of the family and the placement of poor children in "better homes." If D. W. Griffith were alive today to see what time has done to the structure of society, maybe he would realize how insignificant Camelot sets are in social realism. Griffith got the brightest Hollywood luminaries and tiger tank budgeting to help him create this magnificent, awkward thing. Early filmgoers were just dazzled by what they saw. Well, there are touching scenes and sad moments that last long enough for us to ask ourselves how life got so messed up. And the industrialist who cut his workers' wages so he could donate money to charity was surely a shocking insight.

Also recommended: *Metropolis*.

JACKKNIFE

With Robert DeNiro, Ed Harris, Kathy Baker, Sloane Shelton, Tom Isbell. Produced by Robert Schaffel and Carol Baum. Directed by David Jones. Screenplay by Stephan Metcalfe, based on his play *Strange Snow*. Photography by Brian West. Music by Bruce Broughton. USA. English. Color. 102 minutes. 1989.

Vietnam vets help each other adapt to civilian life.

When you put tremendous talent on the screen, the way Jones has done here—in roles stripped of all theatric pretension, in a story about people simply baffled at the agony of living—audiences will divide. Many will restlessly presume they are bored. Others will sit motionless at the spectacle of Robert DeNiro as Joseph "Megs" Megessey, a Vietnam vet who went into the war a madman and came out a dissonant child; his friend (Ed Harris), who can't face himself or his life because he left Megs for dead on the battlefield and Bobby died rescuing him; and Martha, the frantically quiet schoolteacher buffering her repulsions with monotony. Harris has no soul in this loner performance. He takes out his torment on everybody, especially himself. He has shut Megs out and particularly does not want Megs seeing his sister. She's his family. She lives with him. She takes care of him. They are all lonely people. DeNiro has forgiven Harris and fallen clumsily in love with his sister Martha (Baker). He shaves and puts on a tuxedo, which drives Harris to bust the glass out of all the trophy cases at the high school where he used to be a sports wonder. His guilt and warshock have almost destroyed him. But, DeNiro walks through fiery hoops to get him into the local support group where men talk about their implausible lives. Harris is not a fiend after all, just a common forgotten commodity of war. *Jackknife* showcases DeNiro, Harris, and Baker—actors unafraid to act. They suffer universal embarrassments and frustrations for us. In *Jackknife*, nothing is lost in translation. The characters in the film take the first steps toward rehabilitation. But we know and they know that they aren't the same people anymore, and it isn't the same world.

Also recommended: *In Country*.

JESUS OF MONTREAL

With Lothaire Bluteau, Gilles Pelletier, Johanne-Marie Tremblay, Catherine Wilkering, Remy Girard, Robert Le Page, Yves Jacques. Produced by
Roger Frappier and Pierre Gendron. Written and directed by Denys Arcand. Photography by Guy Dufaux. Music by Yves LaFerriere, Francois
Dompierre, and Jean-Marie Benoit. Canada/France. In French and English with English titles. Color. 119 minutes. 1989.

A passion play hits too close to home for church leaders.

For a film like *Jesus of Montreal*, Lothaire Bluteau is the reality that sur-
passes illusion. He is the holy nexus between divine innocence and
earthly good, with bones showing through his sackcloth suit and eyes
reflecting the universal soul. He has been hired by the Catholic church
to restage their annual passion play. Bluteau—blessed with final creative authority and a budget windfall—rewrites the script based on
simple biblical truths about the time of Christ. His stations are reckless
exaltations beckoned from a myth-enshrouded past—ethereal images,
low-vaulted chambers awash in serpentine torch light, mesmerizing Is-
lamic arias, and promontories of sacrificial carnage. Amidst the fervent
opulence and daring excavations of the word of God and the agonies of
the crucifixion are oratories against the Romans who crucified thousands on posts set along the most travelled roadways. Money changers
defied the essence of godly ardor and perverted the teachings of Christ.
"Too realistic," say church officials. Too real, too relevant, too true.
Pandemonium erupts when the actors perform their "illegal" play
against orders of the church. There are riots. Bluteau is injured and later
dies. Denys Arcand floods the margins of the drama with callow commercial sins of Montreal today. Bluteau is an actor playing an actor in
the viciously competitive performing arts market. Art, like life, is a commodity. The works of great novelists are used to promote perfume:
"Give me more Kundera." Talent, technology, and science all fuel the
parody of progress, as commerce restrains everything into material
bondage. The abstractions are real people selling out in the war between altruism and commerce, good and evil. The two forces are like
giant, unseen opponents, enormous as nebulae. Arcand says all this
with architectural elegance. He puts everything he needs in front of the
cameras, most especially the deeply craven, hungering, beautiful

Bluteau—the embodiment of carnal divinity. It's an artful, philosophic effusion, with more social commentary than the mind can grasp.

Also recommended: *Man Facing Southeast.*

JOHNNY GOT HIS GUN

With Jason Robards, Timothy Bottoms, Kathy Fields, Marsha Hunt, Donald Sutherland, Diane Vars. Produced by Bruce Campbell. Written and directed by Dalton Trumbo, based on the novel. Photography by Jules Brenner. Music by Jerry Fielding. English. Color. 111 minutes. 1971.

War veteran returns from combat with multiple war injuries.

This perhaps unnecessarily unrelenting screenplay reveals Dalton Trumbo's deep resentment of war and the military, the religions that serve them, and the families that send their children off to fight. His war veteran returns home without legs, arms, or a face. It's meant to be an anti-war film, but the emphasis soon leans toward human reflex response to the abnormal. Johnny is hidden away in the hospital behind locked doors and shuttered windows, under a sheet, and behind a mask. Some caregivers have compassion; some are repulsed. He gets routine care punctuated by rare acts of kindness. He can neither move nor speak. No one is sure who he is. No one is sure he can think. But, of course, he can. He dreams and fantasizes, unable to tell one from the other, unable to express his fears and questions. As Johnny the young war veteran, Timothy Bottoms is perfect in the role of a pious youth gone off to fight for freedom. In bed all day, Johnny thinks back over his life. He remembers his father (Robards), part neurotic, part fishing buddy—at times sensitive, at times stewing with closely guarded grudges. In one scene with pre-war Johnny he says, "My life is so poor and shoddy that without this [fishing] pole, why, I'd have nothing to set me apart from other men, nothing to give me distinction. Nothing at all. I love this pole." Johnny asks, "Do you love it more than me?" "Ha, ha," Robards responds, "of course I do." He's great at whatever he's doing. Donald Sutherland is Jesus the carpenter, making crosses that he loads into wagons, taking care to get a receipt for every one. Of Johnny's deplorable condition he confesses, "It would be cruel to suggest that anyone can help you." When Johnny manages to communicate by morse code, he asks the astonished hospital staff to put him in a carnival so people can see him and he can support himself. When the request is denied, he taps out another message, "Kill me, kill me, kill me." Johnny wants to die, and Dalton Trumbo wants you to know that in the paradoxical warlike society in which we live it would be murder to kill him.

Also recommended: *Fires on the Plain.*

JUAREZ

With Brian Aherne, Bette Davis, Paul Muni, John Garfield, Gale Sondergaard, Gilbert Roland, Henry O'Neill, Claude Rains, Donald Crisp. Produced by Hal B. Wallis. Directed by William Dieterle. Screenplay by John Huston, Aeneas MacKenzie, Wolfgang Reinhardt, based on the play *Juarez and Maximilian* by Franz Werfel, which was based on the novel *The Phantom Crown* by Bertita Harding. Photography by Tony Guadio. Music by Erich Wolfgang Korngold. USA. English. Black and white. 132 minutes. 1939.

The Archduke Maximilian becomes the emperor of Mexico and is deposed by Benito Juarez.

Even though the title is *Juarez*, Maximilian (Brian Aherne) reigns in this film about the crossfire of history played out in Juarez's Mexico. Max is a dupe and a puppet of Napoleon III. He is a benevolent man who goes to his post with his wife Carlotta (Davis), believing he has been elected by a popular majority to work with the people of Mexico to create an independent state. In his first cabinet meeting, he refuses requests to return land bought from eighty-five landholders and given to peasants. "We cannot very well set our hand to an instrument which might well be against the best interest of a majority of our subjects. In a case where it's eighty-five individuals versus the nation, the nation must prevail." If the landowners work to win him the election, "We are indebted to no political party." He loves Mexico and will repay the trust voted to him by the people. Max's government, set up by Napoleon in artless noncompliance to the Monroe Doctrine, is marked from inception and will soon be defied by Benito Juarez, leader of the resistance to French imperialism and the greatest national hero in Mexican history. Maximilian wants to work with Juarez, but they are inevitably pushed into revolution, and Max's forces are overcome. With Carlotta safely in Europe, he foregoes the privilege of leaving Mexico with the retreating French troops and is captured and executed by a Juarez firing squad. His last request is to hear the song "La Paloma" one more time—his wife's favorite. A woman sings this radiantly beautiful song at daybreak outside his cell—ranges of green pasture-lands unfolding behind her in the distance. Max listens at the window before walking to his execution. Carlotta lives out her life obsessed by madness. The collaborated screenplay is loaded with historic legitimacy about the two men, including many references to Juarez's idolatry of President Lincoln, who promised aid but was assassinated before he could give it. Muni's overresearched performance dims opposite Aherne, who plays the Archduke as if he is the son of God. Garfield hashes up every scene, and as for Davis, well, Carlotta just wasn't like that.

Also recommended: *Viva Zapata!*.

JUDGE HORTON AND THE SCOTTSBORO BOYS

With Arthur Hill, Lewis J. Stadlen, Ken Kercheval, Vera Miles, Rony Clanton, Tom Ligon, Richard Backus, Afemo Omilami, Michael Adams, Larry Butts, Frank Bettis, Roy Cooper, Joe Dorsey, Louis Fox. Produced by Paul Leaf. Directed by Fielder Cook. Screenplay by John McGreevey. Photography by Mario Tosi. USA. English. Color. 96 minutes. 1976.

Nine young black men are arrested for the rape of a white woman.

It's 1931 in Decatur, Alabama. Nine black men are pulled from a boxcar and accused of raping two white women. They range in age from thirteen to twenty. They are tried together. Eight are found guilty and sentenced to die. The jury is split, seven to five on whether Olen Montgomery, thirteen years old and nearly blind, should receive the death penalty. It is the first time in the history of the Union that eight men are sentenced to die on the same day. Due to the disagreement on sentencing of the ninth defendant, a mistrial is declared and a new trial for each defendant is scheduled in the court of Judge Horton. One by one the boys are convicted with "no corroborating evidence." One of the women in the original complaint withdraws her charge and testifies for the defense. None of the witnesses, either for the prosecution or the defense, substantiates the testimonies of the remaining complainant— Victoria Price. The doctor who examined Price the day of the arrests found no evidence of motile sperm. Witnesses were unable to place the men in the railcar where the two women were riding. Notwithstanding the likelihood of their innocence, the nine are again found guilty in separate trials. Judge Horton's compassion for the accused men overwhelms him. "I saw them as vulnerable, broken human beings, doomed sheep helplessly stumbling toward the slaughter bin." He saves them from the electric chair and destroys his own career by ordering new trials and allowing every appeal in a quest for a fair verdict. Horton loses his 1934 bid for reelection to the court and returns to private law practice. The Scottsboro boys are sentenced. The shortest sentence of six years is given to Olen Montgomery. The longest term— nineteen years—is served by the most defiant, outspoken member of the group, Haywood Petterson. Although they are paroled one by one after serving a total of 130 years in prison, they are doomed to live in the shadow of the memory of injustice. The case of the Scottsboro boys resulted in a change in the state's trial law—all white juries can no longer sit against black defendants in the state of Alabama.

Also recommended: *Sacco and Vanzetti.*

JUDGEMENT AT NUREMBERG

With Spencer Tracy, Burt Lancaster, Richard Widmark, William Shatner, Marlene Dietrich, Judy Garland, Maximilian Schell, Montgomery Clift, Edward Binns. Produced and directed by Stanley Kramer. Written by Abby Mann. Photography by Ernest Laszlo. Music by Ernest Gold. USA. English. Black and white. 187 minutes. 1961.

Dramatization of the trials of the judges who ruled the courts in Nazi Germany.

After the well-publicized trials of Hitler's generals and field marshals came the not-so-well-publicized trials of the judges who enforced the Nuremberg laws during World War II. The laws were judged to be crimes themselves, and the judges who enforced them were judged to be criminals of war. These Nazi laws criminalized intimate social interchange between races. In the National Socialist state, the death penalty was expanded to cover crimes of racial pollution. The judges who resisted were forced out of the courts or resigned. Those who pledged loyalty to the fascists wore the swastika and ordered political dissidents to be sterilized and condemned men and women to death for falling in love. Spencer Tracy officiates the trials. Prosecution exhibits chronicle the appalling cruelties of the Nazis and their taste for savage relics of their hate—shrunken heads, desk ornaments made from human bones, drawing "paper" made of human skin. There are close-ups of Zyklon-B, the poison used in the extermination ovens. There are young children compliantly baring their tattooed arms for the cameras. Two-thirds of the Jews in Europe—over six million people—were killed by the fascists. They left behind mountains of shoes, purses, and eyeglasses. The gold from their teeth was reformed into jewelry. The evidence is overwhelming. In their defense, the judges testify that it was not their job to write the laws, but to preside over the courts. Others talk of trying to soften sentences. Victims testify to personal tragedy. Montgomery Clift plays a man who was sterilized by the Nazis after being classified as mentally retarded. Some say it was poor health that made Clift's performance, for which he took no money, so memorable. He wasn't well, but he was one of America's greatest performers, and this is his greatest role—concentrating more pathos into seven minutes than the rest of the cast will in the remaining 180. His scene is a movie in itself. He seems to embody the suffering of all war in his fragile innocence. His scarred memories surprise him, and there is a question in his eyes that nobody can answer. Almost as impressive is the wonderful Richard Widmark. Not so wonderful is an artificially bloated script, swollen to three hours by including romance, Sunday sightseeing, and lots of dinner talk about whether it's the judges who are on trial or Germany and Germans. I would have preferred a less exclusive use of English in a drama of some historic urgency.

Also recommended: *Hotel Terminus.*

JULIA

With Jane Fonda, Vanessa Redgrave, Hal Holbrook, Rosemary Murphey, Maximilian Schell, Jason Robards, Meryl Streep. Produced by Richard Roth. Directed by Fred Zinnemann. Screenplay by Alvin Sargent based on the story in the book *Pentimento* by Lillian Hellman. Photography by Douglas Slocombe. Music by Georges Delerue. USA. English. Color. 118 minutes. 1977.

The true story of two friends during World War II—one who wrote about fascism and one who died fighting it.

Unintentionally to be sure, Hellman exaggerates her own superfluousness in this true-life story of friends in World War II. Even as girls, Hellman envied Julia's intensity and her unwavering, confrontational intellect. As an adult, Hellman (Fonda) lives a safeguarded if not sheltered life in a cottage by the sea with fellow writer Dashiell Hammett, writing stories and screenplays reflecting her humanitarian philosophies. Julia (Redgrave) has gone to Austria to study under Freud and become a professional anti-fascist, fighting the advance of the Nazis. Now all Lillian sees of Julia's intellect is an occasional postcard or letter from Europe. And even these stop after she is attacked by a Hitler youth group and disappears from her hospital bed, presumably to work with the resistance underground. Just as she is planning a celebratory trip to Europe and the Soviet Union, and having heard nothing for months from Julia, Hellman is visited by an agent of the resistance, who asks her to transport money across the border into Germany to buy freedom for political prisoners. Julia will meet her in Berlin. Terrified, Hellman crosses the German border with $50,000 sewn into a chinchilla hat. In Berlin, she meets Julia—a wizard of controlled obsessions whose broken body harbors a ferrous will. She accepts the money and asks Hellman to take her daughter out of the German war zone and to the U.S. Before this can happen, Julia is killed by the fascists and her daughter disappears. Hellman returns to the cottage by the sea to ponder the past, outlive Hammett, write screenplays, and become famous. Director Zinnemann narrates deep indigo tensions into this film, adulating Julia (or perhaps Redgrave) and ratifying himself as a disciple of her heroism, holding her in permanent acute focus. When Redgrave is not on the screen, Fonda stands in for her remote energies of radicalism. Vanessa Redgrave triumphs. Everything about her personifies fanatic resistance to totalitarianism and confirms her as the greatest English language actress alive today. And Fonda, perhaps overqualified for the role, must settle for being the perfect Hellman, safe at home, and soon to write the story about how her close friend died fighting for human rights while she wrote about it from a beach chair. Too bad Julia wasn't the writer; maybe whe would have written herself a bigger part.

Also recommended: *The White Rose.*

JUNGLE FEVER

With Wesley Snipes, Annabella Sciorra, Ossie Davis, Ruby Dee, John Turturro, Spike Lee, Anthony Quinn, Lonette McKee, Samuel L. Jackson, Frank Vincent. Written, produced, and directed by Spike Lee. Co-produced by Monty Ross. Photography by Ernest Dickerson. Original score by Terence Blanchard. Songs by Stevie Wonder and the Boy's Choir of Harlem. USA. English. Color. 131 minutes. 1991.

Interracial love, racism, and cultural head-ons in New York City.

A close friend of mine finds Spike Lee's films depressing. After *Do the Right Thing* he said, "It's hopeless." Meaning interracial fellowship. As much as Lee wants to brand it into our brains that blacks and whites are unsuited to cohabit the same hemisphere, I'm still hoping it will work out. I'm hoping that despite Lee's cynicism, audiences will learn *something* from his movies that will help make change happen. In the meantime, Angie (Sciorra) is such a nice person that the only thing Lee can think of to do with her is beat her up, break her heart, and dump her on the street at midnight. The meek shall bite the dust. And what about Flipper (Snipes)—attracted to a white woman? Sinners pay heed. He and Sciorra can't go anywhere without being hassled by cops and turbaned waitresses. He loses his lucrative job. His wife kicks him out. His brother goes so far overboard on drugs that his father (Davis) shoots him, and he dies on the living room floor with his mother (Dee) lost in hysteria. The bad news? Don't cross the color bar. The good news? It's not just them. The world isn't falling in on Angie and Flipper. It's falling in, period. There's lots of graffiti and urban slang to prove it. The elderly are husks of metropolitan mind-sucking monsoons. Young men O.D. on testosterone. Women are victims. Children are hep. And Hades could be no worse than the Taj Mahal—den of crack depravity. There are rumblings along the fault-lines of civilization. Lee is willing to notice this without noticing that differentiating between black oppression and general working class oppression denies the common source of both and limits the hope of overcoming either. After all, whites also breathe contaminated air, drink polluted water, pay taxes for war, have no health insurance, own no property, have no voice, and live in a world overwhelmed by commerce. The unions, democracy, the standard of living, and the quality of life are being degraded, and corporations control the governments for everybody. Not just for whites. Not just for blacks. That's why Flipper and Angie need each other. Well, Lee runs the zoo. I just write about it. Stevie Wonder is wonderful. As for the rest of the score, I'm surprised that all those violins and angelic choir overtures didn't divert the marabou from their seasonal migrations. Stellar performances by all the leading talents, with Ruby Dee due for a Hollywood nod.

Also recommended: *Sayonara*.

KAMERADSCHAFT
(COMRADESHIP)

With George Chalia, Alexander Granach, Davaid Mendaille, Fritz Kampers, Ernest Busch, Andree Ducret, Gustav Puttjer. Produced by Seymour Nebenzahl. Directed by G. W. Pabst. From the screenplay by Karl Otten, Ladislaus Vajda, and Peter Martin Lampel. Cinematography by Fritz Arno Wagner and Robert Baberske. German. German and French with English titles. Black and white. 93 minutes. 1931.

An international rescue effort saves miners and generates renewed cultural understanding.

Kameradschaft is dedicated to "The Miners of the World," in memory of the 1,200 miners killed by pit gas in French border mines in 1906. The movie was filmed in French and German to retain authentic integrity and to dramatize the differences and the ultimate unity of the French and German miners (which puts Pabst fifty years ahead of

American filmmakers, who would not release a major subtitled film until 1984). In 1906, pit fires deep in the mines were walled off and left to burn sometimes for years. Moments before they ate through old walls, new ones were built. But the fire of 1906 burst through the brickwork before the miners could retain it and flashed through the tunnels, burning supporting beams and killing miners by asphyxiation and catastrophic cave-ins. Shots of mine interiors are by the unstoppable Erno Metzner. Wagner's suspended camera angles and impulse-lighting ricochet through the audacious sets, compelling art to serve life. The miners are trapped by startling dangers in a world of coal walls and oak beams conforming to Pabst's taste for visual grandeur and reflecting the burnished specter of threat. For the outdoor scenes, which were all shot at an actual mine, Pabst strikes many deftly sculpted portraits of mothers and children poised for all time and waiting for news from the mines. The film is more than a personal trip to the ground floor of fossil fuels, it also apprehends the power of internationalism, as German miners defy a government order and go unrequested to the aid of the victims of the French mine disaster. A proletarian solidarity forms in the mine rescue mission and culminates in a pageant of unity spotlighted in the film's closing scenes. Here, a spokesperson for the French workers and their families stands to make an impromptu declaration of brotherhood. Neither side understands the other, but a German speaker rises and repeats the French message word for word. They crowd cheers unknowing, responding to the emotion of unanimity and cooperation to which the words are merely a shadow, "We are all miners together."

Also recommended: *Matewan* and *Strike*.

KAMIKAZE '89

With Rainer Werner Fassbinder, Gunther Kaufman, Nicole Heesters, Petra Jokisch, Boy Gobert, Arnold Marquis, Franco Nero. Produced by Regina Ziegler. Directed by Wolf Gremm. Screenplay by Robert Katz and Wolff Gremm, based on the novel *Murder on the 31st Floor* by Per Wahloo. Photography by Xaver Schwarzenberger. Music by Edgar Froes of Tangerine Dream. West Germany. In German with subtitles. 106 minutes. 1982.

A gigantic, possibly multinational communications conglomerate controls all, seven years in the future.

"The year is 1989. The Federal Republic of Germany is the richest country. Law and order are permanent to the last detail. General industry has solved all its problems. All is green. There is no energy problem, no pollution, no inflation, no unemployment. The chemical industry has found the solution for sweet dreams. There are no harmful drugs." So far, either I'm in a tuna mind melt or this doesn't sound that bad. But wait, "In the press and on television, all entertainment and information is formulated and transmitted by one single combine." This beast monopolizes the air waves and possibly the political process, war, peace, hunger, famine, and other social phenomena. The president of the Combine is the Blue Panther. He has an enemy—Krysmopompas, a popular comic book hero. Combine programming gravitates toward voyeuristic, semi-candid events involving real people. Marathon laugh-ins are big. Video cameras are big. It's scientific fiction placed seven years in the future. Detective Jansen (Fassbinder) has an unbroken record of solved cases and is assigned to check out bomb threats on Combine executive offices. He has a mere four days to solve the case but moves through scenes like a lizard off a leash. He dresses in fake leopard skin. He carries a pill-box notebook. His motto is, "Eliminate unnecessary words," at which he excels. His assistant, Anton (Gobert), uses all the words he omits. The clashy punkoid atmosphere of the near future is populated by people who misuse microwaves and never mean what they say. Jansen is very good, but *things* are very bad. The bomb blows up the secret thirty-first floor of the Combine, which was a penthouse prison for radical intellectuals. Jansen couldn't save them and is fired from the police force of the future. It's Fassbinder's opaque magnetism along with the circus of extravagant characters, uncharted interior decor, and the Katz/Gremm citron screenplay that park this plot at the end of the pier in the moonlight. If it had gone any further, it would have disturbed the deep, deep sea of monopoly.

Also recommended: *Max Headroom.*

KANAL

(THE SEWER)

With Teresa Izewska, Tadeusz Janczar, Emil Karewicz, Teresa Berezowska, Tadeusz Gwiazdowski, Wienczyslaw Glinski, Wladyslow Sheybal. Produced by Stanislaw Adler. Directed by Andrzej Wajda. Written by Jerzy Stefan Stawinski, based on his play. Photography by Jerzy Lipman. Music by Jan Krenz. Poland. In Polish with English titles. Black and white. 93 minutes. 1956.

Polish resistance struggle against fascism in World War II.

Wajda more or less obscures his tremendous talent with drain pipes, trying to show us what the sewers were like in Poland during World War II. There's not much creative leeway in drainage tunnels, and we just feel bad watching everybody try so hard to relive for us this unpalatable part of the Polish resistance effort. The Nazis couldn't have designed a less appealing strategy. People are combing their way through tunnels of murk, never too sure where they are going or how they're going to get there. *Kanal* is about how the Poles used the sewers to move around in the cities without the Nazis observing them—although the Gestapo often waited outside sewer covers to arrest or kill anyone crawling out. Of those who do go down into the sewers, few survive their journeys through the gruesome mazes. The film opens in the charred ruin of a bombed-out town. Here, things are bad, but at least there is air, sunlight, and a dry place to sleep. And the people are working together against something they can aim their weapons at. In the sewers, this noble force is reduced to lying, hysteria, and murder. It's Donner Pass in reverse—a completely repulsive environment of foul air, disease, rats, darkness, and claustrophobia. If you needed another reason to hate Hitler, here it is. It's hard to imagine why anyone would want to make such a film much less be in it—sloughing through fungal slush for more than an hour. It's just a morose, unhappy drama with characters who are interesting at first, but hard to tell apart once they are covered in raw sewerage.

Also recommended: *Fires on the Plain.*

KANGAROO

With Colin Freils, Judy Davis, John Walton, Julie Nihill, Hugh Keays-Byrne. Produced by Ross Dimsey. Directed by Tim Burstall. Written by Evan Jones, from the novel by D. H. Lawrence. Photography by Dan Burstall. Music by Nathan Waks. Australia. English. Color. 104 minutes. 1986.

An inside look at Australian revolutionaries.

Kangaroo is a well-costumed, uniquely suave, hash-heavy film about what revolution is, what revolutionaries are, whether revolution is possible, and, if so, who cares? Is it a game, a power fest, a social cause, or purely a noble gesture? It all takes place in the life of D. H. Lawrence, who was a real person who left Cornwall, England, around 1922 to escape fascism and war-mindedness, saying, "I hate my own country. No one who has lived through this war [World War I] can believe again in democracy." He winds up in Australia and becomes acquainted with various revolutionaries there, none of whom agrees with any other about anything any radical philosopher ever said. He settles familiarly into the hazing of idealistic theories with his wife (Davis), paying only enough attention to discount them all. Each of the Australian groups wants "Richard" (Freils) to join with them and promote their cause through his writing. His job is to decide which one to support. His wife's job is to accuse the men of simply hunting for "power out of the depths of your weakness." Richard goes to work for a socialist newspaper that allows him complete editorial control. The other revolutionaries descend, as Davis seems to have predicted they would, into petty struggles, pushing each other off philosophic mountain tops, while the world they will save spins on through the depths of space. We get the idea that liberty is not a bad thing to aim for, but to aim is to miss, especially when mere mortals are involved, so why bother? Progress toward good is progress toward a Saharan mirage. There is no particular beginning or end or middle to the film apart from the occurrence of the trip to Australia, which in Lawrence's real life lasted six weeks. Freils and Davis are putty in the hands of director Burstall, and photographer Burstall is awfully good at keeping our eyes on the screen. *Kangaroo* is a technical gem—all the decorations are there. There's just no tree to hang them on.

Also recommended: *Swept Away*.

KATHERINE

With Sissy Spacek, Art Carney, Jane Wyatt, Henry Winkler, Julie Kavner, Hector Elias, Jenny Sullivan. Produced by Gerald I. Isenberg. Written and directed by Jeremy Paul Kagan. Photography by Frank Stanley. USA. English. Color. 98 minutes. 1975.

A woman from the bourgeoisie becomes a member of the radical Weather Underground.

A friend once told me, "If I were any further left, I'd be putting bombs in phone booths." There aren't enough phone booths on earth these days to hold all the nuclear warheads set to go off on a moment's notice. They are the latest generation of weapons in the history of world firepower. The body count from the wars that all the world's weapons have fought is impossible to tally. Much of the slaughter is glorified in pageants and parades. Enter Katherine—enemy to peace. Americans shiver. She's a former coed who went from the girl's social choir to being a professional revolutionary member of the Weather Underground in eight years. "I love this country . . . I'm committed to making America a better place, no matter what the cost. . . . I grew up a princess in a fairy tale. Everyone should be so lucky, but they aren't. I lived in a protected shell so long. . . . My white skin has given me a lot of privileges." As each new year flashes on the screen, Katherine becomes more radical and her parents more frantic. There are two tragedies going on in this film—the justifiable breakdown of Katherine's faith in the American system and her parents' inability to see how their affluence "depends on somebody else's hardship." She cannot communicate to them "the contradiction in their goodness." It is the era of the Vietnam war, race riots, and President Johnson's promises that "we have the opportunity to move, not only toward the rich society and the powerful society, but upwards to the great society. . . . The great society rests on abundance and liberty for all. It demands an end to the poverty." Johnson, in his quest to make "all the people . . . free," orders the air mobilization to Vietnam. Katherine joins the armed resistance to capitalist imperialism at home. "I think it's senseless to help the victims of a cruel system if you let the system remain cruel." By 1970, Nixon is masterminding secret bombings in Cambodia. Four students are shot by the National Guard at Kent State University. Bobby Kennedy is dead. Martin Luther King is dead. And Katherine is a professional revolutionary, advising other Weathermen to "take up arms against imperialism." She has severed all ties with her privileged past. In 1972, she dies carrying a parcel bomb meant for a government office.

Also recommended: *Underground*.

KENT STATE

With Talia Balsam, Charley Lang, Jane Fleiss, John Getz, Keith Gordon, David Marshall Grant, Roxanne Hart, Michael Higgens, Jeff McCracken. Produced by Lin Ephraim. Directed by James Goldstone. Written by Gerald Green and Richard Kramer, from the books *Kent State: What Happened and Why* by James A. Michener, *Mayday, Kent State* by J. Gregory Paynes, and *The Kent State Coverup* by James Munves and Joseph Kelner. Photography by Stevan Larner. Music by Ken Lauber. Additional music by Neil Young. USA. English. Color. 120 minutes. 1981.

Chronicles the events leading to the shooting deaths of four student anti-war protesters at Kent State University by the Ohio National Guard.

In May of 1970, the American people learned of President Richard Nixon's secret bombings in Cambodia. News of the Cambodia bombings generated anti-war hysteria on college campuses. As part of their protest, Kent State activists burned down the campus ROTC (Reserve Officer's Training Corps) building. This action was followed by gatherings and ungatherings of protesters throughout the next day. There was perhaps a sense of power arising from the success of anti-war actions and civil disobedience around the U.S., but no crisis of activism premeditated the National Guard armed attack on unarmed students at Kent State University. From the standpoint of resistance to the Vietnam war, it was a day of nonevents. The thing that was different on this day was the National Guard. They were pulled into Kent State on short notice, worn down by sleep deprivation on the days prior to the killings. Many of the young men of the Guard had no strong feelings about the activists or the war. But they were tired, and they were commanded by a war-minded officer who believed he was a field marshal at war. Instead of giving the men the rest they needed, he sent them back and forth across the campus, tracking rumors and the nearly aimless grouping and movement of activists. Neither the students nor the members of the Guard had any premonition of the tragedy to come. There were conversations between the two groups at the periphery. The camera wanders in and out of dorms and barracks and substantiates the incremental and unrelated events that positioned some students within the line of fire. There is an overwhelming sense of circumstance. The rifle assault is a bewildering event measurable only by the bodies left behind. Confusion outweighs the terror. Only the headlines seem to know what it means. *Kent State* sees the whole thing as innocence and accidents. This is its limitation. The deaths are in no way the blame of premeditated acts of aggression against the people of Southeast Asia. Blame submerges. It's a guilt-free tragedy limited to the campus. Along with the thematic pitfalls of *Kent State* are less-than-stellar performances by all but a few members of the cast in this drama that describes the players and the setting of the Kent State killings.

Also recommended: *Berkeley in the '60's.*

THE KILLING FIELDS

With Sam Waterston, Dr. Haing Ngor, John Malkovich, Julian Sands, Craig T. Nelson, Spalding Grey, Graham Kennedy, Bill Paterson, Athol Fugard. Produced by David Puttman. Directed by Roland Joffe. Screenplay by Bruce Robinson, based on the magazine article, "The Death and the Life of Dith Pran" by Sidney Schanberg. Photography by Chris Menges. Music by Mike Oldfield. USA. English and Cambodian. Color. 142 minutes. 1984.

Two men struggle to escape the Khmer Rouge in the allied evacuation of Southeast Asia.

The war is in its waning days. Compared to the terror of this decay, the combat was a revelry. Now all covenants are broken. Saturation bombing has been replaced by delirious crowds; long, monotonous wailings; forgotten corpses; and death masquerading as life. Whole villages are in exile along roadways. Helicopters crowd into the skies. Black smoke rises. Embassies are overrun. Bullets kill people who don't know they are shot. It is the infinite uncertainty of the end of war. As the Khmer

Rouge presses south, Cambodia becomes the edge of the world. Sam Waterston is journalist Sidney Schanberg, who with Dith Pran (Ngor) is trying to reach evacuation points through the malignant pandemonium. Waterston faces down Khmer Rouge soldiers, suppressing fear that is sharper than pain. Hundreds crowd the French embassy, which is giving sanctuary to foreign nationals. Cambodian citizens must surrender themselves to guerrillas who have lost all human attributes. Pran's family has flown to safety. Waterston and an international coterie of civilians are flown to safety. Pran is left behind. And now there is peace; and there are the killing fields and concentration camps. Pran is being reeducated into communist ideology. Schanberg is in New York, writing for the *New York Times* and trying to predict whether his friend survived and is alive somewhere. The rest of the film follows Pran's struggle for life in the prison camp, where he never loses hope he will be free again. He escapes to France and then to the U.S. and is reunited with his family and joins the staff of the *New York Times*. If you're too young to remember the Vietnam war, some of the early drama will outpace you. But the plot remains tightly intact. Waterston, who did this film for very little money, is a raving hero; he is driven. Cinematography is by the superb Chris Menges and is accompanied by Oldfield's nerve-crippling electronic score.

Also recommended: *Hearts and Minds* and *Vietnam: In the Year of the Pig*.

KING: MONTGOMERY TO MEMPHIS

Introduced by Harry Belafonte. Directed by Ely Landau. Music coordinator, Coleridge Taylor Perkinson. USA. English. Black and white. 90 minutes (shortened from the original 177 minutes). 1970.

The career of Martin Luther King, Jr., from 1955 to his death in Memphis in 1968.

In spite of the fact that the Reverend King was shot down by an assassin in 1968, this film unfolds like a victory celebration of the human energy for social transformation. From the bus boycotts of 1955 to the triumphant march on Washington D.C. in 1963 and the protest marches in Selma, every defeat is met with revitalized commitment and enthusiasm to see change come. King led a movement of "nonviolent passive resistance" as an open "weapon of love." The bus boycott in Montgomery, which pushed the movement into the headlines, achieved 99.9 percent participation from blacks and led to statewide boycotts and sit-ins and a withdrawal of support from businesses failing to conform to demands of desegregation. As the movement spread across the country, infecting city after city with activist vitality, the KKK and white supremacists rose up to meet it. "They want to throw white children and colored children into the melting pot of integration out of which will come a conglomerated mongrel race of people. I will die before I'll yield an inch." Churches were blown up. Dr. King's home was bombed. Cars and buses were bombed. Crosses were burned. Each crisis swelled the numbers of men, women, and children marching for human rights. "No man is free who fears death," King preached, "I may not have much. . . . but I have the capacity to die." His "Letter from a Birmingham Jail" is read in full. He wrote of blacks "forever fighting a degrading, degenerating sense of nobodiness." Police dogs, fire hoses, billy clubs, tear gas, and brute force were used against peaceful marchers and against blacks trying to register to vote. As innocent people were beaten bloody in the street, King promised, "We will wear you down by our capacity to suffer." In D.C., his historic "I have a dream" speech stirs the hundreds of thousands gathered on the mall into a spectacular demonstration of the ecstasy of social righteousness. But back in Selma, racists followed every march, taunting blacks with insults, threats, and violence. President Johnson called on the National Guard to protect the peaceful, direct actions of black and white civil rights workers. In April of 1968 in Memphis, Tennessee, King was killed by an assassin's bullet. In a speech just days before he died, having read the hate mail and heard the death threats, he told supporters, "I don't mind . . . because I've been to the mountain top, and I've seen the promised land."

Also recommended: *The Long Walk Home*.

KOYAANISQATSI
(life out of balance)

Produced and directed by Godfrey Reggio. Photography by Ron Fricke.
Music by Philip Glass. USA. Color. 87 minutes. 1983.

The decay of industrial civilization.

Godfrey Reggio has got to be more than human. The only way to watch
his movie is to be possessed by it. *Koyaanisqatsi* (from the Hopi) is a
gesture of omniscient, creative awe. It is the spectral memory of a being
without form that has perhaps seen many worlds, but now sees this one
inventing itself out of shadow, rhythms, mythic moods, and infinite, exhilarating silence, like a god might see the surface of the Earth. Translat-
ing itself from light and stone, shaping by motion, and perspiring from
volcanic pores and vaporizing remote rivers. Never to be touched except by the sun and protected by time. Willing to sing through the bodies of birds and breathing out clouds across the open skies. Resolved
into inaudible thunders. Consuming nothing in the mirage of evolution.
Persuading trees to push away from gravity. Sinking canyons into cold,
clear riverbeds. Without ceremony. At home in space. Not slowing its
rotation of day and night to hear the engines diverting the currents, in-
terrupting the wave, reconsecrating the abyss, prodigiously controlling
it. Melting diamonds in nuclear flashes of backward energy. There is a
motorized industrial purpose speculated on by a billion binocular irises
genuflecting anew. The people are platelets for the death of objectivity.
The moon can only flash in slices of glass preservatories. And daylight
is digested by vacant rooms in which people have renounced hope.
The carcasses of buildings rupture with elegant pain. And roadways
flow with gray blood pumping carbon monoxide through the cell walls
of the new machine. Capable of striking at its own parts, consuming its
parts. Retaliating on the thing it is—an intercontinental body of bombs.
Remembering nothing about not wanting to be touched except by the
sun. Smoke like a dying dust. Punctures through which the exhaust refuses to escape. Elaborate tortures and bloated lights that blind no one
and erase the stars. Infection of monotony. Measurable cataclysmic
document. Accurate catastrophe. Unstoppable intricacy of sameness.
Days pass unrecognized. Seasons monument into pages. Salvage nothing, but addiction. The poverty of space flight. Out there are the answers to urgency. Burning at the bottom of the sea. And on an ancient

cave wall an earlier culture predicted it all. *Koyaanisqatsi.* Some say it has no powerful narrative. Has no narrative. Has no power. Because these are verbal times. And we are the ones who need words.

Also recommended: *Powaqqatsi.*

LA MUERTE DEL CHE GUEVARA

With Francisco Rabal, Howard Ross, John Ireland, Ricardo Gomez, Susana Martinoka. Produced by Inducine Productions: Enrico Varga, Conrado Ferlaino, Daniel Castrellon. Directed by Lewis E. Ciannelli. Dialogue by John Hart and Daniel Castrellon. Photography by Luciano Trassati. Music by Nico Fidenco. Spanish. Color. 92 minutes. 1968.

Dramatization of the capture and murder of Che Guevara.

In 1968, Che Guevara left Cuba to go to Bolivia to generate revolution. This movie concentrates on the international cover-up regarding the events of Guevara's murder by the Bolivian right wing and the CIA. But audiences might want to know that popular supporters of Guevara marched under banners of "land or death" in "the homeless citizens' revolution." In many countries in South America, most of the arable land was held by large landowners, and squatters were often killed resisting eviction. Che spent eleven months in the jungles of Bolivia with a small force of men and was hunted down by rangers of the Bolivian right-wing military assisted by the CIA. In his diaries, from which much of the film is taken, he confesses his fears, "I have confidence in no one. . . . I am afraid." He feels cut off from revolutionary leaders of other countries. There is a chronic shortage of weapons and supplies. He and his few men sleep under trees and beg from villages for handouts and support as an enormous international campaign gears up to find him. "Wanted" posters offering a reward of fifty million Bolivian pesos for information are posted on storefronts and town halls across the country. Travel in or out of villages is banned under orders of "military emergency." The CIA operative (Ireland) and leaders of the Bolivian military track Che's movements and mobilize their combined forces of helicopters, jet fighters, and convoys of ground troops to close in on the small rebel force. Indians and campesinos are ordered to report sightings of any guerrillas. Everything the revolutionaries do gives away their location. In the final assault, all his men are killed and Che is wounded in both legs and carried to a schoolhouse in a nearby village. News of his capture is wired secretly to the U.S. as he sits untreated in an empty room. Here Ciannelli borrows loosely from Sergei Eisenstein in scenes suggesting the indulgent wealth of the capitalist bourgeoisie who sit at tables heavy with crystal and caviar casually deciding the fate of the captured land reformist. A trial might generate unpredictable public opinion and political repercussion. The decision is made to reinvent the capture sequence. Che is shot with an M2, and his body is transported by helicopter back to the mountains. The news is then released to the world press. "Che killed in combat." No subtitled version available.

Also recommended: *Malcolm X*.

THE LAST SEVEN MONTHS OF ANNE FRANK

Written, produced, and directed by Willy Lindwer. Music by Gary Goldschneider. English. Color. 73 minutes. 1988.

Interviews with schoolmates of Anne who knew her before her family went into hiding and saw her only days before she died in 1945.

The Nazis kept records of all the people they sent to concentration camps during World War II. In the pages of their record books are the names of Anne Frank and her family—shipped out with the last train-load of prisoners to Bergen Belsen. Anne's fate was to push her one step ahead of liberation armies from the attic hideout in Holland to the deportation train and to the camps. As the trains carried the prisoners away from freedom, many aboard prayed that they would be bombed before they could reach their destination. Arriving at night, they were kicked and beaten by other prisoners who ordered them off the train, whispering, "You're healthy, run for it." The elderly and children were sent directly to the ovens. Teeth were checked and heads were shaven.

Women were forced to undress and remove sanitary napkins in front of guards. "You saw things with your eyes, but no further. Feelings were totally repressed." One lady confesses, "I was glad my mother and all my other relatives went into the gas chambers right away. I've always said that—it was over for them." Friends who had known the Franks in Holland in 1942 thought they had found asylum in Switzerland until Anne, her sister Margo, and her mother arrived at Women's Block 29. Survivors remember how Mrs. Frank struggled to keep her daughters alive. She saved food for them and tried to protect them, but she died early, leaving the girls alone. They both developed scabies and skin rashes over their bodies. When winter came, typhus raged through the barracks. Everyone was cold. There weren't enough clothes or blankets. Anne was seen wearing nothing but a coat on a bitter cold day. She told a friend she'd given away her clothes because they were infested. One woman describes their lives as a "natural disaster unconnected to the S.S." "It was as if we'd been shipwrecked." Death selections were made every morning after roll call—an ordeal that could last for hours in any weather. People died standing in line; then the roll would start again from the beginning. Margo and Anne Frank died within days of one another in March of 1945. The camp was liberated in April. Their father, Otto Frank, survived.

Also recommended: *Witness to the Holocaust.*

THE LAST WAVE

With Richard Chamberlain, Olivia Hamnett, Gulpilil, Nandjiwarra Amagula, Frederick Parslow. Produced by Hal McElroy and James McElroy. Directed by Peter Weir. Screenplay by Peter Weir, Tony Morphett, Peter Popescu. Photography by Russell Boyd. Music by Charles Wain. Australia. English and aboriginal language. Color. 106 minutes. 1978.

Weir's classic film of tribal magic, mysticism, and aboriginal Dream Time.

Who else but Weir could have directed this excavation of "unseen qualities" emanating from a parallel universe of nonform that controls the material plane, which is, after all, only visible reality? In the area around Sydney, Australia, the weather has become violent and unpredictable—wild thunderstorms bring huge hail, "black rain," and impenetrable, all-immersing fog. The violent weather is a harbinger of the presence of dream forces. As he works to build a defense for five men accused of murder, a lawyer (Chamberlain) learns about aboriginal culture and the Dream Time. "The tribal aboriginals of Australia recognize two forms of time—normal time and Dream Time—an infinite spiritual cycle more real than reality itself." His wife (Hamnett) is a fourth-generation Australian who has never met an aborigine. When Chris (Gulpilil) and Charley (Amagula) come to dinner, she withdraws from their intensity. They are more obviously alive and in tune with unheard and unseen things. Chamberlain pleads with them, "You must tell me the truth. You are in terrible trouble." "No," they tell him, "You are in terrible trouble, you don't know what dreams are any more. . . . A dream is a shadow of something real." As Chamberlain loses his battle to allow the convicted men to be tried under tribal law, he also loses touch with his own culture and begins to believe the "myths." He slips away from his life into the aura of 50,000 years of aboriginal Dream Time. "I've lost the world I thought I had." He learns he is a Mulcrul—a being with "incredible premonitory dreams." His visions come with the severe weather because water links the material and nonmaterial planes. It is the ancient, unconquerable, portentous connective tissue of the vision body. It is the blood of timelessness. Weir has put everything into this film—his love of Australian aboriginal culture; his love of the hidden, the obscure, and the intangible; and his gift of dramatic omen and the thrill of fear. *The Last Wave* grafts implausibilities together until they resemble absolute truth. Insatiable photography by Russell Boyd; indeed, something surrounds the characters and begins to breathe.

Also recommended: *Where the Green Ants Dream.*

LATINO

With Robert Beltran, Annette Cardona, Tony Plana, Gavin McFadden, Ricardo Lopez, Julio Medina, Juan Carlos Ortiz, Luis Torrentes. Produced by Benjamin Berg. Written and directed by Haskell Wexler. Photography by Tom Sigel. Music by Diane Louie. Theme song by Jackson Browne. USA. Spanish with English titles. Color. 105 minutes. 1985.

A recruit to the U.S.-backed war against the Sandanistas in Nicaragua defects and surrenders to the other side.

The United States government recruited Vietnam vets to fight in South America, convincing them that they were saving the world from Marxism. Having served in Southeast Asia, many of these servicemen were already desensitized to the brutalities of their own acts. Beltran plays a Hispanic-American fighting with the contras. He's like many Americans in a lot of ways. He doesn't know anything about Nicaragua, and he trusts U.S. foreign policy decisions completely. But after witnessing kidnappings, tortures, sadistic executions, bombings of family farms, raids on church sancturaries, undocumented war crimes, assaults on unarmed civilians, and so much compromise of common justice, he begins to question U.S. strategies and the ideologies for which they stand. His girlfriend (Cordena) fills him in on other offenses. To hide the extent of American involvement, U.S. troops were often required to participate in offensives without carrying any I.D. Many were killed, and without proof of nationality, families back home were informed that their loved ones were "missing in action." On an attack of a coffee cooperative, Beltran, now completely disillusioned, publicizes U.S. complicity and drops out of the war by wearing his dog tags and surrendering to the Sandanistas. Haskell Wexler directed this fictionalized historic drama. He's a radical creative talent, but his films are full of people it's difficult to care about and issues we know to be important but which fail to alarm. Perhaps some of the romance footage could have been invested in enlightening audiences about the extent of corporate craving for third-world governments.

Also recommended: *The Uprising*.

THE LEARNING TREE

With Kyle Johnson, Alex Clarke, Estelle Evans, Dana Elcar, Mira Waters, Joel Fluellen, Malcolm Atterbury, Richard Ward, Peggy Rea, Carole

Lamond. Produced, written, and directed by Gordon Parks, based on the novel by Gordon Parks. Photography by Burnett Guffey. Music by Gordon Parks. USA. English. Color. 107 minutes. 1969.

A young black boy walks a tightrope of heroism in the U.S. south.

The Learning Tree sits on a list in the Library of Congress as one of the twenty-five greatest films of the American film era apparently because the main character, a young, black boy named "Newt," is so good-natured that he can watch the white sheriff murder one of his friends without it ruining his day. "You didn't have to go and kill him." Oh, Newt, he was just asking for it. You're supposed to like Newt and bring your family to see the film, but I don't think I want anyone I'm related to to remain calm while I'm being gunned down without a trial for maybe stealing an apple. The year 1969 was not a year of strong minority statement in film. As the civil rights wars set major cities ablaze and threatened to destabilize white authority and perhaps eradicate racism from the dictionary of human definitions, film media proffered such pathetic ware as this—evidence that blacks were, after all, born to good parents whose values ruled out revolution but not congenital courteousness. *The Learning Tree* is full of cruelties, injustices, and racial slurs, to which Newt submits himself because that's the way he's been brought up. He's the ideal child, if not the ideal black actor, whose clothes are ironed and whose shoes are shined. His is the perfect family. But they live in an imperfect world—a world of weak moral fiber and great abuse of power. There are a lot of people with bad attitudes walking around loose who should be locked away. There are innocent people running futilely from the long arm of the law. There are uncorrected confusions. There is poor muscle tone. There is flab. There is cellulite. There is cellulose. There are uncut forests of pole barns. Of course, writer, producer, director, music maker Gordon Parks is black and male, and I am not. But I can tell a morbidly swollen nursery rhyme when I see it, especially after it has exploded out of the bread box. I'm not saying, "don't go to this movie." I'm just saying, I wouldn't take anybody to see it, except maybe Gandhi after a good meal.

Also recommended: *The Autobiography of Miss Jane Pittman.*

THE LIBERATION OF L.B. JONES

With Lee J. Cobb, Lee Majors, Anthony Zerbe, Roscoe Lee Browne, Yaphet Kotto, Chill Wills, Lola Falana, Barbara Hershey. Produced by Ronald Lubin. Directed by William Wyler. Screenplay by Stirling Silliphant and Jesse Hill Ford, based on the novel by Jesse Hill Ford. Photography by Robert Surtees. Music by Elmer Bernstein. English. Color. 101 minutes. 1969.

A black man is unjustly condemned by a white criminal justice system.

The actors gathered in the small town of Sommerton, Tennessee, are enough to transform this film into something remarkably better than the plot outline would imply. "Undertaker wanting divorce" is maybe not the way to headline the diametrically diverse talents stoking the coals of this unique little story about how far wrong you can go once you start giving in to white supremacy. Falana is the incandescent wife of undertaker Browne, who wants Cobb to represent him in a divorce since Falana is having an affair with a white policeman (Zerbe). The problem is that in Sommerton in 1960, the system is not set up to allow white men to testify in black divorce suits. What happens instead is that Zerbe kills Browne to save his good name, but an innocent black man is jailed for the crime. They won't arrest Zerbe even when he begs them to after he realizes what he's done. "I killed him Mr. Hedgepath [Cobb]. It was either the nigger or me. Take me, book me, lock me up. Lay it on me. Otherwise I'll never sleep again." But his wish is not granted and Lee Majors, who has come to town to work with Uncle Cobb in his law office, packs up and leaves in disgust. Kotto simmers in the shrubberies of every scene and will avenge a long-ago crime.

Also recommended: *Judge Horton and the Scottsboro Boys*.

LITTLE BIG MAN

With Dustin Hoffman, Faye Dunaway, Martin Balsam, Richard Mulligan, Chief Dan George, Jeff Corey, Amy Eccles, Kelly Jean Peters, Carole

Androsky, Robert Little Star. Produced by Stuart Millar. Directed by Arthur Penn. Written by Calder Willingham, based on the novel by Thomas Berger. Photography by Harry Stradling. Music by John Hammond. USA. English. Color. 147 minutes. 1970.

A 121-year-old man tells the story of his life with the Cheyenne.

It's tempting to wonder how the stars were aligned for director Penn, who in a mere 147 minutes manages to surgically conjoin two formerly single birth babies into an unambulatory union, which he then names *Little Big Man*, but which I think should have been named Arthur Penn Man after its creator. Save a seat for Mary Shelley when you watch the story of the man (Hoffman) who has lived 121 years and has had a lot of experiences that are supposed to be funny but really just make us wonder about the future of American filmmaking. Hoffman has been taken by the Indians and partially raised by them. He has listened to Chief Dan George's Cheyenne legends and philosophies for twenty or thirty years but still has to witness a massacre of the Indians before he realizes which culture he prefers. The movie is a comedy about genocide. At least it's supposed to be funny watching sex-starved Faye Dunaway bathe the youthful orphan man while Wild Bill Hickock, Buffalo Bill, and George Custer are outside reordering the west. And so chiquita mia peeking under her petticoats after the massacre at Washita. The many comic furloughs into the tidewaters of vaudeville do not make more tolerable the sight of women being burned alive, women being killed naked in the snow, women having babies shot from their arms, and women breathing out chilled last breaths of life as fifes and drums play somewhere. *Little Big Man* wants the Indians *and* the whites to look realistically conjured from impaired clay. We bow to enlightenment. There is a very nice rain scene at the end, with quiet gray-green hills where an Indian culture used to be. In step with the sleight-of-hand historic legitimacy of the film, the script insists on referring to Custer as General George, when at the time of the Battle at the Little Bighorn River and the time of his death, Custer carried the rank of lieutenant colonel.

Also recommended: *Dances with Wolves.*

THE LITTLE FOXES

With Bette Davis, Herbert Marshall, Dan Duryea, Richard Carlson, Teresa Wright, Charles Dingle, Carl Benton Reid, Patricia Collinge. Directed by William Wyler. Written by Lillian Hellman, Alan Campbell, and Dorothy Parker, from the play by Lillian Hellman. Photography by Gregg Toland. Music by Meredith Wilson. USA. English. Black and white. 116 minutes. 1941.

A woman's obsession with material wealth dominates her life.

If there is one thing Bette Davis does with the skill of a surgeon it's play the evil woman. In *The Little Foxes*, she defies the laws of thermodynamics, draining every last drop of human warmth from the character of Regina Giddens. She's odious, but you can't take your eyes off the chalky-faced demoness. Davis has a piquant maliciousness that repels and attracts at the same time. We know she's going to take over the world, but we don't cover our eyes. Her dying husband, piously underacted by Herbert Marshall, might as well be walking along a slippery cliff blindfolded as try to defeat his craven wife. This is the story of Regina and her two greedy brothers, who want Mr. Giddens' $75,000 of Union Pacific Railroad stock so they can build a cotton mill and become millionaires. Giddens doesn't want to invest in this potential sweatshop. He's too nice a guy to make money that way (no talk about how the Union Pacific Railroad makes its money). Davis hounds Marshall through his last gasping days of life on earth, but he will not relent. This movie is full of flamboyant direction and cinematography, with drama dangling over spiral staircases, built especially to cater to Davis's haughty posture. Marshall clings to banisters while Davis floats up a step at a time to tower over him. On his part, Marshall suffocates her in purity. "I'll die my own way, and I'll do it without making the world any worse." "You'll wreck the town, you and your brothers. You'll wreck the world you and your kind, if they let you." (Was he right or what?) In *The Little Foxes*, all the nice people are saints who wouldn't make a cent off the labor power of others unless they were personal friends. It seems that some people are just born mean, and those are the ones who make it to the top. It's not the free market that turns people into zombies. It's zombies who turn the free market into a bottom-line war zone. Of special note is Richard Carlson, here playing the idealistic newspaper reporter. How many remember him from "I Led Three Lives" of 1950 television fare? So the budding revolutionary became a double agent. That's Hollywood. Director Wyler and Gregg Toland (photographer for *Citizen Kane*) have created a dreamy jewel of a movie that moves from scene to scene like a rose blossoming a petal at a time—proof that you can make a social statement that is a work of art.

Also recommended: *Ship of Fools*.

THE LONG WALK HOME

With Sissy Spacek, Whoopi Goldberg, Dwight Schultz, Ving Rhames, Dylan Baker, Erika Alexander. Produced by Howard W. Koch, Jr., and David Bell. Directed by Richard Pearce. Screenplay by John Cork. Photography by Roger Deakens. Music by George Fenton. USA. English. Color. 115 minutes. 1990.

The civil rights bus boycott in Alabama pulls families together.

There are a few wars that filmmakers don't care too much about. The civil rights war of the 1960s is one of them. This film was released behind such a media smokescreen that few Americans ever heard about it and a lot fewer ever saw it. One reviewer explained that the theme was historically of limited interest. I guess there just wasn't enough cumulative firepower going off in Montgomery, Alabama, in 1955 when Rosa Parks declined to sit in the back of the south's segregated buses. All it amounted to was a boycott that in conjunction with the work of other freedom-fighters precipitated the civil rights movement. Sissy Spacek is the Junior League socialite who's gathered the courage to pick up her maid Odetta (Goldberg) whenever she's on *that* side of town. She will later be astonished to see other white women working openly with the blacks in the city-wide carpool program. According to Spacek's close Junior League cousins to the Klan, anyone who helps blacks is working against their own race and promoting anarchy. The film divides its time between Spacek's elegant family life and Goldberg's very humble home and family life as they prepare quite differently for the holidays. The festive harmonies waver when a friend sees Spacek driving Goldberg to work and accuses her of treason. "When you pick her up, you are saying she's just like us, and she isn't." When her husband also discovers what she's up to and demands she stop, Spacek responds by volunteering to drive whole carloads of black house servants back and forth to help the boycott succeed in ending segregation. In the end, Spacek must choose between her husband's hate-filled fiats and the notion of equal rights. When she and her daughter join Goldberg and others in a face-off against a mob of angry racists, she has rejected the racist yoke that whites impose on each other and sees conformity for what it is. *The Long Walk Home* survived the flaming-arrow ambush of well-armed critics and will surely also survive the lull in America's interest in American history.

Also recommended: *You Got to Move.*

LOS OLVIDADOS
(The Forgotten Ones, Pity for Them, the Hooligans)

With Estela Inda, Miguel Inclan, Alfonso Mejia, Roberto Cobo. Produced by Oscar Dancigers. Directed by Luis Buñuel. Screenplay by Luis Buñuel and Luis Alcoriza. Photography by Gabriel Figueroa. Music by Rudolfo Halffter and Gustavo Pitaluga. Mexico. Spanish with titles. Black and white. 88 minutes. 1951.

Poor people try and fail to survive their lives of urban poverty.

"The large cities of the world are pits of misery, poverty, and homeless children." Buñuel's special talent is creating depravity, but here it is so well-disguised that you may not even know it's happening. He finds comfort in surrounding himself with the heartless, the soulless, the toothless, the limbless, each with their own twisted outlook on life and self-centered distrust of others. If at any time we begin to suspect we have found a good person in *Los Olvidados*, then we have fallen into Buñuel's trap. He wants to get our hopes up; otherwise, how can he pound them back down with his stupendously negative pontifications? As for the wasteland of tortured souls in *Los Olvidados*, they are incapable of understanding why life has worked out for them the way it has.

There are no hunches surfacing as to where things may have gone wrong or how they might be made to go right. And the textbook on economic imperialism is in a spaceship on the way to Pluto. With a cast of malcontents and degenerates, it could be that Buñuel himself doesn't believe in a better world. If *Los Olvidados* has any point at all, it's that society pulls itself down just by waking up in the morning, and that if leprosy didn't already exist, Buñuel would have invented it. I'm lost trying to find anything to like about this debauched commentary on life, which seems aimed at convincing us that human beings were put on earth to attract vultures out of a cloudless sky, provoke evil misfortune, suffer a glory death, and wind up buried in a solid waste dump. Buñuel is one of the outstanding Spanish filmmakers of the century, but if anyone had ever asked me, I would have called it destructive social commentary. He has a gift. It's there in every frame. And he clearly objects to poverty, but you get the impression that as a filmmaker, he'd miss it if it were gone.

Also recommended: *Pixote.*

THE LOST HORIZON

With Ronald Colman, Jane Wyatt, John Howard, Thomas Mitchell, Edward Everett Horton. Produced and directed by Frank Capra. Screenplay by Robert Riskin, from the novel *The Lost Horizon* by James Hilton. Photography by Joseph Walker and Elmer Dyer. Music by Dimitri Tiomkin. USA. English. Black and white. 132 minutes. 1937.

English refugees find utopia in the mountains of Tibet.

"In these days of wars and rumors of war, have you ever dreamed of a place where there was peace and security, where living was not a struggle but a delight?" Only all the time. In *The Lost Horizon*, a group of white people board a plane to escape from war-torn China. They are kidnapped by the pilot and taken to a valley in the mountains a thousand miles outside the explored regions on the map. It is an enchanted kingdom cut off from imperfection by endless square miles of snow-capped peaks. It is Shangri-La, where raging blizzards cannot enter. The luxurious marble palace where Conway (Colman) and his friends are taken overlooks the Valley of the Blue Moon. It's a land without crime or punishment or regular mail service, radio, telegraph, or baggage handlers for the potential overland traveler. To arrive is never to leave or want to leave. Everybody has all they need and no fear of want tomorrow. "We do not seek personal fortunes," says the benevolent overseer, standing amidst jade and ivory splendors. "We have no money as you know it." They only have gold as we know it, glittering up the cliff walls, which is fortunate because if it wasn't falling on them, they'd need miners—probably not the people of the marble mansion—to dig it out and refine it. Gold is a heavy thing to pack out across the blizzard-fed mountain peaks to exchange for marble colonnades, but, in Shangri-La, such things happen. Jane Wyatt lives in the palace. She has read one of Conway's books and has decided he is the best person to take over rulership for the elderly Lama when he retires. That's why they were kidnapped. The contented working classes (the ones hoeing the vegetable gardens) do not hunger for representational democracy. None of them yearns for a congressional seat, although the children Wyatt leads in sing-alongs of old American classics could grow up to lead some kind of bigger sing-alongs, who knows? While discussing Shangri-La's religion of moderation, Conway is advised that if someone else wants his woman, the decent thing to do is let him have her, and vice versa. Conway is a pacifist and a very nice guy. So, paradise, let me in. And there's no aging. How could there be in a climate of constant violin music? What's wrong with *The Lost Horizon*? Everything. Except the weather. And the cinematography, direction, acting, drama, and film editing. It's a movie marvel weakened by indifference to social theory and perpetuating myth upon myth about the causes of social discord. Utopia ought not be racist, sexist, elitist, or dictated to, even benevolently. And it should not bear such a chilling resemblance to colonialism the world over.

Also recommended: *Our Daily Bread*.

LOVE AND ANARCHY

With Giancarlo Gainnini, Mariangela Melato, Eros Pagni, Lina Polito, Pina Cei, Elena Fiore. Produced by Herbert R. Steinmann and Billy Baxter. Written and directed by Lina Wertmuller. Photography by Giuseppe

Rotunna. Music by Nino Rota. Italy. Italian with English titles. Color. 108 minutes. 1973.

Neither love nor anarchy can catch up with Benito Mussolini in this Italian romp.

There are only two things wrong with this film. First, there's no anarchy. Second, there's no love. And as a bonus, there's nothing in-between. There's no reason for this film to exist except as a model for unsuccessful humor based on exploitation and poor taste. Socialist director Wertmuller's expressions of radicalism (in this film anyway) fall far short of any meaningful standards of artistic excellence or social relevance. If I hadn't known who the director was, I would have pictured a guy in a trench coat under a dim street lamp. From a flashy Mussolini montage beginning, the film jackknifes into an ear-splitting, over-rehearsed vaudeville act, most of which takes place in a villa-esque brothel populated by females who flutter up and down stairways in waves of chiffonette. There are two kinds of women in this film—those who can't speak above a throaty whisper and those who've stood around on flight decks too long. One of the women *is* an anarchist, and she does plot with a guest to kill Mussolini, but they never make it because they wind up thinking it might be bad luck. Yes, Benito was a ghoul. But what's new, you fool? There's nothing to redeem *Love and Anarchy* from its own crowning ineptitudes. I wouldn't take a dog to see this film about how *homo sapiens* can only inflict tyranny but never manage to resist it as long as there's a double bed tempting them and their honey bun's to so much fun. I could recommend it, though, as an example of how to miss Moon River by wider than a mile.

Also recommended: *Good Fight.*

MACARTHUR'S CHILDREN

With Masako Natsume, Takaya Yamauchi, Shiori Sakura, Shima Iwashita, Yoshiyuki Omoro. Produced by You-No-Kai and Masato Hara. Directed by Masahiro Shinoda. Screenplay by Tsutome Tamura, based on a novel by Yu Aku. Photography by Kazuo Miyagawa. Music by Shinichiro Ikebe. Japan. In Japanese with titles. Color. 115 minutes. 1984.

The story of how some schoolchildren in Japan cope in the post-World War II climate.

Director Shinoda calls Japan, "America's fifty-first state." He says his film has nothing to do with revenge but goes on to say, "America came to Japan to destroy the old Japanese system. . . . We are still defeated. We are still occupied. They haven't left yet." In *MacArthur's Children*, the sixth-grade class is listening to surrender announcements on a radio at the front of the room. From the abstractions of the news will come orders for the students to erase the "forbidden parts" of their school texts. The United States has certain ideas about what Japanese children should be allowed to learn. Some of these students decide to form a union to protect the people of Japan from American control. They call themselves the Japanese Guard. But their anxieties about Americanization cannot really hold up to the charm of U.S. servicemen. After seeing a baseball, the students form the Inland Sea boys' baseball team. They play against adult American servicemen. The ball park is the new battleground. Based on recollections of the director's childhood, Shinoda must have led a sheltered life if the worse thing he can put to film about World War II is that women were unfaithful to their soldier husbands and children hated the Americans until they tasted their chewing gum. Nothing really seems to be happening in the film except unnecessarily subtle shifts in the children's perceptions of surrender. If deep tragedies were inflicted by the war, they are serenely resolved off-screen. One of the young girl's fathers is on trial for war crimes, but he's really only a martyr and a hero caught up in the times. Shinoda is an elegant storyteller, apparently content to fill the screen with heavenly beauty to give the impression that "We are still occupied." Americans will consult their Sunday gazetteers. Back in the classroom, we do fall momentarily sentimental watching the children work through their English lessons, "I am an American boy." But when the war hero is executed and his daughter is sent away to live with her aunt, the leader of the children's Japanese Guard stands on the pier waving to the departing ship and singing a Japanese song of goodbye. It's a luscious, lamentable moment, soaring splendidly wide of our observable theme. Shinoda's film is a delicacy of full-spectrum sunlight illuminating something perhaps only he can see.

Also recommended: *Twenty-Four Eyes*.

THE MAGIC CHRISTIAN

With Peter Sellers, Ringo Starr, Raquel Welch, Isabel Jeans, Richard Attenborough, Caroline Blakiston, Christopher Lee, Wilfrid Hyde-White, Spike Milligan, John Cleese, Peter Graves, Lawrence Harvey. Produced by Dennis O'Dell. Directed by Joseph McGrath. Written by Terry Southern, from the novel by Terry Southern and Joseph McGrath. Additional material by John Cleese, Graham Chapman, and Peter Sellers. Photography by Geoffrey Unsworth. Music by Ken Thorne. Great Britain. English. Color. 95 minutes. 1970.

Outrageous parody of money and civilized pretension.

Iconically rich Guy Grand (Sellers), while feeding the birds in the park one morning with park bum Ringo Starr, decides he'll adopt him as his new son, Youngman Grand. Spiral stairways full of household servants chorus, "Welcome, welcome, Youngman Grand, to the finest family in the land." Youngman and Guy traipse into drawing rooms and partridge huts with wads of money to test its power, which turns out to be vast. Snobs will grovel, cops will eat tickets, crew teams will battle with their paddles, and boxers will fall in love in the ring. "The crowd seems to be sickened by the sight of no blood." The daring duo live out the destiny wealth places on them—Sherman-tank quail hunts, multiracial head transplants, cruise ships with a female slave crew in the engine room. In the background are television and radio broadcasts about some of the less whimsical things money does—the Vietnam war, executions, riots, poverty, disaster, and starvation. On the maiden voyage of *The Magic Christian*, Guy and Youngman take note of the "few people of color aboard" as the boat is hijacked to Cuba, sending passengers into a spree of violence, looting, graffiti ("Smash capitalism"), and posters of Mao Tse Tung. After the cruise, having grown bored, Guy and Youngman fill an open vat with blood, urine, and manure. As the goop purifies in the sun, they litter the curdled surface with pound notes and advertise, "Free Money." Soon the vat is full of businessmen in three-piece suits diving for loot. Purged by this gross discovery, Guy and Youngman return to live in the park with sleeping bags, buying off park guards with fists full of dough-ray-me. *The Magic Christian* dares to be obnoxious; it dares to be nonlinear. Sellers and Starr could have been related in a former life. But stabs at wealth and privileged seem odd coming from the wealthy and privileged who don't sleep in parks and don't give their money away—who probably travel first class, are afraid of Castro, and live in restricted zoning areas.

Also recommended: *Head Office.*

MALCOLM X

Produced by Marvin Worth and Arnold Perl. Based on the book *The Autobiography of Malcolm X.* USA. English. Black and white. 92 minutes. 1972.

**A Black Muslim revolutionary teaches black power
to Americans.**

This film documentary biography of the activist career of Malcolm X is a revealing portrait and the definitive tribute to a man who was ultimately hero to black and white alike, preaching racial tolerance and proving that leadership is nothing more mysterious than total commitment to a personal ideal. *Malcolm X* is a deft archival reconstruction, recapturing the zeal and the charisma of Malcolm X and the times in which he lived. He grew up in Michigan during the Klan heyday and took the low road to prison where he read the writings of the Black Muslim leader Elijah Muhammad and became committed to the nation of Islam. He took "X" as his last name, symbolizing the African name he could never know. Out of prison, he became a leader in the black consciousness and back-to-Africa movements. He named his daughters after Attila the Hun and Kublai Khan. His speeches condemned all whites and their religions as inferior and white society as oppressive and racist. He taught that whites were inherently evil and that the possibility of living peacefully with them in a just society did not exist. He preached violence as a defense against racism. He preached segregation. But he was soon to undergo another dramatic transformation of personal philosophies. On a pilgrimage to Mecca in the 1960s, Malcolm X met white Muslims who knelt down beside him in the holy city and prayed to Allah. In these blond-haired Muslims he could find no trace of the inherent evil. In his autobiography, he wrote, "Never have I witnessed such sincere hospitality and overwhelming spirit of true brotherhood as is practiced by people of all colors and races here. . . . The pilgrimage has blessed me with new insights." Back in the U.S., he began to promote racial understanding and became alienated from the black Muslims and Elijah Muhammad. When he spoke out publicly against Elijah, Elijah's son, Wallace, issued an open invitation to black Muslims to "bring him the ear of Malcolm X." Although he was not indifferent to danger, for personal reasons Malcolm refused offers of police security and was shot and killed while speaking at the Audubon Ballroom in Harlem on February 21, 1965.

Also recommended: Spike Lee's movie on Malcolm X.

MAN FACING SOUTHEAST

With Lorenzo Quinteros, Hugo Soto, Ines Vernengo, Cristina Scaramuzza. Produced by Lujan Pflaum. Written and directed by Eliseo Subiela. Photography by Ricardo de Angelis. Music by Pedro Aznar. Argentina. In Spanish with yellow English titles. Color. 105 minutes. 1986.

A mysterious man appears in a mental hospital teaching love and understanding.

It's either the perfect delusion or he is an extraterrestrial sent to Earth to teach humans how to respond to their innermost humane urges. He's come directly to the mental home to save everyone the trouble of putting him there. For Rantes (Soto), it's a time saver. Apart from the space story, he's normal in every way, except that he stands out on the sunny lawn for hours facing southeast. This is how he receives his transmissions. He says he's visiting Earth to rescue the victims of human stupidity. He says there are "Rantes" all over the world doing the same thing. It's a copybook case for Dr. Dennis (Quinteros). Impossible to prove, impossible to disprove. Rantes says the entire society is insane for failing to carry through on impulses to help the needy and the poor, the sad and the fearful. He sees people all around him rejecting their spontaneous ideas—holding back kind words and repressing the urge to help others. This denial of identity is a disease, he says. Repression of spontaneous impulse is destroying all hope for human happiness. "Rantes," the doctor explains, "you are sick. I want to cure you." "Doctor," Rantes explains, "I don't want you to cure me. I want you to understand me." His influence on the patients is strong. They become disciples. But the hospital staff thinks Rantes should be sedated. He could be dangerous. The strong tranquilizers disorient him and disrupt his transmissions from the southeast. His health declines. A "friend" intervenes to no avail. The doctor seduces her. She tells him that she is a "Rantes" too. He rejects them both. Rantes asks, "Doctor, why have you forsaken me?" After he dies, the patients form a circle on the lawn and wait for his return in a ship from space.

Also recommended: *Jesus of Montreal.*

MANDELA

With Danny Glover, Alfre Woodard, Warren Clarke, Allan Corduner, Nathan Dambuse Mdledle, John Natshikiza, Julian Glover. Produced by Robert Berger. Directed by Philip Saville. Written by Ronald Harwood. Photography by John Coquillon. Music by Richard English. USA. English. Color. 135 minutes. 1987.

Made for American television, the life story of Nelson Mandela.

Back in 1943, Nelson Mandela was already a member of the African National Congress (ANC). He promoted nonviolent opposition to the white supremacist government following the example of Gandhi, who once lived in South Africa until he was deported to his native India. We don't hear the word "Gandhi" in this movie. Nor do we hear much about an independent black state, forced relocations, the Mixed Marriages Act, and so on. We do see many zoom shots of the budding romance between Minnie and Nelson—their first meeting, their courtship, their marriage, their babies. All the newsworthy events in Mandela's life, including bannings and arrests, are revealed, not as setbacks to the fight for home rule, but as blows to their romance. As Nelson goes off to jail, Winnie's sad but brave face fills the screen, leaving little room for background details about the inequities of apartheid. Even after the sequence on the 1960 Sharpeville massacre, no death toll figures are given and not one actual news photo is shown. There *is* coverage of the history and development of the Suppression of Communism Act, which evolved as a multi-purpose tool of legalized racial oppression—one act in an ocean of supremacist legislation, including the Mixed Marriages Act, the Morality Act, the Group Areas Act and so on. The ANC is mentioned—the banning of the group and its members, the harassment of members and the shift from pacifism to terrorism are sketchily laid out. But once Mandela is arrested for leaving the country without valid papers and violating his banning orders, the movie lapses contentedly into prison visits—each one sadder than the one before. This takes up so much of Winnie's screen time that when she is arrested, a voice-over has to tell us that she has been active in politics "in her own right." As time goes by, the kids grow up, have kids of their own, and take turns visiting. Occasionally Mandela refuses offers for freedom if the offer entails limits on his political activities. In real life, Nelson Mandela was released from prison in February of 1990 at the age of 71. This made-for-American-T.V. movie was billed as a love story and remained oh-so-true to its word.

Also recommended: *Master Harold and the Boys*.

THE MANHATTAN PROJECT: THE DEADLY GAME

With John Lithgow, Christopher Collet, Jill Eikenberry, Cynthia Nixon, John Mahoney. Produced by Jennifer Ogden and Marshall Brickman. Directed by Marshall Brickman. Screenplay by Marshall Brickman and Thomas Baum. Cinematography by Billy Williams. Music by Philippe Sarde. USA. English. 117 minutes. 1986.

Youth versus adults in the game of nuclear deterrence.

John Lithgow is almost too nice to be building advance lasers for the refinement of plutonium. There are a lot other people like him working at jobs they haven't thought too much about. He's a valuable nonthinking link in the cold war. Writer-producer-director Brickman has filled the screen with ordinary, likable people who live near a plutonium refinery. The drama tightens, contrasting homespun happenstance to weapons manufacture. That "Metatomics" is being sold as a medical research facility is possibly an allusion to the G.E. "Re-Entry Systems Di-

vision" plant in King of Prussia, Pennsylvania—formerly secret manufacturing sight of Mark 12A first-strike nuclear warheads. Lithgow's
young friend Paul (Collet) will break into Metatomics and steal enough
plutonium to make "the first privately built nuclear device in the history
of the world." He will take the amateur weapon to the annual science
fair hoping to win the grand prize and alert everyone to the risk of
weapons technology. Chased back to Metatomics, Paul's courage pre-
vails. He won't back down. When the military surrounds Paul and Lithgow, Lithgow grasps the meaninglessness of human life to the war
mind. He and Paul stare at each other from opposite sides of a narrow-
ing crevasse. Paul knows by instinct that he has to obey the dictates of
his conscience the same way he would if he had witnessed a crime of
violence. Lithgow has been one of the morally blind. If the boy dies, it
will be in part owed to his own work—he has lent his mind and his humanity to forces of destruction. Filmmaker Brickman was interested in
making a film dramatizing the threat of nuclear weapons. Perhaps he
chose a child star to save money, or maybe he wanted the innocence
and vulnerability of children measured against the undiscriminating
potential of hydrogen bombs.

Also recommended: *Amazing Grace and Chuck.*

MAPANTSULA

With Thomas Mogotlane, Marcel Van Heerden, Thembi Mtshali, Dolly
Rathebe, Peter Sephuma, Darlington Michaels, Eugene Majola. Produced
by Max Montocchio. Directed by Oliver Schmitz. Written by Oliver
Schmitz and Thomas Mogotlane. Photography by Rod Stewart. Music by
the Ouens. South Africa/Britain/Australia. In English, Afrikaans, Zulu, and
Sotho with titles. Color. 102 minutes. 1988.

A black South African becomes radicalized by
black consciousness.

As the Internal Securities Act drones out over loud speakers, police dis-
perse a gathering of blacks in Soweto (*South West Township*), Johannesburg's largest black township. Panic (Mogotlane) is arrested and
thrown in a common cell with political protesters. He's a petty criminal

and police informer, but it is not purely an accident that he came to be at the public funeral where the arrests were made. Afrikaaner police are pressuring him to confess what he knows about the labor movement. He is beaten and bribed. They want the names of organizers they can arrest under the Suppression of Communism Act. But once content to steal from black and white alike, Panic has begun to understand what the resistance is all about. In the final scene, even though his life has been threatened, he refuses to sign the "statement" they set before him. *Mapantsula* places heavy emphasis on the dominance of women in black society and the diversity of native cultures that makes black unity so difficult to cultivate and so unconquerable once attained.

Also recommended: *Come Back Africa.*

MASTER HAROLD AND THE BOYS

With Matthew Broderick, Zakes Mokae, John Kani. Produced by Iris Merlis. Directed by Michael Lindsay-Hogg. Screenplay by Athol Fugard, adapted from the play of the same name. Music by David Franco. United Kingdom. English. Color. 90 minutes. 1984.

A young, white South African stands at the crossroads of apartheid.

For non-South African audiences the first tremor from *Master Harold and the Boys* is the title. In the world of de jure racism, who are the boys and who is the master? The contradictions of apartheid move every South African child toward the age of controlled intimacy. Here Harold (Broderick) will lay down the first bricks in the wall of supremacist restraint between himself and the two black men who helped raise him. Until today, Sam (Makoe) and Willy (Kani), "the boys," were co-conspirators in a friendship of secret loyalties and blood-felt affections. The crime of being different was not powerful enough to bend Master Harold to the temptations of hate. This undisguised stage play contents itself with one room and a cast of three. The raptures of the dance are gliding Makoe and Kani back and forth across the tiled floor when

"Hally" comes in out of the rain to debate with them the historic craving for choreography. The dance, says Sam, makes life go the way you want it "as long as the music plays." The trouble with the world is that there is no music, no harmony. From here, their conversations range from literature to sociology to science. But a family crisis soon subdues Hally's enthusiasm for scholarship. His father is being released from the sanatorium where he's been treated for alcoholism. Hally's strong resistance to his father's release turns him against Mokae, who has warned him to be careful. "It's your turn to be careful," Broderick rallies, "You're treading on thin ground. . . . My mother warned me about getting too familiar. It's going to stop right now. You're only a servant here." He reminds Sam that all white men are his boss—an allusion to the now-repealed law requiring blacks to use the title. "Think of it as a little lesson in respect, long overdue." He tells the boys his father's favorite joke: "You know what's not fair? A nigger's ass." "How do you know it is not fair?" asks Sam, "You've never seen it." He lowers his trousers, ". . . this is about as nigger as they come, and. . . . you have made me feel dirtier than I have ever felt in my life." He confesses a promise he made years before. "I felt sorry for that little boy picking up his drunken father. I promised to keep you from feeling ashamed of yourself. I wanted you to be proud." Harold gathers his books and walks back into the rain, leaving Sam and Willy hoping for better weather tomorrow.

Also recommended: *Country Lovers, City Lovers.*

MATEWAN

With James Earl Jones, Chris Cooper, Mary McDonnell, Will Oldham, Nancy Mette, Gary McCleery, Ken Jenkins, Bob Gunton, Kevin Tighe, Jane Alexander, David Strathairn, Maggie Renzi, John Sayles. Produced by Maggie Renzi and Peggy Rajski. Directed by John Sayles. Written by John Sayles. Photography by Haskell Wexler. Music by Mason Daring. USA. English. Color. 130 minutes. 1987.

Miners defy coal companies in West Virginia—leading to the Matewan massacre and the coal wars.

"It were 19 an' 20 in the southwest fields, and things was tough. . . . Them was hand loadin' days. They paid you by the ton and they didn't care no more for a man than . . . for a daft mule." Mingo County, West Virginia, was the heart of coal country and the scene of the great coal wars of the 1920s. "The miners was trying to bring the union . . . and the coal operators and their gun thugs was set on keepin' 'em out." In those days, coal companies owned every building in the town, and they owned the people, too. Miners were paid in company "script" that was valid only at the company store. Union men came undercover to Matewan to organize strikes for fair pay in recognized currency, for safety standards, and for health benefits. Strikers were evicted from company housing, arrested, ambushed by mercenaries, and gunned down on the railroad tracks. Box cars full of scabs were shipped in along these rails—desperate blacks from the cities and Italian immigrants who barely spoke English. The scabs were quick to see through the company line and forged an alliance with the striking miners. Chris Cooper is the former Wobbly who talks through the racism and gets blacks voted into the union. Sayles' strong message of racial and cultural understanding is one of the best things about this film. In the camps at night, the music of the mandolin, fiddle, and harmonica brought former enemies together for worker's rights. The film is narrated by fifteen-year-old Danny (Oldham), a miner and a preacher who speaks out from the pulpit for the union effort. Boys ran coal raids, gathering fuel for camp fires, and were captured, tortures, and executed in the cold-blooded campaigns of greed. Sayles has enriched this tumultuous period in American history with the power of authentic illusion. He has recreated Appalachia, drawing on mountain heritage, West Virginia dialect, and stunning *a capella* singing, reflecting the independence and the courage of the Appalachian people. Chris Cooper's character, Joe Kenahn, did not die in a shoot-out, as depicted in the film, but went on to organize unions and strikes for many years.

Also recommended: *Harlan County, USA.*

MEDIUM COOL

With Robert Forster, Verna Bloom, Peter Bonerz, Marianna Hill, Harold Blankenship, Sid McCoy. Produced by Jerrold Wexler, Haskell Wexler, and Tully Friedman. Directed and photographed by Haskell Wexler. Written by Haskell Wexler, based on the novel *The Concrete Wilderness* by Jack Couffer. Music by Mike Bloomfield. USA. English. Color. 110 minutes. 1969.

A story about some people disoriented by the Democratic National Convention of 1968, or at least by the crowds outside.

I'm not sure where they got the title, but it does fit. Forster is a photographer suffering from some kind of photographer's disease, which has turned him into a Hoover vacuum, sucking up the visual spectrum but unable to react to it. He's a professional opportunist but dumps his gorgeous girlfriend for telling him so, and he sets out to prove her right. He will visit some black people in a tenement in the ghetto and learn all about them. He will meet a young widow from the hills of Appalachia who has moved to the city but will never fit in—she dresses wrong, doesn't wear make-up, and talks with an accent. She works in a factory, so it's love at first sight. It's 1968, so they can make a social comment just by getting lost in a crowd of protesters. There's no such thing as getting though a scene without civil disobedience or some comment on the poor quality of urban life. If there was a gravitational center to the protest movement of the 1960s, it must have been Haskell Wexler. The crowd scenes in this film are *real* crowds. This was Wexler's idea. If he had asked these *real* people what they were up to and why they were out there, we'd have a document on our hands instead of a slow-tone fade off a roadbank. The causes of exploitation and poverty and the breakdown of the family unit and all those other issues are not investigated in *Medium Cool.* Maybe that's because creative people are just as confused as everybody else. Some critics would say this movie is a slice of the 1960s. For me, it was more like an instrument fly-over. Harold Blankenship is good as the boy. About the cinematography, the less said the better. It's not that kind of movie. There are a few pleasantly cynical moments along with a suggestion that social chaos devours blindly in cycles. But it's hard to warm to the rambling chronicle attitude Wexler seems to enjoy getting himself into. Still, who knows—centerless, possibly random, paceless narrative could become the mode of choice for audiences of the future, in which case Haskell Wexler comes out ahead of his time.

Also recommended: *Zabriski Point.*

MEET JOHN DOE

With Barbara Stanwyck, Gary Cooper, Edward Arnold, James Gleason, Walter Brennan, Gene Lockhart, Spring Byington. Produced and directed by Frank Capra. Written by Robert Riskin, based on the story "The Life and Death of John Doe" by Richard Connell and Robert Presnell. Photographed by George Barnes. Music by Dimitri Tiomkin. USA. English. Black and white. 122 minutes. 1941.

Depression-era newspaper tries to push sales by dramatizing the suicide promise of a desperate man.

Gary Cooper is no more desperate than a lot of other guys who interview for the job of pretending to be the "John Doe" so down on his luck that he wrote to the newspaper promising to kill himself on Christmas Eve. Cooper's sheepish good looks get him in over a hundred others. He is the perfect fake, posing for photographs while Barbara Stanwyck writes pathetic letters to the editor every week. Readers wolf down the bogus copy and besiege the paper with job offers, marriage offers, places to live, and potential adoption. John Doe speaks to millions over the radio, "We're the people and we're tough...a free people can beat the world at anything. I know some of you are saying, 'I'm just a little punk, I don't count.' Well, you're wrong. The sum total of a country is the sum total of its little punks." Of course he doesn't write this remarkable stuff, he just reads it, but listeners don't know that, so he becomes a celebrity, and depression-era masses begin reaching out to each other through the John Doe Clubs that spring up by the dozens overnight. The newspaper foots the bill for the good will. It looks like a miracle. But wait. The newspaper owner wants Cooper to announce the formation of a third political party of which the John Doe Clubs will be the seedling impetus. If he refuses, they'll kill the clubs. "You can't kill it," Cooper protests, "it's bigger than whether I'm a fake. It's bigger than your ambition." But the headline reads, "John Doe is a fake!" And Cooper disappears. The holidays approach, the few who still believe in him are convinced he will jump off of City Hall on Christmas Eve, even though it wasn't really he who said that. It's a peaceful, snowy evening when he walks out on the rooftop. Stanwyck is there professing her love. Some John Doe clubbers dressed like soda jerks swear they'll keep their club going. The haunted look in his eye fades. The bells toll, and the spirit of hope is born again on the roof top. As improbable as this film seems at times, especially Stanwyck's raving sales pitches, you *will* walk out of the theater being nicer to people than when you walked in—even HUAC plebes like Cooper can make you want to be a better person.

Also recommended: *All the King's Men.*

MEPHISTO

With Klaus Maria Brandauer, Rolf Hoppe, Gyorgy Cserhalmi, Ildiko Bansagi, Krystyna Janda, Peter Andorai, Karin Boyd, Christine Harbort. Produced by Manfred Durniok. Directed by Istvan Szabo. Screenplay by Peter Dobai and Istvan Szabo, based on the book by Klaus Mann. Photographed by Lajos Koltai. Music by Zdenko Tamassy. Hungary, West Germany, Austria. German dubbed in English. Color. 144 minutes. 1981.

An actor compromises everything to become a star in Nazi Germany.

Is there any difference between selling your soul to the devil and taking a vow of loyalty to the Third Reich? Klaus Maria Brandauer wants to play Mephisto and become a director of the National Socialist Theater even if it means being devoured by the fascist state. Once a compassionate liberal working to create "a revolutionary theater for the workers," he retreats into denial of fascist brutalities. Many of the best talents leave Germany. If he stays, he will dominate German theater. He is stunned by the possibility. He has the perfect rationale, "It's out of the question to say 'no.'" He advises friends not to speak out and refuses to become involved in the resistance. He will not follow his wife to Paris, where she publishes an anti-fascist newspaper. He takes a black lover and learns, "She is different than what is allowed. You should not even keep a picture of that woman in your apartment." She accuses him, "You are a showcase. You legalize these people, and you'll never be able to cleanse yourself. You took an oath." "I didn't take the oath." To him it's a game. "I only moved my lips." He is consumed by self-deception. "I never was political, why should I start now . . . The real values in theater will rise above all this, believe me." He accepts fame and awards on behalf of racial purity while friends are gunned down fighting fascism. He is a star without moral equivocation. As the swastika replaces all former symbols and murder and cruelty rise up to sustain Hitler's state, the actors are exhibited to prove that art is alive in Germany. Brandauer's personality pales. He is a dazzling jewel in the crown of tyranny, with nothing left inside. In the end he will be blinded by floodlights in a massive amphitheater observed by a flank of officers. His face has lost the power of expression. He can only whisper, "What do they want of me. I am only an actor." Brandauer is super-human in this complex role of acting within acting. The dubbed version unfortunately obscures this and floods your skull like a powder-puff drenched in saturated fat. Learn German or find a subtitled version.

Also recommended: *Slave of Love.*

METROPOLIS

With Gustav Frohlich, Rudolph Klein-Rogge, Brigitte Helm, Theodor Loos, Alfred Abel, Heinrich George, Fritz Rasp, 750 bit players, 30,000 extras. Directed by Fritz Lang. Screenplay by Fritz Lang and Thea Von Harbou, based on the novel by Thea Von Harbou. Photography by Karl Freund and Gunther Rittau. Special effects by Eugen Schufftan. Germany. Silent with English titles. Tinted. 87 minutes. 1926.

Heir to the industrial revolution joins the workers in their fight for occupational justice.

This 1984 rerelease of the 1926 classic has been magnificently restored by Giorgio Morodor. Missing segments are built up by still photos. On-screen titles largely replace the black-screen titles of the silent era. The color tinting is marvelous. Restoration has saved one of the most astonishing films ever made—a monumental and visionary accomplishment. This is Fritz Lang's greatest film, permanently ahead of its time and now rededicated to audiences of the 21st century. A new soundtrack highlights the talents of contemporary rock musicians. This often intoxicating musical score has turned some critics' hair white overnight. But *Metropolis* is set in the year 2026, so the music of 1984 is still forty years out of sync for this predictive history classic. It's 2026. The fangs of the free market have created towering urban landscapes, great wealth, and total suppression of the 30,000 extras whom Lang directs like a filmic messiah. *Metropolis* captures the peripheral images—the overlooked subtleties, the monstrous evils, the gothic splendor and vacuousness of advanced industrialization. Human is subordinate to machine, and machine is subordinate to the fiats of commerce. The workers' dreams of revolution are inspired by Maria (Helm), who preaches to them from the pulpit of an underground cathedral, and by Freder (Frohlich), heir to Metropolis, who has traded places with one of the workers of find this woman and now sees the cruelty of the system he will inherit. Helm and Frohlich work together in the caverns and steamrooms of the vast underground, industrial machine, Brazen scenes are staged with the thousands of worker-extras. Hundreds of children are almost swept away in a flood scene that will simply never be surpassed. The wonder of Lang's talent and human rights message is an artistic and ethical beacon. If Lang does not go far enough in suggesting compassion from the owners of the means of production, he at least copes with the realities of capital accumulation. And perhaps leniency is, in the end, all we can expect. *Metropolis* is a mesmerizing film, which critic Pauline Kael called "almost incredible" and which I will call truly incredible, if any film ever was, or ever shall be.

Also recommended: *The Crowd.*

MILAGRO BEANFIELD WAR

With Chuck Vennera, Sonia Braga, Julia Carmen, Carlos Riquelme, Roberto Carricart, John Heard, Daniel Stern, Ruben Blades. Produced by Robert Redford and Moctesuma Esparza. Directed by Robert Redford. Screenplay by David Ward and John Nichols, based on the novel by John Nichols. Photography by Robbie Greenberg. Music by David Grusin. USA. English. Color. 118 minutes. 1988.

The story of how a guy named José diverts water from the Miracle Valley Recreation Group to grow beans.

"Milagro" means "miracle". "Beanfield" means that Jose (Vennera) Mondragon is illegally siphoning off water controlled by the big landowners to water his father's former beanfield. Behind the locked doors of the Miracle Valley Recreation Company, executive officers debate the felonious theft of Miracle Valley water. It's clearly illegal, but negative publicity might make them look like the frosty-freeze land grabbers they are. They need to divert Jose in some covert way. But all their schemes backfire—even the one where they buy up all the newspapers before anyone can read what the town's hippie lawyer (Heard) has said about the beanfield, the water, and Jose. They buy the papers all right, but before they can burn the collected bundles in an old oil drum, a magic wind comes along and blows them up, up into the sky. Next thing you know, they are drifting down into all the right places with full orchestral backup. I guess that's the "milagro" part. Of course, there are plenty of other miracles. It is miraculous that the two leading ladies could have eaten all those beans and still fit into size five jeans. It's a miracle and a half that the guy Jose thought he killed in a fit of frustration survives to tell about it. It's one stroke of luck after another for the bean sprouters because they can communicate with the next world. There's no way the Miracle Valley people can top that. They are outmaneuvered by the medicine men and ancient flutists. Robert Redford directs, so it's easy to see why the condos are selling so well in Miracle Valley. It's very beautiful. It's wide-screen. But apart form divine intercession, there's not a lot of practical advice for ordinary people to go on in this film. It's sort of a lesson in traditional culture, but the only time I felt like I was seeing any really traditional people was in the background of the dance scene in the last two minutes of the film.

Also recommended: *Our Daily Bread.*

MISSING

With Sissy Spacek, Jack Lemmon, John Shea, Charles Cioffi, Melanie Mayron, David Clennon, Joe Regalbuto, Janice Rule, Richard Venture. Produced by Edward and Mildred Lewis. Directed by Constantin Costa-Gavras. Screenplay by Constantine Costa-Gavras and Donald Stewart, based on the book *The Execution of Charles Horman* by Thomas Hauser. Photography by Ricardo Aronovich. Music by Vangelis. USA. English and Spanish. Color. 122 minutes. 1982.

An American national is assassinated in South America by a U.S.-supported military dictatorship.

This film was denounced by Alexander Haig, and it doesn't take too long to figure out why! The tempest of intervention in Central and South America has by now destroyed so many lives that the movie industry could divert all its energy for the next decade into telling the stories and still leave thousands of stories untold. *Missing* is the true story of Charlie Horman (Shea), who disappeared in an unnamed South American country (Chile) during a time of political unrest. Shea is the overinquisitive American who discovers that the U.S. is supplying military aid to the Pinochet regime and begins a personal investigation into the extent of U.S. involvement. He is detained by the military and is never seen alive again. As his wife (Spacek) and father (Lemmon) begin a futile and often grisly search through diplomatic evasion and underground corpse depositories, it becomes obvious that the authorities, both theirs and ours, are transfused with indifference to either the truth or the family's anguish. During the travesty of their search, the psychopathy of military rule takes shape—the unconscionable acts of violence, disdain of the law, desperation, and incomprehensible cruelties. *Missing* dramatizes the political metamorphosis of one American father—Ed Horman—whose patriotism turns to distrust, anger, and finally radicalism. Until U.S. intervention killed his son, Horman had relied on his government to make humane foreign policy decisions. Like many deluded Americans, he believed democracy was a steadfast constellation in the night sky. Now democracy is a corporate designer country where Madison Avenue ad campaigns are no longer enough to crush popular movements that might lead to nationalization of industry. The disposability of human life is a function of the international corporate "monopoly" game, moral invisibility, and a lapse of all social reason. *Missing* is a vena cava reenactment of one family's loss and dizzy descent into disillusionment. Shot on location in Mexico, it is a mainline political horror film, where street executions and the stench of odium will hit as hard as reality. Intuitive acting. The best direction possible. Vividly memorable. Popularly received.

Also recommended: *Salvador.*

THE MISSION

With Jeremy Irons, Robert DeNiro, Aidan Quinn. Produced by David Puttman. Directed by Roland Joffe. Written by Robert Bold. Photography by Chris Menges. Music by Ennio Morricone. USA. English and Indian languages. Color. 126 minutes. 1989.

South American Indians suffer the approach
of European imperialists.

"I was trained as a mercenary." Robert DeNiro killed his own brother in a duel and now works in perpetual penitence with the missionaries. He is driven by self-loathing to pull tin goods up waterfalls with his teeth. In his eyes is something so desolate that he will forfeit his life to it. He works with the Jesuits at San Carlos Mission above the falls, trying to save the Indians from the advances of time. He and Jeremy Irons are lost in a lost world, bringing God to the people of the rain forest. The innocence of nature and the allure of primitive life infects them, and they will watch everything they work for, everything they pray for, and everything they live for be crushed by the Portuguese colonialist slave traders. To these commerce-minded invaders into the sanctuaries of traditional life, the Indian is nothing but "an animal with a human voice." The last priest was killed, tied to a cross, and sent downstream over the falls. Irons has replaced him. "They are not naturally animals," he tells the Portuguese, "they are naturally spiritual.... We are going to make Christians of these people." But on the trade routes, animals with human voices are good for something. Christians are not. The mission is attacked and burned to the ground. The Guarani populations are ravaged. The priests are killed. DeNiro rejects his vows to lead a futile retaliation. The entire last half-hour of the film is a genocidal bloodletting—children are shot down in choir robes and the remnant of the San Carlos Mission is left smoldering with corpses and relics of faith and trust in God. Morricone's score suspends *The Mission* over an abyss of uncertainty, at the edge of which angels are lamenting to heaven about the transcendent sins of humankind. In *The Mission*, the rain forest's intoxicating natural beauty is a sanctuary for imperial crime. Nothing is on the screen that does not glorify idealism and then sacrifice it at the stake of economic totalitarianism. DeNiro, at last, is frozen in death, a symbol of subjugation and defeat. "The world is thus." "No. Thus have we made the world."

Also recommended: *Raoni.*

MISSISSIPPI BURNING

With Gene Hackman, Willem Dafoe, Frances McDormand, Brad Dourif, R. Lee Ermey, Gailard Sartain. Produced by Frederick Zollo and Robert F. Colesberry. Directed by Alan Parker. Written by Chris Gerolmo. Cinematography by Peter Biziou. Music by Trevor Jones. USA. English. Color. 112 minutes. 1989.

The FBI solves the mystery of who killed three northern civil rights workers in Mississippi in the 1960s.

This is one of the few films made about the civil rights movement. Still, critics lashed at it with whips, wondering whether a film that rewrites the truth about the civil rights movement is better than no movie at all. *Mississippi Burning* supposedly tells the story of the investigation of the murders of civil rights workers Chaney, Goodman, and Schwerner, which was a national scandal in the headlines for weeks after it happened. So, if you are going to organize cameras, and a film crew, to tell this well-known story, you should probably tell the truth. Instead, Alan Parker made a film about a fictionalized organization that is supposed to be true. The truth is, however, that the FBI appeared on the scene only under some duress because J. Edgar Hoover really didn't believe civil rights was the FBI's problem. Blacks have been risking their lives and giving their lives for centuries, and the FBI comes along and takes the credit. The film could have focused on how blacks have struggled and died, which would have been astonishing enough to most viewers. Instead, in this film they are all but helpless and the FBI is the savior of the world. Maybe next they'll make a film about how the CIA was down there, too. Another problem is that the civil rights movement was an honest-to-God calamity raging across the country and the nightly news throughout the 1960s, but you don't get any sense of that in this film. There are just a few sad, secret things that happened to blacks in the south because of racism and the venom of the Klan. But the FBI fixed all that. As a story the film succeeds. Gene Hackman succeeds. It's not a bad film. It's well-acted, but possibly to the wrong point. You have to praise the intent of the filmmakers. You have to give them the benefit of the doubt and assume that their intentions were the best. I would recommend that people see this film, but not without having first read this review.

Also recommended: *Betrayed.*

MISTER JOHNSON

With Maynard Eziashi, Pierce Brosnan, Edward Woodward, Denis Quilley, Nick Reding, Jerry Linus, Beatie Edney. Produced by Michael Fitzgerald. Directed by Bruce Beresford. Written by William Boyd based on the novel by Joyce Cary. Photography by Peter James. Music by Georges Delerue. U.K. English. 103 minutes. 1990.

Black man in British colonial Africa loses everything in his effort to be British.

What we all dream for in films is that they not be too subtle nor too obvious. This one succeeds so well at both that we aren't precisely sure about much except that we should have felt sorry for Mister Johnson (Eziashi) and did not. This is a film about materialism and cultural confusion and people trying to swim upstream to some idealized social spawning ground. It's about the minor clerk playing the fall-guy, the way minors do worldwide and maybe always will. It isn't so much the tragedy of colonialism as it is the tragedy of classism. The widespread barbarities typically inflicted on aborigines by French, British, Dutch, and other quick-tempered imperialists were not parceled into this film. British Harry Rudbeck (Brosnan) is a wise and forgiving cultural interloper. He wants to build a road—people have done worse. He's single-minded, but not cruel. He believes in civilization the way a lot of people still do. There is a racist in the film who will be killed trying to prevent Mr. Johnson from grand theft of his cash drawer. And Johnson, who cons black and white alike, is happy to die trying too hard to be white. The trouble with the film or perhaps the genius of it, is that we feel sorrier for the road-builder than we do for the desperate clerk. Brosnan is caught between two worlds. He is both subject and object—a misfit with poise and polished survival skills. We get the feeling that although the story was filmed in Africa and is full of drop-dead shots of Nigeria, it isn't about Africa or Mr. Johnson at all, but about something ruinously more common. Frames are joltingly cut artifacts, blisteringly beautiful earthen empires sheltering unknowable black beings in ruby-red robes. It's a place where darkness descends at night and roads are built by bare-backed workers pounding the bush with log poles. The place dominates the characters. It reduces them, and thus we focus on the wrong thing. We find ourselves wishing that the slight drama would take its flags and bugles and move on. Delerue dims his genius to match the awesomely unlikely ending with Lassie music—sad things have happened, after all, and nothing is the way is should be.

Also recommended: *Black and White in Color.*

MODERN TIMES

With Charlie Chaplin, Paulette Goddard, Stanley J. Sanford, Henry Berg-man, Allen Garcia. Writing, production, direction, and music by Charlie Chaplin, assisted by Carter De Haven and Henry Bergman. USA. Silent and English. Black and white. 10 reels. 1936.

A factory worker is overcome by the tools of industrialization.

You've heard of continuous motion syndrome? How about continuous employment disorder? How about chronic brute bolt fatigue? How about the days before robotics deified mass production when Charlie Chaplin worked somewhere near the epicenter of monotony in a plant with gears through the floor that didn't know the difference between sheet metal and the hired help? The man is defenseless. The age of giant mammals has been replace by the age of gigantic machines. The sad difference is that humans didn't have to *live* with the dinosaurs. There's a boss with a big screen who easily singles out Chaplin since he's wan-dered off the assembly line with his dino pliers and is tightening or threatening to tighten everything his man-eating wrench jaws hunger for. It's off to the mind-refinery detox depot for Charlie. After the gruel-ing cure, he's back on the streets, meeting Paulette Goddard playing an orphan waif who is to orphan waifs what super novas are to corn-cob pie. She's a big, big star, in case you didn't know. She teams up with Chaplin who manages to get mistaken for a communist because he has been mistaken for a union leader because he was standing (where else?) in a working-class riot. So now he's in jail for sabotaging the in-dustrial domination of the world. At this point, he would just as soon stay there. It's steady work. When they put him out, he wants back in, but he can't make it. So he and Goddard do this and that. He gets a job as a night watchman and puts on a precision roller-skating exhibition. And he gets fired again. It's the Depression. A mill opens, and thou-sands clamor for jobs. How did the working class go so wrong? Goddard and Chaplin are joined at the hip despite it all. For daring to capitalize on the industrial age, *Modern Times* was banned in Italy as communist propaganda.

Also recommended: *Strike.*

MOTHER

With Vera Baranovskaya and M. Batalof. Directed by Vsevolod Pudovkin. Camera by Anatoli Golovnya. From the book by Maxim Gorky. Sound effects track added in 1968. USSR. Silent with English titles. Black and white. 75 minutes. 1926.

A peasant woman is transformed into a revolutionary hero in Tsarist Russia.

While other Russian filmmakers focus on instruments of domination and the sociologic uproar of revolution, Vsevolod Pudovkin singles out the nascent spark of purpose in a woman bent to the will of her husband and the will of the state. Pudovkin enters the prison of the working poor to create a legend of the potential that is nurtured at the lowest ranks of oppression and to reveal why women are the most powerful revolutionaries. Her husband and son are factory serfs. They live in a severe world and are the bedrock of totalitarianism. They possess only one precious remnant of another time. On the bare walls of their room is a hand-carved clock, which her husband pulls down and threatens to sell. It falls to the floor, spilling out its hope. As she gathers the delicate pieces in her hands she sees that there is nothing left now to treasure, nothing to prize. There is nothing but the terror and the emptiness of absolute poverty. The military has been mobilized by the factory where the men's stamina and strength is used to keep them poor. Unions have formed. She begs them not to join the strike. But her husband is killed, and when the police come, she shows them where her son hides the gun he used in the protests. To yield is to survive. To yield is to win something from them. Submission—to succeed—must be unconditional. At her son's trial, she sits in the courtroom, waiting for new decrees of subjugation. When the verdict comes, "hard labor," her eyes reflect nothing, but she stands and raises her fist and cries out from the asylum of her urgency, "No!" This solitary action restores her. The weariness recedes. The anger rejuvenates her. She joins the strikers and leads an attack on the prison to liberate the workers. Her son is freed to fight beside her against the advancing military guard. His is shot down in the battle, and she wipes the blood from his face before lifting his banner high in defiance of the Tsarist state. Her courage and rebellion have made her young again. She dies beautiful in her passionate love of freedom and is trampled under the hooves of the cavalry horses—a symbol of the immortal voice of liberty never to be silenced. Only Pudovkin could do it this way.

Also recommended: *No Regrets for Our Youth* and *Our Daily Bread*.

THE MOUSE THAT ROARED

With Peter Sellers, Jean Seberg, David Kossoff, William Hartnell. Directed by Jack Arnold. Screenplay by Roger MacDougall and Stanley Mann, from the novel *The Wrath of the Grapes* by Leonard Wibberley. Produced by Walter Shenson and Jon Pennington. Photography by John Wilcox. Music by Edwin Astley. English. U.K. Color. 83 minutes. 1959.

A small country invaded the U.S. and winds up controlling the future of the world.

The Mouse that Roared is not the best movie in the world, but it doesn't care. It's amazingly modest, but that's how mice are. It shuns the limelight on principle. It. doesn't want to defy the law of gravity; it just wants to talk about defying it. The idea is to declare war on the U.S., lose, and collect foreign aid. So the diminutive Republic of Fenwick sends a group of combatants under the leadership of Peter Sellers to attack New York City. Once in New York, nothing goes according to the plan, which was to lose. The force of ten defeats the mighty industrial nation by accidentally capturing the Q-bomb and its creator and taking them back to Fenwick as diplomatic hostages. The Q-bomb, while only the size of a football, has an explosive capacity capable of destroying the world. The U.S. has no alternative but to give in to Fenwick's demand for one million dollars in aid, part of which needs to be in the form of indoor plumbing fixtures. Then Sellers refuses to return the bomb. He patiently explains to the U.S. agent, "Now there's a Q-bomb, soon everyone else will invent one. Then there'll be an X, Y, and Zed bomb. We thought things would be better after the war [World War II] but in many ways they weren't, what with all these bombs and so on." He wants total disarmament. He wants the United Nations to let the little nations of the world look after the bomb, ". . . we want this League of Little Nations to watch over things to make it all go smoothly." "How will you talk them in to it?" the emissary wants to know. "Well, otherwise, we'll blow up the world." "Then you'll blow up, too." "The way we see it, we'll be blown up eventually if we don't get disarmament." The big nations comply. Peace comes and the arms race stalls and everyone on Earth can stop stockpiling and start wondering what to do with all the spare money. It's just crazy enough to work. Peter Sellers gives the impression of being the only person in the world who could have played the part of the Fenwick mouse. Filmmakers cleared the streets of New York City by scheduling street filming for Sunday.

Also recommended: *Dr. Strangelove.*

MR. HOOVER AND I

With Emile de Antonio, John Cage, and Nancy de Antonio. Produced, written and directed by Emile de Antonio. Cinematography by Morgan Wesson. USA. English. Color. 90 minutes. 1989.

A close-up look at J. Edgar Hoover and Emile de Antonio.

"If I were asked to choose a villain from the history of this country, I would choose Hoover." According to de Antonio, John Edgar Hoover was a rabid anti-communist who pushed for the electric chair for Ethel Rosenberg. He conceptualized "custodial detention," which was responsible for the unconstitutional imprisonment of thousands of Japanese-Americans during World War II. When this idea became unpopular, he changed the name of the program to "do not file." Records for future custodial detentions were to be kept "unfiled" and known only to a few trusted workers. De Antonio's FBI file was opened when he was sixteen years old and joined the Young Communist League.

Later, Hoover tried to interfere with de Antonio's production of *Vietnam: In the Year of the Pig*. There were bomb threats, and Hoover was instrumental in preventing the film from being seen by large audiences. De Antonio tells us all this while standing perhaps a little unvaryingly in front of the camera. His monologue is interrupted by a few still photos of Hoover, a few scenes of himself lecturing before a high school class, and several segments with friend John Cage, with whom he talks while Cage makes homemade health bread. These discussions and the discussions with Nancy de Antonio as she gives her father a haircut seem to be quite off the topic of Mr. Hoover altogether. It's a temptation to conclude that they have nothing to do with Hoover or the CIA. But there is something edgy about quick assumptions in the land of well-kneaded dough. Men who have concerned their entire lives with perfecting reality are busy at something. The way I see it, if Emile de Antonio wants to film himself getting a haircut and chatting with Cage, it's fine with me. After all, the title is *Mr. Hoover and I*. I get the general idea about Hoover, and if I feel I need to know more, I guess that's what libraries are for. This was de Antonio's last film, released to festivals just a few weeks before he died in 1989. Perhaps his appearance in front of the camera was a way of saying goodbye.

Also recommended: *Point of Order, Vietnam: In the Year of the Pig,* and *Underground.*

MR. KLEIN

With Alain Delon, Juliet Berto, Michel Lonsdale, Suzanne Flon, Massimo Girotti, Francine Berge, Jeanne Moreau. Produced by Raymond Danon, Alain Delon, Robert Kupferberg, and Jean-Pierre La Brande. Directed by Joseph Losey. Screenplay by Franco Solinas. Photography by Gerry Fisher. Music by Egisto Macchi and Pierre Porte. France. In French dubbed into English. Color. 123 minutes. 1977.

A man is arrested by the Nazis in a case of mistaken identity.

"She is of a non-European race . . . of Semitic origin—Judaic, Armenian, or Arab. Case is questionable." In France in 1942, desperate men and women hired doctors to determine if they were Jews. Skin type, bone structure—these things could exalt you or condemn you. Mr. Klein (Delon) is not subject to such invasions of his vanity. He has never had to prove who he is. He's an Aryan in the business of under-pricing goods brought to him by Jews raising money to leave France. He buys heirlooms and works of art, sometimes spilling the coins on the floor so the seller must bend to gather them up. He's done well from the war. But somewhere in the sea of documents generated by fascism, he is mistaken for another Robert Klein—a Jew. He is unable to find this man or excise from his records this lesion of injustice. Without his grandmother's birth certificate, he can't even use a public toilet. He plans to sell certain things to raise money to escape France, but before he can arrange it, he is arrested and herded into a boxcar with hundreds of others being transported to the Nazi camps. The film is heavily into method and is tensionless in parts, but it contains a cogent character-ization by Alain Delon, as a victim of intolerance.

Also recommended: *The Blum Affair*.

MR. SMITH GOES TO WASHINGTON

With Jimmy Stewart, Jean Arthur, Claude Rains, Beulah Bond, Edward Arnold, Guy Kibbee, Thomas Mitchell, Eugene Pallette, H.B. Warner, William Demarest. Produced and directed by Frank Capra. Screenplay by Sidney Buchman, based on the book *The Gentleman From Montana* by Lewis R. Foster. Photography by Joseph Walker. Musical score by Dimitri Tiomkin. USA. English. Black and white. 125 minutes. 1939.

A big-hearted politician from a small town gets elected to the United States Senate and goes to D.C. with a lot to learn.

Mr. Smith Goes to Washington is one of America's "corruption in gov-ernment" classics. It's a simple story of a simple guy who idolizes stat-ues and believes anything he reads, as long as it is carved in marble. He goes to D.C., like others before him, to find out how democracy really works. He's been appointed as a "born stooge," "boy ranger," "bird lover," "young patriot," "simpleton of all times," replacement for Senator Sam Foley, who was a team player on the Willard Creek scam and who chose a very bad time to die. Smith arrives on the Mall in such a patriotic thrall that he sees all the monuments through soft-focus lenses. What with the "Capitol dome sparkling away under the old sun," his only wish in life is to introduce legislation to establish a national boy's camp on the graft-infested banks of Willard Creek. But even though all those industry smear artists and corrupt politicians are now in cahoots to drive him back to boy's town, Smith filibusters for twenty-three hours, reading from the Constitution, reciting long-neglected democratic ideals, pleading his innocence, and crying about the decay of trust in government, until, badly in need of a shave and treacherously hoarse, he faints into a heap of purely bogus hate mail from home. This performance wins everyone to his side and clears his name. It busts the land grab deal. Even though the movie ends here, we presume that industry will never sway the Senate again and that a national boy's camp will be built from the pennies, nickels, and dimes sent in by America's "boys of all creeds and *kinds*." It's too daring to be fiction. Appropriate acting on all sides. I see the world is run by white males, who keep glamorous females as pets. Jimmy Stewart is his own clone cousin in this role. There are lots of pretty shots of Washington, D.C., too.

Also recommended: *Advise and Consent.*

MUSIC BOX

With Jessica Lange, Armin Mueller-Stahl, Frederic Forrest, Lukas Haas, Donald Moffat. Produced by Irwin Winkler. Directed by Costa-Gavras. Screenplay by Joe Eszterhas. Photography by Patrick Blossier. Music by Philippe Sarde. USA. English and Hungarian with titles. Color. 124 minutes. 1989.

Woman lawyer discovers her father is wanted as a Nazi war criminal and chooses to represent him in court.

Legitimacy is the tangible evidence of innocence. In *Music Box*, nothing is tangible, and innocence will disintegrate under the combined talents of Costa-Gavras, Mueller-Stahl, and Lange. Her father is accused;

she will defend him because he is innocent. She will defend him against the special investigator (Forrest) and against the witnesses sobbing of tortures and lists with certain names and wild incriminations. The law protects him against hysteria. Lange is a magnificent apostle of the gospel of truth. Stories of cruelties told by men and women with faltering memories hazed by the pain of unbearable events register nothing inside her. Instead she registers only terror that someone, perhaps herself, will misinterpret the intensity of her cross-examination of victims of persecution. She discredits the anguish and disallows evidences of atrocities and Mueller-Stahl is acquitted. Headlines announce the verdict. Children who didn't quite understand are now happily embraced. And she drives to the address on the canceled checks. She would like to ask about the money sent for so many years to this house. She might have asked her father but prefers to drive and talk to whoever she finds there. The lady gives her an antique music box. As she lifts the lid to hear the chiming classics, photos of her father wind out of the machine one by one. He's wearing an SS uniform and aiming his field revolver at the heads of innocent Jews including children. The photos are falling because she can't hold them. Her talent had confused the sobbing witnesses. And the jury was eased into a verdict defined by precedent and limitations of the introduction of exhibits. She shows him the photographs—pointing at the child, asking about the child. He's sorry to see that she's been brainwashed by the communists. His prejudice is subterranean. His evil is invisible, but now it is the only thing she can see. Jessica Lange is an actress of such depth of talent that her body and her mind seem dominated by it. The film is dominated by it. She gives the film all the energy it has. She is brilliant.

Also recommended: *QB VII*.

MY BRILLIANT CAREER

With Judy Davis, Sam Neill, Wendy Hughes, Robert Grubb, Max Cullen, Pat Kennedy. Produced by Margaret Fink. Directed by Gillian Armstrong. Screenplay by Eleanor Witcombe, from the novel by Miles Franklin. Photography by Don McAlpine. Music by Nathan Waks. Australia. English. Color. 90 minutes. 1979.

**A young girl rejects all expectation to pursue
her career as a writer.**

Somehow director Armstrong has made such a powerful case for both possible outcomes of this feminist drama that audiences will be unsure what should become of Sybylla Melvyn (Davis). Should she remain in the flamboyantly rustic decay of the outback, writing novels full of sensual melodrama? Or should she choose to marry the man carved out of marble (Neill), wear dresses that refine her body, and view inviting expanses of farmland from a trellised promenade while nursing iced limeade? Will she forget about her hair and lean over a small black typewriter in a darkened room? Or will she wrestle with Neill in orchards and dare both him and herself to be tempted? She seems capable of both. There is something so fierce and intricate about the love between them that it seems incapable of being split by dramatic device. *My Brilliant Career* is a film of feral visual beauty. It moves from canopy bed to the howling wilderness and back again at the very best moment. Davis is a little too wild wherever she goes, pressing at invisible limits. That is what fascinates Neill. They intrigue one another. He would have let her write books, and live in a tree, bear no children, and demand more if she wanted and still they would have been happy. But she prefers a thing closer to total freedom, closer to abandoned limits. She rejects him and seems suddenly not such a potentially great writer after all because she can't see the weak thing inside him that is shattering as he looks at her too long because he can't believe she has refused him. This fabulously beautiful film is a milestone in Australian cinema, a milestone for Davis, a milestone for Armstrong, and a tribute to the creative spirit.

Also recommended: *Slave of Love.*

NASHVILLE

With David Arkin, Barbara Baxley, Ned Beatty, Karen Black, Ronee Blakley, Timothy Brown, Keith Carradine, Geraldine Chaplin, Robert Doqui, Shelly Duvall, Allen Garfield, Henry Gibson, Scott Glenn, Barbara Harris, Jeff Goldblum, Michael Murphy, Christine Raines, Bert Remsen, Lily Tomlin, Keenan Wynn, Elliot Gould, Julie Christie, Donna Denton, James

Dan Calvert. Produced and directed by Robert Altman. Written by Joan Tewkesbury. Photographed by Paul Lohmann. Music by Richard Baskin. USA. English. Color. 159 minutes. 1975.

Not just a slice of the 1960s; more like the whole cherry pie.

Nashville is Altman's anti-establishment leviathan, substituting inspiration, as usual, for good reviews. The film is towering in an unapologetic micro-genre, understanding that good actors make good films no matter what year it is and that character development never went out of style and never will. It's got no pretensions because it's a film about people learning that there is no logical order to the universe and that brains mean nothing next to talent, and talent means nothing next to ambition, and ambition means nothing next to popular opinion, and popular opinion means nothing next to blind luck, and blind luck means nothing at all. The undeserving fame of some is balanced by the undeserving anonymity of others. As for *Homo sapiens*, some die, some fly, and some write home about it. And insanity, as they say, is a normal person's reaction to mass mental mania. *Nashville* follows the political campaign of Hal Phillip Walker (played by Michael Murphy—champion of unpretentiousness) as he puts together country-western hoedowns for his tremendously uncharismatic campaign. He is not particular which political party performers have signed with as long as they show up and perform. There are a couple dozen major characters in *Nashville*, plus a couple dozen minor ones connected to each other by the Tewkesbury script—an elaborate device of interlaced stories and sub stories of love, fear, ambition, infatuation, and bad electrical wiring. Each character has his or her own plot. Each is a misfit in history. Each is choking on destiny. *Nashville* is a commentary on the 1960s that carries over to the eternity of the present. Fame is fleeting. Power is fleeting. Love is fleeting. If you want it done right, call the plumber. Never give up. Lead—do not follow. Trust no one, especially Keith Carradine beckoning you from the doorway of an alternative universe.

Also recommended: *Buffalo Bill and the Indians*.

NASTY GIRL

With Lena Stolze, Michael Gahr, Monika Baumgartner, Elisabeth Bertram, Fred Stillkrauth. Produced, written, and directed by Michael Verhoeven. Photography by Axel de Roche. Music by Mike Herting. Germany. In German with English titles. Color. 92 minutes. 1989.

A young girl upsets hometown residents by researching local events during the Third Reich.

She's adorable. She's articulate. She's not nasty, until she starts asking around about what went on in Pfilsing during World War II, which does not happen until halfway through the movie. Before this she is just the oldest daughter in a very photogenic, open-minded family, with many cute laughs folded into the offbeat fabric of her young life. We are charmed. We anticipate great things. But greatness is not thrust upon us. By the time the nasty girl (Stolze) gets around to writing "My Hometown During the Third Reich" for her school paper, the story slips into very calm waters. Part of the reason for this is that nobody wants to talk to her about the Reich. Few give interviews. Some are hostile. Others hint that Pfilsing has secrets. After uncovering a few references to "Aryan purity" and concentration camps, she descends into a living, breathing limbo of squelched efforts to find the truth. "The files are closed." "The files are on loan." "The files are lost." "The files will be inaccessible until fifty years after the deaths of all the people involved." Voices over the phone advise: "Leave town." "Pack your things, commie bitch." "I'm proud to be a German." "I'll ruin you." Even her husband soon runs out of patience with a wife who won't stop. The ham-a-minute beginning is perhaps meant as a comparison to how things change when you ask unpopular questions. Once she was a harmless child. Now she's a nasty girl, graduating from a student essay to an adult book in her "fearless struggle for truth." But her rise to nasty fame is repetitive, unenlightening, and at times confusing ramble between the courts and the archives and the deep blue yawn. We are very clear on how whopping a cover-up can be, but maybe some of the footage could have been put to more revelational use. Director Verhoeven does everything possible to jazz things up. There are remarkable gray-grained, photo-enlarged sets that make history seem to be looming all around these deplorable acts of deceit. There are far fetched visual "events." It is clear Verhoeven has a rapport with Stolze, who is very good. It's an unusual movie in a lot of ways but perhaps less indicting than audiences might have withstood.

Also recommended: *The White Rose.*

NETWORK

With Faye Dunaway, William Holden, Peter Finch, Robert Duvall, Wesley Addy, Ned Beatty, Arther Burghardt, Bill Burrows, John Carpenter, Jordan Charney, Kathy Cronkite, Darryl Hickman. Narrated by Lee Richardson. Produced by Howard Gottfried. Directed by Sidney Lumet. Written by Paddy Chayefsky. Photography by Owen Roizman. Music by Elliot Lawrence. USA. Color. 120 minutes. 1976.

In the future, networks will sacrifice anything for a clean rating share.

Howard Beale (Finch) is a successful news anchor with a 28 share dropping to 22 and to 12 and then off the UBS payroll. He's given a week's notice and decides, "I'm going to blow my brains out right in the middle of the seven o'clock news." William Holden is fascinated. "Helluva rating—50 share easy. We could make a series, 'Suicide of the Week,' 'Execution of the Week,' 'Terrorist of the Week.' Assassinations, mad bombers, auto smashups . . . 'The Death Hour.'" Hmmm. It would be funny if the new programming zealot (Dunaway) wasn't already interviewing the Ecumenical Liberation Army hoping to get someone on the air to "articulate the popular rage." The revolutionary ELA has sent videotapes of a bank heist and Dunaway wants more—authentic acts of political terrorism. "I want angry shows. I want counterculture. I want anti-establishment." And she wants Finch on the air as a "latter-day prophet, a magnificent messianic figure inveighing against the hypocrisies of out time" and articulating the popular rage, "The air is unfit to breathe, food unfit to eat, things are worse than bad. We sit in the house and say, 'Please, just leave us alone in out living rooms with our toasters ovens and T.V.'s and steel belted radials.' . . . I want you to get mad. I'm a human being, goddamn it. My life has value. I want you to get up, go to the window, stick your head out and yell, 'I'm mad as hell, and

I'm not going to take it any more.'" He's a 42-rating share sensation. And so are the Ecumenicals. Diane Christiansen—"racist lacky of the imperialist ruling class"—meet Maureen Hobbs—"bad-ass commie nigger." Hobbs is a nonviolent communist party leader, but she will host the terror hour if it means she can speak to fifty million people a week. Off-screen she rages about contract negotiations. "Don't fuck with my distribution costs. I'm making a lousy $215 per segment. I'm paying William Morris 10 percent off the top. I'm giving this turkey ten thou per segment, another five for this fruitcake, and don't start no shit with me about a piece again. I'm paying Metro 20 percent for all foreign and Canadian distribution, and that's after recruitment. The Communist Party is not going to see a nickel of the goddamned show until we go into syndication. I'm not giving the pseudo-insurrectionary sectarian a piece of my show, I'm not giving them script approval and I sure ain't cutting them in on my distribution charges." To which the ELA responds, "You fucking fascist." Meanwhile, Finch's anger has turned toward the corporate takeover of UBS. He is locked in a low-lit boardroom with Ned Beatty, who gives one of the greatest speeches ever written for film. "There are no nations. There are no people. There are no Russians, no Arabs, no Third Worlds, no West. There is only one holistic system of systems. One vast interwoven, interacting multi-varied, multi-national dominion of dollars—petro dollars, electro dollars, Reichmarks, rubles, pounds, shekels. That is the atomic and sub-atomic and galactic structure of things today. . . . There is no democracy. There is only IBM, ITT, AT&T, DuPont, Dow, Union Carbide, Exxon—these are the nations of the world today. The world is a business, Mr. Beale. Democracy is a dying giant, a sick, sick decaying political concept. It's a nation of two-hundred million totally unnecessary human beings as replaceable as piston rods." So Beale inveighs against the tube itself. "You dress like the tube, you eat like the tube, you raise your children like the tube. It's mass madness. You maniacs. You are the real thing—turn them off. Right in the middle of this sentence I am speaking." His rating plunge and he's gunned down by the Ecumenicals on the Mao Tse Tung Hour in a "fuselage of automatic rifle fire." "This was the story of Howard Beale, killed for lousy ratings." Screenwriter Paddy Chayefsky was a man of prophetic insight and unswayable philosophic integrity whose screenplays were a creative manifestation of his powerful intellect. He feared nothing. In one of his few public appearances at the 1976 Academy Awards ceremony, he charmed some and annoyed others. When called to the podium to accept the award for best actor on behalf of the recently deceased Finch, he said, "I don't know what I'm doing up here," looking down at

Finch's widow (the black half of an interracial marriage) "There's only one person who should accept the award for Peter, and that's his wife, Eletha. Come up here, Eletha, and accept your award."

Also recommended: *Max Headroom.*

NEVER CRY WOLF

With Charles Martin Smith, Brian Dennehy, Samson Joran, Zachary Ittimangnaq. Produced by Jack Couffer, Joseph Strick, and Lewis Allen. Directed by Carroll Ballard. Photography by Hiro Narita. Screenplay by Curtis Hanson, Sam Hamm, and Richard Kletter, based on the book by Farley Mowat. Narration written by C.M. Smith, Eugene Corr, and Christina Lueshcer. Music by Mark Isham. USA. English. Color. 105 minutes. 1983.

A man goes to Alaska to study wolves and stays on to protect the wilderness and animals.

Charles Martin Smith is a nerd-hero-scientist, alone and terribly tiny on the tundra, surrounded by crates of supplies and a canoe full of beer in a frozen valley vanishing into mountain crags. There's nothing but him and the creaking glaciers and a haunting sound, possibly the howling of a thousand wolves. Possibly the ones he's here to study, *Canis lupus Arcticus.* As Dennehy coasts away in the bush plane, Smith trots alongside, "Remember my position." "Sure." "And . . . what . . . is my position?" As the plane chugs into the air, the answer chugs into the air, "Beats the hell out of me-e-e-e." It's getting dark, and the howling is getting closer. The object of his study is the object of his terror. To build "Lupus Base One," he will need help from the Eskimos. He'll need to read government rules and ignore them all. He will collect dung instead of stomach contents to see if wolves are eating caribou. He will reject "inconspicuous distance" and camp directly across from the den. He will do as they do—he pees on all the boundaries. He will eat as they eat—mice, boiling little bodies in chemical beakers or roasting them on toothpicks. He apologizes to the Eskimos, "I don't eat fish." He names his two wolves George and Angelene. Their white winter coats contrast strikingly to that of the dusty brown cubs. He notes,

"Wolves mate for life. There is a constant, varied display of affection." He mimics the howling on his oboe. The sounds echoes through far-away canyons. Now that we've almost forgotten them, the caribou thunder up over a hill and surround Smith, who is sunbathing on the tundra. The caribou are a symphonic and imperial sight. Their breath hangs in the air around them. If Narita's photography is not the best in the world, it's very, very, close. And when we've almost forgotten him, Dennehy returns, piloting would-be entrepreneurs into the sparkling lakebeds to consider hotels and bottled water. Smith fires into the air to drive them away from Lupus Base One. Have they already killed George and Angelene? When the parent wolves never return, he plays the oboe to attract other adults and writes, "There are no orphans among the wolves." Cunning simplicity all around. The filmmakers should receive some kind of reward for filming very far north of Hollywood, California. Isham's score seems to emanate from the very lungs of the wolves and the caribou and the wild, wild, wilderness.

Also recommended: *Dances With Wolves*.

1984

With John Hurt, Richard Burton, Suzanna Hamilton, Gregory Fisher, Cyril Cusack. Produced by Simon Perry. Directed by Michael Radford. Written by Michael Radford and Jonathan Gems, from the book by George Orwell. Photography by Roger Deakins. Music by The Eurythmics and Dominic Muldowney. United Kingdom. English. Color. 115 minutes. 1984.

"Who controls the past, controls the future. Who controls the present, controls the past."

1984 is set in the ravishing bombed-out ruins and ruthless misery of the year 1984, where "everything fades into mist, the past is erased, the erasure forgotten, the lie becomes the truth, and then becomes a lie again." Big Brother is on the wall T.V. in every home twenty-four hours a day, every day. You can lower the volume, but you can't turn off the commercial-free propaganda. Big Brother opposes marriage, families, and sex because they erode public oneness. Women in the Anti-sex League are celibate vessels of artificial insemination for the state. Thought control means language control. Vocabularies are shrinking. New dictionaries are smaller than old ones. With no revolutionary words, there can be no revolution. Winston Smith (Hurt) works at the communications center, rewriting news stories for the glory of the state. At home, he has a secret. "Thought crime is death. Thought crime does not *entail* death. Though crime *is* death. I have committed, even before setting pen to paper, the essential crime that contains all others in it." He is a Citizen of Oceania, still human enough to write his thought crimes into a diary. He is illegally in love. He tells his girlfriend, "I hate purity. I hate goodness. I don't want virtue to exist anywhere. I want everyone corrupt." They meet in a gray room in a gray city. Their puncturable pink skin is obvious for miles. Their love is a new kind of pain. They are betrayed, tortured, and trained to think away the love, and they submit. They even deny there was a torment as physical as sex. Now they pull the yoke of uniformity, which rests on them as evenly as air pressure. It is not a story about communists. It is not a story about fascists. *1984* is not a story about other people. It is a story about us. And it's not Orwell's fault that the two hands clasped on the INGSOC symbol are black and white, even though no black actors appear on screen. In movies about oppression, it's especially important to cast the other way. *1984* was made in 1984, which is obvious but meaningful.

Also recommended: *The Crowd.*

1900

With Robert DeNiro, Gerard Depardieu, Donald Sutherland, Burt Lancaster, Sterling Hayden, Dominique Sanda, Laura Betti, Roberto Maccanti, Romolo Valli, Anna-Maria Gherardi, Alida Valle, Werner Bruhns, Francesca Bertini. Produced by Alberto Grimaldi. Directed by Bernardo Bertolucci. Screenplay by Bernardo Bertolucci, Giuseppe Bertolucci, and Franco Arcalli. Photography by Vittorio Storaro. Music by Ennio Morriconi. Italy. English and Italian dubbed. Color. 255 minutes. 1976.

Two young men grow up on opposites sides of fascism during World War II.

Liberation Day, 1945. April in Italy. Young farm women with haying forks are chasing a desperate couple across a field. When they catch them, they stab them. Two-hundred and fifty-five minutes later, we will understand why. This is a story about Alfredo (DeNiro), a fascist, and Olmo (Depardieu), a socialist. Alfredo thinks socialism is a fine idea, but he is unable to part with inherited wealth, passed down from a tyrant father (Lancaster) who blasphemed workers and stole their labor. When they laid in the road in protest, he called them Bolsheviks—he called them semi-Asiatic, mongol subversives. Alfredo will marry Dominique Sanda, and she will come to despise him and be consumed with unhappiness and alcoholism. He accuses her of being in love with Olmo. She says, "Do you think Olmo would have anything to do with the wife of a fascist?" "I am not a fascist. If you call me that again, I will kill you. . . . I'm going to have you locked in an asylum." She's unleashed, "You are disgusting. You are surrounded by arrogant bullies, murderers." "I think I have a heart condition." "You don't have a heart." Partisans are arrested. Olmo cries after them, "The party will not abandon you. We are hundreds, we are thousands." Olmo and Ada disappear from Alfredo's life on the same day. When Olmo returns after the liberation, he pushes Alfredo to the ground shouting, "The Padrone is the enemy of the people." DeNiro looks up from the dirt, "Ada is gone." He has the power to think only of himself. The workers' tribunal charges, "We made the money, you spent it." "I never hurt anyone." *1900* sustains its 255-minute running time by draining the potentially simple saga away into a litany of side stories, none of which can obscure the unobscurable: Morriconi is a sensation; DeNiro is a sensation; Storaro is a god; Sanda gives off gamma rays. It's too bad that Bertolucci wasn't willing to save these creative geniuses from his lost quest for epic grandeur.

Also recommended: *Tree of Wooden Clogs.*

NO REGRETS FOR OUR YOUTH
(WAGA SEISHUN NI KUI NASHI)

With Setsuko Hara, Susumu Fujita, Akitake Kono, Takashi Shimura, Haruko Sugimura, Denjiro Okochi. Directed by Akira Kurosawa. Screenplay by Eijiro Hisaita. Photography by Asakazu Nakai. Music by Tadashi Hattori. Japan. Japanese with English titles. Black and white. 110 minutes. 1946.

A young woman is transformed from a self-absorbed coed into a proletarian hero.

In 1931, in an act of imperialist aggression, Japan invaded Manchuria. Japan would rule over the Chinese people of Manchukuo until pushed out by the Soviets in 1945. Student protests in Japan opposed the "Manchurian Incident," and universities were torn by bitterly repressive opposition movements. As the riots at Kyoto University are struck down and "freedom [is] destroyed, independence buried," Yukie allows the tempest of political unrest to convulse around her. She is a manufactured beauty in western clothes and make-up. She's a perpetually flowering rose fed on flattery. Kurosawa endows Yukie with rare and radiant indifference to anything but her own self-possession. She presumes attention. The heroism of resistance only detracts from her own notoriety of allure. To men, she is an ephemeral beauty. But school is transient. Graduation delivers the students into private life. Yukie's vacuity absorbs her and soon depletes her, and nothing she does has meaning. She's embarrassed to knock on Nogi's door and ask him if she can work with him in his fight against imperialism and against the war. The character is pulled by the power of the narrative toward the dawn of a new rebellion. She will go to prison for marrying a "spy." She will desert pretension and be guided by inner courage. She will wear kimonos and then peasant pants and a straw hat. She will work in rice fields and endure poverty, slander, vengeance, and hardship. Now her long hair is pulled back in braids. Her face is brown from the sun. All traces of vanity and uncertainty have faded. A friend from the city does not recognize the worker archetype. Her face is astonishingly changed. She has become wholly different. From a bourgeois ingenue, Kurosawa creates a model from a billboard of the people's campaign. Witnessing the startling metamorphosis does not make it any less a sensation. *No Regrets for Our Youth* is certainly the most remarkable transformation film ever made.

Also recommended: *24 Eyes*.

NORMA RAE

With Sally Field, Beau Bridges, Ron Liebman, Pat Hingle, Barbara Baxley, Gail Strickland. Produced by Tamara Asseyev and Alex Rose. Directed by Martin Ritt. Screenplay by Irving Ravetch and Harriet Frank, Jr. Photography by John A. Alonzo. Music directed by David Shire. USA. English. Color. 114 minutes. 1979.

A female textile worker fights a courageous battle to form a union in her plant.

Sally Field is Norma Rae—an ordinary person with a "gone wrong" family life and a nonunionized textile plant job. She's not well read. Except for her kids, she's never thought much about anybody but herself. But she will find herself listening to the big city organizer (Liebman) when the bosses at the plant start leaning hard on the employees. They need a union. Why? Same sad story—low pay, poor conditions, bad attitude. The employees are generally law-abiding and acquiescent to the union on the first strike shut-down, prompted by Field standing in her dungarees on a tabletop and holding a cardboard "UNION" sign. Beau Bridges is Field's husband. His function is to feed the kids and stoke his paranoias while Norma is down at the union offices night after night falling a little bit in love with Liebman. If I had been high up in the casting hierarchy of *Norma Rae*, I might not have hired Liebman in the first place to push the talents of Bridges into the background. Liebman's not that plausible as the union organizer being so close to someone's idea of the type—tense, wan, and dreary from so much social-cause thinking. He's from the big city, where apparently all radical leaders are born. There's no way to believe he and Field love each other; and in fact, it's hard to picture Field loving anyone or caring about a union. *Norma Rae* gets four stars in *The Motion Picture Guide*, while other, much better union films are not included at all and novelties of insight like *Buffalo Bill and the Indians* get a blazing zero. I'm here to correct that. I'm giving *Buffalo Bill* as many stars as there are. I'm giving *Norma Rae* fewer—maybe two. Well, there is a lot of sex talk in *Norma Rae* and some fleeting nudity and various conversations about how Norma's life got to be that way. She is a union maid. She does not back down. She's not scared off. That's our Norma, starring in this underlit, less than terse, less than edifying pretension of low-pop nobility.

Also recommended: *Silkwood*.

NORTH BY NORTHWEST

With Cary Grant, Eva Marie Saint, James Mason, Leo Carroll, Martin Landau, Edward Binns, Jesse Royce Landis, Philip Ober. Produced and directed by Alfred Hitchcock. Screenplay by Ernest Lehman. Photography by Robert Burkes. Music by Bernard Herrmann. USA. English. Color. 136 minutes. 1959.

An international intelligence mix-up almost ruins a man's life.

There's something about Cary Grant. At times you want to slug him and at times you want to *be* him. Is this guy ever flustered or confused? Is he ever at a loss? Where does he find all these debonair roles? In *North by Northwest*, his whole life flashes before his eyes, but the only thing he's ever anxious about is that he may appear to be rude. He's kidnapped, arrested, and accused. His life is threatened, and, worst of all, no one believes him, not even his mother. He's Roger Thornhill—a business executive mistaken for a spy, which leads him into a veritable maze of life-threatening, but always surmountable misadventures. And, of course, there's romance. Grant is cast opposite Eva Marie Saint, who loses the struggle to appear less than deified. She is Eve Kendall, bored socialite turned double agent. I am surprised that this pair didn't become joined at the hip in Hollywood movie mythland—they melt into each other's arms, they smile in unison, they outshine the sun. But there's more. The effortlessly galvanizing James Mason is one of the most suave screen personages of all time. He's Phillip VanDamm, spy of a nameless country. This dramatically harmonious troupe lives through one tantalizing escapade after another in their individual quests for the right-living. They drift north by northwest on the trial of the nonexistent George Kaplan, a dummy set up by the CIA to throw James Mason off the trail of the real agent. This plan works splendidly inasmuch as the real agent turns out to be his mistress, Eva Marie Saint. Of course she doesn't really love him. She's faking it for national security. When she meets Mr. Thornhill, she really falls for him while pretending to fall for him while luring him to his doom in Hitchcock's legendary cornfield sequence. This cast must have been a daydream to direct, and we see Hitchcock's genius lavished in one pre-cut scene after another, inventing drama in the movement of a pair of hands, promising and delivering the best he has to offer, which, in this movie, is easy to believe is the best there is. The action scenes aren't apt to be eclipsed in this millennium. A thousand years from now, when people are plugging into 360-degree holographic energy fields, Cary Grant will be there, outrunning a crop duster across an empty Illinois cornfield. In this classic scene, it isn't just man versus plane. It's man alone on a cornfield planet. It's the mutant other-worldliness of road signs and the prairie sky. It's a blacktop to nowhere that reflects no light. It's Hitchcockian alchemy, where crop dusters coalesce from motionless, zirconian skies. It's time, space, and the elements that have waited four billion years to lure Cary Grant into the open. Here Hitchcock pumps expectation into the sonic boom of seconds and magnifies our unborn fears (can he read our minds?). This scene and the finale, filmed atop Mt. Rushmore, will engrave images on your cranial template that no know solvents will ever erase. In a Hitchcockian plot, everything happens for a reason. When you begin to think things are too easy, or too convenient, or too coincidental, the story doubles back and layers everything that's gone before with murky intrigue. Why would progressive thinkers want to see this film? Well, it's irresistible, that's why. We do hear the words "CIA" and "INTERPOL" occasionally, and we get the impression that they are almost indistinguishable and that they inconvenience innocent men like Cary Grant who, through no fault of their own, become the center of attention.

Also recommended: *Slave of Love.*

THE NORTH STAR

With Dana Andrews, Anne Baxter, Farley Granger, Erich von Stroheim, Jane Withers, Walter Huston, Dean Jagger, Walter Brennen, Eric Roberts. Produced by William Cameron Menzies. Directed by Louis Milestone. Written by Lillian Hellman. Photography by James Wong Howe. Music by Aaron Copland, with Ira Gershwin. USA. English. Black and white. 106 minutes. 1943.

Russian peasants struggle to hold back the Third Reich.

This Academy Award winning jumble of everything it pretends to be about was concocted after Franklin Roosevelt suggested that someone make a film about our Allies resisting the Nazis. So, Hellman and Milestone got together and made *The North Star.* The Russians are the ones singing classic folk songs like, "Parents dear, use your tact, if you don't like how we act, do not fret, do not mourn, is it our fault we were born? Tittleeum tum tum." The women all wear babushkas and embroidered blouses and chortle to soaring Copeland overtures while peasant men somehow perform the mazurka to the same thing. Conversations are searing voids. "Wars do not leave people as they were." "The earth belongs to us, the people, if we fight for it, and we will fight for it." "Do men all make noise when they sleep?" "I don't know, I haven't heard all men sleep." Tittleeum. When the Russian peasants are ordered to burn their houses because the Germans are coming, it is sad, so sad— sad as a Gershwin tune can be. The philosophic encounters between von Stroheim and Huston are just plain far-fetched. The only thing I liked about *The North Star* was a scene of some sheep coming up over a hill, but even then they sounded like humans making sheep noises. About as much effort toward historic and cultural accuracy went into this film as the Mad Hatter put into the press releases for his tea party. Screenwriter Hellman called it "a big-time, sentimental, badly directed, badly acted mess." Newspaper magnate William Randolph Hearst called it a Bolshevik film, backed by Stalin. The filmmakers, having created this awesomely aimless box office smash, were called before HUAC to explain what they were up to. It's hard to believe the Committee found enough in it to justify cutting out twenty minutes (every use of the word "comrade," for example) and renaming it *Armored Attack*.

Also recommended: *How Green Was My Valley*.

OCTOBER

With Nikandov and N. Popov. Produced by Sovkino. Directed by Sergei Eisenstein and G. V. Alexandrov. Script by Sergei Eisenstein and G.V. Alexandrov, based on the book *Ten Days that Shook the World* by John Reed. Photography by Eduard Tisse. Music by Dmitry Shostakovich. USSR. Silent with English titles. Black and white. 141 minutes cut to 102 for U.S. release. 1926.

The last days of the 1917 revolution and the formation of the Union of Soviet Socialist Republics.

The USSR wanted a filmic record of the revolutionary struggle for a socialist state. Eisenstein had great resources made available to him to make this film—eleven thousand extras, streets blocked off, power diverted. Many scenes from news archives are replicated virtually to a person. Eisenstein was an artistic fanatic who appreciated the shock value of motion versus stillness—tidal waves of movement awash in clouds of smoke or steam, collages of momentum and power followed by stopclock pauses. All his films are colossal creations of his genius. They testify to the extraordinary talent that was there at the beginning of the film and that validates silent films as being relevant to contemporary problems and the future of filmmaking. If silent films were made for others to tower over, we are still waiting for someone to tower over this one. Anybody who sees *October* will know that film was a monumental power right from the beginning, and Eisenstein had a monumental facility to command it. He has inspired every new generation of filmmakers to the present day. He was a social realist who believed in the people's revolution. He followed changes within the new USSR and he was willing to allow history to back up in scene after scene, removing all references to Trotsky in the film. But if Soviet governments veered from their own ideals, the oppression in Russia at the time of the last Tsar was genuine, and Eisenstein contrasts the fabulous wealth of the empire with the revolutionary's hard want. The spectacle of peasants occupying the Winter Palace pushes contrast to its limits. Eisenstein created with sound—horses' heavy breathing, cannon volleys, snow creaking underfoot, battle cries. He built in extremes—cold, fear, pain, the joy of victory, hunger, ennui, pettiness, and hate. *October* is an almost unbelievably vivid and vital chapter in Soviet history and the history of film.

Also recommended: *Strike.*

THE OFFICIAL STORY
(LOS DESAPARECIDOS)

With Norma Aleandro, Hector Alterio, Analia Castro, Chela Ruis, Chunchuna Villefane, Hugo Arana, Patricio Contreras, Guillermo Battaglia. Produced by Marcelo Pineyro. Directed by Luis Puenzo. Photography by

Felix Monti. Screenplay by Aida Bortnik and Luis Puenzo. Music by Atilio Stampone and Maria Elena Walsh. Argentina. In Spanish with English titles. Color. 112 minutes. 1984.

A conservative woman discovers her daughter was stolen from a "disappeared" mother.

Alicia has led a privileged life. She is married to a successful businessman who grew rich during the military dictatorship of the 1970s. She has lived insulated from the political upheavals of Argentina. In her classes at the high school, she continues to teach the Official Story. Her students increasingly refuse to accept her version of history and challenge her with the truth about the death squads and atrocities of the dictatorship. She turns to another teacher for support. "What does it matter?" he responds, "What does it matter to you if it is true or not? It's not your problem, is it?" When a close friend visits and tells stories of arrests and torture, Alicia begins a tentative investigation that will substantiate the truth of the ruthless repression and the disappearances of thousands of innocent people, "Los Desaparecidos." During the campaign of terror between 1976 and 1983, 30,000 people disappeared in Argentina. Even young children disappeared. Newborn babies of pregnant prisoners were taken at birth and were often adopted by those sympathetic to the junta. Inevitably, Alicia begins to suspect that her own daughter, adopted under unusual conditions, was the daughter of one of the disappeared. She tries to trace details of Gaby's birth. She searches through the photo catalogs—page after page, thousands of faces of disappeared people. She goes to the Plaza do Mayo where mothers march with pictures of their missing children. Her husband demands that she stop her hysterical searching. She tells him that she can't bear to think of a grandmother who is not marching for their daughter, because she doesn't even know the child exists. She continues searching until, finally, there are no illusions left. On that day, Alicia sends Gaby to her mother's. When her husband comes home, he looks in Gaby's room and asks, "Where is she?" Alicia answers, "How does it feel?" "How does what feel?" "How does it feel to not know where your daughter is?"

Also recommended: *Salvador.*

ON THE BEACH

With Fred Astaire, Gregory Peck, Ava Gardner, Anthony Perkins, Donna Anderson, John Tate, Lola Brooks. Produced and directed by Stanley Kramer. Written by John Paxton and James Lee Barrett, based on the novel by Nevil Shute. Photography by Giuseppe Rotunno and Daniel Fapp. Music by Ernest Gold. USA. English. Black and white. 133 minutes. 1959.

Survivors of World War III, living in Australia, cope with the end of human civilization.

You've heard of Donner Pass? Take away the snow, the mountains, the starvation, and the wagons and you end up on a beach in Australia, waiting for fallout to visit the southern hemisphere. However, you are not lost. You know where you are, but that's no consolation. There will be no spring thaw. It's a fascinating premise. Everything *looks* O.K. The people *look* O.K. But the only sign of life left in the rest of the world is a soft drink bottle rocking back and forth on a morse code key at a military base in L.A. It took the nuclear age to set it up. The remnants of humanity in Australia cling unwholesomely to life, faced with the mad enormity of a war that crushed billions into a solitary shoreline. Every sunrise is like a dragnet of doom. If it wasn't for this, though, it wouldn't be that bad—it would be like heaven. There's no working, no money, no private ownership, no pretense. Lots of canned foods and candlelight. No rush hour. The roadways are quiet all the time. Why go places? *On the Beach* doesn't fill our heads with information on the war, about which we presumably know all we will ever need to know. It focuses on these few survivors to see what they're feeling about global thermonuclear campaigns and to find out what they may want to do with their lives, if anything, before they die. If people didn't break into tears at tender moments and carry death pills everywhere they go and pay acute attention to weather reports, we might forget about the RAD thing. For the brave, beautiful, confused survivors, time is not on their side. They are to be pitied because even though they are all U.S. military personnel, or married to someone who is, it was not their fault. I liked Anthony Perkins. Actually, I liked everybody. Only the best people have outlived World War III so far. I had to admire the planet, too—casual enough at the loss. The scenes of Los Angeles void of all life had an uncanny, planetoid spookiness. *On the Beach* has a mellow, snow-drifting plot and is about the most watchable movie of its type. And it would have been even better with fewer refrains of "Waltzing Matilda," even if the lyrics fit the occasion so ironically well.

Also recommended: *The Day After.*

OUR DAILY BREAD

With Karen Morely, Tom Keene, Barbara Pepper, John Qualen. Produced and directed by King Vidor. Written by King Vidor, Elizabeth Hill, and Joseph Mankiewicz. Photography by Robert Plank. Music by Alfred Newman. USA. Silent. Black and white. 74 minutes. 1934.

A Depression-era couple teams up with the migrant homeless to survive on the land.

This is one of those films in which everyone starts out busted and through a series of individually fortunate but cumulatively outlandish lucky breaks rewrites the laws of probability. In King Vidor's version of utopia, he has a married couple with no jobs, no money, and of course, no place to live. It is the middle of the Depression, the stock market has nose-dived, and there are four men to every apple that needs picking. Time for Uncle Success to loan out a farm sitting empty in Vidorville where they can live rent-free if they will just pray for a miracle and sit back waiting for it to happen. Vidor's solution to world economic inequality is to place a sign at the end of the driveway inviting the homeless nomads to drive down the driveway in a steady stream. Some have tools. Others have seeds. Some have money. There are electricians, mechanic, barbers, and just about everything you'd need to open up a good mall. The outside world is just a memory. Until Uncle wants his farm back. Ingenious courtroom antics result in the couple gaining title to the farm. That's how things are in utopia. The little guy can outsmart capitalism just by planting corn. The film is exuberantly overacted by a cast of ecstatics. The whole thing makes me want to run blindfolded off a cliff. If *Our Daily Bread* is Vidor's hint about the radical potential of communes, he actually sustains the myth of the bounties of capitalism and the opportunities waiting for losers in the contest of free enterprise.

We are only to guess how those of us with no rich uncles, situated on farms uphill rather than downhill from crucial water supplies, would make out.

Also recommended: *The Milagro Beanfield War.*

THE OX-BOW INCIDENT

With Henry Fonda, Henry Morgan, Dana Andrews, Mary Beth Hughes, Anthony Quinn, William Eythe. Produced by Lamar Trotti. Directed by William Wellman. Screenplay by Lamar Trotti from the novel by Walter Van Tilberg Clark. Photography by Arther Miller. Music by Cyril J. Mockridge. USA. English. Black and white. 75 minutes. 1942.

A few good men try to save innocent drifters from a lynch mob.

The Ox-bow Incident is a surprising film—surprising that is got made at a time when westerns were dominated by Roy Rogers, Johnny Mac Brown, and jeeps named Nelly-bell. During the 1940s, the good guys won, the bad guys lost, and the hero kissed his horse. In *The Ox-bow Incident*, the horses are usually standing around listening to philosophic conversations about right and wrong. The only heroics are the words spoken, often eloquently, for truth, justice, and the courage it takes to stand by personal beliefs in the face of mob rule. Circumstantial evidence incriminates the three drifters whom Fonda and Morgan try to save from execution. The deputy refuses to wait for the sheriff after a local rancher is killed. He organizes a posse that gives in to the temptations of prairie jurisprudence. Fonda does not believe in the three drifters so much as he believes in the system created to judge the guilty and protect the innocent. Dana Andrews is enveloped in an aura of innocence as a man wrongly accused. They will not beg for their lives. Fonda and Morgan never give up trying to save the three for trial. His two hired hands are suspiciously belligerent and uncooperative. Even as the lynch knot is tied, they convince the mob to think it over until morning. Andrews writes a letter to his wife and children. At dawn the murders take place as planned. The bodies still hang in the tree when the sheriff arrives with proof that they were innocent. He arrests the deputy and all the co-conspirators. Morgan reads Andrews' letter. The simple, honest words ring out over the tragic scene.

Also recommended: *Twelve Angry Men.*

PAISAN

With Carmela Sazio, Robert Van Loon, Dots M. Johnson, Maria Michi. Directed by Roberto Rossellini. Screenplay by Sergio Amidei, Federico Fellini, Roberto Rossellini, and Annalena Limentani, based on the stories by Victor Haines, Marcello Pagliero, Sergio Amidei, Federico Fellini, and Roberto Rossellini. Cinematography by Otello Martelli. Music by Renzo Rossellini. Italy. In English, Italian, and German with titles. Black and white. 120 minutes. 1946.

World War II in vignettes.

An international team of technicians worked at getting this curiously nondescript anti-war film on the screen. It follows the trail of the American advance through Europe, filming various people, most of them nonprofessional actors, coping with war. There are romances turning bad, friendships failing, and orphans without homes. Dots Johnson, a black soldier befriended by an Italian boy, gives the film its only high-echelon performance as a man awakened to the hardships that war inflicted on the children of Italy. This segment also showcases the talents of cinematographer Otello Martelli—the smoldering ruins of Italy, incinerated by the war, awash with shadows and fleeting sunlight and hulking artifacts of chaos. In another segment, Maria Michi is an American health aid hunting for her lost Italian lover. Most of her screen time is spent ducking for cover and running from peril. The last episode takes place in a real monastery with real monks, and you can pretty much forecast the dialogue between the monks and the soldiers on themes of peace, love, and harmony, over a humble supper, of course.

Also recommended: *Western Front 1918.*

THE PARALLAX VIEW

With Warren Beatty, Hume Cronyn, William Daniels, Paula Prentiss.
Produced and directed by Alan Pakula. Screenplay by David Giler and
Lorenzo Semple, Jr., based on the novel by Loren Singer. Photography by
Gordon Willis. Music by Michael Small. USA. English. Color. 102 min-
utes. 1974.

**Warren Beatty faces off with the corporate assassination
machine.**

This film is a feast for the paranoid senses. Yes, you too can have your
worst fears acted out for you on the screen by Warren Beatty, amateur
superhero. Three years after a popular political candidate is assassinated in Seattle's Space Needle, under conditions approximating the
murder of Bobby Kennedy, Beatty learns that of all the witnesses present that day, only three survive. In tracing down possible clues of a conspiracy and cover-up, what Beatty discovers is an extermination
depot—a sort of assassination fellowship, going by the name of the Parallax Corporation, which employs hit men for all important assassinations. At Parallax, potential employees are given psychologic profiles to
identify homicidal tendencies. Beatty fakes his way onto the payroll by
posing as a psycho. They test for this, and he excels on the written part,
having gotten the questions ahead of time. And perhaps the set of his
jaw-line gets him through the visual part—a montage of Depression
mothers, Hitler, apple pie, amber waves, skeletons, puppy dogs, Castro, Mao, the Washington Monument, naked lovers, all geared to detect
the killer instinct. I don't believe even Warren Beatty could have passed
the montage test, so I don't believe the rest of the movie, which has to
do with him getting hired out to do stuff he never winds up doing and
evading the kiss-of-death kismet that's filling the mortuaries until
there's no one left who knows what's going on but Beatty and the disciples of doom. Only they know that the world is dominated by the death
cartel. Pretty scary. The film manages to make conspiracy theories in
general look as plausible as invasions from space.

Also recommended: *Winter Kills*.

A PASSAGE TO INDIA

With Dame Peggy Ashcroft, Judy Davis, James Fox, Alec Guiness, Nigel Havers, Victor Banerjee, Saeed Jaffrey. Produced by John Brabourne. Directed by David Lean. Screenplay by David Lean, based on the novel by E. M. Forster. Photography by Ernest Day. Music by Maurice Jarre. United Kingdom. English. Color. 163 minutes. 1984.

Cultures clash when English tourists visit colonial India to become acquainted with the Indian people.

David Lean made this film with a mood of hallowed deference for India and lulled the scenes into such thermal updrafts of beauty that we know it is a radiance too excellent to last. Amid a London fanfare, Ashcroft and Davis board a luxury liner that will sail them across two oceans to India and to a train that will take them 1,000 miles inland to Chandrapur—land of subliminal strangenesses. They are ordinary, sincere people who want to meet Indians and immerse themselves in the Indian culture. But in 1928, British imperialism still extends to the subcontinent. Fellow passengers caution, "east is east. . . ." From a railway car, it is easy to visualize "egalitarian colonialism." But when the train pulls into the station, the true meaning of colonialism is clear. Chandrapur is rigidly stratified and segregated into exclusive neighborhoods, country clubs, and social assemblages. The British demean even the notion of convivial interaction with the people over whom they presume to rule. They have imported British furnishings and clothings and seem oblivious to the thrust of India, even as they press through culture-crowded roadways in their extravagant automobiles. Only one of the colonials has taken the trouble to learn Hindi. All this bewilders Ashcroft and Davis, who still want to bend the rules far enough to allow them to acquire Indian friends. The Matabar Caves, full of thundering echoes that are unsettling to the European mind, will displace these incautious ideals and cause a narrowly escaped miscarriage of justice. Vows were made before the menaces of India were known. The alien land and the aliens in it are inconceivably unknowable and impossible to trust. British law immunizes innocent guests of the Empire against the threats of the subcontinent. A Passage to India is an intuitively forceful drama, flamboyantly shot, and it's too bad the Indians in it often seem to want the dramatic dignity Lean intended them to have. In the court scenes, particularly, only the English are extended the latitude of sorting the calamity out. Alec Guiness, usually so crafty, is awkward here.

Why Lean chose to dress up an Englishman to play the part of an Indian in a film about cultural and racial integrity I have no clue. The nuance of a generously ambient plot allows viewers the option of torturing themselves wondering how it all went so wrong.

Also recommended: *Gandhi.*

PATCH OF BLUE

With Shelley Winters, Elizabeth Hartman, Wallace Ford, Ivan Dixon, Sidney Poitier. Produced by Pandro S. Berman. Written and directed by Guy Green, based on the book *Be Ready With Bells and Drums* by Elizabeth Kata. Photography by Robert Burks. Music by Jerry Goldsmith. USA. English. Black and white. 106 minutes. 1965.

A young blind woman meets a black man who tries to help her escape an oppressive home life.

This film is absolute proof that provocative, well-performed films were made about race relations in the 1960s. It has talent on top of talent. Poitier was never better (but often as good). The Hartman/Winters/Ford triangle balances the energy of the intricate drama. When Poitier meets blind Selina in the park under a tree, where she sits stringing beads, he is astonished that she can't read braille, has never been in an elevator, has never been to a school of any sort, cannot cross the street alone, and cannot use the phone. She's never had a corned beef sandwich. She's never had pineapple juice. He likes her and is distressed to learn that she's living in feudal servitude, cooking, cleaning, washing, and ironing for her mother (Winters) and her grandfather (Ford) and stringing beads for the beadman to pay her way. Winters is a tyrant whose daughter was blinded when she threw a glass at her boyfriend and missed. Selina was "done over" by another of her mother's friends. And so much more. Poitier takes her to restaurants. He brings her treats. He buys her sunglasses to hide her eyes. He takes her to his apartment to hear classical music. She calls him "a fine and tolerant friend." When Winters discovers that Selina has been seen with a black man, a crisis builds. Meantime, Poitier is investigating schools that will take a woman of Selina's age with no school background. He has a brother who says, "Let white educate their own women." There is a showdown in the park. When Selina stands up to her mother's tantrums and walks away with Poitier, bystanders applaud. Selina has fallen in love with him even if he is black, and she wishes she'd never been done over. She would like to stay with him and not go to school. He tells her to try the school for one year to meet new people and to have life experiences before she decides. The on-screen kiss they share was daring for the time and helped pave the way for Spike Lee and others in-between.

Also recommended: *Guess Who's Coming to Dinner.*

PATHS OF GLORY

With Kirk Douglas, George Macready, Adolph Menjou, Ralph Meeker, Wayne Morris, Richard Anderson, Joseph Turkel, Timothy Carey, Susanne Christian. Produced by James B. Harris. Directed by Stanley Kubrick. Written by Stanley Kubrick, Calder Willingham and Jim Thompson. Photography by George Krause. Music by Gerald Fried. USA. English. Black and white. 87 minutes. 1957.

The boasts of heraldry the pomp of pow'r,
And all that beauty, all that wealth e'er gave,
Awaits alike th' inevitable hour.
The paths of glory lead but to the grave.
(from "Elegy, Written in a Country Churchyard,"
by Thomas Gray)

Anyone who's seen *Paths of Glory* knows that to call it a war film is to be watching it form the wrong side of the photon emissions. Stanley Kubrick dazzled the movie-going public with this inspired treatise on human behavior under unspeakable conditions. The opening scenes in the magnificent headquarters of General Mireau (Macready) gleam in exotic contrast to the blasted-to-bits moonscape of the front-line trenches. The footfalls of Mireau and his staff echo throughout the vast marble chamber. In these rococo surroundings, Mireau tallies kill ratios and artillery movements and choreographs the atrocities of war. Salutes fly in perfect harmony with the deadly decrees they finalize. All is calm. All is well. Until General Broulard (Menjou) visits with the news that it has become important to someone at the pinnacle of the military hierarchy to take the "Ant Hill" in two days time. Mireau apologizes. He wishes he could comply, but his ranks are not strong enough to take the Ant Hill. He excludes paternalistic compassion—"the life of one of those soldiers means more to me than all the stars and decoration and honors of France." Macready breathes out these words in his own patented ferocity. But a promotion is pending—a very big promotion, big enough to transform Mireau from a reasonable leader of men into a tyrant who besieges his own troops in his merciless quest for glory. What follows is a study not of war, but of the struggle that goes on in each man's soul as he contemplates a destiny he cannot change and from which he cannot escape. Rational men enter valleys of psychological darkness where they battle their fears and their conscience and jeopardize their sanity. In these shadows, they will triumph or be vanquished. Mere life or death is but a superficial phenomenon beside this test of will and character. The irony of righteousness, the futility of logic, and the screaming certainty of injustice are themes laid open in metronomic precision in this Kubrick masterwork. From the opening scene to the final credits, this psycho-drama descends relentlessly into a maelstrom, drawing everything toward the vortex, where callous ambition at least must meet the seminal resoluteness of ordinary man. Kirk Douglas (as Colonel Dax) sees all his faith and trust destroyed as he tries to comply with Mireau's outlandish demands. Ultimately, he must place himself between the general command and the 8,000 man of the 701st Infantry. It's a war of clinical attrition—the military versus Kirk Douglas in his most powerful role. It's the performance of a lifetime. But if Douglas stands out, it is not at the expense of the supporting cast, each one of whom gives equally moving portrayals of war-worn men at the edge of their endurance. Certainly, Macready outdoes himself as a man obsessed beyond all humanity with his desire for glory. (Macready and Douglas worked together again in *Seven Days in May*, ten years later.) Wayne Morris is unforgettable as the woozy and pathetic alcoholic, Lieutenant Roget, who has sacrificed every shed of self-esteem in his struggle to survive the war. Carey, Meeker, and Turkel play three condemned soldiers chosen to be sacrificed to Mireau's drooling fanaticism. Typical of the sensibility of the plot to the most mundane self-absorbed anxieties of the characters is a scene in the prison cell where the three await execution. Meeker sees a cockroach on the table and complains, "Tomorrow, I'll be dead, and that cockroach will still be here, alive." Carey reaches out and smashes the bug, saying, "Now you have the edge on him." Adolph Menjou moves in and out of scenes with unsubdued enthusiasm for war from on high. He yelps out his lines with an android jangle—a perfect example of the general command's distant mechanics of the game of war. Kubrick directed this excellent cast in what feels like one continuous, uncut shot. Like a seismograph, the film registers the flickering whispers of human pathos on a scale as remarkable for its ambitiousness as for its dramatic success. When Douglas confesses that he is ashamed to be a member of the human race, we also nearly give up all hope for our kind. This bitterness is shattered in the mesmerizing and incompatible pub scene, which alone would have made this film a classic. The viewer should know that *Paths of Glory*, a tremendous work of art and one of the greatest anti-war films of all times, is the story of actual events of World War I. It was banned in France upon release, banned briefly from U.S. military bases, and failed to win any recognition from the American Academy of Motion Picture Arts and Sciences. Asked which film he would name as his favorite form a distinguished career in the performing arts, Douglas answered, "*Paths of Glory*, because I played a nice guy." There's a saying that a good movie is one with at least three good scenes and no bad ones. *Paths of Glory* has only one good scene. It lasts 87 minutes.

Also recommended: *Harp of Burma*.

PAUL ROBESON

With James Earl Jones. Directed by Lloyd Richards. Written by Phillip Hayes Dean. Original staging by Charles Nelson Reilly. USA. English. Color. 118 minutes. 1988.

One man tells the story of his life, with piano accompaniment.

At Rutgers, he couldn't even get directions to the cafeteria until he pretended to be the dishwasher. White teammates on the football team broke his nose, hand, and shoulder. They wore gloves so they wouldn't have to touch the ball after he did. Ridicule and race hate followed him to Columbia Law School. He explained, "College men in those days didn't have much social conscience." Appointed to a New York law firm, he wrote "brilliant" briefs in a converted storage room. "I learned that all he secretaries were quitting. They wouldn't take dictation from me." He couldn't appear in court because his presence would have jeopardized the cases. "I was the only negro in the firm except for Miss Minnie, the cleaning lady." She convinced him that his job was nothing but a high-paying prison. He quit with no prospects and went on to become an actor, singer, and blacklisted radical socialist with a circle of friends that included George Bernard Shaw, Jomo Kenyatta, the Coolidges, the Barclays, and Eugene O'Neill. At the height of his popularity, he appeared in Moscow and experienced for the first time in his life "no tension of black." This unanticipated taste of social equality drove him toward conscientious political activism and away from capitalism. He spoke out wherever he went. He raised money for the Spanish Civil War. British intelligence warned him to stop talking during his concerts. "If I can't speak out here," he answered, "I will speak elsewhere." In the U.S., he urged Truman to ban lynchings in the South. He refused to sing in clubs barring black customers. When the U.S. went to war, Robeson was appalled to see black troops shipped to the front. "I find it inconceivable that American negroes could go to war on behalf of those who have oppressed them for generations against a country like Russia which acknowledges the full dignity of the negro." To increasingly negative press, he responded, "I'm only for peace and anti-fascism." His passport was revoked. Record royalties were cut off. Rutgers removed his name from their All-American list. But in 1952, the Soviet Union awarded him their highest honor—the Stalin Peace Prize. The State Department refused to let him travel to accept the award. The IRS intercepted the $25,000 prize. But Robeson was not intimidated. "No fascist-minded people are going to drive me anywhere. I happen to believe in the principles of scientific socialism. A socialist society is economically, culturally, ethically superior to any system based on production for private property." He was HUAC subpoenaed in 1954. "Are you a member of the Communist party?" "Well, it's a party, like the Democratic party, or the Republican party. My vote is no one else's business. I invoke the fifth amendment." Forced to live on the charity of his brother, he told the press, "Even if (they) socially politically, economically assassinate me, I will still speak out." Which he did all over the world until his death in 1976.

Also recommended: *Swimming to Cambodia.*

THE PEDESTRIAN

With Gustav Rudolf Sellner, Peter Hall, Ruth Hausmeister, Maximilian Schell, Dagmar Hirtz, Elsa Wagner, Manuel Sellner. Produced by Maximilian Schell and Ziv Braun. Written and directed by Maximilian Schell. Cinematography by Wolfgang Treu and Klaus Konig. Music by Manos Hadjidakis. West Germany. In German with English titles. Color. 97 minutes. 1974.

A German industrialist comes under suspicion for war crimes.

Heinz Geise has temporarily lost his driver's license due to a minor traffic violation. Now he has to walk or ride the bus. He's a little intimidated by his dependency. He is suddenly vulnerable. Today, he is taking his grandson to the museum to see the lightning simulator. Bolts of light energy ignite the air between two towers. Geise is under suspicion for war crimes, but he doesn't know this. He doesn't know that a survivor of a massacre stands pressing against him on the bus. He doesn't know that photos of men in Nazi uniforms are being spread out on tables, and that people are looking hard into the eyes of faded faces to find him there. It's been so many years. In fact, it's impossible to make a positive identification. Still, a story is run in the local paper implying that he's a Nazi. Protesters demonstrate outside his office building. A veteran comes forward to identify him as the local commander. The way he remembers it, Geise could have issued an order to kill them all, or maybe he just passed on the order. He could have fired shots. He was definitely present during the Third Reich. At the same time, proof of guilt surfaces about a less well-known, less wealthy man. Newspapers choose not to run the story. Who cares about him? Who cares how many people he murdered? Geise considers suicide. He has a beautiful family, an extraordinary home, a career. He's remembering a conversation he had with his eldest son, who was killed in an auto accident. They were driving together at the time of the tragic event. They were arguing. Geise was explaining something about the confusion of war. "Do you think whoever killed that child wanted to kill that child? How can you understand the constant fear of instant decisions of life and death that slip out of hand before you've made them?" And there is an accident. Geise is, perhaps, familiar with the way life and death slip out of hand. His concern now is that the media is behaving irresponsibly. After all, his reputation is at stake. *The Pedestrian* is part of a finely tuned genre that studies the mutability of truth. The drama sways on a delicate fulcrum at the opposite ends of which are innocence and guilt. The possibility of justice often seems outweighed by the implausibility of truth.

Also recommended: *The Blum Affair.*

PLATOON

With Tom Berenger, Charlie Sheen, Willem Dafoe, John C. McGinley, Kevin Dillon, Johnny Depp, Tony Todd, Francesco Quinn, Keith David, Reggie Johnson, Mark Moses, David Neidorf, Forest Whitacker. Produced by Arnold Kopelson. Directed by Oliver Stone. Screenplay by Oliver Stone. Photography by Robert Richardson. Music by Georges Delerue. USA. English. Color. 120 minutes. 1986.

The experiences of Army paratroopers in Vietnam in 1967.

"Somebody once wrote, 'Hell is the impossibility of reason.' That's what this place feels like—hell. I don't even know what I'm doing. . . I'm so tired. I think I made a big mistake coming here." Charlie Sheen is Chris, the rich, white boy who volunteered to fight in Vietnam because he didn't think the poor people should have to do it all. "I've always been sheltered and special. I just want to be anonymous, like everyone else. Well, here I am, anonymous alright, with guys nobody really cares about. . . . They are poor, they are the bottom of the barrel, and they know it. Maybe that's why they call themselves 'grunts.'" So now he sleeps in the pouring rain, fights off leeches, and witnesses the decay of human decency among the men of Bravo Company. These guys take bites out of beer cans and shoot anything, even each other, which does tarnish Sheen's self-obligatory chivalry. *Platoon* is about combat duty in the Vietnam war. There is battle scene after battle scene—flares, bombings, machine gun fire, booby traps. It's an insecure world that brings out the worst in everybody. When the beasts of Bravo enter a village, they brutalize and murder whoever they find there. The film is a ponderous montage of war fought by people who've grown to love it. The few who don't enjoy killing lack the courage to say so. Except Dafoe, who says, "You aren't a firing squad, you piece of shit." And Sheen, "She's a human being, you fucking animal." The sol-diers torch what they leave behind. The burn everything and retreat into slimy jungles—home to snakes, snipers, and blood soaked fox-holes. They survive by hiding under the bodies of the newly dead while everyone around them attracts enemy fire. Stone is aiming for and in-dictment of war and war-mindedness in this film reminiscence of his own experiences in Vietnam. But it's hard to stick to the point with so much tempting heroics. Between soulful letters to his grandma, Sheen fits in a rabid, killing rampage of the Viet Cong, leaving witnesses open-mouthed. He's a war hero—a man saving us from other men. Berenger is the prototypical subhuman who thrives on hate and violence. He's surrounded by grunts in every stage of war psychosis. Stone's direction is visceral, and the film may be cathartic for combat veterans. Others will despair for the future of the species and wonder how anyone once sane could stay that way after being "in country." Although not central to the energy of the film, *Platoon* screens the fragile nature of hope and despair caught in the spectral vacuum of war.

Also recommended: *Apocalypse Now.*

POINT OF ORDER McCARTHY: DEATH OF A WITCH HUNTER

Narrated by Paul Newman. Produced by Emile de Antonio and Daniel Talbot. Directed and edited by Emile de Antonio. USA. English. Black and white with color introductory sequence. 97 minutes. 1964.

The Army-McCarthy hearings destroy the career of Senator Joe McCarthy.

On December 2, 1954, the McCarthy era ended. Senate resolution 301 found Senator Joe McCarthy's conduct to be contrary to senatorial tra-dition and "tending to bring the Senate into disrepute." McCarthy's acts were condemned, and his sway of personal influence and power was over. What conduct were they talking about? Well, not the part where he made practicing one's constitutional rights a criminal offense. The Senate reprimanded and, as it turned out, ruined McCarthy for seeking military favors for his assistant in terror, David Schime, and perhaps, but without really saying so, for aiming his Red bait at the wrong target. Hollywood is one thing, but fishing for Reds at the Pentagon is the road to ruin. Emile de Antonio edited thirty-six days of hearings into a ninety-seven-minute, time-lapse photograph of the decline and fall of Senator Joe McCarthy. Hunched over his microphone, he threatened to expose the Red core of the Pentagon, crying "point of order" at real or imagined departures from court decorum. To McCarthy, everybody was out of order. While the cameras rolled and the nation looked on, he fell from tremendous power to pathetic ruin, unaware of what was happening, unaware that he wasn't making sense and almost surely unaware that he never did. During recess, he spoke on blindly to a slowly emptying room. Even his sidekick, Roy Cohn began to withdraw from this spectacle of unspontaneous human combustion. Other witnesses to the epic cave-in included: Senator Mundt, Ray Jenkins, John McClellan, Stuart Symmington, and Robert Kennedy. Paul Newman introduces the spectacle and provides closing commentary, "McCarthyism did not die with the man [Joe McCarthy died on May 2, 1957], but lives on in many forms in this country." He defines McCarthy as a "reckless, brilliant gambler, who never found a communist, but never stopped looking."

Also recommended: *Hollywood on Trial*.

POWAQQATSI

(Entity which consumes the life force of other beings in order to further its own life)

Produced by Mel Lawrence, Godfrey Reggio, and Lawrence Taub. Directed by Godfrey Reggio. Written by Godfrey Reggio and Ken Richards. Photography by Graham Berry and Leonidas Sourdoumis. Music by Philip Glass. USA. Color. 97 minutes. 1989.

The dehumanizing urbanization of the Third World.

A lot of people are mystified by and therefore cannot relate to Godfrey Reggio's recent work. And that's O.K., because in *Powaqqatsi* and *Koyaanisqatsi*, Reggio is not speaking to everybody. He's speaking to the ones who have become suspicious of advanced metropolization. He's speaking to the ones who have begun to question everything, who no longer accept everything, who no longer accept that they have to accept everything. He's speaking to the universal sensation of existence through the fluid catalog of visual momentum and auditory invention. He's experimenting with film to speak to the few who see the world as a holistic system of life pulsing in cycles, but which current tendencies are leading toward an utterly predictable and intolerable end. He's speaking to people who have begun to perceive the built environment itself as a construction seducing the tonality of existence. He's speaking to people who fathom the insanity of the division of labor, the eight-hour day, and the assembly line—redundancy for which the only real purpose is the inflation of productive capacity. He's speaking about a sacred planet that this mechanized capacity is destroying. This productive, destructive capacity is destroying the people and their planet. He's speaking to those who see the routinization of humanity as the onset of the darkest age of all dark ages, where the horror of the aimless, alienated, commercialized life is outweighed only by the horror of its unascertainability. If only everyone would just refuse to do it. If they would just stop building the roads and driving the cars and buying the bombs. If they would just let it all collapse—that would be the one true chance for ecstasy. Masses of motion, rivers of life, and compressed and retarded time are the indispensable method to Reggio's theme. He is not suggesting millions, but showing millions, sluggishly repressed or frenzied with nothing beyond the desk top, nothing beyond the work station, nothing but the deadly dictums of time. Of course, all this is a photo montage, nonnarrative, wordless, visual, musical investigation of the deformities of the world's advanced life systems. It's a silent film to the power of ten, and I sadly lament and pity those so lost to visual and moral sensation that they cannot get lost in Godfrey Reggio's magnificent philosophic dream.

Also recommended: *Koyaanisqatsi.*

PROJECT X

With Matthew Broderick, Helen Hunt, Bill Sadler, Johnny Rae McGhee, Jonathon Stank. Produced by Lawrence Lasker and Walter Parks. Directed by Johnathan Kaplan. Screenplay by Stanley Weiser, from a story by Stanley Weiser and Lawrence Lasker. Photography by Dean Cundey. Music by James Horner. USA. English. Color. 107 minutes. 1988.

U.S. Air Force animal experimentation is stopped by two young people.

Anyone who thinks *Project X* is just a filmmaker's fancy way of exploring plots against the U.S. military needs to reenter the Earth's atmosphere. This film is a rosy rendering of U.S. Air Force irradiation studies and generously omits most atrocities of experimentation, including small arms testing on target dogs and cats (*perhaps* stopped by public outcry), flame-thrower practice involving conscious pigs, and Hydrogen bomb blast-zone exposure studies too cruel for mere dramatic counterforce. Skipping over all of this as it does, *Project X* could easily win Miss Manners' biggest trophy of the year. The film is based on the real-life experiences of former military experimenter, Donald Barnes, who watched chimps die a lot less euphemistically than they do in this movie before he resigned from the military to go to work for the National Antivivisection Society. *Project X* stars Matthew Broderick as the young career cadet assigned to care for U.S. Air Force chimps. The animals are trained in flight simulators to prearranged skill levels and then are exposed to lethal doses of radiation while in the simulators in order to determine how long they can stay an accurate course before they die. In *Project X*, some of the chimps have learned American Sign Language in a former experiment, allowing them to communicate with humans. Broderick and fellow trainer Helen Hunt become so attached to the chimps that they lose their enthusiasm for "Project X." As the chimps die one by one, they begin to feel they ought to do something to stop the testing, even if it could ruin Broderick's military career. However, the chimps aren't as helpless as everybody thought they were. They spearhead their own minor revolution, and the movie ends on an enthusiastic upswing, but not without tragic overtones for all the lives lost so far. That's one small step for a chimp, one giant leap for chimpkind. The five chimps purchased especially for *Project X* were liberated after filming by 20th Century Fox and sent to the Primarily Primates sanctuary in Texas. When accusations of animal abuse were leveled at set chimp handler Ron Oxley, who apparently carried an electric prod to work with him every morning, the film became a doubly profound petition for sensitivity to the rights of nonhuman animals, not only in a research setting, but also in the entertainment industry.

Also recommended: *The Animals Film.*

A QUESTION OF SILENCE

With Cox Habbema, Nelly Frijda, Henriette Tol, Edda Barends, Eddy Brugman, Kees Coolen, Onno Molenkamp, Dolf de Vries. Produced by Matthijs Van Heijningen. Written and directed by Marleen Gorris. Photography by Frans Bromet. Music by Lodewijk De Boer and Martijn Hasebos. The Netherlands. Dutch with English titles. Color 92 minutes. 1983.

Three women murder a shopkeeper in defense of self-defense.

Three women (Frijda, Tol, Barends) are arrested for murdering a shopkeeper. They are neither repentant nor apprehensive. They don't know each other. The question is, why did they do it? They have no motive. The would rather talk about anything except the case. Their court-appointed psychiatrist (Habbema) is assigned to find them legally insane and unfit to be tried. She finds them to be normal. When she asks them about the crime, they talk about their lives. They all worked for men or were married to men or were dependent on men. They were taken for granted, belittled, criticized for small things, treated like children and suffered slights too small to mention, but not too small to remember. In prison, their lives are no less humiliating and demeaning than in the outside world of institutionalized sexism. The more Habbema talks to them, the more she grows to resent the "natural" dominance of her husband. In court, she testifies that the women are sane, responsible, and capable of standing trial. The court protests. Her husband warns her that she's ruining her career. "You all keep overlooking one important detail," she testifies. "The man was a shopkeeper." The judge answers, "The fact that he was a shopkeeper means nothing. Nor would it have any meaning if the victim had been a woman. For that matter, it could have as easily been three men that murdered a woman shopkeeper." As this concept sinks in, the three defendants begin to laugh. Habbema laughs. The women spectators in the courtroom laugh. The judge bangs his gavel until they are all laughing out of control. "It's really very funny." They are picturing men distraught enough at the daily humiliations pressed upon them by women to push a female shopkeeper over and beat her with their billfolds. It has comic value. Of course, some people don't think so. Some people were unable to consider the allegorical gist of the film. But, clearly, neither the death of the shopkeeper nor the technique of the murder have any mundane corollary. They represent the attempt to eradicate the male presumption of dominance. And the funny part is how even "second-degree murder" alerts so few to how tiring this dominance has gotten to be. *A Question of Silence* reaffirms feminism as a philosophy with something for everyone—even men.

Also recommended: *The Handmaid's Tale.*

RAIN MAN

With Dustin Hoffman, Tom Cruise, Valeria Golino, Jerry Molen, Jack Murdock, Ralph Seymour. Produced by Mark Johnson. Directed by Barry Levinson. Screenplay by Ronald Bass and Barry Morrow based on the story by Barry Morrow. Photography by John Seale. Music by Hans Zimmer. USA. English. Color. 134 minutes. 1989.

A young man loses his Lamborghini, finds his brother, and sees the light.

"The whole world is choking in smog, and they are going to correct the situation by keeping my four cars off the road?" Hot-shot hustler Charlie (Cruise) has four Lamborghinis without smog controls to cash in on in a hurry if he's going to get himself out of the pit all his former scams have dug him into. Instead of smog clearance, what happens is that Charlie's father dies and leaves the family fortune not to Charlie, but to someone "residing at the Wallbrook Home for the Mentally Handicapped." "Did you hear what I just read" "No, I didn't," says Charlie, "so why don't you read it again because I can't believe my fuckin' ears." All Charlie gets is a 1949 Buick Roadmaster convertible with a Straight 8 and a dyna-flow transmission. He drives the Buick to Wallbrook and finds Raymond, a brother he never knew he had, but who he now kidnaps to force the executors to agree that he, Charlie, should get at least half of the three-million dollars since he needs it and since Raymond "does not understand the concept of money." "That is fuckin' poetic." Raymond is autistic. Hustle doesn't work on him. Charlie can't push him around. He tries though, and that convinces his beautiful girlfriend (Golino) to pack up and leave. "They tell you for the first time that you have a brother and I don't see in your face one little reaction. I'm not saying joy, I'm just saying *something*. You're using Raymond, Charlie. You're using me. You use everybody." And, maybe without really noticing it, Charlie starts giving in to Raymond. Raymond won't travel in the rain. He has the Wallbrook menu memorized along with every airline accident in the history of flight. "You tire me, Raymond." "You're killing me. I gotta be in L.A. in three hours, and it's gonna take me three days." At an isolated farmhouse on a road between two deserts he is squinting through the screen door. "This is my brother, ma'am, and if he doesn't get to see "The People's Court" in exactly thirty seconds, he's going to throw a fit right here on the front porch. Now you can help me, or you can stand there and watch it happen." Charlie is astounded that he has a brother he never knew he had. "Why didn't anyone ever tell me I had a brother? Because it would have been nice to know him for more that just the last six days." Finally, he rips up the check Wallbrook sends him. "This is my family, don't you understand?" *Rain Man* is a movie about a nice thing that happened to Charlie and Raymond. It probably didn't deserve to be dragged over the burning coals by the critics the way it was.

Also recommended: *The Coca-Cola Kid*.

RAONI

Narrated by Marlon Brando. Written and directed by Jean Pierre Dutileux. Photography by Carlos Saldanha. Music by Egberto Gismonti. France/USA. English and native languages with titles. Color. 82 minutes 1978.

A personal look at the Indians of the Amazon basin and how progress is threatening their culture and way of life.

In 1978, two thousand Native Americans walk three thousand miles across the U.S. to dramatize the plight of Indians in the United States and to speak out against the Native American Equal Opportunity Act, which would "abrogate all the treaties, close all the schools, all the hospitals, and, in fact, extinguish American Indian identity as a separate people." Washington, D.C., is the destination point of the five month odyssey. Marlon Brando walks among them and talks to them about their hopes and concerns. Native Americans have the highest infant mortality rate, the lowest income, and the highest suicide rate of any American people. Brando is concerned about the trends in cultural genocide. "I don't know why white men want everyone to be like them. They don't want anyone to be different. We just keep imposing our will on others. The tribal people all over the world just want to survive." The scene shifts to South America. Raoni is the chief of the Txucarramae Indians, who have been attacked by machine gun assault and poisoned in an effort to drive them off the land. Their culture, based on the opulence and certainty of nature, is an exotic mixture of sounds—the music and the language—and the striking artistry of their traditional environment—body painting, legends, ceremonies, myths, and the weapons of people who "just want to survive." They have seen the cities. The prefer the rain forest. They resent the film crew and consider killing them. Raoni convinces them that the film may help keep other whites away. He has talked to Carlos Villas Boaz about a united Indian front to oppose the invasion of technology and progress and to save the Amazon basin forests and the tribes whose lives depend on them. Boaz explains to Raoni, "White people are not like you. They live in total confusion. They do not share. They cannot explain their life. They are not free to do what they want to do." Boaz and his brother have worked with the Indians for years to establish sanctuaries for the indigenous people and to develop programs to help them cope with progress when it comes. The cameras follow the work crews of invading industries as they cut swaths in the rain forest with bulldozers dragging enormous chains. The shallow-rooted trees offer no resistance to this simple technique, which opens fresh acres of the rain forest to farmers, the beef industry, water diversion schemes, and the boom towns that spring up behind them. Four hundred thousand beef farms now prosper in the open sun. The scope of the devastation is inconceivably vast. Brando's compassionate narrative blames the developed countries. Consumer tastes have had a tragic impact, and commerce is only a reflection of market trends.

Also recommended: *The Emerald Forest.*

RATE IT X

Produced by Lynn Campbell, Claudette Charbonneau, Paula de Koenigsberg, Lucy Winer. Directed by Lucy Winer and Paula de Koenigsberg. Scenario based on an idea by Claudeette Charbonneau. Photography by Paula de Koenigsberg. Music by Liz Swados. Interviews by Lucy Winer. USA. English. Color. 95 minutes. 1985.

Sexism, oppression, racism and violence become one in this revealing and candid film of how commerce shapes culture.

From humble beginnings, George now closes in on the American dream. He has created "The Ugly George Show," which "consists of me flexing up to innocent young voigens [virgins] and asking them to flex into a hallway and pose nude." He prefers blondes. "I don't particularly consider darker people sexy." Other independent entrepreneurs have noticed the advantages of sexist novelty in business. "Do you ever put heads on these cakes?" "No, because the head is superfluous to . . . the idea of the cake." Just the torso, with room to write "Happy Father's Day." *Rate It X* is a world of cleavage-promoted electronics and underwear magnates who know that women want "frilly, functional, sexy undergarments that make them feel like women." "Advertising in America has always been heavily oriented toward . . . well-endowed, blue-eyed blondes." Helpful female hints are even passed out by appliance repairmen—things a woman should know like how to look like a girl, act like a lady, think like a man, and work like a dog. The repairman explains that some women complained about the hints because they couldn't see that they were not to be taken literally. The white-gloved, tweed-coated arm of the interviewer holds the microphone out to ask men, "What would you do if your little seven-year-old boy wanted a doll?" "Holy moly, I'd have him checked over." The inspiration behind *Hustler*'s "Chester the Molester" is a caveman with a baseball bat, whose every conscious moment is spent luring little girls into his lair with candy and money (candy for the gentiles, money for the Jews). Chester doesn't actually *need* the bat. He could hit the little girls if he had to—the bat is for the cave image. *Hustler* has just released its woman-in-the-meat-grinder issue. Inside are women on platters, looking butchered or dead. Winer and Koenigsberg take their cameras to a shop next to the XXX theater where adult amusements are for sale. "All she needs is sex from you . . . stroke her nude flesh-like skin and her warm, water-filled breasts . . . while her warm . . . I can't read this . . . while her warm sucking mouth and deep, penetrating anal opening awaits . . . I'm not going to read this." The marquee next door flashes, "24 hours a day." The theater has just shown the popular slasher/horror film, *Blood Sucking Freaks.* "I was surprised the Women Against Pornography opposed this movie. . . . It's just light, good-hearted wholesome sado-masochism." *Rate It X* so demoralizingly chronicles male malignment of females and female sexuality that it helps us understand how culture has contributed to increased sexual assaults and abuse against women in the U.S.

Also recommended: *Roger and Me.*

RED BEARD

With Yuzo Kayama, Terumi Niki, Toshiro Mifune, Yoshio Tsuchiya. Produced by Ryuzo Kikushima and Tomoyuki Tanaka. Directed by Akira Kurosawa. Written by Ryuzo Kikushima, Hideo Oguni, Masato Ide, and Akira Kurosawa, based on the novel *Akahige Sinryo Tan* by Shugoro Yamamoto. Photography by Asakazu Nakai and Takao Saito. Music by Masaru Sato. Japan. Japanese with English titles. Black and white. 1985 minutes. 1965.

A new doctor resents placement in a rural clinic but grows to love the people and develop a social conscience.

Red Beard (not his real name) is an ambitious graduate of medical school in Shogun-era Japan. His career goals are derailed by a temporary assignment to a charity hospital. His selfishness and indifference to the needs of the underclasses are manifested by such un-Hippocratic oaths as, "I'll just break every rule and be asked to leave." He begins by refusing to do anything, but he's surrounded by trauma and uproar. There aren't enough doctors. That's why he's there. There are men, women, and children in every stage of emotional and physical distress. Maybe one small act of kindness wouldn't ruin his life. And, by the way, what's the story on the lady secluded in the garden house? And the child with no parents? He never heard such stories of hardship and privation. Red Beard, the patients call him. He can't stop his heart from breaking. People are dying from sheer neglect. He rescues a young girl from a brothel and comes to rely on her when he falls sick from overwork. Poverty, it would seem, breeds crime and shortens lives. Kyojio Niide (his real name) begins to see that, "Poverty is a political problem." And he questions the unequal distribution of wealth in society. He discovers qualities he never knew he had—true healing qualities and the ability to care. From old country doctors he learns a dietary prescription for health; "no meat, no eggs, no fowl, not too much fish or salt, no white rice, wheat mostly." But the world has not forgotten Red Beard. His position with the Shogun opens at last. His life of prestige is waiting, but he can't leave the poor. He tells his bride he will never be rich or important—he will never leave the people. Director Akira Kurosawa reaffirms his stature in world cinema as a master of style, poetry, tragedy, and character transformation. The narrative is a mosaic of the seven faces of poverty and the degenerative levels of social stratification acted out by a tremendously credible cast.

Also recommended: *The Citadel.*

REDS

With Warren Beatty, Diane Keaton, Edward Herrmann, Jerzy Kosinski, Jack Nicholson, Paul Sorvino, Maureen Stapleton, George Plimpton, M. Emmet Walsh, Ian Wolfe, Bessie Love, Nicholas Coster. Produced and directed by Warren Beatty. Written by Warren Beatty and Trevor Griffiths, from the book by John Reed. Photography by Vittorio Storaro. Music by Stephen Sondheim. USA. English. Color. 200 minutes. 1981.

The story of the life of radical, revolutionary John Reed.

Warren Beatty wanted to make a film about John Reed because he read the book and was excited about the heroic potential of his love life backed by incidental historic events, such as the fall of the Romanov empire in Russia and the rise of radicalism in the U.S. The intercontinental saga of the Reed/Bryant romance is a veritable discovery to be sure, without which the three-hour film would have fit into its own preview clips. As a love story, it has some power about it, dramatically set, as it is, against the plate tectonics of war, radical politics, and Reed's failing health. But if Beatty was impressed with Reed's life, Reed might not be impressed with the movie of it—a portrayal of a misled thinker who believed in economic democracy but came to his senses before he died of typhus and kidney failure in the USSR. Not only is Reed exonerated of revolutionary thoughts in this Beatty co-scripted film, a host of other individuals important to the most revolutionary era in American history are typecast as self-absorbed bohemians, bickering, cheating on each other, uncorking vino, and dressing up for totally homespun stage skits put on at somebody's seaside bungalow. George Eastman, a dynamic radical thinker for the cause of socialism, casts no shadow as played by Edward Herrmann. Perhaps he was just a camera heir. I give Maureen Stapleton all the credit for generating a passionate revolutionary zeal on behalf of the incomparable Emma Goldman. *Reds* is a true love story, passing itself off as historical realism and trivializing economic democracy both as a theory and a movement capable of shaping history. The candid interviews of real people who knew Reed—Eastman, Goldman, and others—give us the simply sorry idea that resistance to market economy hangs on by an unraveling thread of DNA to the last generation. Those conservatives who protested the film knowing only the title need not have bothered. Beatty is not trying to annoy conservatives or liberals with this ambitious, costly film. He just doesn't seem to know the difference. It should not go unreported that the extras in *Reds* went on strike for higher pay, which they did get. I guess the workers of the world have Beatty to thank for that.

Also recommended: *Good Fight.*

THE RIVER NIGER

With Cicely Tyson, James Earl Jones, Louis Gossett, Jr., Glynn Turner, Roger Mosely, Jonelle Allen, Hilda Haynes. Produced by Sidney Beckerman and Isaac L. Jones. Directed by Krishna Shah. Written by Joseph A. Walker, based on his play. Photography by Michael Marguiles. Music by War and Jerry Goldstein. USA. English. Color. 104 minutes. 1976.

A black family and its friends live from day to day in a post-civil-rights era inner-city home.

Cross-cultural scavenge has replaced the normal family, and the tempestuous, in-house life-fest in *The River Niger* is going absolutely nowhere toward recreating it because there's no social, religious, or political unity left to work with. Direct-action racialism is also dead in the trenches. Out on the streets, Moe (Mosely) is heading up the remnants of a revolutionary black movement whose followers are being consumed and transformed by the very system they once dreamed of changing. Moe and his small band of misfits exemplify, either intentionally or through a sorry script screw-up, how none but the dangerously deranged believe in anything anymore except fashion and the fast lane. Jeff is a reformed radical who is no longer into subverting the status quo. He's into law school and wish-fulfillment. The lost-cause message is camouflaged so comfortably by the ad hoc extended family of *The River Niger* that some reviewers thought the "Moe" guys were "over the edge" gang members from ghetto America. Well, there *are* a lot of other things going on—there are grandmothers and prodigal sons and amigos from compass points galore, including Jamaica and Africa, most of them over-anxious, over-dressed, and wearing us out with their florid accents. James Earl Jones, who is *not* anxious, gives a powerful performance as a worker-philosopher-poet. In fact, he is too good, measured against the rest of the cast. Mosely and the gang hold out, assailed as they are by manic bacteria. Glynn Turner is also good, but the rest of the cast fades a bit. And *The River Niger* classifies itself as a sort of hydra-headed, root-bound ancestor to *Roots*.

Also recommended: *Watermelon Man.*

THE ROAD TO 1984—GEORGE ORWELL: THE LIFE THAT SHAPED THE VISION

With James Fox, Janet Dale, Julia Goodman. Produced by Steve Morrison. Directed by David Wheatley. Screenplay by Willis Hall. Music by Bill Conner. United Kingdom. English. Color. 88 minutes. 1985.

The life of George Orwell, author of *Animal Farm* and *1984*.

The man we all know as George Orwell was born Eric Arthur Blair to English parents in colonial India. He served with the Indian Imperial Police in Burma, overseeing the execution of men for "crimes" he would have committed himself. His radicalism was a personal thing, "driven by demons that I can neither resist nor understand." The abuses of power in Burma drove him to England. "In order to hate imperialism, you've got to be a part of it. Then you recognize it as an unjustifiable tyranny." But in England he discovers, "I don't need to go as far as Burma to find tyranny and exploitation." In the leprous clutches of the industrial revolution, the English working classes are drudging underground with their throats full of coal dust. He saw "the curse of class difference, like a wall of stone." To Orwell, social hierarchy of any kind was intolerable. He was anti-imperialist, anti-totalitarian, anti-Stalinist. In 1937, he fought with the Republicans in the Spanish Civil War. Here, for the first time in his life, in the trenches, he was treated as an equal by the working class. "Every line I have written since the Spanish Civil War was written against totalitarianism and in favor of democratic socialism." Back in England, he wrote *Animal Farm*, reenactments of which are included here, effectively using real animals in favor of clips from the animated film. The rule of *Animal Farm* after the animals revolt against their capitalist owner is, "All animals are created equal." The first publishers to whom he submitted his manuscript turned it down complaining, "It can only apply to Russia." There was concern that the choice of pigs as the ruling class "would prove offensive to many people." When his first wife died, he took his infant son to the Hebrides and wrote, "It was a bright cold day in April and the clocks were striking thirteen." His dystopian classic *1984* features Winston Smith and his feeble efforts at personal expression during "hate week" in Oceana. Fox stands in for Smith in reenacted scenes from the story, again in preference to clips from the film. Debilitated by tuberculosis, Orwell married his second wife from a hospital bed in a sanatorium. As an artist, he lived immersed in his philosophies and his writing. His one wish for oppressed people was, "If only they knew their own strength."

Also recommended: *1984* and *Animal Farm.*

ROGER AND ME

With Michael Moore. Written, produced, and directed by Michael Moore. Cinematography by Christopher Beaver, John Prusak, Kevin Rafferty, and Bruce Schermer. USA. English. Color. 90 minutes. 1989.

A major auto corporation pulls out of Flint, Michigan, leaving joblessness, poverty, and social upheaval behind.

Following five years of tremendous growth and profits, General Motors, the largest corporation in the world, closed down plants in Flint, Michigan, at a cost to Flint of approximately 30,000 jobs. GM then opened plants in tax-free zones in Mexico, outside the reach of the UAW. Press releases indicated that market factors were behind the move. *Roger and Me* is a "docucomedy" about the effects of this closure on the legally terminated and unpensioned GM workers, some of whom had been with the giant auto company for thirty years. "Roger" is Roger Smith, the (then) president of GM. Moore wants to talk to him about the plant closings and the 30,000 jobs, but Smith does not return his calls. Armed guards prevent Moore from entering the elevator to Smith's seventh-floor offices. When they meet, at last, Moore asks Smith about the evictions in Flint (going on at the rate of sixteen a day) in the weeks preceding the Christmas holidays. Smith resents the intrusion into a celebratory gathering of stockholders and the implication that there is any connection between General Motors' policy and the difficulty some people have paying their rent. Filmmaker Michael Moore follows the Flint deputy sheriff on his eviction rounds—a knock on the door and suddenly homeless children are piling their toys by the curb. After the film's release, GM pulled ads from any television programs featuring Moore or *Roger and Me.* GM also mass-distributed negative reviews of the movie. Moore pledged to pay the rent for two years for all families evicted on film and agreed to save one seat for Smith at all screenings of *Roger and Me*. Denied recognition by the Academy of Motion Picture Arts and Sciences at Oscar time for disrupting minor chronologies of his film, Moore also absorbed public flack for aiming his cameras at the Flint bourgeoisie. They did not appreciate the one-sided coverage sensationalizing plant closings: "... people should quit concentrating on the negative part of this whole thing and look at some of the positive things going on." Like the opera and the ballet. On the sunlit, country club golf course, they nod in agreement. If you lose your job, just get another one. That's what they would do. They aren't uncaring. They participate in fund raising galas to raise money for a new prison, and they hire people to pose as statues at their patio soirees. Some critics were insulted by whatever camera tricks Moore used to make certain people look foolish. For example, Pat Boone and other celebrities immortalize their bedrock insensitivity to the hardship of the auto workers. Michael Moore believes in economic democracy and has taken his film east of the iron curtain so transitional economies can take a look at the free market.

Also recommended: *H-2 Worker.*

ROME OPEN CITY

With Anna Magnani, Aldo Fabrizi, Marcello Pagliero. Produced and directed by Roberto Rossellini. Written by Sergio Amidei, Federico Fellini, and Roberto Rossellini. Photography by Ubaldo Arata. Music by Renzo Rossellini. Italy. Italian with English titles. Black and white. 101 minutes. 1945.

Italians cooperate to resist Nazi occupation in World War II.

The revolutionary film techniques of *Rome Open City* will surely make a greater impression on the future than the simple story of resistance to the Nazis in occupied Italy. With this film, Rossellini turned filmmaking away from the theatrical Hollywood standard, liberating filmmakers from bourgeois technique, bourgeois styles, bourgeois values, and establishment funding. He rejected elitism in favor of radical application of the film media. He "altered forever the development and aesthetics of film" (Magill) and moved filmmaking one step closer to Robert Flaherty's prediction made in 1922, that "truly great films have yet to be made. They will not be the work of large studios, but . . . of passionate people . . . without commercial aims, and these films will be made with art and truth." Rossellini was so broke when he made *Rome Open City* that it was shot as a silent film and the sound was dubbed in later. For the same reason, he cast nonactors, creating several stars of world cinema whose performances have helped alter the aesthetic of acting. The instinctual, minimalist-under-compression Anna Magnani became an instant star. The furtive, intense camera and directing techniques gave rise to the rumor that the movie was shot during the occupation. Filming actually began two months after liberation. The dramatic nucleus of *Rome Open City* is the resistance movement smuggling money to the partisans. The Catholic priest working with the Committee of National Liberation is accused by conservatives of helping atheist, Marxist anti-fascists. He defends his work saying, "I believe that he who fights for justice and truth walks in the path of the Lord, and the paths of the Lord are infinite"—possibly the screen debut for the theories of liberation theology.

Also recommended: *The Battle of Algiers.*

ROMERO

With Raul Julia, Richard Jordan, Ana Alicia, Tony Plana, Harold Gould, Alejandro Bracho. Produced by Ellwood E. Kieser. Directed by John Duigan. Written by John Sacret Young. Photography by Geoff Burton. Music by Gabriel Jared. USA. English and Spanish. Color. 94 minutes. 1989.

The life and death of catholic Archbishop Oscar Romero—a believer and promoter of liberation theology.

Archbishop Oscar Arnulfo Romero was a conservative who believed the government propaganda and preached tolerance and endurance before becoming radicalized by the military brutalities he witnessed in El Salvador. Human rights violations were a staple tactic of the regime of government terrorism. Rebel leaders were kidnapped, tortured, murdered, or they "disappeared." The assault was funded, in part, by wealthy landowners protecting their estates against nationalization. Land reform motivated revolutionaries in El Salvador and other Central and South American countries to fight for the right to survive on the land. These freedom campaigns were cruelly put down. In Argentina alone, 30,000 people disappeared in the people's struggle. Many Catholic leaders began to study Marxism and to preach "revolutionary theology." These brave men and women were often castigated by the church and targeted for execution. Archbishop Romero was assassinated in 1980 for speaking out against human rights abuses. He encouraged soldiers to refuse to obey orders that went against the teachings of the church. He worked in the struggle for human rights against a U.S.-backed regime and was shot down in his church while saying mass. *Romero* was independently produced by Paulist Pictures, the Catholic media branch of the Paulist order. Father Ellwood E. Kieser turned to the order and to various Catholic bishops to raise money for the film when Hollywood studios and all three American television networks turned him down. The Paulist monks have salvaged this story for the screen. Unfortunately, funding limitations come through in the film, which neglects to confirm for the camera the genuine scope of the fight for economic liberty in Central America. Isolated events fail to define the whole, and rebel forces lack the fervency of the moment. Under Duigan's direction, Romero is often afoot from here to there, not uncommonly helming a silent throng. Raul Julia, keen to play the role, stiffens charitably into the tempo of the frames. Thanks to cinematographer Geoff Burton, the film is set with still sequences, which inject a potent visual impact into this profound story.

Also recommended: *Salvador.*

THE ROSENBERG-SOBELL CASE REVISITED
(THE UNQUIET DEATH OF JULIUS AND ETHEL ROSENBERG)

Narrated by Barton Heyman. Reported by Alvin H. Goldstein. Produced by Sue Ballou. Directed by Alan Moorman. Photography by Ben Tubb, Peter Hoving, John Camie, Jim Furlong, Kip Durrin, and Lee Kenower. USA. English. Black and white and color. 89 minutes. 1978.

Chronicle of the arrest, trial, and execution of Julius and Ethel Rosenberg.

On June 19, 1953, at Sing Sing prison in New York, Julius and Ethel Rosenberg were executed for "conspiring to commit espionage in war time." They were the only civilians put to death in U.S. Civil Court history. They left behind two sons, ages six and ten. Laws specific to the charge of "conspiracy to commit espionage" required the testimony of only one uncorroborated witness to justify a guilty verdict. They were accused of passing hydrogen bomb secrets to the USSR, enabling the Soviets to build a nuclear weapon. Scientists interviewed by the filmmakers deny there was any "secret" to the bomb at all. "When the bomb went off in Hiroshima, everybody knew, fusion would do it." And, anyway, "The bomb is an industry, not a recipe. There are thousands of little secrets, and sixty ways to do every one of them. It's too much for one man to know, too much for one book to tell, to much to write on any piece of paper. Volumes of technical skill, laboratories full of people, factories of machinists and machines—that's what it takes." A rough sketch on a single sheet of paper was all that was needed to condemn the Rosenbergs to die. The judge justified the death penalty saying, "I consider your crime worse than murder." The prosecutor is Roy Cohn, Joe McCarthy's aid throughout the 1950s. This film follows the Rosenberg trial through its many staggeringly obscure incarnations. There are reprieves and reversals of reprieves, reversals of testimony, a conservative jury of non-Jews, and unreliable witnesses. A CIA document reveals that the Rosenbergs could have saved their lives up to the last minute by appealing ". . . to Jews . . . to get out of the communist movement and seek to destroy it." In exchange for making such a proc-

lamation, Julius and Ethyl Rosenberg were promised "a generous com-
mutation." For the CIA the Rosenbergs were pawns in an "international
psychological warfare campaign against communism primarily of the
Jewish issue." National and international rallies of support were held
up until the execution deadline. Ethel was electrocuted three times before the coroner pronounced her dead. Although this film is an indictment of the American criminal justice system corrupted by nationalism,
the filmmaker's goal is not to prove that the Rosenbergs were innocent,
but to substantiate the illegitimacy of their deaths.

Also recommended: *Daniel.*

RUNNING ON EMPTY

With River Phoenix, Judd Hirsch, Christine Lahti, Martha Plimpton, Jonas
Abry. Produced by Amy Robinson and Griffin Dunne. Directed by Sidney
Lumet. Screenplay by Naomi Foner. Cinematography by Gerry Fisher.
Music by Tony Mottola. USA. English. Color. 115 minutes. 1988.

**Anti-war activists who bombed a napalm plant in the 1960s
cope with life underground in the 1980s.**

The feeding frenzy this film incited among critics can be traced to two
things. For one, most of the critics don't get it that activism is not just a
bomb, it's a movement. Second, because of this, there's very little interest in (and perhaps even an aversion to) the moral values that inform
the production. For some critics, it's quite workable simply to reverse
the content of their reviews. If one critic says *Running On Empty* "does
not show us how to live with radical ideals in this society," just take
that to mean that it does. If a review says that radicalism was the background, you can read that as "all the ground." If we don't know what
the Popes feel about their past crime—well, you get the idea. Everything
that happens to the people in this drama is shadowed by the fugitive
status of Arthus and Annie Pope (Hirsch and Lahti), who are wanted by
the FBI for crimes against the military state. *Running on Empty* reveals
the activism of the Vietnam era as it has settled into the modern lives of
people like the Popes—people who work for the unions, the food co-
ops, and the environment; who are vegetarians; who are nonmaterialis-

tic; who live their ethic every day; and who used to be called the counterculture (which did not disappear but became the alternative movement). It's an introduction to a socially relevant lifestyle, and for most audiences, this is a lot. It's a culture of conscience, in this case dramatically elaborated by the fact of the family's fugitive status. As a result of the bombing, they live underground, pursued by the FBI. The Popes and their two sons (Phoenix and Abry) move on a moment's notice, never use their real names, and periodically change their appearances to avoid arrest. Although the Popes regret that a janitor was injured in the bombing of the napalm plant, they never regret their acts of conscience, and they never convert to acceptance of militarism or imperialism. They do regret that their fugitive status has kept them apart from their own families, and the crisis of the narrative comes when Phoenix decides he wants to leave the family to pursue a career in music. Righteous performances all around. The novel theme of the story stands effortlessly on its own philosophies of sacrificing personal well-being for humanitarian ideals.

Also recommended: *The War at Home.*

SACCO AND VANZETTI

With Gian Maria Volonte, Riccardo Cucciolla, Cyril Cusack, Milo O'Shea, Geoffrey Keen, William Prince. Produced by Arrigo Colombo and Giorgio Papi. Directed by Giuliano Montaldo. Written by Giuliano Montaldo, Fabrizo Onofri, and Ottavio Jemma. Photography by Silvano Ippoliti. Music by Ennio Morricone. Italy/France. English and Italian dubbed into English. Color and black and white. 120 minutes. 1971.

Dramatization of the arrest, trial, and execution of two suspected revolutionaries.

In August of 1927, Bartolomeo Vanzetti and Nicola Sacco were electrocuted by the state of Massachusetts. They were Italian immigrants convicted of a South Braintree payroll robbery in which two men were killed. Overwhelming evidence as to their innocence and public outcries in the U.S. and in Europe could not save the two immigrant anarchists in the conservative Massachusetts court. In this case, the prosecution preferred to indulge their own agenda of racial and political persecution. During the seven years of trials, judges habitually overruled the admission of critical evidence, prosecution witnesses perjured themselves, and defense attorneys were denied retrial and appeal rights. The courtroom was transformed into an arena of intolerance and injustice and became a forum for the assassination of judicial ideals. Defense counsel, overwhelmed by this misuse of "legal" procedure, were unable to save their client's lives. Not only was the Massachusetts court prejudiced against anarchists and immigrants, but also against minorities. Sacco and Vanzetti *were* guilty of being all three. It's almost intolerable to watch Sacco and Vanzetti be murdered by state-supported henchmen who were so immune to public sentiment that they could ignore petitions with hundred of thousands of signatures, resolutions from every major university in the country, and 17,000 personal letters and telegrams to the governor's office. All these were simply set aside. In his sentencing statement, Vanzetti makes an impassioned plea for life. He wants to live, but only "in a better world." "Help the persecuted and oppressed," he said. "They are your best friends." *Sacco and Vanzetti* not only articulates the appalling shortcomings of the criminal justice system and the unconstitutionality of the death penalty, it is an impassioned call for a system more obedient to democratic ideals. The technical quality of the film provides hazards worth mentioning. You may find, for example, that the dialogue of *Sacco and Vanzetti*, having been dubbed with thick Italian accents, is often a challenge to understand.

Also recommended: *Who Killed Vincent Chin?*

THE SACRIFICE

With Erland Josephson, Susan Fleetwood, Allan Edwall, Valerie Mairesse. Produced by Katinka Farago. Written and directed by Andrei Tarkovsky. Photography by Sven Nykvist. Art direction by Anna Asp. Music by J.S. Back and Watazumido Shuoo. France/Sweden. Swedish with English titles. Color. 145 minutes. 1986.

A bargain is made with God. A sacrifice is made for life.

A man and his young son are watering a tree with buckets of water from a lake. As they work, the man tells the boy that he believes if a person were to do precisely the same thing every day at the same time, day after day, the world would be changed. The man's name is Alexander. He lives with his family in a house on the steppe. Today is his birthday. In the evening, as they are preparing his birthday dinner, an explosion shakes the house. Before the electricity fails, news comes on the black-and-white television screen—war has been declared. People begin to cry. His wife is screaming. Candles guide their way from room to room. The little boy is asleep upstairs, the moonlight shining on his bed, the windows open to the night. Alexander prays to God. He bargains with him—he will give up his house, his wife, and his son—if time will turn back and remove the bomb and the war. A friend comes to the house and tells him to lie with the maid, Maria, in her cottage. If, while making love to her, Alexander wishes the world to be right again, it will be so. He spends the night with Maria, but wakes up in the house on the steppe. The lights are lit. Breakfast is being cooked. No one speaks of the events of the night before. There is no war; no bomb has dropped. Alexander waits for his family to leave on an outing; then he sets the home ablaze. When they return, the house is enveloped in flame. They run helplessly back and forth. Alexander explains that he set the fire to keep his promise to God. An ambulance carries him off into the mist. Maria follows for a while on her bike. Smoke rises and is visible for miles. Someone asks where the little boy is. As the ambulance passes the lake, we see the child there pulling buckets of water out, watering the tree and lying beneath it to contemplate a world where sameness and constancy will coax miracles from life. *The Sacrifice* is a rare work of art pondering a parallel universe of nonform. It is symbolism, grace, novel hopes, lenient whispers, and elegant intangibles, drawing on a deep wellspring of suspicions, temptations, and terror. Tarkovsky is a master. If something seems to be missing from *The Sacrifice*, we can be sure the fault is in us, not the movie.

Also recommended: *Savages*.

SALT OF THE EARTH

With Will Geer, Juan Chacon, Rosaura Revueltas, David Wolfe, Melvin Williams, and David Sarvis. Produced by Paul Jarrico, Sonja Dahl Biberman, and Adolfo Barela. Directed by Herbert Biberman. Screenplay by Michael Wilson Biberman. Photography by Leonard Stark and Stanley Meredith. Music by Sol Kaplan. USA. Black and white. 94 minutes. 1953.

The true story about striking International Mining and Smelting Union, local 890, in Bayard, New Mexico.

For the reasonable and legal action of striking for better living conditions and higher pay, Mexican-American zinc miners were harassed by the mining company; the local sheriff's department; the citizens of Bayard, New Mexico; the FBI; the CIA; and the House Un-American Activities Committee (HUAC). Force and threat of force were used to try to break the strike and stop production of the film. Through an injunction of the Taft-Hartley Act, it became illegal for men to stand in the picket line. The wives of the miners evaded compliance to the intent of the injunction by standing in for their husbands while the men stayed home, watched the children, did the laundry, and cooked the meals. Some of the husbands were embarrassed to be doing housework and depending on women in the strike line. Our hero (Chacon) is humiliated by the role reversal. He tells his wife (Revueltas) to stay home so he'll be free of the degrading chores. She refuses, "The mine owner pushes you down. Do you feel better having someone lower than you? Who's neck will I stand on to make me feel superior? I don't want anyone lower than I am. I want to rise up and push everything up with me as I go." The moving performance by Revueltas would be her last. During filming, she was arrested for a minor passport violation and deported to Mexico where HUAC blacklisting ended her acting career. The processing of the film was also plagued by interference. The completed film was taken to eight processors before it was developed under an alias title. Throughout production, the townspeople of Bayard refused to do business with anyone involved in the film. Fights were picked with the crew. There were death threats. A local teacher wrote to Walter Pidgeon, then president of the Screen Actor's Guild, telling him someone was making an "anti-American, racial issue, propaganda film" out in New Mexico. It was Pidgeon who notified the CIA and the FBI and HUAC. HUAC promised to do all it could to prevent the screening of the "communist-made film." Part of the reason for the tidal wave of negative reaction to *Salt of the Earth* was its timing. In 1953, producers, writers, actors, and extras were all being harassed by HUAC. Producer Paul Jarrico was blacklisted when he made this film, as was Will Geer. Biberman was one of the Hollywood Ten—he served five months in jail for refusing to cooperate with HUAC. Most of the cast parts are played by actual miners. Geer and Revueltas were the only professional actors used. When it was released, *Salt of the Earth* was boycotted in most theaters across the U.S. Only thirteen theaters showed the film. Advertisers refused to carry promotionals. But it ran to enthusiastic audiences in the USSR, China, Germany, Canada, France, and several other European countries. During the 1960s and 1970s it was discovered by the civil rights generation, feminists, and anti-capitalists.

Also recommended: *The Wave.*

SALVADOR

With James Woods, Jim Belushi, John Savage, Michael Murphy, Tony Plana, Colby Chester, Elpedian Carrillo, and Cindy Gibb. Produced by Oliver Stone and Gerald Green. Directed by Oliver Stone. Screenplay by Oliver Stone and Richard Boyle. Photography by Robert Richardson. Music by Georges Delerue. USA. English. Color. 122 minutes. 1985.

The experiences of American photographer Richard Boyle in El Salvador during American intervention.

Richard Boyle (Woods) is a photographer, a free spirit, and a paranormal liar living on borrowed film stock on his way to El Salvador to cover the war down there for anybody who will pay his way. The only thing that could possibly stop him is a state trooper. "Mr. Boyle, your license has been revoked. You're driving without a license, registration, or insurance. You've got four outstanding speeding tickets, all gone to warrants, forty-three unpaid parking tickets, and your press card is out of date." "Out of date? Shit." Dr. Rock (Belushi) bails him out and winds up riding down to El Salvador with him since they only have three dollars between them and no place to live. It's a war zone in a foreign language, with terrorists, government madmen, death squads, and poverty. But assignments are scarce. Boyle and fellow photographer John Cassady (Savage) go on a shoot to El Playon, the city dump for the war dead, where bodies decompose along with the mountains of garbage. There are 10,000 "disappeared" people in El Salvador. There are kids with no arms. Back home Ronald Reagan is saying, "We are trying to halt the infiltration into the Americas by terrorists who are aiming at the whole Central and possibly South and eventually North America." There is "humanitarian assistance" money for the military. There are U.S. troops sent in to train killers. Boyle borrows enough film to document the carnage of the U.S.-supported regime. He nails the power elite, "I'm not a communist. I love my country; that may surprise you. You trained these butchers. They created El Playon. You let them kill whoever they want, all because they aren't commies. You've created a Frankenstein. . . . All you're doing is creating misery here. The U.S. stands for something—human rights, for everybody on this planet." When Archbishop Romero is gunned down in his church and Katharine Moore and three nuns are raped and shot dead on a country road, U.S. Ambassador Tom Kelly (Murphy) cuts off U.S. aid. On its own, the right wing sinks under the people's assault. Cassady will die proving that U.S. military support has been restored. In *Salvador*, Oliver Stone, John Savage, Michael Murphy, James Woods, and Jim Belushi have executed an unflinching tactical strike on U.S. puppet regimes and the atrocities inflicted by them on the people of El Salvador.

Also recommended: *Missing*.

SAVAGES

With Sam Waterston, Susan Blakely, Lewis J. Stadlen, Kathleen Widdoes, Martin Kove, Russ Thacker, Eva Saleh, Anne Francine, Ultra Violet, Neil Fitzgerald, Thayer David, Salome Jens, Margaret Brewster, Asha Puthili. Narrated by Lilly Lessing and Claus Jurgen. Produced by Ismail Merchant. Directed by James Ivory. Written by George Swift Trow, Michael O'Donoghue, and James Ivory, based on an idea by James Ivory. Photography by Walter Lassally. Music by Joe Raposo. Black and white, sepia, and color. U.S.A. English, Greek titles, and German. 106 minutes. 1972.

A band of stone-age people experience accelerated cultural evolution.

"In the forest where perfect spheres are unknown, the arrival of a croquet ball causes astonishment." Somewhere in a parallel universe, the
"Mud People" are interrupted on the verge of human sacrifice when an
errant, airborne croquet ball lands in their midst. A seer picks it up and
traces its aura through the woods to a deserted mansion on a lawn.
Someone lived here moments before the cobwebs grew in doorways.
The Mud People examine the paintings, mirrors, clothing, fur, jewelry,
globes, magnifying glasses, and books. They learn to speak and come
to know the secrets of electric trains: "The little engine is Edrue, the Fire
God, and the bands of steel are Elba, his lover. They are enchanted.
Edrue is condemned to travel on the body of his lover without ever finding her." And the secrets of plants: "This is a misshapen octahedron.
This is as many as you will ever see in one place. Don't touch it. Don't
breathe on it. Don't do anything with it because it will turn brown.
Don't touch the flowers. If you touch them, they will die." And the secrets of plums: "Duplicity, remorse, glandular imbalance, an illegible
missive, a soiled kimono, an explosion at the mill, disinterment, rubber
sheets, rubber sheets, trench warfare, worthless endearments, ink eradi-
cator, ant farms, webbed fingers, a punctured thumb, sheep emotions,
faded carpets." Their curiosity solves riddles of history: "Toward the
middle of the 16th century, a woman attracted attention. . . . She was
possessed of the art of modulating her voice so that it seemed to emanate from her elbow, her foot, or a place it would be improper to name.
She was possessed of the devil. But, as a special favor, instead of being
burned at the stake, she was banished to the island of St. Thomas forever." "As a favor to whom?" "What?" "Well, as a special favor—
instead of being burned at the stake—as a favor to whom?" "I don't
know. I've repeated the story exactly. There's nothing more to say."
They have discovered and interpreted civilization. It's a world of moral
isolation, lesbian love, suicide, petty cruelty, and indulgences of style.
But it is only the apogee of a perishing orbit. It is a delicate vista low-
ered too low on its own horizon—so low they are pulled back into the
world of blood wounds and human tribal sacrifice. *Savages* is a stunning anthropological witticism about the origins of myth, mystery, culture, and civilization. The persuasion of its ingenuity is a minor miracle
of sight, sound, and ideas under the poetic direction of James Ivory and
indulged with Lassally's lavish colorless, sepia, and color photography.

Also recommended: *The Sacrifice.*

SAYONARA

With Marlon Brando, Red Buttons, James Garner, Miyoshi Umeki, Martha Scott, Miika Taka, Kent Smith, Douglas Watson, Soo Young, Patricia Owens, Ricardo Montalban, and Reiko Kuba. Produced by William Goetz. Directed by Joshua Logan. Written by Paul Osborn, based on the novel by James A. Michener. Photography by Ellsworth Fredericks. Music by Franz Waxman. USA. English. Color. 147 minutes. 1957.

A story of love that overcomes racism and red tape in post-World War II Japan.

Sayonara means good-bye. Part of U.S. government policy after World War II was to force American military personnel to say good-bye to their Japanese spouses when their tours of duty were over. The U.S. government could not prevent Americans from marrying Japanese nationals, but they could deny U.S. resident visas to the husbands, wives, and children of these unions. Pamphlets were distributed to service men and women summarizing the hardships of an interracial relationship. "Think it over Americans." "But will your family accept her?" "Things you need to know before marrying an oriental." Even appearing at the officer's club with a Japanese friend was "out and out fraternization . . . a disgrace to the uniform." Marlon Brando is a career aviator who is beginning to lose interest in the "splendid" sport of shooting other human beings out of the sky. Maybe he doesn't want to buck for a star and do the right thing for the great white race after all. He only went to West Point because his father expected it. And now he's supposed to talk Kelly (Buttons) out of marrying Katsumi (Umeki), but he prefers to stand up for them at their wedding and to explain to the general that they weren't to be stopped, "They were very much in love." He will eventually lose all willingness to comply with racist military standards that condemn love and ruin lives. He breaks off with his fiancée and falls in love with Hana Ogi (Young) after seeing her perform for the Matsubiashi Dance Troupe. The general *and* his wife are appalled, "Don't you think it's time you got back into the mainstream of your life?" "If I had a million years," says Brando, "I don't know if I could explain how all this happened." It's hard to think of a role Brando has played with more affection and tenderness than the part he plays in this anti-military, anti-racist story about love besieged by racism and red tape in post-war Japan. Astonishing club-car cultural excursions and Kabuki, Matsubiashi, and puppet theater segments throughout.

Also recommended: *Camila.*

SECRET HONOR: A POLITICAL MYTH

With Philip Baker Hall. Produced and directed by Robert Altman, with the cooperation of the University of Michigan Department of Communications and the Los Angeles Actors Theatre. Written by Donald Freed and Arnold M. Stone, based on their stage play, "The Last Will and Testament of Richard M. Nixon." Photography by Pierre Mignot. Music by George Burt. USA. English. Color. 90 minutes. 1984.

A fictional Richard M. Nixon spills all there is to spill.

You want to make a movie. All you have is a tape recorder, a loaded revolver, four closed-circuit television monitors, and a bottle of Chivas Regal. Oh, yeah, and Richard Milhous Nixon, who's defending himself to a mythical judge in a mythical trial by fire. And he's taking everybody with him if he can. "The founding fathers were nothing more than a bunch of *snotty English shits* that never trusted any elected president in the first place." They "caused the White House to be built in a swamp...for Christ's sake, and Congress up on a *Goddamn hill!*" "Yes, I'm crawling down here in the swamp where the founding, fucking fathers put the White House in the first place." It's a type of absolution. He feels so alone. To "Henry Asshole Kissinger: They gave you the Nobel Peace Prize and they called me the Mad Bomber." "That fat fuck is walking around telling everyone that I'm nuts and he all the time thinks that he's Napoleon or Metternick." As for Uncle Sam: "He's the American nightmare. He's nothing but a pitiful giant—an old man being eaten alive by armies of Ellsbergers, Ralph Naders, Jane Fondas, and all led by Hiss...Alger Hiss-s-s-s!" On his mother's baby grand piano ("the fucking museum is *not* going to get you"), he accompanies himself, "The Reds, the Reds, the Reds, the Reds, atheists, godless, spying Reds, hiding under democratic beds. Oh the Reds, the Reds...." My mother said, 'there is no path to peace, peace *is* the path.' That's what my mother said." "I wanted to grow up to be Abraham Lincoln, but you know what I found out? I found out that the world is nothing more than a bunch of second-generation mobsters and their lawyers and the PR guys and the new money crooks...and the old money crooks... that's what public life is all about." He tells the tape recorder he leaked the Watergate tapes through Deep Throat to escape a quagmire of corruption that was exhausting him. "They needed Nixon in the White House for eight more years. It involved what else...money, power...millions for the Bohemian Grove guys. And billions for the mob, because of the...the heroin...to keep the war in Vietnam going until 1976 at all cost, to accept the draft in '76 for a third term, seal the deal with China against the Soviet Union and carve up the market of the rest of the world....You know what I did? I sold my soul at Bohemian Grove for shit...." "Your Honor, my client is guilty of one thing—being Richard Milhous Nixon!" Secret honor is what Nixon was supposed to have had while suffering public shame—a giant among well-kept secrets.

Also recommended: *Millhouse: A White Comedy*

A SENSE OF LOSS

Written, produced, and directed by Marcel Ophuls. France/USA. English. Color. 120 minutes. 1972.

The Irish Republican Army and the war for an independent Ireland.

The enthusiastic celebration of the St. Patrick's Day Parade in New York City effectively emphasizes the lack of awareness and sensitivity in America for the tragedy in Northern Ireland. The festivities are interrupted by a small group of people trying to join the parade carrying a coffin. The police surround them, causing many to fall. The coffin is thrown aside. The parade sweeps on. It was just an easily overwhelmed intrusion of radicals at the gala annual even. In Northern Ireland, a real funeral is in progress for one of the children lost to the struggle for a unified and independent Ireland. Ophuls' camera pieces together a story of violently repressed campaigns for independence, religious persecution, and British imperialism that has divided the people and the country. By 1972, terrorism has become so commonplace in Belfast that troops patrol the streets on Christmas day. Whole rows of houses burst into flame. A trip to the market could kill you. None of this causes either shock or despair. Parents raise their children at war. Their lives revolve around it. The proudest families are the ones with both mother and father in prison or dead. Political activist Bernadette Devlin sits on an empty beach. She says the people of Northern Ireland "have forgotten the things they used to do for fun. It's not that they don't do them anymore, it's that they have forgotten that they ever did them." The quiet beach stretches behind her. Every open wall is covered with political graffiti. The Special Powers Act has legalized the massacre of people struggling for freedom. Catholics feel persecuted, but no one admits persecuting them. Magistrates are insensitive to their own decrees. *Sense of Loss* documents the magnitude of the British retaliation against the freedom fighters in Northern Ireland—and the magnitude of the cover-up. People on the streets in London simply don't know or don't believe that there is repression. Members of the Irish Republican Army talk about arrests, police brutality, and family tragedy. One young mother of three has been crippled by gunshot wounds. Another family has lost their seventeen-month-old son. A young girl lies in the street in a pool of blood. A widow sits with her seven children. An IRA member says, "If you treat people like animals, you can't complain if you get a bloody revolt." Devlin calls England "an empire on which the blood never dries."

Also recommended: *Hidden Agenda*.

SEVEN DAYS IN MAY

With Burt Lancaster, Kirk Douglas, Ava Gardner, George Macready, John Houseman, Martin Balsam, Frederic March, Edmond O'Brien. Produced by Edward Lewis. Directed by John Frankenheimer. Screenplay by Rod Serling, based on the novel by Fletcher Knebel and Charles Waldo Bailey II. Photography by Ellsworth Fredricks. Music by Jerry Goldsmith. USA. English. Black and white. 120 minutes. 1964.

A political drama: who's the better choice for running a country—the elected representatives or the military?

Kirk Douglas, George Macready, and the Kirk Douglas production company are together again (see *Paths of Glory*, 1957), along with a cast of Hollywood greats, to present us with the reasonably probable premise that the U.S. government is in danger of being taken over by the U.S. military. Burt Lancaster is General James Matton Scott of the U.S. Air Force who will destroy the world if necessary to save us from the Russians. It's all so very plausible. Lancaster, responding to the President's move to negotiate a disarmament treaty with the Soviets, lays the gridwork for a military coup. His personal friend and long-time associate Col. "Jiggs" Casey (Douglas) eventually becomes suspicious enough to explain his paranoias to the President (March), who calls in his most trusted associates to investigate the warnings. It's intriguing. How is the President going to dislodge war thoughts from the head of the war man? It's got to be like dislodging egg ideas from the head of Humpty Dumpty. To Lancaster, the proposed disarmament treaty is an act of "unsupportable negligence." "We've stayed alive because we've built up an arsenal, and we've kept the peace because we've dealt with an enemy who knew we would use that arsenal. Now we are to believe that a piece of paper will take the place of missile silos?" Heavy, very heavy. Paper versus missiles. That's a tough one. But the President can take it. When someone refers to Lancaster as "the enemy," the President responds, "Scott is not the enemy. The enemy is the nuclear age. It happens to have killed man's faith in his ability to influence what happens to him. And out of this came a sickness—a sickness, a frustration, a feeling of impotence, helplessness, weakness. And from this, this desperation, we look for a champion. . . . for some it was Senator McCarthy; for some it was General Walker. Now, it's Scott." The bomb made everyone feel small—too small to live without the bomb. The President makes another hit when he and Scott come face to face. "If you have such a fervent, evangelical affection for your country, why, in the name of God . . . don't you try to get it through the normal democratic process the flag represents?" Lancaster remains unmoved. For him, E does not equal MC^2. But he does begin to suspect that things are going against him. He suspects a leak, and when he meets Douglas in one of the final scenes, he levels his gaze and asks, "Do you know who Judas was?" There's a pause. Douglas's shoulders are exceptionally broad, his waist exceptionally thin. "Yes," he answers, "*I* know who Judas was." For some reason it's a very sad moment. Sad to see the cold war at work among friends, dividing the people, dividing the country, dividing this world and worlds to come. It would be a good idea not to underestimate films like this that grapple with the awesome and opposed philosophies of our time.

Also recommended: *Paths of Glory*.

SHERMAN'S MARCH
A Documentary Meditation upon the Possibilities of Romantic Love in the South during an Era of Nuclear Weapons Proliferation

Written, produced, directed, and photographed by Ross McElwee. USA. English. Color. 161 minutes. 1985.

Ross McElwee tries and fails to get a girlfriend even though he's got a movie camera on his shoulder. Or, a young man starts out tracing Civil War casualties and gets derailed by a nesting urge.

"In 1864, Sherman began his famous march to the sea with an army of 60,000. He swept into the South, destroying Atlanta, Georgia, Columbia, South Carolina, and dozens of smaller towns. His troops plundered houses, destroyed livestock, burned buildings, and left a path of destruction sixty miles wide and seven hundred miles long before finally forcing a Confederate surrender. Traces of the scars he left on the South can still be found." But not by McElwee. After he mentions the sofa stabbed full of holes in his aunt's attic, we discover that Sherman is a detail irrelevant to all that goes on in the rest of *Sherman's March*. This is a film about Pat and Kathie and Cindy and Jackie and Claudia and some other women Ross knows. If we hear anything socially relevant after the opening quote, it will be from one of them. Jackie is an activist working to stop bomb plants, nuclear waste dumping, and nuclear reactors in South Carolina. This prompts Ross to tell about witnessing a nuclear test in the Pacific as a child. "We were eight hundred miles from the test sight. But at 11:00 P.M., a white flash turned the night sky whiter than noon. Honolulu behind us was visible as if it were broad daylight. The flash gave way to lingering green light that faded to a deep red." And then there's Claudia, who wants to be an actress. And Kathie, who does odd squatting exercises while wearing no underwear. This one lives almost alone on a bug-bitten island and thinks about linguistics. That one is hugging him while the camera goes wrong. "Pat is gone. I have no idea what to do. The color T.V. is broke." "Should I stay here and film Claudia or continue to trace Sherman's march as I originally planned?" There are women's legs, women's arms, women's underarms. "Both my life and my film seems in limbo." "Why aren't you in love with me?" Hmmmm. Male critics predict: "You will be in a pleased delirium." "It's wonderfully goofy." The highlight of Ross' hormone quest is a visit to a monument in South Carolina. Etched on a granite block, in twelve languages is a message in case the world is destroyed by nuclear weapons: "Seek Harmony." "Avoid Petty Laws." "Have a World Court." "Leave Room for Nature. Leave Room for Nature."

Also recommended: *Speaking Directly.*

SHIP OF FOOLS

With Simone Signoret, Jose Ferrer, Lee Marvin, Oskar Werner, Elizabeth Ashley, Jose Greco, Michael Dunn, Charles Korvin, Vivian Leigh, George Segal, Heinz Ruehmanns, Lilia Skala, Barbara Luna, Alf Kjellin, Werner Klemperer, John Wengraf, Olga Fabian, Gila Golan, Oscar Beregi, Karen Verne, Paul Daniel, David Renard, and Henry Calvin. Produced and directed by Stanley Kramer. Written by Abby Mann, based on the novel by Katherine Anne Porter. Photography by Ernest Laszlo. Music by Ernest Gold. USA. English. Black and white. 148 minutes. 1965.

Passengers on an oceanic voyage come face to face with their illusions, desperation, and hate.

A *Ship of Fools* is populated by dwarfs, Jews, political dissenters, Spanish laborers, dogs, working girls, Nazis, socialites, cowboys, and artists. Each is on a journey toward submission or temptation. Each is part of a puzzle that will not be solved. Each will struggle but be unable to remain unchanged. The random price of sugarcane, the strong right arm of the law, the health of a despised wife, passion, and hard cynicism have brought them together. Here, the sincerely sinister meet softhearted dupes. Lonely hearted women stand by railing in the night. Cabin mates are cruelly matched. A pampered pet may strike a pitiful revenge. Open confessions go unheard. Simone Signoret is sailing to prison. She's done too much for freedom to have freedom for herself. She's a candle glowing in human form. She's too ripe with superlatives for Oskar Werner to forgo. He's the ship's doctor supplying her with "medications" to help her forget enough to sleep. He loves her for being all that he never was. His whole life has been emptier than a shell. "I was the perfect dupe. I believed anything anybody ever told me. I was full of the highest hopes and the most unbelievable innocence." For Signoret, it was very different. "I realized that every bit of food I ate, every piece of clothing I wore came from them. I began hiding agitators in the chapel of the house, and I ended by helping them get arms." He will follow her to prison, but the anchor of his existence holds him back. As he despises himself, he despises everything false, everything destructive, all cruelty, hypocrisy pointed unkindnesses, and the bigotries of society. He's outraged at last with anti-Semitic seating charts and cold stabs at vanity. "You good people can't even exist without your prejudices, and the worse thing is, you can't even recognize what you are. . . . I wonder if it's true that life is really as stupid and meaningless as it seems to be on this ship." He's haunted by the power of his discontent. Whole decks full of migrant workers sleep on cots so others can demean them. One of them will die too ennobled for their gratitude. He despairs that he can neither change these things nor change himself. "We are the intelligent, civilized people who carry out orders we are given, no matter what they are." He's a marvelous, sympathetic, selfdevouring archetype, with a face from a Greek myth. Oskar Werner and Simone Signoret. And Vivian Leigh in bleary-eyed charm, smiling her southern-comfort smile at crag-faced Lee Marvin, who maybe will believe she's young again. And Jose Greco, cooking up fascist attitudes like a referee at a bomb factory. Whoever was in this movie was never as good again, except Signoret, who knew no other way. *Ship if Fools* is an unsurpassable film of social exploitation, futility, and paradox. Few films try as hard to do so much and succeed so well. Stanley Kramer deserved an Oscar; he brought the stars down out of the sky to give us this exquisite, unforgettable film in which he balances the darkness and the light and all the shadows in between.

Also recommended: *Paths of Glory*.

SILKWOOD

With Meryl Streep, Kurt Russell, Cher, Craig T. Nelson, Diana Scarwid, Fred Ward, Ron Silver, Charles Hallahan, and Josef Sommer. Produced by Mike Nichols. Written by Nora Ephron and Alice Arlen. Photography by Miroslav Ondrecik. Music by Georges Delerue. USA. English. Color. 131 minutes. 1983.

Dramatization of the life of Karen Silkwood, who helped fight nuclear power industry corruption.

The Kerr-McGee Nuclear Power Plant in Cimarron, Oklahoma, doesn't have time to spare for real drills. At KM, workers eat birthday cake off the floor and ignore emergency sirens because every single one of them "is only a test." The plant is running twenty-four hours a day, double shifts, overdrawn on a deadline. Beneath the Buck Rogers overalls and last week's gossip is the fear of contamination. There is external contamination and internal contamination. Dolly, Drew, and Karen (Cher, Russell, and Streep) are just in it to make a living like everybody else. Secret exposure catastrophes and doctored negatives are company business. If people snoop around asking questions about trucks burned in pits or radiation leaks, someone may put a few micrograms of pluto fluid in their urine sample kit. And if you are in a hurry getting ready for work in the morning, you might spill the urine kit and spread plutonium everywhere, without even knowing it. You may become externally and internally contaminated at the same time. When Kerr-McGee becomes a threat to Karen Silkwood's health, she tries to investigate the counterfeit X rays as an agent of the local union. The real Karen was on her way to an interview with the press to discuss what she had found when her car was hit from behind and plunged over an embankment, killing her and effectively quieting the investigation. Nevertheless, the KM plant was closed down barely a year after Silkwood's death. On the charge of criminal negligence in the radiation contamination of their daughter, Karen Silkwood's family won a sizable settlement from Kerr-McGee. This film is a milestone work of art that helped stall nuclear power enthusiasm in the U.S. Beyond that, it is a sophisticated dramatic achievement, in which all the principal stars give unadorned performances as people whose lives are dominated by an industry under no one's control. Director Nichols has created a film memorial to Karen Silkwood and a testament to the tragedy of nuclear power.

Also recommended: *The China Syndrome.*

SLAVE OF LOVE
(RABA LYUBVI)

With Yelena Solovey, Rodion Nakhapetov, Aleksandr Kalyagin, Konstantin Grigoryev. Directed by Nikita Mikhalkov. Screenplay by Friedrich Gorenstein and Andrei Mikhalkov-Konchalovskiy. Cinematography by Pavel Lebeshev. Music by Eduard Artemiev. USSR. Russian with titles. Color. 94 minutes. 1976.

A pampered silent-screen star becomes a Bolshevik revolutionary.

Olga (Solovey) is a luscious, soliloquy-starved luminary of the silent screen in Czarist Russia in 1917. She's ravishing, but her beauty does not discourage her soul from craving meaning. Movies are trivial. There is a revolution going on. She lisps out compassion for the "Bolshies." To directors, revolution lacks the fascination of film media. Civil uproar is cutting off film stock supplies. They want raw film. They want the guards to quit disrupting the sets. Whether the Czar falls or the Bolsheviks rise or the peasants are freed from bondage, why does it have to disrupt their film? Viktor Ivanych Pototsky (Nakhapetov) is the cameraman/revolutionary smuggling films of Czarist war atrocities to the Bolsheviks in the south. He needs someone to help him hide films for the couriers. Olga sits with him in the park between takes, lounging in the warmth of his adoration. Will she hide films in her dressing room and work for the revolution? She teases him. She should tell everyone he's a Bolshie. The thrill of purpose possesses her as she smuggles film past befuddled Czarist guards. Her beauty empties their minds. She's a national treasure. She wheels revolutionary footage around in doll buggies. She asks Ivan, "What would they do if they caught you?" He smiles and says, "They would kill me." At a showing of one of the films, Olga arrives in a princess gown and leaves humiliated with her life and despising her own existence. She wants to go to Moscow and help show the films, but she lacks the power to liberate herself from stardom. She is sitting at an outdoor cafe the day Ivan drives up in a yellow convertible and hands her a package before being shot down in the street. His death shatters her last resistance to revolutionary life. She will fight for the people and come to be on a runaway trolley on her knees, hair streaming in the wind, watching Czarist horsemen gaining on the carriage. She talks to them, her voice drowned to a whisper by the roar of the trolley and the thunder of hooves. "You are worse than beasts." "You will be cursed by your country and soldiers." She has lost everything and becomes more exotic as a martyr for the Soviet Socialist Republics than wealth, fame, or beauty could have made her.

Also recommended: *The Official Story.*

SOLDIERS OF ORANGE

With Jeroen Krabbe, Rutger Hauer, Peter Faber, Derek De Lint, Eddy Habbema, Lex Van Delden, Edward Fox, Dolf DeVries, Susan Penhaligon, Andrea Domburt, Huib Rooymans, Rijk De Gooyer, Belinda Meuldijk, Gus Hermus, Del Henny, and Rene Koldehoff. Produced by Robert Houwer. Directed by Paul Verhoeven. Written by Robert Verhoeven, Gerald Soetman, and Kees Holierhoek, based on the autobiography of Eric Hazelhoff Roelfzema. Photography by Peter De Bont and Jost Vacano. Music by Rogier Van Otterloo. Holland. In Dutch and English with English titles. Color. 165 minutes. 1979.

The story of how Dutch college students helped resist fascism during World War II.

This screenplay is based on actual diary entries, which makes it pretty hard to complain about how much the resistance effort resembles a college fraternity hazing. I wasn't there. Eric (Hauer) was. So maybe I should have my eyes examined. Part of the problem is that the Soldiers of Orange *were* college students. And I guess the moviemakers didn't want us to forget that. They *aren't* ordinary. They are clever. They have steel-banded, radial nerves. They refuse blindfolds. They overdress, and they associate with sex-starved nymphs who direct history lying naked between two men. In this war, there's always time for sensuous innuendo, even if you have to double up. I did admire the guy who risked his life sending radio messages to England from occupied Holland. He led a less venturesome life and maybe didn't even own a tux, but seemed dedicated and mortal. Hauer is the incarnation of valorous savoir faire, saving the day with a saber smile. Let's just say that Zorro lives. It's fun fighting the bad guys, risking your life, perhaps losing your life, and being a blase hero whom the Queen will want to sit beside. There are scenes of Nazi cruelties. In one, a German professor is giving a demonstration in a large auditorium. He has a live human subject, whom he prods impassively with an electric probe to every part of his body. If these scenes are disturbing, it is somehow even more tragic to suspect that they exist in history only to generate matinee adventures and cinematic fame. Typical of the focus of the narrative are closing scenes in which the surviving Soldiers of Orange are looking at a picture taken of the whole group before the war. They are no more moved by this photo than they were by anything else in the movie, and neither are we. We have already forgotten the missing faces and why there are only two left living. Fighting fascism was never less of a drag, and future resistance efforts can maybe live and learn.

Also recommended: *24 Eyes.*

SOMEBODY HAS TO SHOOT THE PICTURE

With Roy Scheider, Arliss Howard, Bonnie Bedelia, Robert Carradine, Andre Braugher. Produced by Alan Barnette. Directed by Frank Pierson. Screenplay by Doug Magee. Photography by Bajon Bazelli. Music by James Newton Howard. USA. English. Color. 105 minutes. 1991.

Death-row inmate Raymond Aims has a last wish.

Roy Scheider travelled to showings of this film around the United States to raise consciousness about death row and the death penalty. He also fought Warner Brothers throughout production, intolerant of any compromise that would lessen the impact of Magee's willfully relevant screenplay. Magee based the character of Raymond Aims (Howard) on dozens of personal interviews with death-row inmates. Only when he saw the completed film did he realize how closely Aims resembled Virginia death-row inmate Joe Giarratano, whom the film was promoted to save. Arliss Howard truly withdraws into the character of Aims, coercing every gesture and expression to project his wild reconciliation to death. "All I ask is, if they are going to kill me that they have the guts to look me in the eye when they do it." He wants full television coverage of his execution, but settles for front-line photographer Paul Marish (Scheider). His camera is the innovation that lets the film stalk close-ups and arrest the torment of the execution process. Howard sits for his last portrait like a phantom child in psychic remission from life. On death row, every day is part of a gradual battle against memory, purpose, and hope. Scheider tours the electrocution chamber listening to a guard chat impassively about the death routine. "They hire a man from an ad in the personals and pay him $150 to throw the switch. He wears a hood so nobody knows who he is, and he's paid in cash so he won't have to cash a check. Twenty-two hundred volts will pass through the prisoner's body." For the execution, Aims changes into a white dress shirt. As the leather straps tighten across his arms and chest, a governor's reprieve sends him back to his cell. He's in a fury of elation. "The only thing worse than thinking about dying is thinking you might have a chance to live." The stay has been granted for "ineffective assistance"—a plea common to prisoners assigned court-appointed counsel. The film acquaints us with other death-row inmates—the impaired, the insane, the psychotic, who are unable to understand either the crime or the punishment. It's a film about the mechanics and the fallibility and the utter desolation of institutionalized homicide. Photography by Bajon Bazelli contrasts the remote world of color to Scheider's black and white freeze-frame images. This film ran in Virginia as an organizational point for public rallies and played and important part in getting Joe Giarratano's death sentence reversed.

Also recommended: *The Thin Blue Line*.

SONG OF FREEDOM

With Paul Robeson, Elizabeth Welch, George Mozart, Esme Percy, Arthur Williams, and Joan Fred Emney. Produced by H. Fraser Passmore. Directed by Elder Wells. Story by Claude Wallace and Dorothy Holloway, adapted to the screen by Ingram D'abba and Fenn Sherie. Photography by Eric Cross, Thomas Glover, and Harry Rose. Music by Eric Russell. Great Britain. English. Black and white. 80 minutes. 1938.

A black opera star makes a trip to Africa to trace his roots and help his people.

Well, that's what it says on the box. Paul Robeson was an outspoken anti-fascist and human rights martyr, hassled by the State Department, HUAC, the IRS, and British Intelligence. But before he became a radical socialist, he made this feature, which begins as an enthusiastic success story, tracing the rise of a longshoreman (Robeson) on his way to becoming an international opera star, and ends in an artistic flambe of native African culture. Robeson is such a talented actor and singer that he easily wins audiences to his side as an overnight opera sensation. When he starts talking about returning to Africa, to trace his roots, the film teeters ahead of its time, but it decays into a castration of traditional black culture when Robeson steps off the boat onto African soil. The Zinga people are outrageous, fright-wig parodies—savages best suited to colonial rule. They fall on him and take him captive, upsetting one of the subsections of Robeson's dream, which was to teach his people and help them become less primitive, backward, and barbaric. They tie him to a stake and are gathering firewood when he starts singing the king's song, which was "born in him," in Zingaese. He *must* be their true king. They stop torturing his wife and look upon him astonished. Robeson is freed to dismantle the pathetic primitive culture and to introduce education and modern technology to help lift the native people out of the stupor of the stone age. Darling film all around if you fancy low-level ink eradication missions over the history books of the African subcontinent.

Also recommended: *Paul Robeson*.

THE SORROW AND THE PITY

With Pierre Mendes-France, Sir Anthony Eden, Prof. Albert Speer, Dr. Claude Levy. Directed by Marcel Ophuls. Scenario and interviews by Marcel, Ophuls and Andre Harris. Photography by Andre Gazut and Jurgen Thieme. France. In French and German with English titles and overvoice translations. Black and white. 260 minutes. 1969.

The French respond to the German occupation of France.

Former German officer Helmuth Tausend is celebrating a family wedding. He wears his SS uniform with service ribbons. He admits that Germany should have won the war. Inflated Jewish death statistics are a slander against the National Socialist state. Asked why he wears field medals when many of his own countrymen would not approve, he explains, "They still give out medals for the same things." Across the border in Clermont, Ophuls considers the many strategic miscalculations that led to the defeat of France. Of special note, the French aristocracy collecting money to plant rose bushes on the front lines. As Hitler advanced, thousands fled along the roadways to the southern borders only to be bombed on the open roads by Nazi artillery. It was a "continual river of people, flooding south, stopped only by bullets." Mile after mile of ruin, wreckage, horse carts, baby buggies, cars, bicycles, and bodies. As the war intensified, treason spread in France. Many believed the massacre would never end. In a haze of national desperation, Marshall Petain surrendered France to Hitler. The Fuehrer rode victorious through boulevards of bombed ruins. He denied German soldiers the right to marry French women, whom he found misshapen. He controlled the film industry, producing odious propaganda disguised as art. These films—often presented as French-made—promoted the vision of German heroes cleaning up the anarchy of France. Many featured the execution of Jews guilty of violating racial purity laws with French nationals. But while many boycotted the film industry and thousands went underground to work with the resistance, others gave in to the occupation. Anti-Semitism surfaced in France to match the Nazi standard. Newspapers portrayed Jews as an unpure mixture—a deteriorated race. The French, "collaborating all along the way," introduced racist laws that were worse than the Nuremberg laws. France was covered with concentration camps filled with Jews, gypsies, communists, and Free Masons, who were handed over to the Germans on command. They rounded up children as young as sixteen years old. The Gestapo arrested over 4,000 children in France and gassed them immediately. Members of the French resistance were labeled "terrorists" and "misfits" who couldn't adapt to the new situation. Ophuls' film sorts out the roles of communism, Marxism, fascism, and German nationalism as they crossed paths in France. *The Sorrow and the Pity* is not only an incrimination of the Third Reich, war, and racist rationale, it is filmmaking according to the highest ideals of truth. It is a remarkable testament to human war fallibility.

Also recommended: *The Exiles.*

SOYLENT GREEN

With Charlton Heston, Edward G. Robinson, Leigh Taylor-Young, Joseph Cotton, Chuck Conners, Brock Peters, Paula Kelly. Produced by Walter Seltzer and Russell Thacher. Directed by Richard Fleischer. Written by Stanley R. Greenberg based on the novel *Make Room, Make Room* by Harry Harrison. Photography by Richard H. Kline. Music by Fred Myrow. USA. English. Color. 97 minutes. 1973.

New bad world food choices.

The perils of overpopulation are legion. Overpopulation is nothing more than a tiny, time-capsule H-bomb going off right at your feet. It bombs out everything and saves the people for last so they don't even care that much if they die. First the animals, then the land, then the plants. Clean air, water, flowers, strawberry jam, goat farms, and parks all get blown away, eaten away by humans. Did you think the future was going to be rosy? Well, in *Soylent Green* it's green. Charlton Heston and Edward G. Robinson (his last movie) are new bad world police detectives assigned to investigate the death of Joseph Cotton, an executive of the Soylent Company. Preliminary investigations indicate treachery. People are afraid for their lives. They're not talking. Heston has his ways though, that's what makes him so good. He gathers clues and gives them over to Robinson, his counterpart and roommate, to check out at the local book depository/research archive. What Robinson discovers there convinces him to turn himself in to the euthanasia center. Heston runs through the gloom-littered streets of New York City, reaching the death depot just in time for Robinson to whisper something in his ear before he dies. What he whispers is that Heston should follow his body out of the center to see if it goes directly to the Soylent Company. There's no time to mourn the loss of his only friend. Heston hides among dead bodies, risking his life to make a grisly discovery. All the other soylents were produced from plants, but there are no more plants. There is no more anything. There is only people. At the Soylent factory, the recent dead are converted into food chips. Back outside, Heston, pursued by Soylent gunmen, manages to tell one person what he knows, "Soylent green is people." What he sees in the other man's eyes is not disbelief, it is not disgust. It is indifference. Nobody cares what they eat as long as they eat. Or maybe they care a lot but have a family to support. Or maybe they're afraid. What a relief that this is just a movie and that we don't live in a world of such passive, degenerate submissiveness. This could *never* happen to us. It's just a science fiction movie—not even a *real* movie that some guy by the name of Stanley R. Greenberg thought up, probably after a bad fish dinner.

Also recommended: *Blade Runner.*

SPARROWS

With Mary Pickford, Roy Stewart, Mary Louise Miller, Gustav von Seyffertitz, Mary Louise Miller, Specs O'Donnell, Charlotte Mineau. Directed by William Beaudine. Screenplay by C. Gardner Sullivan, based on the original story by Winifred Dunn. Photography by Charles Rosher, Karl Struss, and Hall Mohr. Music by Rosa Rio on the organ. USA. Silent with titles. Black and white. 111 minutes (corrected speed version). 1926.

Orphans escape the clutches of oppression and fall into the lap of luxury.

This is the tale of a group of orphans being kept as slaves in a swampland in the South. America's sweetheart, Mary Pickford, is the oldest of the slave kids. She protects and fights for the younger ones and finally leads them on a perilous escape through gator-laden bogs and swampy, quicksand death traps. The entire film is eerie and supernatural, with ghostly swamps oozing away in the back of every scene. When the kids escape, they land on what appears to be the bad side of Transylvania. Back in 1926, actors worked hard for their money—even little ones. Here, they are crawling across rotting branches and swinging on ropes from tree to tree. They are falling into goo; they are covered in mud. King-sized alligators lurk nearby to eat them. They are pathetic. They are pitiable. And the most pathetic, pitiful one in the bunch is the curly-headed baby whom the arch-evil slavemaster stole from a very rich family. Her little petticoats are sodden and will probably never be white again. She's a precious little actress, never complaining about being tied to Pickford's back and dragged through the mire. She points wherever she's supposed to and is generally just yummy. When the poor children are finally found by the police and the baby is taken away by her daddy to their mansion home, we are subdued, thinking about the poor kids left behind. But the baby will not eat or drink without "Mommy Molly" (Pickford) to hold the bottle. When Molly shows up, she's offered a permanent job, which she won't take unless all the orphans can come live there, too. "Won't they wreck the house?" they ask Mommy Molly. "No, they wouldn't," she responds. "They are perfect little angels."

Also recommended: *Streetwise*.

SPEAKING DIRECTLY

Produced, directed, written, and photographed by Jon Jost. USA. English. Color. 110 minutes. 1973.

Independent, semiautobiographical film devoted to themes of war and communication.

Halfway through this film we learn from an acquaintance of Jon's that *Speaking Directly* is about the implausibility of speaking directly, which is a relief of sorts since we were swimming five sizes too small in a non-narrative muumuu and feeling inadequate for it. The friend goes on to suggest that if he's right, we shouldn't take the time to see the rest of the film. Then he walks out. Jost seems to relish the whole incident and is clearly pleased that audiences now know for sure that he is over their heads. And to prove it, here comes a double-tracked segment— two voices saying completely different things on the same inches of video tape. A litany on the history of U.S. involvement in Vietnam is joined with another voice. Those who can block out this voice will learn that in the 1940's it is Ho Chi Min versus the French; 1950, the U.S. begins funding France; in 1954, the Geneva Accord temporarily divides Vietnam at the 17th parallel; in 1955, the U.S. lends a hand training the military; in 1962, the U.S. begins MAC—Military Assistance Command; in 1963, seven Buddhist monks self-immolate protesting foreign presence; in 1964, the Gulf of Tonkin; in 1967, elections; in 1968, the Tet Offensive; in 1970, Cambodia; in 1971, Lt. Calley. And the other voice? I didn't care; I never will care. I'm set up to hear one thing at a time and tire easily at contrivance. Next are interviews of random content with random people, static close-ups of the filmmaker's erect but withering penis, not-so-static masturbation episodes, and five minutes of blank screen for viewer input. Even though Jon's friend has by now become sort of a cult hero, something *does* get communicated in this film. *Speaking Directly* is all about how Jon sees the world, how isolated he feels because no one else sees it that way, how unique this makes him, and how we should pity him for it. The person I pity is the girlfriend who gave him enough money to expose himself and this film to light of day. I pity myself for watching it. I don't pity Jon. And I don't believe any of his cryptic insights were worth the trouble it took and the resources he used to make *Speaking Directly*.

Also recommended: Check local collections of other films Jost has made.

STATE OF SIEGE
(ETAT DE SIEGE)

With Yves Montand, Renato Salvatori, O.E. Hasse, Jacques Weber, Jean Luc Bideau, Maurice Teynac, Harold Wolff, Nemesio Antunes, Evangeline Peterson. Produced by Jaques Perrin. Directed by Constantin Costa-Gavras. Written by Franco Solinas and Constantin Costa-Gavras, based on the real events of Daniel Mitrone. Photography by Pierre William Glenn. Music by Mikis Theodorakis. France/USA/Italy/Germany. French dubbed into English. Color. 120 minutes. 1973.

Terrorists kidnap a corporate executive to exchange for political prisoners in Uruguay.

"If one is to believe this movie," *Motion Picture Guide* reviewers write, "the U.S. is like an infestation of cockroaches, rubbing its legs together." When *State of Siege* was released in 1973, it was denied screening at the American Film Institute theater in Washington, D.C., owing to its "glorification of assassination." It was also labeled anti-American for depicting Uruguay in 1970, where terrorism is being used by Uruguay's people's police to combat the right-wing, American-supported government. The "Tupamaros" have kidnapped three hostages, one of whom is the American Phillip Michael Santore, sent to

Uruguay by the American government as "traffic control personnel." The Tupamaros accuse him of being a CIA agent who has trained 100,000 police to help repress popular movements in Santo Domingo and Brazil. Wearing hoods to conceal their identities, the Tupamaros confront Santore with details of the CIA-backed U.S. Marine action on behalf of the United Fruit Company in Costa Rica. They talk to each other from opposite sides of a philosophic abyss. Santore has a clear conscience. Capitalism is a good thing. Imperialism is the hope of the third world. The Tupamaros explain to Santore and the other hostages what a people's revolution would mean to the politically and economically disenfranchised employees of foreign corporations. They offer systematic expositions on the hazards of the free market. The captives persistently justify their ideas and actions. If they are responsible for tortures and repressions, it is as a necessary defense against terrorists such as the Tupamaros and the threat they represent to world stability. "We are conservatives, so we don't care for change." Santore is also charged with organizing the arrest of people who went on strike when their wages were cut. Santore accuses, "You are terrorists and communists. You are against everything I stand for." If the CIA intervened to overthrow popular governments in Brazil or Santo Domingo, it was because they threatened to nationalize U.S. corporate land holdings in those countries. American industry, Santore reminds the terrorists, means jobs. He does not understand why the people are landless. To Santore, "the people" is just a euphemism for armed ingratitude. As the talks continue, the Tupamaros demand an exchange of 150 political prisoners for Santore's life, which offer the government of Uruguay rejects. Santore is executed by the people's movement.

Also recommended: *The Battle of Algiers*.

STORM OVER ASIA

From the story by I. Novokshenov. Photography by A. N. Golovnia. Directed by V. I. Pudovkin. USSR. Black and white. Silent with English titles. 98 minutes. 1928.

Mongol herders overthrow the dictatorial rule of white capitalists.

Beethoven, da Vinci, Pudovkin. They all had the same idea—just exhaust the possibilities and wait around a few hundred years for everyone else to catch up. Of course, there's one sad difference between
Pudovkin and the others. The public worships da Vinci and Beethoven
while lumping all early filmmakers together in clod-land, where they
lived groping their way into a novel medium about which they were
not expected to know a darn thing since it was just invented. Anyway,
there's no *sound*! Americans have the ideal alibi for thinking this way.
During the first decades of the 1900s, most U.S. filmmakers were busy
speeding the film through the cameras so keystone cops could run
faster (some of these movies have since been speed-corrected). While
Americans went to the movies to be entertained, the Russians were living through every phenomenal social disaster known to humanity. Film
was used to revel at revolution, decry totalitarianism, and elevate peasants to their rightful status as celebrities of the century. It's 1918. The
descendants of Genghis Khan are herders living in solitary yurts in the
depraved emptiness of the Shamo steppe. Pudovkin drains away footage into the solitude, which is the living spirit of independence to these
nomadic people. The Dali Lama is dead and his soul has transferred to
a two-year-old boy—the Buddha "whose soul eternally transmits from
the dead body into the living." Nomads and chieftains alike kneel before the child-god. But as the chiefs bow, their corrupt henchmen are
occupied stealing cattle from herders to pay the British tax. Even on the
Mongol steppe, trafficking in profit has arrived. In the civil war that follows, a common Mongol herder is mistaken for a descendent of Genghis Khan and appointed as an ally to the white government. He uses
his power to win a victory for the peasants. Ousted capitalists are belligerent, beef-fed, fur-bearing opportunists with wives festooned in jew-
els. They'll be relinquishing their unrighteous domination here and
finding other sanctuaries to invade. *Storm over Asia* is filmed through
Novokshenov's mindlessly magic lens. He and Pudovkin could overcome any imperialist invasion any time by the combined potency of
their artistic and moral euphorias.

Also recommended: *Mother.*

STREET OF SHAME
(AKASEN CHITAI)

With Machiko Kyo, Aiko Mimasu, Ayako Wakao, Michiyo Kogure, Yasuko Kawakami, Kenji Sugawara, Kumeko Urabe, Eitaro Shindo. Produced by Masaichi Nagata. Directed by Kenji Mizoguchi. Screenplay by Masashige Narusawa, based partly on the short story "Women of Sasoka" ("Susakino Onna") by Yoshiko Shibaki. Photography by Katsuo Miyagawa. Music by Toshiro Mayuzumi. Japan. Japanese with English titles. Black and white. 88 minutes. 1956.

Prostitutes in Japan struggle to change their lives.

If you're tired of films about prostitutes who love their work, here's one about women in post-World War II Japan who indenture themselves to brothels as a survival strategy and spend the entire film trying to pay off the indenturement. Family responsibilities make it hard for many of the women to save money. There are emergency medical needs and housing expenses to be met out of the modest wage each woman earns after deductions for the debt. The narrative turns strongly on the intricacies of Japanese culture. One husband tries to kill himself, explaining that he is unworthy of his wife's sacrifice. Narusawa's screenplay interprets prostitution as a flaw in society, which individuals are compelled to accommodate any way possible. The women are uncomplicated, obvious people whom audiences want to succeed. When legislation is introduced to control prostitution, they prematurely celebrate their anticipated freedom. Asked how they will survive if prostitution is banned, they realize no law can save them while society fails them.

Also recommended: *24 Eyes*.

STREETWISE

Directed by Martin Bell. Photography by Mary Ellen Mark. Written and produced by Cheryl McCall, from the *Life* magazine story "Streets of the Lost". USA. English. Color. 92 minutes. 1984.

Documentary of children surviving in the streets of Seattle, Washington.

There are common elements to homelessness anywhere in the world: panhandling, theft, drugs, guns, prostitution, rolling drunks, pimping, eating garbage, fights, arrests, selling blood, hopping trains, suicide. *Streetwise* is about children who have fallen off the edge of childhood and off the bottom of the income graphs to become the most tragic cost of a capitalist state. The film crew follows young Seattle street kids around, listening in on their conversations and philosophies of life. A fourteen-year-old prostitute says, "I don't know why these old guys like little girls, but they do. They're just dirty old men." Her casual talk about her "dates" defeats all social evolution. In Seattle, there are case workers, medical clinical staff, juvenile court, and police patrols—they know these kids by heart, but they can't help them. They are the products of broken homes, sexual abuse, and poverty. They drop out of school and never go back. They come from dysfunctional families—mother missing, father in jail, father missing, father unknown, mother alcoholic, parents that never wanted them around and so on. But even these kids have hopes for the future. They have dreams they share as they sit on the curb—they want nice homes, swimming pools, cars, jobs, and a normal family. Someday they'll be happy. Meanwhile, they sleep in abandoned buildings or in a shelter, making attachments that never last to people who move on or go to jail or die. When Dewayne visits his Dad in jail, they talk about what they'll do when his sentence is up. They want to open a shop of their own. "I love you a big, big bunch," his father tells him, as he checks for needle tracks on the boy's arms and looks to see if he's quit biting his fingernails. "You're all I've got, and unfortunately, I'm all you've got." Before his father is released, Dewayne, to whom the filmmakers have dedicated this film, hangs himself in the juvenile detention center. His case worker arranges to have his ashes scattered over the bay. He can't bring himself to put Dewayne underground. "All he ever wanted was a normal family—a mother, a father . . . he wanted to be normal and have normal things."

Also recommended: *Salaam Bombay*.

STRIKE: TOWARD A DICTATORSHIP OF THE PROLETARIAT

(STRACHKA)

With Maxim Shtraukh, Grigori Alexandrov, Mikhail Gomorov, I. Klukvin. Directed by Sergei Eisenstein. Screenplay by Sergei Eisenstein, Valeri Pletniov, and I. Kravchinovski. Photography by Edouard Tisse. USSR. Silent with English titles. Black and white. 84 minutes. 1924.

Working-class people in pre-revolutionary Russia struggle for survival against capitalist dictators.

Sergei Eisenstein was a genius. His films were monuments. But the 21st century promises faint fanfare for movies with no soundtrack. The good news is that in silent films, all languages are equal, so it really doesn't matter that *Strike* is in Russian. The setting of *Strike* is a large factory in tsarist Russia. The bourgeois capitalist managers are depicted as being viciously indifferent to the condition of the working class and criminally self-indulgent at the workers' expense. In one scene, bloated capitalists sit before a lavish banquet table pouring floods of wine into inadequate glasses as midgets perform on the table top while the workers outside in the woods are run down by the Tsar's cavalry soldiers. Eisenstein sets the workers against a backdrop of giant instruments of production. The scale of human life is mutable, first miniaturized by colossal artifacts of industry, next magnified in close-ups of human anguish and suffering. The workers' vulnerability and submission to the appetites of the machine kingdom are so complete and individual existence is so degraded, tentative, and redundant that workers only precariously avoid being devoured by the monstrous iron jaws of the workplace. There are wave-like rivers of motion throughout the film—sensuous and serpentine. Melodically paced. The afterimage is of turmoil raging in the membranous chambers of the digestive tract of the industrial revolution. Eisenstein's technique shrouds the action in a kind of gothic spirituality, accentuated by the iconic use of light in reverent close-ups of the workers' faces. The romantic elevation of the proletariat is in keeping with Marxist-Leninist theory and social realism, which aims to "reinforce the credibility of presentations of working class nobility, strength, and victory." Time will not diminish Eisenstein's achievements. If he had lived into the sound era, his name would surely be more common to American fans of film media. Today, he remains a dynamic champion of the workers' revolution and the equality this revolutionary theory promises.

Also recommended: *October.*

SUGAR CANE ALLEY

With Darling Legitmus, Garry Cadenat, Douta Seck, Francisco Charles, Marie-Jo Descas, Joby Bernabe. Produced by Michel Loulergue and Alix Regis Sumafa. Written and directed by Euzhan Palcy, based on the novel *La Rue Cases Negres* by Joseph Zobel. Photography by Dominique Chapuis. Music by Groupe Malavoi, Roland Louis, and others. Martinique. In French with English titles. Color. 103 minutes. 1983.

The lives of black sugarcane workers in Martinique.

Sugar Cane Alley is the first feature-length film of French filmmaker Euzhan Palcy. She sets her cameras up in the Caribbean—on Martinique, where wage labor now enslaves the islanders of the French colonial empire. Sugar production must match sugar markets that have escalated for a hundred years. It's a paradox of progress that multinationals and wage slavery have taken over most beautiful tropical regions and transformed paradise into havens of oppression, racism, and poverty. Sympathetic direction and against-type photography work together to fill the screen with this contradiction. The people of Sugar Shack Alley die poor so we can have affordable sugar. Children grow up working beside their parents in the fields. José (Cadenat) is not one of these. He's being raised by his grandmother (Legitmus), who will save him from the company because she sees beyond the poverty to the tyranny that perpetuates an unjust system. When a friend's baby is stillborn, she says, "That's one less black back to bend in their cane fields." She despises the white landowners and will keep José in school any way possible to be educated for a better life. When he wins a scholarship to the local school, Legitmus thanks God for a miracle, but then she discovers that the money offered covers only half the tuition. To people with no money, half is nothing. Her anger and commitment take her and José to the city where José can attend the free public school. They leave Sugar Shack Alley for a hut in the slums. José impresses his new teachers with his talent as a scholar. He wins friends and a timely stipend just as his grandmother's health prevents her from working. The tension of *Sugar Cane Alley* simmers in the background, warning us to expect misfortune to eat these dreamers alive. Palcy maybe leans a little too hard on the harpsichord with her idealized resolution to poverty—after all, all of the less-gifted young workers are still in the fields, and moving to the city might not work for every cane worker on this Earth. Still, this is a sensitive drama that navigates over dangerously unfamiliar territory.

Also recommended: *H-2 Worker.*

SWEPT AWAY

With Giancarlo Giannini and Maiangela Melato. Produced by Romano Cardarelli. Written and directed by Lina Wertmuller. Photography by Giulio Battiferri, Giuseppi Fornari, and Stefano Ricciotti. Music by Piero Piccioni. Italy. Italian dubbed into English. 116 minutes. Color. 116 minutes. 1975.

A bourgeois socialite is marooned on a deserted island with a thuggish, Marxist deckhand.

She's rich, blonde, and insensitive. She's a dragon to the hired help, who fear and despise her. She's the beauteous beast of the bourgeoisie, soon to be shipwrecked on a deserted island with Gennarino—the thug-like Marxist. On the island, "Those who eat must work for it." If she washes his pants, he will catch her a fish. She's been in a tower. Now she's at sea level, hearing lectures on fairness and sharing, experiences the humiliations that Gennarino has been saving up for her in his dreams. She has to call him Signor Carunkio and kiss his hand. She has to crawl. She's lower than a slave. She now regrets complaining so much about his cooking and having taken off her top to lie in the sun. "You did it to torture and excite us." Now he tortures and excites her. In *Swept Away*, she likes it. Somewhere along in here, between the surprises of interclass togetherness, the combined cynicisms of this film pull it away from promising commentary and toward toxic waste treatment. He slaps her for not paying taxes and for the high price of milk. If she should anger him too much, he will kill her. She is only an object of pleasure. He's abusive and cruel. So much for the dictatorship of the proletariat. She calls him her lord and master. It's very unhealthy. They never knew love could be so drastic. They are calling it love and exchanging crude vows against a background of endless sand, endless sun, and endless decay of socialist philosophy. Eventually, they are rescued and revert back to their former identities, which don't seem so bad any more. Director Wertmuller wastes another opportunity to say something about economic theory. Perhaps long ago, the world reached peak utopian potential and the thing to do now is to analyze the sadistic tendencies of Marxists who would enslave the female of the species if capitalism ever fell.

Also recommended: *Love and Anarchy.*

SWIMMING TO CAMBODIA

With Spaulding Gray. Produced by R.A. Shafransky. Directed by Jonathan Demme. Screenplay by Spaulding Gray. Photography, by John Bailey. Music by Laurie Anderson. USA. English. Color. 87 minutes. 1988.

Toxic war facts by Spaulding Gray—genius of dark truth.

He sits behind a desk. He opens a notebook. "Saturday, June 18th, 1983." He's heard about a film called *The Killing Fields.* He wants to be in it. "I'm not political at all. I don't know anything about secret bombings. In fact, I've never even voted." "Perfect, we're hunting for someone to play the American Ambassador's aide." Behind him is a scene of clouds in a blue sky. Over this he pulls a map of Cambodia. "It's the size of Missouri. . . . Ninety percent of the land was owned by the people. They knew how to have a good time. They had a good time getting born, a good time growing up . . . a good time falling in love, a good time staying in love, a good time getting married, a good time having children, a good time growing old, a good time dying. They were so open and tantric and loving they were defenseless. . . . They lost touch with evil." He pulls down another map—U.S. bombing targets of North Vietnamese sanctuaries along the Cambodian border. "The Cooper-Church amendment went through, and I found out we weren't living in a democracy." The bombing of Cambodia lasted five years. In the notebook are stories of mass murders, crazed presidential plots, body counts, Khmer Rouge, Pol Pot, cover-ups, genocide, hate, fear, broken trust, lost patriotism, deceit, defoliation, profiteering, moral chaos, and the meaningless of all that once had meaning—everything he learned while playing John Gunther Dean's aide in a film about the U.S. evacuation of American personnel from Southeast Asia. From a helicopter hovering over the rain forest floor he realizes, "My God, look how much of the jungle this movie controls.... Of course!!! War therapy—every country must and should make a major motion war film every year.... It's very much like the real event." In the major film he explains to Sam Waterston about accidental bombings. "The flier was fined $750. U.S. agents came in passing out $100 to people who had lost relatives, $50 to those who had lost legs and arms." The light dims, a fan chugs, and there is a high-pitched wavering drum sound or cello being destroyed. The film crew were "pleasure seeking colonialists... in a barbed-wire enclosed.... oasis for hedonists, a pleasure prison... surrounded by bandits and rabid dogs." The film crews venture out to stage scenes of carnage. Extras get $5 a day—$7.50 if they're amputees. Nixon is hanging on by a rip-cord. "Let the rumor get out that I've gone mad." Fifteen are wounded and four dead at Kent State. One hundred thousand protest in front of the White House. Gray turns a page in the notebook. Pol Pot—"five years of bombing, a diet of bark, leaves, and lizards up in the Cambodian jungles, an education in Paris environs in strict Maoist doctrine with a touch of Rousseau, and other things that we will probably never know about in our lifetime, including, perhaps, an invisible cloud of evil that circles the Earth and lands at random in places like Iran, Beirut, Germany, Cambodia... America...." And the Khmer Rouge—"the worst case of auto-homeo-genocide in modern history.... Who needs metaphors for hell when all this happened here on this Earth?" He met a Navy man who got high on blue-flake cocaine to sit chained to a wall in a waterproof missile silo. There is a Nuclear Destruction Club—the brotherhood of fear—and Navy pamphlets telling Navy people where to go to avoid radiation. On the train home from Bangkok, he adjusts his purple Thai sleeping mask and suddenly understands why Marilyn Monroe killed herself.

Also recommended: *The Killing Fields*.

TANNER '88

With Michael Murphy, Ken O'Conner, Mat Maloy, Veronica Cartright, Pamela Reed, Cynthia Nixon. Cameos by Pat Robertson, Robert Dole, Gary Hart, Waylon Jennings. Produced and directed by Robert Altman and Garry Trudeau. Written by Garry Trudeau. Photography by Jean Lepine. USA. English. Color. 120 minutes. 1988.

A good guy runs for the presidency in 1988 and loses.

I've said it before and I'll say it again, I love Michael Murphy. I wish he *was* president. But in 1988 he has a fat chance, because he's too nice, too honest, and too decent to fire his election committee. He believes in them. In return, they send him to the wrong places at the wrong times on buses that break down. They order inappropriate foods for rooms full of Republicans. It's not easy pushing a major candidate through every cow town on the campaign trail. There is confusion and bad weather and press hounds sucking up all the bad news even if they have to invent it. It's a tempest of ideals and images and portable sound systems, where the rules were never written down so they never stay the same. The cameo appearances of real candidates are *deja vu* and a little disorienting. Which one is the actor? Seen side-by-side, in all fairness, Tanner seems to have as much of the right stuff as the rest of the candidates. (Maybe that's why they all lost, too.) But audiences will not rip their hair out when Tanner loses his bid for the presidency of the United States. To run a country, you probably have to be able to run a staff of five. For reasons I am sure of, the credits are shown a bit at a time throughout the film. My impression is of something that is over before it starts, of a guy on the way to the campaign boneyard. He's mild-mannered all right, but maybe he wandered too close to the Kryptonite. He's about as low-key as he can get and still have a movie made about him. He gives great speeches, though. He's too good for the likes of us, or he's a couple layers too deep in the sediments of P.R. geology. The Trudeau script is puffy with political goose down. Apparently Trudeau really notices these things, and I'm wondering who he's got slated to lose in '92.

Also recommended: *The Candidate*.

TESTAMENT

With Jane Alexander, William Devane, Kevin Costner, Ross Harris, Lukas Haas, Roxana Zal, Leon Ames, Lurene Tuttle, Gerry Murillo. Produced by Jonathan Bernstein and Lynn Lippman. Directed by Lynn Littman. Screenplay by John Sacret Young, based on the story "The Last Testament" by Carol Amen. Photography by Steven Poster. Music by James Horner. USA. English. Color. 90 minutes. 1983.

**How a family and their friends cope in the aftermath
of a nuclear war.**

"Ladies and gentlemen, this is a real—beeeeep—this is a national emergency notification. Radar sources verify the explosion of nuclear devices in New York and up and down the east coast. Ladies and gentlemen, the—beep—President of the—beep—United States." The people in Hamlin, California, aren't hit by the bomb. They would not even know there'd been a bomb except for the bad television reception and bad milk. Before the bright flash of light, Hamlin used to be an ordinary town, full of fishing trips, quiet weekends, and excellent curbs. The people who run out into the streets after the emergency warning see nothing except lawns, lawn sprinklers, and elm trees shading all the streets. The bomb must have hit somewhere in the distance. It did not hit in Hamlin, which makes me wonder why they wanted to make the movie here. In *Testament*, everything happens off-screen. The war is off-screen. The bombs are off-screen. Everybody dies off-screen. They fall in love off-screen. It's like there is a great movie going on somewhere, but not here. Here, the Weatherbys—mother (Alexander), father (Devane), and kids (Zal, Haas, and Harris)—just go on with their lives, doing everything they were doing before, only now it's ironic to be eating frosted flakes. It's ironic to be having piano lessons. How aberrant to see the home movies of happily overlit, out-of-focus times. Even the symptoms of radiation sickness—gastric problems, fever, dizziness, hair loss, vomiting, skin sores—happen mostly off-screen. People in Hamlin prefer to look fine until they slump over their radios or are suddenly being sewn up in bed sheets. Kevin Costner as the young, bereaved father becomes refreshingly emotional when his baby dies (off-screen). He's pretty sad. But Alexander saves it for her diary. "I write this to keep my sanity." "I don't know what day it is." "The cemetery is full." "I can't write today." She's in the audience when the kids perform the school play. The littlest Weatherby is the Pied Piper (of Hamlin). "Your children are not dead, they will return. They are just waiting 'till the world deserves them." The real Pied Piper would have turned his flute over to these people and bought property in this land where thermonuclear war is just a bad case of the flu.

Also recommended: *Threads*.

THE THIN BLUE LINE

Produced by Mark Libson. Directed by Errol Morris. Photography by Stefan Czapsky and Robert Chappell. Music by Philip Glass. USA. English. Color. 101 minutes. 1988.

Death row inmate wins a retrial and is acquitted through the investigations of director Errol Morris.

"In October my brother and I left Ohio. We were driving to California...." Randall Adams' words are scored by Philip Glass' wavering and lamentable messianic arias. "In Dallas... I get a job right away.... It's like I'm supposed to be there." Adams has been convicted of killing a Dallas police officer and has been sentenced to die in the electric chair. "Why did I meet this kid? Why did I run out of gas at that time? It happened. It happened." A runaway on a crime spree, driving a stolen car, armed with a .22-calibre pistol and other weapons, sixteen-year-old David Harris gave Adams a ride to the gas station on the night of the murder. Harris would later brag to friends in Vidor, Texas, that he shot "that fucking pig." On Harris' testimony, Adams is arrested. Police in Klan-dominated Vidor, under the impression the dead officer was a black man, choose to believe Harris' story and refrain from "ruining a young boy's life." Dallas police recollect, "'[Adams] overacted his innocence. He didn't fight. He didn't resist. He just kept protesting his innocence." Adams is handed a confession at gunpoint and told to sign it. Officer Gus Rose called it a "friendly conversation." Adams remembers, "He pulled his service revolver on me. We looked at each other for, to me... it seemed hours. When he finally saw that he would either have to kill me or forget the signature, I guess he forgot the signature because he put his pistol up." Adams' case is confounded by such wide miscarriages of truth and legal process that his lawyer, Dennis White, resigns from the practice of law. "I just feel like I'll let other people handle these things. If justice can miscarry so badly, I'd rather do something else." The Thin Blue Line is the line of uniformed officers that stands between society and anarchy. In this case, the blue line sends an innocent man to death row and grants immunity to David Harris, who is free to add assault, robbery, burglary, kidnapping, and murder to his criminal record. The legal system of Dallas goes on to obstruct the objective deliberation of evidence by relying on spurious testimony and denying Adams' lawyers the privilege of presenting a reasoned picture of the case. When a possible retrial threatens to reverse the guilty verdict, the death penalty sentence is reduced to life in prison. Errol Morris calls his film a nonfiction feature—a combination of fact and art. As a direct result of the film, a retrial was granted in 1988. In March 1989, the murder conviction was overturned. Twelve years after his arrest, Randall Adams was free to return home to Ohio.

Also recommended: *Sacco and Vanzetti*.

THREADS

With Karen Meagher, Reece Dinsdale, David Brierley, Rita May, Nicholas Lane, Henry Moxon, Jane Hazelgrove, June Broughton. Produced and directed by Mick Jackson. Written by Barry Hines. Photography by Andrew Dunn and Paul Morris. Australia/England. English. Color. 110 minutes. 1985.

The people of Sheffield, England, readjust their lives in the aftermath of global thermonuclear war.

There are two things going on in *Threads*. First, the world is coming to an end. Second, no one in Sheffield takes note. In the background of every scene, television and radios are reporting on missing subs, oil slicks, Iran, the USSR, NATO, western interests in the Middle East, rapid deployment forces, the 84th Airborn, B-52 bombers, or AWAC's early-warning aircraft. Jets are flying overhead, drowning out conversations, but life goes on. The story of Ruth begins on May 5 and ends some thirteen years later. She's pregnant, planning her wedding, and settling things between two socially unequal families. She's scraping wallpaper. Even as she stands on a seaside cliff, a car radio will fill the air with weapons deployment updates. By May 19, a few citizens are buying extra food supplies. By the 20th, protesters are being invited to "go back to bloody Russia." On May 26, a boy walks into a grocery store to say the war has started. Soviet nuclear-tipped defense missiles have been fired. The U.S. responds. Grocery baskets tumble into the parking lot. Protests escalate. Ruth's neighbors are packing to go north. About 100,000 other people have the same idea. Banks fight off depositors. Warning sirens wail. A single warhead explodes high above the North Sea. It burns out electrical systems. Another hits near Sheffield. Hurricane-force fires drown out the howling of dogs and the screams of terror rising into the mushroom cloud that's darkening the sun. Eighty megatons hit the U.K. Two-and-a-half to nine million people are killed instantly. A direct hit stops time and sound—in silence, milk bottles melt like lava, people dissolve in flames, bones turn to powder. Buildings explode. "In the early stages, symptoms of radiation sickness and panic are identical"—vomiting, shivering, loss of bladder and bowel control. May 27—attack day plus one. Control centers are inoperable. Attack day plus one week—water shortages begin. One hundred million tons of smoke fill the air. Temperatures drop as much as 25 percent. Days are dark. Attack day plus sixteen—hospitals are scenes of the greatest horror. There are no drugs, water, or bandages. "Without electricity or medical support facilities, there is virtually no way a doctor can exercise his skill." Attack day plus twenty-two—cholera, dysentery, and typhus are rampant. Looters and vandals roam the streets. Money has no meaning. The more who die, the more food left for the rest. Ten to twenty million people lie unburied in the United Kingdom. The smell attracts rats and swarms of flies. Law collapses. Attack day plus five weeks—no water, transportation, electricity, sanitation, or food. Deaths from fallout reach a peak. Plus six weeks—dead livestock are eaten raw. Seventeen to thirty-eight million are dead. Plus four months—darkness retards the ripening of crops planted without fertilizer or agrochemicals. The world is in permanent shadow. Ruth delivers her baby alone in a stall, cutting the umbilical cord with her teeth. Winter will kill the weak. Attack day plus ten months—rats are a staple food. Intensified ultraviolet light in the atmosphere causes cancer and leukemia. Plus three to eight years—the population is at medieval levels. Plus ten years—Ruth dies prematurely aged; her daughter speaks an English degraded by misuse. Plus thirteen years—the Stone Age has returned. Weather patterns remain tortured. Horrendous black-and-white still photos portray isolated beings stunned to be alive. Ruth's daughter gives birth to the next generation. She pulls back the blood-soaked sheets and screams at what she sees there. *Threads* is an act of tremendous social responsibility and caring on the part of the filmmakers and the many professional advisors, including Arthur Katz, Carl Sagan, Joseph Rotblat, and others, who lent their scientific support to this film. It's ambitious. It's darkly focused vision serves as a critical balance to nuclear weapons promotions and war propaganda. It simply stands alone and deserves the gratitude of the people it was created to warn.

Also recommended: *The Day After*.

TIN DRUM

With David Bennent, Mario Adorf, Angela Winkler, Daniel Olbrychski, Katharina Tahlback, Charles Aznavour, Heinz Bennent, Fritz Hakl, Mariella Oliveri, Tina Engel, Berta Drews. Produced by Franz Seitz, Volker Schlondorff, and Anatole Dauman. Directed by Volker Schlondorff. Screenplay by Jean-Claude Carriere, Volker Schlondorff, and Franz Seitz, based on the book by Günter Grass. Photography by Igor Luther. Music by Fredrich Meyer. West Germany/France/Yugoslavia/Poland. German with English titles. Color. 142 minutes. 1979.

The tale of a peculiar kid who defies his parents in Germany in World War II.

After seeing his uncle touch his mother's breast (which may or may not have had anything to do with the war), Oskar is so distraught that he throws himself down the cellar stairwell in the hope that this will stop his growth. Adulthood offends him. He stays small alright. Little Oskar. This is his most conspicuous idiosyncrasy, but there is also the tin drum he has carried with him everywhere since he perceived how much it annoyed people—especially movie audiences. He uses it for good on only one occasion. While hiding under the bleachers at a Nazi rally, he beats on his drum until all the Hitler parades and posturings are converted into waltzing. It's a clever scene and a very nice gesture, however he did it. But he goes on to have a miniature Nazi uniform made for himself so he can travel to occupied outposts with some other Nazi midgets entertaining the troops. Oskar's specialty in the touring show is breaking glass with his high-pitched voice, another distinguishing, childhood characteristic. Along the road to weirdhood, Oskar's close personal relatives all die grotesque deaths, usually through some thoughtless slip up on his part. The movie is full of richly repelling scenes, such as a decaying horse's head with eels oozing from the eye sockets and mouth, which will later be cooked and served to his mother, who vomits on the first bite and can't look at another eel for the rest of her short, troubled life. Almost as unappetizing is watching Oskar (a little boy in real life) giving oral sex to his father's new young wife or having sex with her under the bedclothes. I got so bogged down on the film's distasteful qualities that I forgot to figure out what it was about. (Someone has suggested that the film explores how the Nazis rose to power through the complacency of ordinary people. Like Oskar?)

Also recommended: *Pixote.*

TO BE YOUNG, GIFTED AND BLACK

With Roy Scheider, Barbara Barrie, Blythe Danner, Ruby Dee, Al Freeman, Jr., Lauren Jones, Claudia McNeil. Produced by Robert M. Fresco. Directed by Michael Schultz. Adapted for the screen by Robert M. Fresco, based on the play and book by Robert Nemioff. Photography by Paul Goldsmith. Music by Howard A. Roberts. USA. English. Color. 90 minutes. 1972.

Reenactments of the life of black playwright Lorraine Hansberry.

"I was born on the south side of Chicago. I was born black and female. While I was still in my teens, the first atom bombs were dropped on human beings. . . . I've lost friends and relatives through cancer, lynching, war, drug addiction, alcohol, and mental illness. I have been personally the victim of physical attacks and was the offspring of racial and political hysteria." By the time Lorraine Hansberry is twenty years old, she is "sick of the universal maltreatment of my people." In this film, the members of the cast read from the journals and act out scenes in the life of Hansberry, who would become an immediate favorite with the production of her first play, *A Raisin in the Sun*, and go on to alienate the literary community when her writing turned first radical and then revolutionary. As the Rev. Martin Luther King preaches nonviolent resistance to oppression during the civil rights movement of the 1960s, Hansberry applauds, but she personally believes that nonviolence is not enough. "The condition of our people dictates revolutionary attitudes. We must use every conceivable means of struggle—legal, illegal, passive, active, violent, nonviolent, harass, petition, sit-in, lie down, debate, strike, boycott, sing hymns, and shoot from windows when the racists come cruising through our community. The acceptance of our condition is the only form of extremism that discredits us in front of our children." The extreme words are read over still shots of civil rights violence. Although she broadens her artistic objectives to encompass universals—poverty, communism, prostitution, modernity—her plays are so controversial as to be unpublishable. The publishers "haven't yet decided who won the Civil War." But as a writer, Hansberry has no illusions about her own contribution to the black liberation movement. "I remain a revolutionary intellectually, but am I prepared to give my body to the struggle?" Democracy and freedom from racist anger are the goals of her intellect, but the realities of social existence are never as clear. "I do not hate all white people. I desperately wish that I did. It would make things infinitely more simple." Speaking to the winners of the National Negro College Fund awards, she tells the young people, "You are young, gifted, and black. I know of no more dynamic combination. . . . Write about our people, tell our story."

Also recommended: *Paul Robeson*.

TO KILL A MOCKINGBIRD

With Gregory Peck, Phillip Alford, Mary Bedham, Robert Duvall, John Megna, Brock Peters. Produced by Alan Pakula. Directed by Robert Mulligan. Screenplay by Horton Foote, from the novel by Harper Lee. Photography by Russell Harlan. Music by Elmer Bernstein. USA. English. Black and white. 129 minutes. 1962.

A lawyer defends a black man against racism and violence.

If you're one of those people who hasn't seen *To Kill a Mockingbird* because you think any film made before the incorporation of Industrial Light and Magic will put you to sleep, you're already asleep. Wake up and check it out. In a 1989 interview, Gregory Peck called it, "Such a splendid production—such a reward. More than the fame, more than the money, more than the status and the honors is the knowledge that something you've put your life and work into is still meaningful to people after twenty-seven years." *To Kill a Mockingbird* brought tears to author Harper Lee's eyes when he saw it on the screen. Common inspirations infuse the Horton Foote script. Along the way to an inspired defense and a guilty verdict, Atticus Finch (Peck) explains racism, poverty, and intellectual prejudice to his children (Peters and Bedham). Why do many of his clients pay their legal fees with garden produce? Why is kindness better than cruelty no matter what color people are or what kind of clothes they wear or what food they eat or how smart they are or where they live or how they talk or who they are or who they know? It's a simple story about a small-town lawyer defending a black man against charges of rape. To hear their father at work, the kids sneak into court and sit in the balcony with the black spectators. When the trial ends, the blacks stand in homage, saying to Peters and Bedham, "Stand up children, your father's passing by." It took only ten weeks to shoot this aria to moral innocence. When Peck was asked to name the most difficult part of the movie, he responded, "I remember this as an easy film to make...no stress, no strain. It just flowed, as though we were flowing downstream. I only wish we had it to do over again." It flows alright. The direction, cinematography, and consummate performances combine to make *To Kill a Mockingbird* one of this country's most exceptional and enduring human rights films. A capstone to the tender qualities of the drama is the character Boo Radley (Duvall)—the man with the child's mind, who is elevated to the status of hero in the end.

Also recommended: *Gentlemen's Agreement*, *On the Beach*, and *Amazing Grace and Chuck*.

THE TREE OF WOODEN CLOGS

With Luigi Ornaghi, Omar Brignoli, Francesca Morigi, Teresa Bres-
cianini, Carlo Rota, Giuseppe Brignoli. Produced by Gruppo Produzione
Cinema. Directed, written, and photographed by Ermanno Olmi. Music
by Johann Sebastian Bach, performed by Fernando Germani. Italy. Italian
with English titles. Color. 185 minutes. 1978.

The lives of peasant farmers in 19th-century Italy.

Landlords take two-thirds of every harvest. They own the buildings,
most of the livestock, the tools, and the land. Families live in the tenant
houses for generations. If they should be asked to leave, their whole
lives would be left behind. They are peasants, uninvolved with the
higher elements of fate. A political speech is an incomprehensible
thing. They are surrounded by the rhythms of the land and the hushed
barbarity of tenant life. The landowners are economic mercenaries,
bent over their books without feeling for the suffering shadowed in the
columns. When a peasant's son breaks a clog on the way home from
school, there is no money to replace it. Without shoes, he cannot continue his education. In the night, the father cuts down one of the land-
lord's trees from which he carves a new clog. When the crime is discovered, his family is turned off the land. I mistakenly watched part two
of this three-hour film before seeing the first part. It didn't seem to make
much difference. It's a pretty long film for what it's saying. The photography is nice, but the characters show few distinctions, and we can
only care about them as part of a bulky footnote in the history of the
cruelty of humanity.

Also recommended: *Los Santos Inocentes*.

THE TRIAL

(LE PROCES; DER PROZESS; IL PROCESSO)

With Anthony Perkins, Orson Welles, Jeanne Moreau, Romy Schneider, Akim Tamiroff, Elsa Martinelli, Arnoldo Foa. Produced by Yves Laplanche, Miguel Salkind, and Alexander Salkind. Written and directed by Orson Welles. Based on the novel by Franz Kafka. Photographed by Edmond Richard. Music by Jean Ledrut and Tommaso Albinoni. France/Italy/Germany. English. Black and white. 118 minutes. 1962.

A man is charged with a crime.

Joseph K has been charged with a crime. It looks bad, but we are on his side because he's articulate and he knows a lot. He's rule-oriented. He's *not* crazy because that would be disruptive. There are procedures. It's the common man versus the common man's bureaucracy. There are code rooms full of codes and rules upon rules and sub-sections to major section and entitlements and limitless requirements and protections and clauses and case histories and legal anomalies and almost-forgotten, precedent-setting litigation. Anthony Perkins is Joseph K. Joseph K is a rational being charged with an unnamed crime. He is human, and that means something. There are things he can do to destroy the credibility of the arresting officers. There are people on his side. There are crowds yelling unheard things. There are possibilities at the outposts of reason, but what are they? Why are all the children trying to touch him through the bric-a-brac wall work? Why must he buy these paintings? Who is the man lounging on the pillows? Will the woman deceive him? Will he lose his apartment? Will he lose his life? What are the charges? What is the defense? Is he guilty? If so, of what? Is it inevitable that society will become so morbidly advanced? Anthony Perkins is stupendous in this spooky and unnerving role. Whatever Welles asks, Perkins gives more—it's like cell division. For two hours, he walks through a valley of clinical terror by instinct, fostering vague anxieties in audiences and willing the earth to sustain his weight. Together Perkins and Moreau and the rest of the cast and the entire production crew have created this intellectual, zombie masterpiece of the new bad world.

Also recommended: *Brazil.*

THE TRIAL OF THE CATONSVILLE NINE

With David Spielberg, Davis Roberts, Gwen Arner, Barton Heyman, Mary Jackson, Donald Moffat, William Schallert, Ed Flanders, Peter Strauss, Richard Jordan, Nancy Malone, Father Daniel Berrigan, Father Philip Berrigan. Produced by Gregory Peck. Directed by Gordon Davidson. Screenplay by Daniel Berrigan and Saul Levitt, based on the play by Daniel Berrigan. Photography by Haskell Wexler. Music by Shelly Manne. USA. English. Color. 85 minutes. 1972.

Reenactments of the actual trial of nine people who destroyed draft records during the Vietnam era.

On October 9, 1969, the Berrigan brothers and seven other Roman Catholic, anti-war activists broke into government offices, removed draft records, drenched them in homemade napalm, and set them afire. Fundamental to their trial defense, the Nine testify that they are innocent based on dictates of their conscience—theirs was a sane response to insane government policy. Defense testimonies recount the criminal nature of U.S. domestic and foreign policy, including American covert action, bombs in Africa, Green Beret murders in Central America, Agent Orange, and napalm in Vietnam. The individual testimony of the nuns, priests, civil rights activists, and anti-war workers, who have exchanged their patriotism for civil disobedience, is an incriminating chronicle of American crimes against humanity. Predictably, the defense is too abstract to fit into the criminal codes. They are accused of breaking and entering and destroying government documents (draft records), to which they have all confessed and which all the crimes of corporate-dominated governments cannot wash away. The priests and nuns are found guilty and sentenced to jail terms—an experience to which these defendants are accustomed. For them to be innocent, the government would have to be guilty. Luckily for the national defense, the peace activists are ordered to jail. And the draft records of the continental United States, Alaska, and Hawaii are safeguarded from marauding ecclesiastics. This trial (filmed in a church chancel) is a workbook on political activism. These people get up in the morning to work for human rights. The courtroom presentation suffers slightly from stage fright. There's not that much animation, color, or scenic variation, but it's still better than reading the trial transcripts (if they happened to be at hand), which would deprive you of a glimpse at these modern-day threats to national security.

Also recommended: *In the King of Prussia.*

TUCKER:
A MAN AND HIS DREAM

Jeff Bridges, Joan Allen, Martin Landau, Frederic Forest, Mako, Lloyd Bridges, Elias Koteas, Christian Slater. Produced by Fred Roos and Fred Fuchs. Directed by Francis Ford Coppola. Written by Arnold Schulman and David Seidler. Photography by Vittorio Storaro. Music by Joe Jackson and various other artists. USA. English. Color. 111 minutes. 1989.

A revolutionary automaker introduces a road-safe car to the American market and is beaten down by the Big Three.

Once upon a pre-monopoly time, there were over three-hundred automakers in the U.S. Preston Tucker (Bridges) was one of them. In 1945, he built an automobile worth being driven—seatbelts, disk brakes, fuel injection, pop-out windshields, padded dash, rear engine, 20 mpg, headlights that turned in the direction of travel. "The car of tomorrow—here today!" He accused the American auto industry of "criminal neglect." "The Big Three don't give a damn about people. . . . They should be indicted for manslaughter." Detroit auto kingpins considered Tucker a "loose cannon." They destabilized his efforts to build a road-worthy car. He couldn't get clay for the models. Steel cost him twice as much as Ford was paying. The Big Three lined up their puppet politicos to stop him. They had a certain way of making cars, and they wanted it to stay that way. Did I mention that this was a true story? When Tucker overcame industry sabotage and began mass-producing his car, he was charged with twenty-five counts of mail fraud, five counts of FEC fraud, and some other fairy tales claiming he had failed to produce that for which he had petitioned stockholders' money. In court, he blinded the jurors with charisma, as the automobiles he was accused of not building were lining up in the street below.

The industry judge advised the jury not to look out the window. The jury finds Tucker innocent of all charges, and he gave them all rides in his fabulous, futuristic fleet. But production of the Tucker was stopped forever, which is why you've probably never heard of it. Until now. Auto safety standards were set back thirty or forty years. Millions lost their lives on America's highways before the U.S. government forced Ford, Chrysler, and GM to invent and incorporate the safety features that were standard on Preston Tucker's car. Of the fifty Tuckers built in 1945, forty-six still exist and were used in the movie. Lined up in front of Vittorio Storaro's sun-glow lenses, they prove there was a Camelot. It's the tropic of Coppola, where giant posters promise the tomorrow of our dreams. Huge billboard faces sell wonder products in a world on the verge of perfection. Everything about this movie saps the legends of limits. Jeff Bridges inhabits Tucker's unquenchably visionary personality. And the real Preston Tucker set out to design a "little kerosene refrigerator, so cheap the poorest people in the world can have one."

Also recommended: *Class Action*.

TWELVE ANGRY MEN

With Henry Fonda, Lee J. Cobb, Ed Begley, E.G. Marshall, Jack Warden, Martin Balsam, John Fielder, Jack Klugman, Edward Binns, Joseph Sweeney, George Voskovek, Robert Webber, Judy Bond, James A. Kelly, Bill Nelson. Produced by Henry Fonda and Reginald Rose. Directed by Sidney Lumet. Written by Reginald Rose, based on his television play. Photography by Boris Kaufam. Music by Kenyon Hopkins. USA. Black and white. English. 95 minutes. 1957.

A jury debates the fate of a Hispanic murder suspect.

In this brilliant Reginald Rose script, each juror betrays his own judgmental vacuity and subjective intolerance for truth. The entire movie takes place in a closed jury room because *Twelve Angry Men* is not about facile sympathy. It is about the plunge through prejudice and indifference to logic and reason, judgment and humanity, and an ideal as illusive as it is imperative. Before the jurors leave the room, we will know that in the question of the death penalty or any other penalty, jurors fear opposition or crave it; they are too angry or too impatient; they don't understand the law or don't think deeply about the evidence; they resent mandatory service or they resent the system; they are in a struggle of personalities, emotions, feelings of responsibility, pride, indifference, confusion, or doubt. The cast was hand-picked by Fonda (who never made a cent off the film), and the performances reverberate. It is just short of spectacular. "If you find him guilty, the death penalty is mandatory in this case." There were two eyewitnesses, a murder weapon, a motive, a porous alibi, and a Hispanic defendant from the slums of Chicago. The characters are on a journey of self-discovery. "... and a witness heard the kid cry out, 'I'm going to kill you,' a body hit the floor. Look, I'm just as sentimental as the next person...." "This kid is 5 for 0. Look at his record. This is a very fine boy." "You couldn't change my mind if you talked for a hundred years." "Children from slum backgrounds are a menace to society. I've lived among them all my life." Klugman grew up in the slums: "... all my life, playing in the garbage, maybe you can still smell it on me." "You think he's not guilty?" "It's possible." "Well, if this isn't the living end." "His own lawyer knew he didn't stand a chance, you could see it." "He don't even speak good English." "*Doesn't* speak good English." "Would you look at the time." "He stabbed his father with *this* knife." "That's not the knife, remember?" "You all come here with your hearts bleeding all over the floor about slum boys." "I don't think it matters what kind of kid it is." "I don't think you understand the idea of 'reasonable doubt.'" "I'm getting sick of your yelling." "Who says you have the right to vote because of a baseball game." In a magnificent artistic coup, Lumet moves the twelve men like Rodin statuary on a moral frontier. "You don't know how these people lie. It's born in them.... Human life don't mean as much to them.... I know all about them."

Also recommended: *The Thin Blue Line.*

28 UP

Produced, directed, and written and Michael Apted. Produced by Steve Morrison. Camera by George Jesse Turner. English. Black and white and color. 132 minutes. 1985.

A filmmaker follows seven-year-old children through the next twenty-one years of their lives.

28 Up is unquestionably the most ambitious and unusual project in the history of film. Producer-director Michael Apted interviewed and filmed a group of English school children from various socioeconomic backgrounds from the time they are seven until they are twenty-eight. It's time lapse photography with real people. For a moment they are young, then teens, then adults, exasperated by Apted. It's alarming how quickly and irrevocably some veer from childish dreams, while others remain effortlessly true to the ideals of youth. Some lose all childish charm, turning overly-rational and refusing to participate in the final episode of filming. One man matures while clinging perilously to his own sanity. Suzie journeys through extremes. At seven, she has a boyfriend. By fourteen, she is cynical about boys. At twenty-one, she thinks the film project is "Ridiculous, I don't see any point to it." At twenty-eight, she is a glowing newlywed, happy, pretty, and talkative. At seven, Nick wants to "find out about the moon and all that." Asked if he has a girlfriend, he responds, "I don't answer questions like that." At fourteen, he's in a Yorkshire boarding school and still not answering. At twenty-one, he is studying physics at Oxford and still not answering. At twenty-eight, he is a happily married nuclear physicist at the University of Wisconsin. "I was the only child of my age in my village. If I'd been in the city, I'd have been busier interacting with people." At seven, Bruce wants to "go to Africa and try to teach people." At twenty-eight, he's living in a flat and teaching east-end kids. "I've found something rewarding. . . . I just see a lack of opportunity for so many. . . . I'm about the only socialist in my village. People say I'm a little innocent or naive, but I feel that's a strength in a way." The one black subject has no distinct life goals at the age of seven. At twenty-one, he is working in a warehouse, but "I can't stay here forever or my mind will go dead." At twenty-eight he's "quite happy" at the warehouse. Tony realizes for a time his dream of being a jockey, but then settles into the congenial satisfaction of life as a London cab driver. He finds good everywhere. "What's the point otherwise?" *28 Up* is a startling voyage for audiences who will feel they are peering into the very souls of these people, who themselves fail to realize what they are showing to the camera.

Also recommended: *24 Eyes.*

24 EYES

With Shizue Natsukawa, Nijiko Kiyokawa, Hideko Takamine. Kumeko Urabe, Chieke Naniwa. Directed by Keisuke Kinoshita. Written by Keisuke Kinoshita from the book *Denunciation of Blind Devotion to the State*. Japan. Japanese with titles. Black and white. 158 minutes. 1958.

Eighteen years in the life of a school teacher and her students.

In April of 1928, Oisha arrives at the Shodoshima primary school riding a bike and shocking parents with her western clothes. The students call her Miss Pebble. Twelve students—twenty-four eyes. As she calls their names, she studies the faces—tranquil as moons, hypnotized by her. They follow her on hikes to hilltops overlooking the sea, through cemeteries, and along beaches. Together they celebrate exploration. Six years later, she will teach the same students at middle school during the escalation of the Manchurian conflict. One teacher has been arrested for circulating radical literature. Oisha is using the literature in her class. When she is warned to stop, she resigns. As the war years pass, some of the children quit school. A few suffer personal tragedy. Others marry and begin careers. Almost all the boys join the war. By now they all wear western clothes, but Oisha wears a kimono. She no longer has a bike. She lays flowers at the graves of the boys killed in combat. When her husband dies at the front, she is forced to return to teaching at the same Shodoshima Island school where she taught that first class. As she calls the names, she is startled at the faces—tranquil as moons, hypnotized by her. Kinoshita has cast the same children playing their own descendants—the cousins, sons, and sisters of the original students in sailor suits and t-shirts. And now there is a party for Miss Pebble given by the survivors of her first class. They have each contributed to buy her a new bike. On the wall is a photo of Oisha in her suit and the twelve original students in miniature kimonos. They pass the snapshot among them laughing. When it reaches one student blinded in the war, they tell him to pretend he can see it. He smiles, "I don't have to pretend. There is Masako there with her arm around Sinio, and Seige is there beside Miss Pebble." As his fingers caress the images, the others begin to cry silently remembering that moment that was the only moment of a day that was the only day. It is a scene of unbearable sadness and overwhelming insight. It is Kinoshita's brilliant social comment on the tragedy of time.

Also recommended: *28 Up*.

THE UGLY AMERICAN

With Marlon Brando, Eiji Okada, Pat Hingle, Arthur Hill, Sandra Church, George Shibata, Philip Ober, Jocelyn Brando, Judson Pratt, Judson Laire, Reiko Sato, Yee Tak Yip, Pock Rock Ann, Kukrit Pramoj. Produced and directed by George Englund. Screenstory by Stewart Stern from the novel by William J. Lederer and Eugene Burdick. Photography by Clifford Stine. Music by Frank Skinner. USA. English. Color. 120 minutes. 1963.

The U.S. Ambassador to Sarkan watches civil war erupt around him.

Marlon Brando is the stunningly self-satisfied Harrison Carter Mac-White, new U.S. Ambassador to Sarkan. His outstanding qualification for foreign diplomatic service is his ability to speak Sarkanese. Like ambassadors before him, he will tell you he has an unconditional compassion for the Sarkanese people and their culture—a compassion subordinated only to the shark-witted sabotage of U.S. corporate-dominated foreign policy. If there aren't as many Sarkanese flags as American flags flying in Sarkan, dissent to U.S. opinion is inconsequential and controllable. After firing someone when riots mar his first day in the country, MacWhite pushes forward with construction of "The Freedom Road." He believes in the road. He thinks it will be good for the country. He disdains the simple citizenry of Sarkan who see the road as a way for private developers to truck the country's natural resources off the continent. The Sarkanese need hospitals more than they need to be robbed. Production of the road resumes. Civil war erupts. Road crews are murdered and machinery demolished. The country's a battleground. It is nether inconsequential nor controllable. Villages are burned, innocent people killed, and aid stations destroyed. MacWhite loves Sarkan so much, but now there are assassination rumors. How did it all go so wrong? A reporter asks, "Are we going to lose this country?" Mac-White, a quick study to the rewards of colonial paternalism, half incredulous, half all-knowing, responds, "We never had this country." He resigns his appointment and in his parting speech implores people to become informed. "I am not blaming my country. I am blaming the indifference that some of us show to its promises." As he begs for understanding, his image flickers on television screens in faraway America. There is an overstuffed chair. A man is so bored by these incomprehensible words that he reaches over and turns off the set. The entire issue dissolves into a dot. *The Ugly American* is not one of the earliest

Hollywood films made about U.S. intervention in southeast Asia—it's one of the only ones. There are plenty of feature-length dramas about the war, but few on why it was fought. In real life, the stunningly self-satisfied MacWhite is the stunningly talented Marlon Brando, who made movies like this all the time and was great in every one.

Also recommended: *Burn!*

UMBERTO D

With Carlo Batisti, Mario Pia Casilio, Ileana Simova, Lena Gennari, Alberto Albani Barbieri. Produced by Giuseppe Amato. Directed by Vittorio De Sica. Screenplay by Cesare Zavattini and Vittorio De Sica, based on the story by Cesare Zavattini. Photography by G. R. Aldo. Music by Alessandro Cicognini. Italy. Italian with English titles. Black and white. 89 minutes. 1952.

An elderly man loses almost everything in the aftermath of World War II in Germany.

I don't think De Sica was aiming for easy cinematic sympathy when he hired a dog to co-star with Carlo Batisti in this story about pensioners and poverty in postwar Germany. By singling out these two most vulnerable members of society—animals and the elderly—he reinvents an axiom: the reach of poverty never exceeds its grasp. In post-World War II Germany, economic crisis has hit so hard that thousands of destitute people on fixed incomes are begging in the streets, selling their possessions, and checking into state-run hospitals under pretense for regular meals and a bed. Umberto, a retired civil servant, is months behind on his rent and has no way of paying it. He's too ashamed to beg. He has nothing to sell. When his dog, Flag, gets lost, he raises just enough money to take a cab to the city shelter to redeem him. The scene at the shelter is a tribute to De Sica's capacity for pathos. Here are the city's most desperate, many of them indigent, leaning in lines of mute anxiety for news of a cherished pet. Clerks with no emotion repetitively process requests for lost animals, many of which the owners lack the money to retrieve. It's a pageant of mercilessness in a society that kills companion animals while the owners stand by. Off-screen is an interminable pathetic whining and barking. One man asks what will happen if he doesn't have the fee. "Do you kill them right away then?" The clerk passes him over to the next in line. Umberto saves Flag but loses his apartment and decides to commit suicide as a final solution to his privation. The only dignity left is to be a loving and responsible owner. Before he can die, he must place Flag in a new home. De Sica responds unashamedly to these inhumane petitions. He notices that the promises of progress have lapsed and that all the advantages human social groupings once held out have been forfeited to commerce. The individual, lost to urban intolerance, is now as helpless as if he or she were alone at the edge of a prehistoric plateau. *Umberto D* is a terribly touching film about the daily heartbreaks that poverty demands of people who have only the companionship they can buy and own. The film is blessed by high production values and deft and endearing performances by both actor and dog.

Also recommended: *The Bicycle Thief.*

UNDER FIRE

With Nick Nolte, Gene Hackman, Joanna Cassidy, Jean-Louis Trintignant, Richard Masur, Rene Enriquez, Ed Harris. Produced by Jonathan Taplin. Directed by Roger Spottiswoode. Screenplay by Ron Shelton and Clayton Frohman, based on the story by Clayton Frohman. Photography by John Alcott. Music by Jerry Goldsmith. USA. English and Spanish with titles. Color. 128 minutes. 1983.

Photographers cover war in Nicaragua, risking their lives in the process.

Between Chad and Nicaragua, these canvas-craving photo-journalists will supposedly win our hearts and make us feel sorrier for them than we do for the people being butchered by the remnants of the Somoza dictatorship. They meet all over the world at big-time disasters, yet they are as cool as crawfish, swapping cynicisms and stealing each other's lovers. You get the feeling that if there weren't any tragedies going on, these folks would be chasing movie stars up flag poles. It's a shame this important chapter in American interventionism couldn't have been hosted by Hackman, which it deserved to be, instead of by Nolte, who just isn't quite the same. He and Cassidy and Hackman wind up in Nicaragua where Nolte learns that U.S. Marines invaded umpteen years ago to protect U.S. business interests and put down a peasant revolt. "We're backing a fascist government again," says Hackman, who's a living, breathing saint when permitted to speak. "How did I know they were CIA? They were wearing name tags, O.K?" Somoza owns one-fifth of all the land in the country. He owns the shipping port, the national airline, and a Mercedes dealership. "Is it a crime to sell cars?" Nolte and Cassidy are going to be shocked to discover that they are beginning to care about the people's movement—so much so that Nolte goes off to photograph the dead remains of the people's leader, making him look alive and keeping the revolution going even if it is unethical photojournalism. Hackman is back in the States making $10,000 a week reading the news. But the picture of the dead Raphael is in every newspaper and on half the t-shirts in the western hemisphere, and Leon has fallen to the rebels. He comes back for an interview and is shot down by government troops in an occupied village. It'll be a long time before Nolte and Cassidy finish running around in utterly bogus battle shock, looking for each other before the movie can end. Hackman walks on water, and Harris is truly a manic, greaser-hating slob.

Also recommended: *Uprising.*

UNDERGROUND

With Jeff Jones, Kathy Boudine, Cathy Wilkerson, Bernadine Dohrn, Billy Ayers. Produced and directed by Emile de Antonio and Mary Lamspon. Photographed by Haskell Wexler. USA. English. Color and black and white. 88 minutes. 1974.

Interviews with members of the Weather Underground.

Cited in 1975 by the State of California for making an "illegal" film, Emile de Antonio defied FBI attempts to subpoena *Underground* to use in their case against the Weather Underground. The members of this radical, direct-action political group—The Weathermen—are filmed from behind or through a gauzy curtain. In 1975, these members have been underground for five years. "The reason we are underground is because we believe we have to overthrow United States imperialism and replace it with a different society." "Our revolutionary consciousness was a result of growing up in the age of the atomic bomb." "Our acts have been against the property and the symbols and the institutions of the ruling class." At the age of seventeen, Dohrn was standing with the cheering crowds in Cuba after the revolution. She was a full-time revolutionary—a national officer of SDS. Billy Ayers started with civil rights and anti-war protests in the 1960s. The others marched in picket lines for integration. When they were arrested, they discovered that even the jails were segregated. "We are not a terrorist organization and we are not adventurists." "We feel our actions have been responsible and accountable." "To not act is . . . violent . . . criminal." Discussions with the activists are cut with scenes of the turbulent 60s and 70s. H. Rap Brown calls violence, "as American as cherry pie. We will be free by any means necessary." Fred Hampton threatens, "You can jail the revolutionary, but you can't jail the revolution." In 1971, Vietnam veterans gather in front of the Capital Building in Washington, D.C., to throw their war medals back where they came from. "I have a Vietnam Campaign Ribbon, a Vietnam Service Ribbon . . . a Purple Heart" "I have taken in nine Purple Hearts, a Distinguished Service Cross, a Silver Star, Bronze Star, and a lot of other shit. . . ." Jeff Jones believes the Weathermen can make a difference. "We study a lot. We think a lot about all kinds of things anybody could do it if they wanted to. . . . Just because people aren't comfortable with the word "imperialism" doesn't make it rhetoric." "Why did you bomb the Capital Building?" "In protest of Nixon's invasion of Laos." They talk about the explosion in the Greenwich Village house that killed three Weathermen members and convinced them to go underground. "We believed in the necessity of building an underground. It was offensive as well as defensive." "They told us, 'you can't win, it can't work. . . .' " But the war in Vietnam ended. "We are special. We are professional revolutionaries. And we are fugitives."

Also recommended: *Katherine.*

UNDER THE WORLD
(DEBAJO DEL MUNDO)

With Sergio Renan, Barbara Mugica, Victor La Place, Paula Canals, Oscar Ferrigno, Gabriel Toscano, Gabriel Gibot. Produced by Jorge E. Estrada Mora and Leo Mehl. Written and directed by Beda Docampo Feijoo and Juan Bautista Stagnaro. Photography by Frantised Uldrich. Music by Jose Luis Castuneira de Dios. Argentina/Czechoslovakia. In Spanish with yellow English titles. Color. 100 minutes. 1986.

Jews take to the woods to evade the Nazis during World War II.

In a beneficent forfeiture of theatricality, filmmakers Stagnaro and Feijoo move their cameras into mordant close-ups of families living in earthen dugouts to avoid forced exodus to the death camps. It is Poland in September 1942. Landowners are ordered to send Jewish workers and their families to the Nazis. Many of the farmers are stunned by the expectations of the fascists and let Jewish workers themselves decide whether to conform to the law. Some Jews submit to the SS guard. The rest go into the woods. These Jewish refugees from Hitler's Reich live "under the world," subject to exposure, contagion, and the privation of chronic hunger and thirst. The damp pits rot the clothing off their bodies. There is no way to keep clean. Their skin is covered with sores and the sores are encrusted with filth. For some, the dugouts are like coffins, built to die in while waiting for peace. "In the grave, nobody bothers you." Those who die are buried beside the living in the pits. The Nazis offer flour and sugar to anyone with information about escaped Jews. By the end of the war, many of the forest people are dead. The rest are unrecognizable. Those who survive have proven that nothing can defile freedom.

Also recommended: *Diamonds in the Night.*

THE UPRISING
(DER AUFSTAND; LA INSURRECCION)

With Agustin Pereira, Carlos Catania, Maria Lourdes Centano de Zelaya, Oscar Castillo. Produced by Joachim von Vietinghoff. Directed by Peter Lilienthal. Screenplay by Peter Lilienthal and Antonio Skarmeta. Cinematography by Michael Ballhaus. Music by Claus Bantzer. Germany and Costa Rica. Spanish with English titles. Color. 96 minutes. 1979.

Nicaragua in the last weeks of the Somoza regime.

The Somoza-backed National Guard is a mercenary band of marauders with little understanding of what a Somoza victory would mean for the people of Nicaragua. They rely on kidnapping, torture, threats, and the state of the country's economy to sustain their fighting force. The Lilienthal-Skarmeta script singles out the injustice of the poverty of Nicaragua that drove the poor into the arms of their own oppressors. Agustin Pereira joins Somoza's National Guard, lured by money and the promise of an education in the U.S. When his fathers orders him to take off "that filthy uniform," Agustin responds, "It is this uniform that pays for this house. It is this uniform that pays for Eugenia's education. . . . If I quit, where will the money come from?" As a soldier in the National Guard, he never fires on his own people and believes he can take from Somoza without giving back. But after a massacre of civilians in a church sanctuary, Agustin takes off the uniform and goes into hiding, working with the Sandanistas to defeat the Guard in Leon. Filmed in Nicaragua four months after the Sandanista victory, Lilienthal casts residents of Leon in this film about the last days of the military dictatorship of Anastasio Somoza.

Also recommended: *Calm Over the Countryside.*

UTU

With Anzac Wallace, Bruno Lawrence, Kelly Johnson, Wi Kuki Kaa, Tim Elliot, Faenza Reuben, Tania Bristowe, Iona Rodgers, Martyn Sanderson.

Produced by Don Blakeney and Geoff Murphy. Written by Geoff Murphy
and Keith Aberdein. Directed by Geoff Murphy. Photography by Graeme
Cowley. Music by John Charles. New Zealand. English and Maori with
English titles. Color. 104 minutes. 1983.

**The traditional people of New Zealand mount a campaign of
vengeance against British colonials who have massacred a
Maori village.**

This film takes place in broad-leafed jungles, where perpetually flowering forests simulate a vegetative heaven opening up here on Earth.
Here, the most unhallowed wars are being waged against defenseless
impediments to the advance of a colonial empire. In New Zealand, in
1870, aborigines are trying to survive the invasion of British profiteers.
Te Wheke is a Maori tribesman who has declared revenge (*utu*) against
all white settlers after a village of Maori are ruthlessly killed by British
colonial soldiers. He and his followers carve a trail of violence and
death through the terrorized colonial population. But *Utu* isn't about
these violent events, no matter how much the war of retribution may
monopolize the narrative. While seeming to wander wide of whatever
mark we think it should be making, *Utu* ponders the fluidity of human
social interactions, unsuited as they are to the demarcations of the
nation-state. It's a film about people in the embrace of destiny and the
legends and the cantilevered traditions that direct human response to
the unusual, novel, threatening clash of cultural realities. It's about Te
Wheke clinging irresolutely to his role as an avenger—knowing as he
does so that the whites he kills are neither guilty nor necessarily in sympathy with the massacre of the Maori villagers. The whites, even those
he injures, comprehend Te Wheke's vengeance even as they plot to destroy him. There's no beginning and no end to the prejudices, attrac-
tions, and loyalties. There are Maori fighting on both sides. Whites and
Maori fall in love across the battle lines. Languages compound and re-
shape one another. Either accidentally or on purpose, filmmaker Geoff
Murphy has created an extraordinary film laced with esoteric themes
and a cast of eccentric unpredictables. It apprehends something about
the chimeric quality of cultural traditions under stress and how con-
fusedly we submit to higher estrangements and apply abstract philosophies to our loves and hates. It's an anthropological pilgrimage artisti-
cally exalted by the ballad of spoken Maori, dazzling ritual tattoo, and
the sensational lens work of Graeme Cowley.

Also recommended: *Cannibal Tours*.

U2: RATTLE AND HUM

With Bono, The Edge, Adam Clayton, Larry Mullen, Jr., and B.B. King. Produced by Michael Hamlyn. Directed by Phil Jaonou. Photography by Robert Brinkman and Jordan Cronenweth. Music by U2 and Jimmy Lovine. USA. English. Color. 99 minutes. 1989.

A rock group sings out against racism, imperialism, and poverty.

It's too bad theater-goers weren't as attracted to the U2 marquee as they were to the oh-so-amusing romantic comedy that ran for months afterward. Commonly singled out as the best concert movie ever made, U2 (after the spy plane) toured with a manifold agenda: to make money, to become more famous, and to project the energy and inspiration of their political radicalism in coliseums, amphitheaters, and churches from the redwood forest to the New York Island. They sing about today. They sing about peace, war, oppression, racism, and the roots of rock and roll. They sing about El Salvador and Ireland and Martin Luther King in New Mexico, where legislation vetoed formal recognition of a national holiday to honor King. Bono drones angrily about South Africa: "'Silver and Gold'" was written about a man in a shanty town outside Johannesburg, a man who's sick of looking down the barrel of white South Africa, a man who's ready to take up arms against his oppressor, a man who's lost faith in the peacemakers of the west while they argue and fail to support Bishop Tutu in his request for economic sanctions against South Africa. Am I bugging you? Don't mean to bug ya. . . . Jesus, say something! I am someone . . . they've come to collect silver and gold." The artists in this film sing about poverty, drug addiction, inequality, materialism, violence, and sexual abuse: "I don't believe in riches, but just see where I live. . . . I don't believe the Uzi just went off in my hand. . . . I don't believe in forced entry but . . . wild thoughts escape." They join the outrageous talents of a Harlem choir in "I Still Haven't Found What I'm Looking For." A street performer sings about "freedom for my people" and gets a spot on the tour album. They're at Sun Studios, recording in the room where rock and roll was born. Bono flaunts his talent and his fury across America. "I can't tell the difference between ABC news, Hill Street Blues, and a preacher from the 'Old Time Gospel Hour' stealing money from the sick and the old. Well, the God I believe in isn't short of cash mister." The exuberant lighting and colossal dynamics of the performances cheered on by sell-out throngs will convince you that outrage is everywhere and the world can be made right again.

Also recommended: *A Vision Shared.*

THE VANISHING AMERICAN

With Richard Dix, Lois Wilson, Noah Beery, Malcolm McGregor. Produced by Famous Players-Lasky. Directed by George B. Seitz. Screenplay by Ethel Doherty, based on Lucien Hubbard's adaptation of the novel of the same name by Zane Grey. Photography by C. Edgar Schoenbaum and Harry Perry. Music by Stuart Oderman. USA. Silent with English titles. Black and white. 10 reels. 1925.

American Indians struggle to survive as the Bureau of Indian Affairs' representatives divert Indian supplies to gold miners.

The predominant tradition in American westerns prior to the 1970s was to present white colonialists as blameless in the American Indian wars. In virtually hundreds of westerns, settlers are seen struggling for survival against unprovoked terrorism from Indian tribes. From this enormous body of cultural and historical heresy in filmmaking, a few dedicated filmmakers have created a small, independent genre: almost a dozen films that are more sympathetic to historic fact. In *The Vanishing American*, employees of the Bureau of Indian Affairs (BIA) are conspirators who spend most of their time trying to divert Indian treaty money and supplies to the back room and divesting the Indians of reservation lands. Our Indian hero, Nophaie, is played by Richard Dix, who is not an Indian in real life, but even as a make-believe Indian is not allowed to kiss "White Desert Rose" (Wilson), the school teacher with whom he has fallen in love. He's the reservation Indian who wants to trust the white man. The time is World War I. Like many misled, real-life counterparts, Dix believes he can win recognition and support from whites by fighting for them. In *The Vanishing American*, White Desert Rose gives Nophaie a Bible, which he takes with him to the front lines. When he returns home to discover the BIA abuses, including the theft of lands and death of many of his people, he rejects his traditional native religion and says a few words he has learned from the New Testament. But his new God does not save the Indians or give them back their lands. They organize a revolt, during which Dix is hit by a stray bullet that goes right through the Bible he has put in his shirt pocket. He dies with his head in White Desert Rose's lap, holding the Bible in the air— perhaps so audiences can see how the hole goes all the way through. *The Vanishing American* was shot on location in the Grand Canyon, the Painted Desert, Monument Valley and other areas of natural beauty. The movie opens with a spectacular chronicle of 2,000 years of Navaho history and has very nice Indian drum accompaniment throughout.

Also recommended: *Indian Agent*.

VERONICO CRUZ
(La Deuda Interna)

With Juan Jose Camero, Gonzalo Morales. Produced by Julio Lencina and Sasha Menocki. Directed by Miguel Pereiro. Written by Miguel Pereiro and E. L. Muller, based on the notes of Maestro M. Ramos. Photography by Gerry Feeny. Music by Jaime Torres. Argentina. In Spanish with English titles. Color. 106 minutes. 1990.

A young boy's life is sacrificed to poverty and war.

A clever statement about the divided values of education and progress, this film follows Veronico Cruz (Morales) off the farm and into the local temple de saber, where he and the Maestro (Camero) indulge their shared enthusiasm for studying ships that sail faraway seas. To Veronico, they are "floating cities of thousands of people." The Maestro and the boy are like father and son, but the Maestro is investigated by the military regime, accused of political dissidence, and transferred to a new school. Throughout the next ten years, he and Veronico correspond regularly. By 1984, the political arena of Argentina is violently agitated by the desire to reclaim the Falkland Islands from Great Britain. "The decision has been taken to put an end to the interminable succession of excuses and delays orchestrated by Great Britain to perpetuate their dominion over the islands." The country's exuberance is broken when British fighters fire on and sink an Argentine warship, the *General Belgrano*. The nation is stunned. The Maestro watches the news reports, remembering happier times. The *Belgrano* was one of the ships he and Veronico studied. He decides to travel to Chorcan and visit the boy, whom he hasn't heard from for some time. He learns that Veronico has left the village. There are recent photos. He's now a young man. The local elder excitedly shows Camero the pictures. "Look how big he is and how handsome." He puts on his glasses to better see Veronico standing, smiling, between two friends; all three are in navy uniforms. Veronico has signed the picture, "From the *Belgrano*." Camero looks over the dry croplands, perhaps remembering how he convinced the parents to send their children to his school. "I don't want them to come to . . . to learn to work for others, but to help them think for themselves."

Also recommended: *24 Eyes*.

VIETNAM: IN THE YEAR OF THE PIG

Produced and directed by Emile de Antonio. Music by Steve Addiss. USA. English. Black and white. 103 minutes. 1968.

Significant details about U.S. involvement in the war in Vietnam.

"I have no army. I have no finances. I have no public instruction. I have no diplomacy. I have only hatred and I will not disarm it." Ho Chi Mihn was a Confucian scholar and a Marxist whose father was condemned as a nationalist by the French colonial government. He led the people of Vietnam to resist French imperialists, who as early as 1946 were bombing villages to "teach [the natives] a lesson." By 1953, at the battle of Dien Bien Phu, the popular front overwhelmed the French. In 1954, the U.S. began sending combat planes and technicians to Vietnam. A puppet government won wide support in the U.S., even from liberals who saw French colonialism as a way to stop communism and support the "cause of freedom" in Southeast Asia. General Curtis Lemay describes the campaign against the people's army of Vietnam: "We're fighting a war. We must use our air power in the most humane manner possible to destroy... harbors, power systems, transportation—roads, bridges—eliminate them. Every industrial installation and factory from the biggest to the smallest—never so long as there are two bricks stuck together, and, if necessary, the irrigation system. We must destroy every work of man, if necessary, to win this war." A major weapon in this "humane campaign" was mass media. Journalists were coerced to comply with official versions of a war in which "democracy" became a propaganda slogan. The Gulf of Tonkin assault was sold as a response to an unprovoked North Vietnamese attack on U.S. cruisers, which were actually on a spy mission twelve miles from the North Vietnamese coast. Search and destroy missions bombed critical food stores and burned entire villages in "retaliation." The U.S. offensive included an ambitious anti-personnel arsenal, including napalm and gasoline vapor bombs. Cluster bombs were used indiscriminately while U.S. politicians such as Hubert Humphrey promised, "Your government is not bombing civilian targets." De Antonio's film exposes the brutalizing effects the war had on U.S. combat personnel. Unable to communicate with the Vietnamese (except with money or a gun), ground forces began to mistrust and eventually to despise the Vietnamese. Young men who seem to have lost all human feeling are filmed torturing unarmed and restrained prisoners of war who submit mutely to their fate. The effect is of total, inhumane abandon. How did the people of Vietnam survive the prolonged campaign of imperialist tyranny? "The village cannot be destroyed, even when it no longer physically remains, because the village lies beneath the ground and will always rise up again."

Also recommended: *Hearts and Minds.*

VIVA ZAPATA!

With Marlon Brando, Anthony Quinn, Joseph Wiseman, Harold Gordon, Alan Reed, Lou Gilbert, Jean Peters, Fay Roope. Produced by Darryl F. Zanuck. Directed by Elia Kazan. Written by John Steinbeck, based on the novel *Zapata the Unconquered* by Edgcumb Pichon. Photography by Joe MacDonald. Music by Alex North. USA. English. Black and white. 112 minutes. 1952.

The story of Emiliano Zapata and the Mexican revolution of 1911.

The darkly indelible Steinbeck screenplay traces the haunting inclinations of history and crowns Emiliano Zapata as a martyr to the people's cause. By 1910, rumors of reform and revolution could not arrest the narcotic monopolization of land in Mexico. Enormous holdings were taken over by land barons living like chartered royalty within the protected orbit of the Diaz state. That the Mexicans thought it presumptuous of Kazan to make a film about one of their greatest heroes did not stop Marlon Brando from being a magnetic, moody messiah, rising to the burden of power. Brando inserted rings in his nose and taped his eyelids down to look like Emiliano Zapata—revolutionary. He will incite the campesinos to wage war for agrarian reform and economic democracy. After a victorious but costly crusade and the establishment of a triumvirate in Mexico City, Zapata, a former plowhand hardly qualified to helm a reformed state for long, and his army of Indians and Mexicans return to the south where his dreams of reform lurch unevenly forward. But the zenith of proletarian potential has passed. In the flush of victory, Zapata's brother (Anthony Quinn) goes so rank that he steals a local farmer's wife and is killed in a shoot-out. While Brando refines his style with the wifely Jean Peters, the kingdom come he fought for burns at both ends. In this movie, he will mark a farmer's name the same way Diaz marked his and not even notice what he has become. He is assassinated by traitors to the egalitarian ideal. His death transforms him from a mortal to the redemptive hero of the Mexican working class. Some distraught critics lavished lamentations over the general "state of disorder in Mexico" obvious in the film. Indeed, it was a stew of constitutional rhetoric, revolutionaries, guerrilla warfare, collapsing governments, overthrows, assassinations, and radical agrarian socialists like Zapata, but it still reads better than U.S. history. Here, the docile masses have been driven off the land without much rumpus and the labor force toils unperturbed by the concentration of capital, wealth, and power and the erosion of the democratic process. For Americans, maybe there's a lesson to be learned from this fine film from the Kazan catalog of classics. For my personal tastes, considering that a large percentage of the population of the U.S. and a much larger proportion of

Mexicans is Hispanic, wouldn't it be nice if *Viva Zapata!* had starred some of them?

Also recommended: *Juarez.*

THE WALL
(LE MUR)

With Tuncel Kuritz, Ayse Emel Mesci, Malik Berrichi, Nicolas Hossein. Directed by Yilmaz Guney. Written by Yilmaz Guney and Marie-Helene Quinton. Photography by Izzet Akay. Music by Ozan Garip Sahin and Setrak Bakirel. France. Turkish with English titles. Color. 117 minutes. 1983.

Turkish prison life reconstructed for the screen.

The Wall was either a catharsis or a curse for director Guney, who served time in Turkish prisons as a political dissident before fleeing to France. The prison environment is this film's only theme, with the narrative hinging on the daily beatings, rapes, deprivations, fears, humiliations, deaths, and the filth of prison life. In Turkey, where no unnecessary state funds are spent maintaining the guilty, "criminal justice definitely has a distinctive interpretation. Behind the ancient crumbling walls, in the dark, damp rooms running with vermin, is the final legacy of the Turkish judicial system. Here, the warden is the pusher supplying drugs to society's most vulnerable victims. The Central Jail houses men, women, and children, all living in a wasteland of depravity and fear. Visitors are admitted only twice a month, and no gift packages are allowed. When a female inmate has a baby, Guney's camera is there between her legs, recording the birth, which is definitely not staged for the film. A bridal couple, on the way to be married, is met by a firing squad instead. But these and other triumphs of torment are just marginal remarks in a film focused on the children living in prison, utterly defenseless to the outrages of penal servitude. They are maimed, beaten to death, shot, raped by the guards, and deprived of food. Those who challenge abuses are victimized remorselessly. When the boys barricade themselves in their dormitory as a protest, they are transferred to a prison that is more like a house of horrors than a house of correction. Like most prison films, *The Wall* is a depleting film to watch. Guney's is the only one included here.

Also recommended: *Do-Des'-Ka-Den.*

THE WAR AT HOME

Produced and directed by Glenn Silber and Barry Alexander Brown. Photography by Richard March and Dan Lerner. Music by Bob Dylan, Phil Ochs, Barry Sadler, Buffalo Springfield, and Delaware Water Gap. Narration by Blake Kellogg. USA. English. Black and white and color. 100 minutes. 1976.

Anti-war protests and the counterculture in Madison, Wisconsin.

Beginning in 1965 when students and peace activists staged a citizens' arrest of local military personnel, protests, and demonstrations at the University of Wisconsin at Madison escalated out of control for the next seven years. They burned draft cards, occupied campus buildings, intimidated government "truth" teams, and picketed Dow recruiters with photos of napalm victims. They marched behind the cries of the times, "Hell no, we won't go." "Bring the troops home now." They sang, ". . . what a field day for the heat." Hubert Humphrey wanted to know, "If you can show us how to get out of Vietnam without destroying what little freedom there is left there. . . ." Police arrived in truckloads. "The whole place was like a war zone." "All I can remember is rage and screaming, 'Sieg, heil!'" The FBI, the Department of Justice, the University Protection Agency, the Sheriff's Department, and military intelligence all sent undercover forces into the streets with a twelve-point master plan to bring down the new left. At the democratic national convention in Chicago in 1968, thousands of troops and Chicago police beat back protesters outside the convention center. "Police came in and just started clubbing people." "It was bedlam." "If they are going to make war on us, we are going to make war on them." Nixon was promising, "I would not invade North Vietnam nor any of the other countries in the area of Vietnam." By 1969, regiments of the National Guard were being shipped to Madison to control demonstrations. Fifteen thousand people were calling for a "total moratorium" on military investment and a reversal of U.S. foreign policy. Senator Gaylord Nelson tallied the destruction in Vietnam: "We have dropped twenty-three million bombs...each one creating a crater forty feet across and twenty-five feet deep. Twenty-five percent of Vietnamese are homeless." AWOLs are up. Less than honorable discharges are up. Antimemorial parades are held on Memorial Day. War medals are thrown back to the White House by soldiers on crutches. By 1972, Nixon had mined North Vietnamese ports and rail routes are being bombed. "I ask you for the same strong support you've always given me." In Vietnam, 58,000 Americans are dead, 185,000 Saigon government soldiers are dead, and 927,124 North Vietnamese dead. And finally the war is over.

Also recommended: *Berkeley in the '60s.*

WARGAMES

With Matthew Broderick, Ally Sheedy, John Wood, Michael Ensign, Dabney Coleman, Eddie Deezan, Dennis Lipscomb, Barry Corbin, William Bogert, Susan Davis, Kent Williams, Juanin Clay, Joe Dorsey. Produced by Harold Schneider. Directed by John Bedham. Screenplay by Lawrence Lasker and Walter F. Parkes. Photography by William A. Fraker. Mini-photography by Jack Cooperman. Music by Arthur B. Rubenstein. USA. English. Color. 113 minutes. 1983.

A computer whiz stumbles across the ultimate war game on a U.S. military computer link.

Fifteen-year-old David Lightman (Broderick) hangs out with brain beings who know more than Einstein and get through life's crises by soliciting microchips to rewrite their grades and undermining the phone company and anything else electrical. They are young people lucky enough to have been born at the right micro-interval in the evolution of artificial intelligence. They anticipate computer generations and then sit back waiting for somebody to create them. In David's case, the waiting is very, very hard. Bored with existing software possibilities, he has broken into Pentagon codes to influence the War Department computer to play "All Out Thermonuclear War." The only little thing wrong is that "Joshua," the war computer, does not understand David's innocent intent, does not know what a *game* is, and is happy to be blowing up the world at last, since he's an Air Force defense computer with no higher purpose. He commands the war screen at NORAD to fill itself with missile graphics depicting the pending obliteration of Moscow and points east. Whatever Air Force defense personnel were doing before, they now sit somewhat distracted at their keyboards, unaware that the atomic age has passed them by, unaware that David Lightman's bedroom is the new command center and that only he knows why the world is coming to an end. When they figure this out and the military police surround David's house and arrest him as a communist spy, it's about the biggest thing that ever hit his neighborhood. None of the NORAD group believes he's just a bored young man with an inquisitive mind. He must escape to find Joshua's creator, who is flying pterodactyl models on an island hideout and is basically uncaring about imminent nuclear annihilation. With very little time to spare, the world is rescued by convincing Joshua to see that with war, "the only way to win is not to play." Broderick is charming as a destroyer of worlds. You can see that his heart's in the right place. It's tough being a kid. He knows too much, but it's not his fault. Through him we see that we shouldn't have all these machines with their primitive understanding of world affairs in charge of the bombing. That's why we have the War Department.

Also recommended: *Dr. Strangelove.*

WATCH ON THE RHINE

With Bette Davis, Paul Lukas, Geraldine Fitzgerald, Lucille Watson, Beulah Bond, George Coulouris, Donald Woods, Henry Daniel. Produced by Hal B. Willis. Directed by Herman Shumlin. Screenplay by Dashiell Hammett and Lillian Hellman, from the stage play by Lillian Hellman. Photography be Merritt Gerstad and Hal Mohr. Music by Max Steiner. USA. English. Black and white. 114 minutes. 1943.

**During World War II, a German anti-fascist and his wife and
three children enter the United States.**

You've heard of World War II? Then you've probably heard of Bette Davis. And maybe you've imagined her playing on the right side for a change, which she does here. She probably could have gone on to save the world, she's so good at it. She's hot off a slow boat to Mama's chateau, with her anti-fascist husband (Lukas) and three kids cooked up by Hellman under a dark and stormy sky. The high-strung, impoverished nuclear family is carrying $10,000 in a locked briefcase to be used to continue the battle against the Nazis. When Davis and Lukas discover a fan of National Socialism (Coulouris) is also a welcome guest of her mother's hospitality, they wrangle deep into moral contention with Coulouris, who eventually blackmails Lukas by threatening to expose his resistance status if they don't hand the $10,000 over to him. To resolve the unresolvable, Lukas kills Coulouris and packs off to Germany to continue his work. In real life, he was supposed to pay for this cinematic crime. Film production codes of the 1940s dictated that, "No movie can be made in which a killer goes unpunished." Lukas, whose character takes the fascist out to the garden and leaves him there, was slated to appear in a retribution sequence later in the film, but preferred never to be seen on the set again. Studio execs were forced to order a script rewrite inventing a capture from afar. It's a refined film except for the kids. Lukas and Davis are the supreme, superb seraphs, existing to extinguish the sins of despotism. Filmed in unreserved radiance by Gerstad and Mohr.

Also recommended: *The Little Foxes*.

WATERMELON MAN

With Godfrey Cambridge, Estelle Parsons, Howard Caine, D'urville Martin, Mantan Moreland, Paul Williams. Produced by John B. Bennett. Directed by Melvin Van Peebles. Written by Herman Raucher. Photography by W. Wallace Kelly. Music by Melvin Van Peebles. USA. English Color. 97 minutes. 1970.

An obnoxious white businessman wakes up one morning to discover he's black.

"Althea, I'm having a nightmare about my sunlamp." But poor, transracial Gerber (Cambridge), it turns out, is not asleep. He's awake in front of the mirror. And he's so black that's it's not easy to believe he ever could have been white. There's no telling how it happened. But there is definitely an evil power in the universe. Oh, how he used to laugh at the race riots. Now he's having a race riot. "I'm black! I'm black!" he screams. "I want my whiteness back!" He's loud, overbearing, and impossible to pity. In fact, if somebody had to be black, it works out pretty well that it's Gerber because he hates not being white. He can't see anything good about it. The bus driver comments, "I never noticed you were colored before." Gerber used to race the bus every morning to keep in shape, but now running causes people to run after him. The police want to search his briefcase. The yacht club does not recall having any black members. He buys twenty-five skin-lightening lotions. None of them work. "No wonder negroes riot." The neighbors ask him to sell his home for the sake of property values. "It's nothing personal," they tell him. "Oh, I'd feel real bad if it was." His wife (Parsons) stands by him for a while, but life with Gerber just isn't the same these days. The job doesn't work out. "We've never had a negro salesman before." There's reverse bigotry from his secretary. Now that he's black, he's desirable. It takes a while for the total conversion, but he does lose his wife, his kids, his home, his job, his friends, and his way of life, and he winds up alone in a part of town with bars on all the windows even though it isn't prison. On the way to the ghetto, he hears every possible cliche and cracks every possible corny joke. *Watermelon Man*. Sometimes you can tell a movie by the title. Cambridge is a clod in both colors, and the movie is caustic about its point—you don't make it in this world by the skin of your teeth, just by your skin.

Also recommended: *The River Niger*.

THE WAVE

With Antonio, Lara, Miguel. Produced by the Mexican Department of Fine Arts. Supervised by Paul Strand. Screenplay by Carlos Chavez, Velazquez, and Henwar Rodakiewicz. Photography by Paul Strand. Music by Sylvestre Revueltas. Mexico. Spanish with English titles by John Dos Passos. Black and white. 90 minutes. 1934.

Fishermen in Mexico strike for better wages.

Concentration of power and capital has pushed traditional workers into wage subordination. Merchants now own the boats, the equipment, and the fish, and without a union or government controls, a fisherman can work all his life below the subsistence level. Miro (Miguel) works the boats. His wages don't allow him the luxury of calling the doctor when his son falls sick. He organizes the men into a united front to petition for pay increases. "Companeros, how long must we endure this injustice and slavery? It is not inevitable. We need to act as one." The merchants listen and deny every appeal. The next day the fishermen dump the catch, and they keep dumping until the army is called in to crush the worker revolt. Shooting erupts. Miro is shot and later dies. His death encourages the others to commit to the union. Cries of "*todos juntos!*" (all together) fill the air. Typical of many union films, *The Wave* is more tender than turbulent and more pause for the proletariat than a dozen Academy Award classics.

Also recommended: *Salt of the Earth.*

WE OF THE NEVER NEVER

With Angela Punch McGregor, Arthur Dignam, Martin Vaughan, Lewis Fitz-Gerald, John Jarratt, Tony Barry, Tommy Lewis, Kim Chiukok, Mawuyul Yanthalawuy. Produced by Gregg Tepper and John B. Murray. Directed by Igor Auzins. Screenplay by Peter Schreck, based on the book by Jane Taylor Gunn. Photography by Gary Hansen. Australia. Music by Peter Best. Australia. English. Color. 132 minutes. 1983.

The first white woman arrives in Australia's land of the Never Never.

In the early 20th century, men in Australia's northwest territories lived completely insulated from the ordeals of polite society. The unwritten but certainly not unspoken law of that land excluded white women completely. Having failed to convince these men that they should accept his wife, having failed to settle the novel idea with the Aborigines, and having failed to explain anything at all to his wife, Mr. Aeneas Gunn (Dignam) brings his bride (McGregor) to the Never Never. He lets her discover for her herself the exotic native tribes and the men in dust-

covered clothes, who fear her more than they resent her. He lets her
discover that she is a cultural oddity and has no home. When a home is
built, it turns out to be a prison. She was to live there and survey the rest
of the world from a rocker on the porch. But Mrs. Gunn walks off the
porch, implying it was not "a cottage in Hampton," and introduces
herself to the Aborigines. She swims with them, and they marvel at the
whiteness of her skin. She eats lizard with them. She makes friends with
them. Mr. Gunn thinks familiarity makes natives forget their place. Mrs.
Gunn thinks, "You're afraid I'll forget my place." She adopts an Aboriginal girl. "Bet Bet needs somebody, and I need somebody." When a fever strikes the reclusive men, they die in the bush rather than come to
her for help, and she loses all resilience to social vanity. Mr. Gunn also
takes on the fever and dies, and her short but novel marriage is ended.
Jane Taylor Gunn stays on in the Never Never, where she influences
human nature to appreciate its own diversity. Soon everybody forgets
their places. If it weren't for Mrs. Gunn's diaries, on which this movie
was based, it would be hard to conceive of iron rules of gender and
race bending so willingly to the lull of friendship. *We of the Never
Never* is a delicate celebration of devotion to land and to human
uniqueness. Cinematographer Gary Hansen matches Auzins' long-ago
mood with passive vistas of colorless and forgotten skies.

Also recommended: *My Brilliant Career.*

WE WILL NEVER GO TO THE WOODS AGAIN
(NOUS N'IRONS PLUS AU BOIS)

With Marie France Pisier, Siegfried Rauch, Richard Le Duc, Jaques
Higelin. Directed by George Dumoulin. Written by Catherine Varlin.
Music by Michel Sendrez. France. In French and German with yellow En-
glish titles. Color. 88 minutes. 1985.

**During World War II in Nazi-occupied France, groups of young
people leave the cities and live in the woods, where they organize anti-fascist resistance.**

From the primitive forest encampment, they attack German forces entering the woods and subvert the Nazi war effort. Many townspeople support them with medical supplies and food. When four Germans surrender to them, claiming to be deserters from Hitler's army, they are suspected of being infiltrators, but are held as prisoners of war, put to work around the camp, and even given turns standing guard. They seem sincere, but often speak German among themselves and are never fully indoctrinated into the resistance. When a German troop force is tracked coming toward the camp, the French quickly assume that the POWs have betrayed their position. They evacuate, leaving the four behind, and later learn that they were executed for treason by the Nazis. The opportunity to trust and cooperate is lost in the paranoia of war. Cushioning Varlin's drama are romances and adoring close-ups of the beautiful Marie France Pisier. She fills many a frame pushing her bike, riding her bike, or sitting next to her bike along scenic rural roadways. But even Pisier seems distant and unknowable, making the German POWs the best part of this film about French anti-fascists.

Also recommended: *The White Rose.*

THE WEAVERS: WASN'T THAT A TIME

With Lee Hays, Ronnie Gilbert, Pete Seeger, Fred Hellerman, Mary Travers, Don McLean, Studs Terkel, Arlo Guthrie, Holly Near, Harry Reasoner. Produced by Jim Brown, George Stoney, and Harold Leventhal. Directed by Jim Brown. Written by Lee Hays. Photography by Jim Brown, Daniel Ducovny, and Tom Hurwitz. Music by The Weavers. USA. English. Black and white and color. 78 minutes. 1981.

The reunion of The Weavers—Pete Seeger, Lee Hays, Ronnie Gilbert, and Fred Hellerman.

Lee Hays is ninety years old and confined to a wheelchair. The Weavers haven't performed as a group for over twenty-five years. But they will do Carnegie Hall one last time. As rehearsals for the reunion concert map out the show, archive footage maps out the history of The

Weavers, which parallels the history of social activism in the 20th century. Harry Reasoner calls them the unifying linkage between the activism of the 1930s and the activism of the '60s and '70s. During their career, they sang authentic folksongs of protest and deliverance. "Union miners...stand together." "We are traveling in the footsteps of those who've gone before." "If I Had a Hammer" was recorded by The Weavers and by more than a hundred other artists around the world. "We sang union songs. We sang songs of hope." "We had the feeling that if we sang loud enough and hopefully enough, it would make a difference." They sang in Spanish about disappearing freedom fighters in Chile. They sang about international understanding. They were so dedicated to activism and radical ideals that they were called before the House UnAmerican Activities Committee in 1952. They refused to cooperate and were blacklisted. Decca records dropped their contract. Radio stations wouldn't air their songs. Television refused interviews. At club dates, vigilante mobs shouted, "Why don't you sing 'The Star Spangled Banner'?" Thirty years later, Lee Hays says, "If it weren't for the honor, I'd just as soon not have been blacklisted." There were years of forced inaction. A Carnegie Hall date in 1965 filled the seats, but no one would distribute a recording of the live performance. "It would be nice for America if there had never been a blacklist," says Pete Seeger. "It would be nice if there were no blacklist *now*." The 1980 reunion concert sells out and generates offers from across the country. But this would be The Weaver's last concert performance. Lee Hays, over ninety and in poor health, died nine months later. As he requested, his ashes were mixed into his compost pile to feed the Earth that always fed him. Nothing could more typify the holistic, self-sustaining, artistic ethic of The Weavers than this final gesture of humility.

Also recommended: *A Vision Shared.*

WESTFRONT 1918

With Fritz Kampers, Gustav Diessl, H. J. Moebis, Claus Clausen, Jackie Monnier, Hanna Hoessrich, Else Heller. Produced by Nero Films. Directed by G.W. Pabst. Written by Ladislaus Vajda and Peter Martin Lampel, based on the novel *Vier Von Der Infanterie* by Ernst Johannsen.

Cinematography by Fritz Arno Wagner and Charles Metain. Germany. French and German with titles. Black and white. 90 minutes. 1930.

The conditions of the French and German troops along the western front in World War I.

There are a lot of interesting and likable characters in this German trench warfare film, none of whom will survive their tour of duty. Along the way, there is love lost, love found, bivouac delirium, and a few very talented people performing in a night spot. Most of *Westfront 1918* is spent in foxholes or trenches with cameras aimed out across fields of coiling barbed wire beyond which protracted battles are being fought in billows of cannon powder so thick that it's impossible to tell who's dying and who isn't. We get the impression that war is hell. We get the impression that making war movies is hell. The soundtrack is frequently monopolized by explosions, machine-gun fire, and distant screaming. The fighting men sink into flooding pits, bodies lie forgotten, and corpses fill the screen. Bombs whistle through the air. Closing scenes are shot in a front-line hospital tent. One of the main characters has died after wishing he had forgiven his wife her wartime infidelities. With no time to remove his body, the doctors pull a sheet over his face and leave him in his camp bed. When they've gone, a blind French soldier on the next cot reaches out and takes his hand. "I am not your enemy," he says in French, his face glowing with the hope of friendship, "I'm not your enemy."

Also recommended: *All Quiet on the Western Front.*

WHEN THE WIND BLOWS

With the voices of John Mills and Peggy Ashcroft. Produced by John Coats. Directed by Jimmy T. Murakami. Screenplay based on the book by Raymond Briggs. Music by David Bowie, Genesis, and Paul Hardcastle. Musical score by Roger Waters. Great Britain. English. Color. 80 minutes. 1986.

The story of Mr. and Mrs. artificially-animated Bloggs, whose

story-board world is rocked by a hydrogen bomb blast, momentarily suspending their animation.

As he belatedly war-proofs the house, Jim Bloggs tries to convince Hilda that what's happened is quite a serious thing. He tells her all he knows about the effects of nuclear war. She tries to listen, but doesn't want him wearing his new shirt to the "bomb," even if white is the best color, since it was supposed to be for a special occasion. They've lived through the blast, but they aren't sure why. "They've probably used too small of a bomb . . . and that's why we've survived." There's no electricity, no water coming out of the tap. Things have probably been shut off temporarily due to emergency conditions. When the newspaper comes, a lot of their questions will be answered and they will have some idea of the extent of the destruction. Focusing on stuff like this keeps their spirits high, even when symptoms of radiation poisoning set in. Jim paints the windows white and puts a lean-to in the hallway as protection against the fallout. Nevertheless, they become tired, dizzy, and nauseous. It must be nerves. Their hair is falling out. They have skin sores. The lettuce in the garden plot is burned into the scorched earth. Hilda is planning a trip into town to buy material for new curtains. They will also need to pick up some water. They need water to wash things up and to cook. There's no need for panic. When they are feeling a little better, they will crawl out from under the lean-to and make the trip. Or they could just wait for the emergency services to arrive. These charming but helpless animated people never give up hope that all will return to normal. they are incapable of comprehending what nuclear war means—making them perfect models for the rest of us. This British production dramatizes a Pandora's box of misconceptions. Interspersed footage of actual atomic blasts is used to tremendous effect, contrasted, as is it with the quaint, cartoon couple.

Also recommended: *The Atomic Cafe.*

WHERE THE GREEN ANTS DREAM

With Bruce Spence, Ray Barrett, Norman Kaye, Wandjuk Marika, Roay Marika, Colleen Clifford, Marraru Wunungmurra. Produced by Lucki

Stipetic. Directed by Werner Herzog. Written by Werner Herzog and Bob Ellis. Photography by Jorg Schmidt-Reitwein. Music by Gabriel Faure, Richard Wagner, Klaus-Jochen Wiese, Ernst Bloch, and Wandjuk Marika. Australia. English. Color. 99 minutes. 1984.

An Australian mine chief meets native land claims and dream philosophies.

The tormented energy of the unknown in a place rare to the camera's eye and more rare to human reason. What's out there? The unknown. Maybe it could kill you. Maybe it could save you. Herzog wants us to imagine things as we pan in on the rooftops of the Ayres Mining Company in Australia's northwest territories. In one of the tin huts is field representative Hackett (Spence), talking to a white-haired lady, sort of apologizing and explaining at the same time that the mining company's seismographic apparatus cannot track down Benjamin Franklin, her lost dog. "Even a footstep," she marvels, handing him the snapshot, "even a footstep will make the needles jump? He's out there alone somewhere, my Ben." Yes, even a footstep, but only if tracers were laid over the whole area. And the phone is ringing and a blast line is set outside to blow Spence and Ayres Mining into unknowable wealth. Uranium is out there, as is a group of Aborigines, sitting on the blast line. If he could see into the future, and I think he does, Spence would know when he steps out the door that he has walked into a story rare to the camera's eye. Who are these natives, and what do they want? "There will be no digging and no blasting here." Spence is on a bit of a deadline. "May I be so presumptuous as to ask why?" "This is the land where the green ants dream." "Green ants?" Ayres Mining executives now squat in the yellow dust to explain contractual legal rights to the ant myth people. The white-haired lady is leading an expedition to the mouth of the mine shaft where her dog was last seen. She suggests ladders. Spence thinks that in that case, Ben would need them, too, "if you catch my meaning." He has a new job—public liaison. He's good with people. He finds a man who holds green ants in tweezers and talks absorbedly about natives, the land, and rhythms of other life. He meets white men living as natives. He see Aborigines sitting in the grocery near the laundry products. The owner acknowledges, "It's a sacred site." It's where the men dream their children. They must dream them before they can be born. A tree once grew there—the only tree for a thousand miles. "When we built the store, we cut the tree down, didn't we? There were none too happy about that, I can tell you." Now they sit by the detergents. And the owner of the dog has a deck chair at the mine shaft and an umbrella and a can of dog food. He's down there somewhere. And the natives still occupy the blast line. Nothing can move them. Not threats. Not the courts. Not a glimpse of Sydney. Not an airplane—the generous gift of Ayres Mining. Spence has had a dream. He kneels by the dog owner to confess. "I dreamt that everybody in the world was running away carrying little lunch boxes full of their precious things. Everyone except me." He has nothing precious—nothing to search for, nothing to protect, nothing to lament if lost. He has only Ayres Mining, which he leaves to walk into the land that could kill him—or save him.

Also recommended: *The Last Wave.*

THE WHITE ROSE

With Lena Stolze, Werner Stocker, Mechthild Reinders, Sabine Kretzschmar, Christine Schwartz, Beate Himmerlstoss, Hans-Jurgen Schatz, Wulf Kessler, Martin Benrath, Peter Kortenbach, Heinz Keller, Monika Madras, Werner Schnitzer, Agnes Csere, Oliver Siebert, Anja Kruse, Susanne Seuffert, Ulrich Tukor, Ulf-Jurgen Wagner, Gerhard Friedrich. Directed by Michael Verhoeven. Germany. In German with English titles. Color. 108 minutes. 1983.

College students work to resist the Nazi invasions of World War II.

Representatives of the Nazi party were not unfamiliar spectacles in college lecture halls. They would arrive unannounced to suggest that women students could be put to better purpose breeding for the Third Reich. *The White Rose* was an underground, anti-fascist newspaper printed and distributed by university students in Germany during World War II. The movie dramatizes real events that led to the arrest and execution of five student dissidents. In Hitler's Germany, information service was possibly the most dangerous form of activism. Anything that could be used against the Third Reich was controlled. The government monitored the sale of paper stock and postage stamps. If you bought large quantities, you could be a traitor to National Socialism. All luggage moving in and out of the country was searched. The Nazis knew about *The White Rose* and worked to trace the distribution routes and locate the press. Lena Stolze plays Sophie. She's a sorceress of controlled fear, buying enormous quantities of stamps and stealing paper, which she smuggles past Nazi street troops back to the press. She and others from the staff race through the pre-dawn city leaving copies of the newspaper in hallways, stairways, street corners, and phone booths. What moves these young people to act when so many others do nothing to resist the destruction of their culture and way of life? This is the question that is never answered. They do not despise fascism more. They do not fear it less. But they risk their lives and, in this case, give their lives. Five of these students were tried, found guilty of treason, and beheaded by the fascist state. They were neither heroes nor martyrs, but ordinary people who stood up for what they knew to be right. They left behind parents, some of whom lost their only children to the nightmare of Hitler. Woven into this film are historic details of the perversion and senselessness of German fascism and the precarious personal balance that will move some to submit and others to dare to oppose repression. Closing scenes are photographs of the five student martyrs. It's hard to imagine how anyone could have made a better film of the German resistance movement.

Also recommended: *Nasty Girl*.

WHO KILLED VINCENT CHIN?

With Ron Ebens and Michael Nitz. Produced by Renee Tajima. Directed by Christine Choy. Photography by Christine Choy, Nick Doob, Kylo Kibbe, and Al Santana. USA. English. Color. 87 minutes. 1987.

Documentary of the vigilante murder of a Chinese-American by auto workers in Detroit, Michigan.

Who killed Vincent Chin? Unemployed auto workers Ronald Ebens and his stepson, Michael Nitz, hunted Chin down after an argument in a local restaurant and beat him with a baseball bat while witnesses, including a police officer, looked on. Chin—the only son of a widowed, immigrant mother—died four days later. For this crime of violence, Ebens and Nitz were sentenced by a Detroit district court judge to three month's probation and a $3,000 fine. The court's ruling cited the murderers as steady workers with no prior criminal records, finding that they had "accidentally" killed Chin in a "fight" following a barroom dispute. Vincent Chin lived in Detroit, Michigan—former auto capital of the world before Japanese imports threatened the dominance of the Big Three. The downfall of the American auto industry and the subsequent loss of jobs for Detroit auto workers had long fomented in Ebens' mind. In the argument that led to the murder, witnesses overheard Ebens accuse "people like you" of costing Americans jobs. The appalling sentence of the Detroit court led finally to a national outcry for a new trial in Federal court to try Ebens for breach of federal civil rights law. The case would focus on the "intent" behind the murder. He could be found guilty only if he attacked Chin *because* he was Chinese. In this trial, held in Detroit, jurors were familiar with the implications of the original accusation. Ebens was found guilty and sentenced to twenty-five years in federal prison. However, only hours after Chin's mother issued a statement of thanksgiving and before Ebens' lawyer could file for appeal, the judge, owing to technicalities never made clear in the film, declared a mistrial and found Ebens eligible for retrial outside the jurisdictional limits of Detroit. This second trial was held in Ohio, where there was little if any understanding of the connection between Ebens' state of mind on the night of the murder, the crisis in auto sales, and the anti-Japanese/Chinese sentiment in Detroit. Ohio jurors found Ebens not guilty of violating Vincent Chin's civil rights. It is a testament to Choy's talent as a documentary filmmaker that *Who Killed Vincent Chin?* contains long interviews with the murderers talking casually in their own living rooms about their ordeal. They are resentful. The one night they spent in jail was not pleasant, and the years of the evolving court cases have been difficult. Ebens loves his country. He is not prejudiced. He doesn't worry about his reputation. All his friends are behind him one-hundred percent. *Who Killed Vincent Chin?* rescues the Chin case from judicial oblivion. It incriminates the vigilante injustice that cost Vincent Chin his life and the prejudices in society that let his murderers go free.

Also recommended: *The Thin Blue Line.*

WILD BOYS OF THE ROAD

With Frankie Darro, Dorothy Coonan, Grant Mitchell, Sterling Holloway, Ward Bond, Ann Hovey, Edwin Phillips, Rochelle Hudson, Robert Barrat. Produced by Robert Presnell. Directed by William Wellman. Screenplay by Earl Baldwin, based on the story "Desperate Youth" by Daniel Ahearn. Photography by Arthur Todd. USA. English. Black and white. 77 minutes. 1933.

The story of young American men and women who rode the rails during the Depression of the 1930s.

Thematically, *Wild Boys on the Road* is undeniably unique, set as it is in a unique time and focusing on a unique aspect of those times— homeless children of the 1930s ranging across the country in packs, segregated by age into their own junior Hoovervilles. The young ho- boes live by handouts and begging, but their spirits remain high. Brief individual lapses into melancholy in this film are buoyed up by friends on all sides bounding with pep and boundlessly recuperative from life's ills. They beam with vitality and enthusiastic vigor. Each kid is poised for the new day fresher than they were the day before. Most are young, white boys, but girls and minorities are out there, too, dodging railroad dicks and the police. They dropped out of school and left home to take a burden off their families and survive on the road. There is misfortune. One of the boys falls under a train and loses his leg, but soon recuper- ates and keeps up with the group as best as he can on crutches. The on- going problem of where to sleep is temporarily solved when the kids set up a sewer pipe city in a field full of pretty nice unused sewer pipes. They've gotten permission, but are hosed out by the police anyway. In an unusually desperate moment, our heroes become involved in a theft ring and wind up before a judge who, instead of sending them all to youth detention, gives them a pep talk on the U.S. recovery from the Depression, walks them to the front door, and waves them off as home- less as ever. Closing scenes are of our Tommy and his best friends, pumped up for another day. They can make it. They have no food, no place to live, no jobs, no prospects, and yet you can tell that Wellman considered this a happy ending. I guess a Depression is not that bad, just a sort of adventure for the kids and a perfect training ground for an appreciation of the free enterprise system.

Also recommended: *Our Daily Bread*.

WINDWALKER

With Trevor Howard, Nick Ramus, James Remar, Silvanna Gallardo, Dusty Iron Wings McCrea, Rudy Diaz, Harold Goss-Coyote, Billy Drago, Serene Hedin. Produced by Arthur R. Dubs and Thomas Ballard. Directed by Keith Merrill. Screenplay by Ray Goldrup, based on the novel by Blaine Yorgason. Photography by Reed Smoot. Music by Merrill Jensen. USA. Native American dialogue (Cheyenne and Crow) with English titles and narration. Color. 108 minutes. 1980.

**A Native American family is split up and reunited
after many years.**

If critics found plenty to gripe about in *Dances with Wolves*, they didn't even lower themselves to talk about this ethno-rip-off from the emporium of filmic improbabilities. So why am I lowering myself? Well, because some people liked it. Some people thought it was the greatest movie about Indians ever made. Some people thought it offered insights into Indian spiritual awareness. But I think it would have been better without the Indians in it—just the snow drifts, the blue sky, and the empty tepees. If it were a scenery special, with flute music and an occasional white horse, I would have enjoyed it more. After acknowledging the almost all-Indian cast and the use of Native American language in dialogue sequences, the preposterous plotting and irreducible Bwana Bwana caricatures of *Windwalker* rankle the critical senses. All young Ramus ever does is swim in forest ponds with his mute bride or traipse through the hills hunting for his son, whom the loathsome Crow stole away. The rest of the movie is divided between peeks into the elderly Ramus' (Howard) tent as he dies or fighting off the Crow in wholesome tribal battles. The scenes of Nature, Our Mother, while perfect as a penny postcard, were so separate from the narrative, and the narrative is so flabby and generationally confusing that I was gratified the filmmakers were limited to only the one planet. The spiritual insights must have been the soft-focus daydreams Howard has about his lost love in the variegated flashbacks of his manhood. Not that you would, but don't grieve when Howard dies and is buried in the sky the way all Cheyenne used to be. From the beyond, he will sense his son needs help. He will climb down off the scaffold and plunge through miles of four-foot snowbanks to save the entire encampment (even though he needed help getting *on* the burial rack). But he makes it through the snow drifts and, well, don't let me spoil the surprise, which has a lot to do with discovering that the Crow they take hostage in battle turns out to be a *close* personal relative to Smiling Wolf. Trevor Howard, honored for his performance here, never actually speaks. All his Indian language lines are dubbed by Nick Ramus, who also does the narration. The musical score of flutes and drums is nicely done. Someone should have introduced Jensen to Kevin Costner.

Also recommended: *Little Big Man.*

WINTER KILLS

With Jeff Bridges, John Huston, Tony Perkins, Sterling Hayden, Eli Wallach, Dorothy Malone, Richard Boone, Tomas Milian, Belinda Bauer, Ralph Meeker, Toshiro Mifune, Donald Moffat, Elizabeth Taylor. Produced by Fred Caruso. Written and directed by William Richert, based on the novel by Richard Condon. Photography by Vilmos Zsigmond. Music by Maurice Jarre. USA. English. color. 97 minutes. Re-edited from the 1979 film. 1983.

**A popular young president's assassination
undergoes unexpected scrutiny.**

By the time the telephone answering machine is invented, the print on the relevant documents is fading, interest on the debt generated by the inquiries is dwindling, and few tears remain unshed about the assassination of beloved former president, Tim Kegan. His apolitical younger brother Nick (Bridges) is king of the recovered, until a man makes a spurious deathbed confession and a gun is found, the gun that *really* killed Tim Kegan. Nick would rather not overturn stones to expose withering secrets and the spoor of vegetative omens. But everywhere he turns there is cruel invention and women on motor bikes and bombed-out buildings. Confidants are dropping dead in the rearview mirror. To know him is to die. He is dazed to be alive. He talks to armored fleets in the same way he talks to his shell of a mother and lizard-lipped father. Fabulous lies make the truth seem cruel. There are fungal motives; maybe one of them is true. Maybe the Hollywood bombshell and the suicide or the outlandish campaign debt or the gambling casinos in Cuba. Motive upon motive. Nick sees it all. At last he will know that the

voices on the answering machine were agents, not of love but of decep-
tion. And he will prepare to face a future that is nothing like the past
and to accept a past that was not what he thought. *Winter Kills*—
whatever that means. Everyone in this film is exceptionally responsive
to the blind faith Richert places in them. Nothing remains ungiven.
Winter Kills depends on audience participation. It's for people who like
to think and for people who don't think that much but like to think
thinking is O.K. The producers suffered baffling funding problems toward the end. It was a struggle to finish filming. The movie was released
during a nationwide power failure, played one week, and was pulled
by Avco Embassy Films.

Also recommended: *The Parallax View.*

WITNESS TO THE HOLOCAUST: THE TRIAL OF ADOLF EICHMANN

Narrated by Joel Grey. Produced by Lori Perlow. A project of the National Jewish Theological Seminary of America. In English, German, and
Hebrew with voice translations. Black and white. 90 minutes. 1987.

Nazi leader Adolf Eichmann is tried for war crimes.

"I do not stand alone. Here with me at this moment stand six million
prosecutors. Their ashes have been piled up in the mounds of Aus-
chwitz and the fields of Treblinka and spilled into the rivers of Poland.
Their graves are scattered throughout the length and breadth of Germany. Their blood cries to heaven. But their voices cannot be heard."
Criminal case #40, Jerusalem, April 1961—Adolf Eichmann is charged
with fifteen counts of war crimes, crimes against humanity, membership in a criminal organization, and crimes against the Jewish people.
(Membership in the Nazi party was outlawed by the International Military Tribunal at Nuremberg in 1946.) Eichmann's lawyer argues that Israel has no jurisdiction, that an impartial trial with a Jewish judge is not
possible, and that Eichmann was arrested under illegal circumstances.

Eichmann pleads "not guilty" on all counts as interpreted "in the spirit of the indictment." Thousand of documents and hundreds of witnesses together recreate the horrendous sweep of Nazi war atrocities. In occupied Poland alone, 2.5 million Jews suffered. Some were burned alive in their prayer shawls in supplication to God. The "final solution" was an "industry of death" and the planned extermination of an entire people. To the accusations, Eichmann responds, "I did my level best to bring order to all the hubbub and turmoil with regard to the immigrations and deportations. . . . What was done was not my doing. . . . I was not guilty because I had to toe the line willy-nilly. This is how I found justification for what I did." Throughout the nine months of the trial, his face wears the expression of denial. He was a Lieutenant-Colonel in the SS, the head of Reich security in Section IV B, the department in charge of "the annihilation of European Jewry." The concentration camps used Ropa gas in the ovens. "The last people, seeing the gas coming, not wanting to enter, were bayoneted." The ovens were jam-packed. "They could hardly close the doors. . . . In thirty-five minutes all were dead." To everything, Eichmann responds, "I had to obey orders. I had to do it." There are testimonies of Jewish children given away to Christian families and of Jews smuggled to freedom ahead of the Nazi invasions. Wartime footage shows roadways littered with the bones of the thousands who never made it to safety. Eichmann explains, "The sight of dead Jews left me utterly shattered. It haunted me all the time. I was in an iron grip of orders to continue. I saw something in this 'Jewish solution,' something illegal, something hideous and heinous. . . . I was compelled . . . by my oath of allegiance and loyalty. I had to deal with the technical aspects." "I had transferred the onus of responsibility to my superiors. I regarded myself as not guilty and was glad that I had no direct share in the physical extermination of the Jews." On December 15, 1961, Eichmann is found guilty and sentenced to death for war crimes, crimes against the Jews, and crimes against humanity. He is hanged on May 31, 1962. His ashes are scattered over the Mediterranean.

Also recommended: *The Nuremberg Trials* and *Hotel Terminus*.

A WORLD APART

With Barbara Hershey, Jodhi May, David Suchet, Jeroen Krabbe, Carolyn Clayton-Cragg, Merav Gruer, Albee Lesotho, Linda Mvusi, Tim Roth. Produced by Sarah Radclyffe. Directed by Chris Menges. Screenplay by Shawn Slovo. Photography by Peter Biziou. Music and lyrics by E. M. Sontonga. Musical score by Hans Zimmer. United Kingdom. English and Afrikaans. Color. 113 minutes. 1988.

Political activists in South Africa oppose apartheid.

They all said it couldn't be done, but *A World Apart* seems to have navigated the seas of studio/distributor caprice and arrived at theaters in one piece. For this reason and because of Shawn Slovo's personalized script, Menges' intuitive direction, and class acting from everyone down to the youngest member of the cast, *A World Apart* sits in a class apart. It is a lucid amalgam of facts about the ANC, Soweto, anthems, flags, people, and the laboriously vile system of apartheid. Part of the reason for this is Shawn Slovo. Her mother, upon whose life the story is based, was a journalist working with the African National Congress to end minority rule in South Africa. Her father was also an activist, the only white member of the ANC executive committee and head of the South African communist party, forced to live in exile in Zambia to avoid arrest under the Suppression of Communism Act. The movie starts in 1963, the year of Nelson Mandela's arrest, the Sharpsville massacre, and the passage of the Ninety Day Detention Act. Her mother (Hershey) will be the first woman detained under the new act. When her time is up, she is detained for another ninety days. That's part of the genius of Afrikaaner "law." Hershey's office is the center of her anti-apartheid work. A sign on the wall says, "The People Shall Rule." As her mother is held in detention, Shawn (May) accuses her of putting black people before the welfare of her own children. Hershey says, "You deserve to have a mother—well, you have one, it's just not the way you wanted her." Ruth First was killed by a parcel bomb in Mozambique in 1982. Shawn, who as a child resented her mother's involvement and who was not an activist herself, joined the ANC after her mother's assassination and today follows in her parents' courageous footsteps. Lacking a tag-line for marketing gurus, *A World Apart* was released in the very calm eye of the storm of *Cry Freedom*, a drama about black consciousness leader Steven Biko. So you may have never heard of *A World Apart*—a film in which apartheid is not a game of wits but a deadly vehicle of repression from which the people cannot escape. Notwithstanding the headline breakdown of petty apartheid, the four pillars of totalitarianism—the land, the laws, the economy, the force—remain in place in South Africa, and blacks still live in a world apart. This film was dedicated to "Diana Roth" and the thousands who have given their lives in the struggle for a free South Africa.

Also recommended: *Sarafina.*

YEAR OF LIVING DANGEROUSLY

With Mel Gibson, Sigourney Weaver, Michael Murphy, Linda Hunt, Noel Ferrier, Domingo Landicho, Bembol Roco. Produced by James McElroy. Directed by Peter Weir. Screenplay by David Williamson, Peter Weir, and C.J. Koch, based on the novel by Koch. Photography by Russell Boyd. Music of Maurice Jarre. Australia. English. Color 115 minutes. 1982.

Journalists cover political upheaval in Indonesia.

Year of Living Dangerously cuts into the subcutaneous layers of a revolution personalized by the operatives of unrest—burned-out journalists, idealistic photographers, anti-Americans, anti-capitalists, mobs of Sukarno henchmen, and streets full of the poor, the disabled, the displaced, the hungry, and the treacherous. Weir exposes the diversity of human opinion and the human condition, beginning with Mel Gibson—an Australian journalist on his first assignment in Indonesia, covering the political unrest and hoping to write the story that will save him from the back pages forever. What he finds in Jakarta is a social and political malignancy reported on by a company of press people to whom the spectacle of spontaneous social decay is little more than fuel for their own cynicism and bravado more terrible than the terror they report. Through the narrative commentary of Billy Kwan (Linda Hunt), Weir dramatizes the innocence of Jakarta's poor. When location journalists leeringly describe the city's large prostitute population, Billy counters, "Yes, starvation is a great aphrodisiac." The screenplay, built of undercurrents and unstable moods such as hate, revenge, trust, and love, reveals history as a thing moved by unpredictable shifts in the energy of time and place. These intangibles move people into war or toward peace. Images reflect their opposition. Few filmmakers are willing to shoot from such a daring sociologic, psychoanalytic perch. For Weir, it is the normal thing. "My interest lies in those unknown areas. There are no answers. No endings." An irrepressible curiosity and interest in the generative forces of sociologic phenomena define Weir's distinctive filmmaking formula. He poses injustice against a wall of fallibility. Right and wrong are mutable interpretations of mutably interpreted historic events. The fate of a nation may rest on a single impulse or whim or loyalty or luck. Utopia is a rumor of unharmonious consensus. Instinctual casting, opulent, sweltering photography, and the sometimes deranged, sometimes presentient musical wizardry of Maurice Jarre help make *The Year of Living Dangerously* an exquisite and unforgettable film—a Rosetta stone in reverse—an intellectually arresting, emotionally engrossing work of rarefied social insight.

Also recommended: *Missing*.

YOU GOT TO MOVE

Produced by Lucie Massie Phenix. Directed by Lucie Massie Phenix and Veronica Selver. USA. English. Color. 87 minutes. 1985.

Political activism rises in southern U.S. states in response to racism and toxic waste dumping.

From the day the Highlander School for Social Activism opened its doors in Tennessee, it has been the target of threats, red-baiting, court battles, and other persecutions from white segregationists and conservatives, who called the school a "communist training center" and wanted it shut down. Standing up against racists and capitalists, however, is not the most compelling thing going on in this film. Fights for human rights and a healthy world take second place to the evolution of the courageous spirit that makes victory possible. The inception point of that courage is targeted by Phenix's cameras, and there's just nothing quite like it anywhere, in any film by anybody. Highlander "dared to give people the belief that they could step out . . . and do something." A woman fighting toxic waste dumping says, "I thought that to do what I needed to do, you'd need a college degree, but I found out that if you don't have it, you'll have to go on without it." Women from Harlan County, Kentucky, have gone to war with the coal companies. "What did the strike accomplish?" "We got recognition as human beings, for one." It is the genesis of social reformation kindled into the ardor of purpose. "'I'm not a leader, they all kept saying. I will follow.' If you don't lead, no one is going anywhere." So this black civil rights activist would coordinate the literacy program, helping to get blacks registered to vote in the south. "It was beyond life and death. We knew what we were supposed to be doing. It was somebody else's job to kill." At the school, they talk about El Salvador, South Africa, and the Duke Mining Company. Women from the hills of Appalachia know that buying bananas supports the circle of poison and U.S. corporate imperialism in Central and South America. They have learned first-hand the cost of opposition, the ache of isolation. "Sometimes we felt like we were the only people in the world, and we were fighting the world." Men, women, and children who once trusted the system now believe, "You can either give in, or you can fight." In *You Got to Move*, all activism is interconnected and consolidated into a singular sensation. The simple acts of urgency are minor revolutions fought by ordinary people, which is the only kind of people there are. *You Got to Move* is a film by women, principally about women—tracing ideas culminating in activism and resistance. The message is elemental to all social change, "People became aware of the power that was in them."

Also recommended: *Harlan County*.

THE YOUNG LIONS

With Marlon Brando, Montgomery Clift, May Britt, Dean Martin, Hope Lange, Barbara Rush, Dora Doy, Lee Van Cleef, Maximilian Schell. Produced by Al Lichtman. Directed by Edward Dmytryk. Screenplay by Edward Anhalt, based on the novel by Irwin Shaw. Photography by Joe MacDonald. Music by Hugo Friedhofer. USA. English. Black and white. 167 minutes. 1958.

The story of two U.S. draftees, one Nazi soldier, and what happens to them during World War II.

It's New Year's Eve, 1938 in Bavaria, Germany. Hitler is in with the in crowd, and Marlon Brando, a German, thinks that the Nazis might make things better for the German people. National socialism promises free university education and the unification of Europe. Brando joins the German army. In America, meanwhile, Dean Martin and Montgomery Clift get drafted and assigned to adjacent cots in the same unit. We learn all about them. They are very different people. They get separated, but eventually come to be on the same road outside the same concentration camp at the end of the war. They encounter Brando, whom Martin shoots on sight. He falls into a small stream, and they watch the last bubbles of his breath come to the surface before they walk away. Brando has died because he has become disillusioned about Nazism and has deserted the army. He has bashed his rifle to bits on a tree stump and wandered carelessly down a hillside into the American fire. It's too bad he dies just as he has come to his senses, especially since he didn't have a gun. And what happened in the other 130 minutes? Martin, Clift, and Brando have romances and get in fights and go to parties. There are also a few battle scenes in North Africa with Brando and Schell. It's one hour and fifty-two minutes into the film before we hear the word "Jew." But it still took three rewrites before the Pentagon would approve the screenplay. Our tax dollars at work.

Also recommended: *Burn!*

Z

With Yves Montand, Irene Papas, Jean-Loise Trintigant, Jacques Perrin, Charles Denner, Francois Perier, Pierre Dux, Julien Guiomar. Produced by Jacques Perrin and Hamed Rachedi. Directed by Constantin Costa-Gavras. Written by Jorge Semprun and Constantin Costa-Gavras, from the novel by Vassili Vassilikos. Music by Mikis Theodorakis. Photography by Raoul Coutard. France/Algeria. French with English titles. Color. 128 minutes. 1969.

Political intrigue about the assassination of a peace advocate.

"Any similarity to actual events or persons living or dead is not coincidental, it is intentional." *Z* is based on the assassination of Gregorios Lambrakis—a Greek liberal activist and peace advocate. It's a story of pro-war military madmen plotting to rid their world of the ideological mildews of pacifism, socialism, communism, and anarchism. "We are not an 'ism,' we are a democracy. We need an antibody for the disease. Property rights are still sacred here. Some would like to change that." They have a preventative program to save democracy. Lambrakis (Yves Montand), the Deputy of the Friends of Peace, is coming to town. All meeting halls become unavailable to him. He speaks in a small room with amplifiers for the crowds outside. Behind the crowds are protesters chanting, "We are the antibodies. We are the healthy parts." Like all antibodies, they are killers. As he leaves the lecture hall, Montand is struck down by a protester and later dies. For the investigation that follows, Costa-Gavras took material directly from trial transcripts—cover-ups, distortions, deviation from medical fact, lies upon lies, intimidation of witnesses, destruction of evidence. Anyone who threatened to reveal the truth was branded a leftist, discredited, and ruined. The principal investigator endures every abuse, but traces Montand's death back to the military. He implicates the entire executive superstructure of the armed forces. He implicates the police department as co-conspirators in the assassination. He generates warrants and a parade of arrests—one official after another, each one wearing heavier brass than the one before. They are charged with premeditated murder. It looks as though this one man can salvage justice and sanity from a well of corruption. Pacifists cheer. "One by one, all the extremists will fall." It is the end of oppression and the beginning of true liberty. But, as the trial date approaches, all the witnesses die premature, violent deaths. The case for the people collapses. The officers are freed and exonerated. Pacifists are imprisoned or executed. Liberal literature is banned—Tolstoy, Mark Twain, Einstein, Dostoyevsky. The letter "Z" is also banned—the Greek symbol for "he is alive." The film itself was banned in Greece until 1974, as well as in many other fascist-loving countries. The musical coordinator was under house arrest in Greece as the filming progressed and was unable to complete the score.

Also recommended: *The Trial.*

ZABRISKI POINT

With Mark Frechette, Daria Haprin, Rod Taylor. Produced by Carlo
Ponti. Directed by Michelangelo Antonioni. Written by Michelangelo
Antonioni, Fred Gardner, Sam Shepard, Tonino Guerra, and Clare
Peploe, based on the story by Michelangelo Antonioni. Photography by
Alfio Contini. USA. English. Color 111 minutes. 1970.

Two young people become disillusioned with the '60s.

If you didn't already suspect that lizards are a lot easier to get along
with than the L.A. bourgeoisie, here's your chance to find out. In
Zabriski Point Antonioni unintentionally captures the irony and the futility of the counterculture movement of the sixties. He takes a pair of
disenchanted young people out of the protest-clogged city and plunks
them down at Zabriski Point in the Arizona desert. Here they can merge
with the paleolithic landscape and give us a chance to see not only
how much simpler things were a million years ago, but how all human
beings, both mythic and real, just want to have unabandoned sex, even
if it means ruining their hairdo and their only set of clean clothes in the
Arizona dust. The cinematography *is* pretty overwhelming, especially if
you have the color adjusted right on your T.V. As we follow our young
people out to lizard land, we see just mile after mile of scenery like you
wish you'd seen on your last vacation, backlit with fairly appropriate
music by Pink Floyd. Of course, I missed most of it because I fast for-
warded through these parts. I don't have all day to meditate on how
great it would be if civilization had never evolved. Daria and Mark
traipse from place to place in a big old Buick, nurturing their impromptu friendship with the kind of dialogue that makes you wonder
how we came to be the dominant species. And what's going on back in
the city? Well, lots of protests and violence between the students and
the police. We might find this sort of thing more moving if we didn't
know by now that the student "revolution" did *not* save the world after
all. Since much of the '70s hype got defused by Madison Avenue, it's
sad, if not annoying to watch. Apart from the hopelessly passe aroma
this movie gives off and the amoebic pace of it, it also has nonactors in
the lead roles, and making a dramatic film without actors is like writing
a book with a hammer and chisel. It's not impossible; you just need a
lot of patience to cope with the finished product. I *like* movies. That
means I like good acting. A great actor, like Richard Burton, can read
the phone book aloud and give you goosebumps for years afterward ev-

ery time you think of it. Halprin and Frechette are not like that. They are spineless and boring on the screen. And it doesn't help to know that Mark went on to rob a bank in opposition to the Nixon administration or that Daria married Edward Hopper. Rod Taylor is not given enough to do to oomph things up. There is a very good blow-up scene at the end of the movie that's supposed to make us see how much Daria hates all wealth and wishes she could bomb it to kingdom come. It's shot in very slow slow-motion, so that you'll have trouble matching it up with your brainwaves. All I could think about was all the wood that they must have used to build this house on the cliff-side, not to mention the workers they employed to do so. Just to blow it up. I tried, and failed, to figure out how many cameras they used to film the shot. Perhaps if you are bored to distraction by *Zabriski Point*, you'll be interested to discover that Sam Shepard co-wrote the script, but I don't know which parts.

Also recommended: *Berkeley in the '60s* and *Underground*.

APPENDIX I: LISTING OF FILMS

A Nous La Liberte, 1
Abandoned Fields, 2
Above the Law, 3
Advise and Consent, 4
Air America, 5
Akropolis, 7
All Quiet on the Western Front, 8
All the King's Men, 9
All the President's Men, 10
Alphaville, 11
Alsino and the Condor, 12
Amazing Grace and Chuck, 13
Angry Harvest, 15
Animal Farm, 16
The Animals Film, 17
Another Country, 18
Apocalypse Now, 19
Arsenal, 20
The Assisi Underground, 21
The Atomic Cafe, 22
Au Revoir Les Enfants, 24
The Autobiography of Miss Jane
    Pittman, 25

The Battle of Algiers, 26
Berkeley in the 60's, 27
The Best Man, 29
Betrayed, 30
The Bicycle Thief, 31
Black and White in Color, 32
Black Fury, 33
Black God, White Devil, 34
Black Like Me, 35
The Blum Affair, 36
The Boat is Full, 37
Border Street, 38
Born on the Fourth of July, 39
Bound for Glory, 40
Breaker Morant, 41

Breaking With Old Ideas, 43
Broken Arrow, 44
Buffalo Bill and the Indians, 45
Burn!, 46
Bye Bye Brazil, 47

Camila, 48
Cannibal Tours, 49
Chapayev, 50
Cheyenne Autumn, 51
The China Syndrome, 52
Chocolat, 54
The Citadel, 55
Civilization, 56
Class Action, 57
The Coca-Cola Kid, 58
Come See the Paradise, 59
The Conformist, 60
Country, 62
Country Lovers, City Lovers, 63
Coverup: Behind the Iran-Contra
    Affair, 64
The Crowd, 65
Cry Freedom, 66

Dances With Wolves, 68
Daniel, 70
The Day After, 71
The Day After Trinity, 72
Dead End, 74
Dear America: Letters Home from
    Vietnam, 75
The Decision to Drop the Bomb,
    76
The Diary of a Country Priest, 78
The Diary of Anne Frank, 79
Dingaka, 80
Distant Thunder, 81
Do the Right Thing, 82

Do-Des'-Ka-Den, 84
Dr. Strangelove, 85
A Dry White Season, 86

Eat a Bowl of Tea, 87
84 Charlie Mopic, 88
El Norte, 89
The Emerald Forest, 90
The End of St. Petersburg, 92
Enemy Mine, 93
Executive Action, 95
The Exiles, 96

Fahrenheit 451, 97
Fail Safe, 99
The Falcon and the Snowman,
   100
Fires on the Plain, 101
Forbidden: A True Story, 102
Forbidden Games, 103
Four Days of the Masai, 104
Fringe Dwellers, 106
The Front, 107
Full Metal Jacket, 108

Gallipoli, 109
Gandhi, 110
Generations, 111
Gentlemen's Agreement, 112
The Gods Must Be Crazy, 114
Good Fight, 115
Gorillas in the Mist, 116
Grapes of Wrath, 118
The Great Dictator, 119
The Great McGinty, 120
The Great Wall, 121
Greed, 122
Guess Who's Coming to Dinner?,
   123
Guilty by Suspicion, 125

Handmaid's Tale, 126

Hanussen, 127
The Harder They Come, 128
Harlan County, USA, 130
Harp of Burma, 131
Harry and the Hendersons, 132
Head Office, 133
The Heart is a Lonely Hunter, 135
Hearts and Minds, 136
Heroes for Sale, 137
Hidden Agenda, 138
High Hopes, 139
Himatsuri, 141
Hiroshima Mon Amour, 142
Hollywood on Trial, 143
The Hollywood Shuffle, 144
The Home and the World, 146
Home of the Brave, 147
The Horse, 148
Hotel Terminus: The Life and
   Times of Klaus Barbie, 149
How Green Was My Valley, 150
H-2 Worker, 151
Hungry for Profit, 152

I Will Fight No More Forever, 154
Imitation of Life, 155
In Country, 156
In the King of Prussia, 157
Indian Agent, 159
The Inheritors, 160
Intolerance, 161

Jackknife, 162
Jesus of Montreal, 163
Johnny Got His Gun, 164
Juarez, 165
Judge Horton and the Scottsboro
   Boys, 166
Judgement at Nuremberg, 167
Julia, 169
Jungle Fever, 170

Kameradschaft, 171
Kamikaze '89, 172
Kanal, 174
Kangaroo, 175
Katherine, 176
Kent State, 177
The Killing Fields, 178
King: Montgomery To Memphis,
    179
Koyaanisqatsi, 181

La Muerte del Che Guevara, 182
The Last Seven Months of Anne
    Frank, 183
The Last Wave, 184
Latino, 185
The Learning Tree, 186
The Liberation of L.B. Jones, 188
Little Big Man, 188
The Little Foxes, 190
The Long Walk Home, 191
Los Olividados, 192
The Lost Horizon, 193
Love and Anarchy, 194

MacArthur's Children, 195
The Magic Christian, 197
Malcolm X, 198
Man Facing Southeast, 199
Mandela, 200
The Manhattan Project, 201
Mapantsula, 202
Master Harold and the Boys, 203
Matewan, 204
Medium Cool, 205
Meet John Doe, 207
Mephisto, 208
Metropolis, 209
Milagro Beanfield War, 210
Missing, 211
The Mission, 212
Mississippi Burning, 214

Mister Johnson, 215
Modern Times, 216
Mother, 217
The Mouse That Roared, 218
Mr. Hoover and I, 219
Mr. Klein, 220
Mr. Smith Goes to Washington,
    221
Music Box, 222
My Brilliant Career, 223

Nashville, 224
Nasty Girl, 226
Network, 227
Never Cry Wolf, 229
1984, 230
1990, 231
No Regrets for Our Youth, 232
Norma Rae, 234
North by Northwest, 235
The North Star, 236

October, 237
The Official Story, 238
On the Beach, 240
Our Daily Bread, 241
The Ox-Bow Incident, 242

Paisan, 243
Parallax View, 244
A Passage to India, 245
Patch of Blue, 246
Paths of Glory, 247
Paul Robeson, 249
The Pedestrian, 251
Platoon, 252
Point of Order, 253
Powaqqatsi, 254
Project X, 256

A Question of Silence, 257

Rain Man, 258
Raoni, 259
Rate It X, 261
Red Beard, 262
Reds, 263
The River Niger, 265
The Road to 1984, 266
Roger and Me, 267
Rome Open City, 268
Romero, 269
The Rosenberg and Sorbell Case
    Revisited, 271
Running on Empty, 272

Sacco and Vanzetti, 273
The Sacrifice, 274
Salt of the Earth, 276
Salvador, 277
Savages, 278
Sayonara, 280
Secret Honor: A Political Myth,
    281
A Sense of Loss, 282
Seven Days in May, 283
Sherman's March, 285
Ship of Fools, 286
Silkwood, 288
Slave of Love, 289
Soldiers of Orange, 290
Somebody Has to Shoot the
    Picture, 291
Song of Freedom, 292
The Sorrow and the Pity, 293
Soylent Green, 295
Sparrows, 296
Speaking Directly, 297
State of Siege, 298
Storm Over Asia, 299
Street of Shame, 301
Streetwise, 301
Strike, 303
Sugar Cane Alley, 304

Swept Away, 305
Swimming to Cambodia, 306

Tanner '88, 308
Testament, 309
The Thin Blue Line, 310
Threads, 311
Tin Drum, 313
To Be Young, Gifted and Black,
    314
To Kill a Mockingbird, 315
The Tree of Wooden Clogs, 317
The Trial, 318
Trial of the Catonsville Nine, 319
Tucker: A Man and His Dream,
    320
Twelve Angry Men, 321
28 Up, 322
24 Eyes, 324

The Ugly American, 325
Umberto D, 326
Under Fire, 327
Underground, 328
Under the World, 330
The Uprising, 331
Utu, 331
U2: Rattle and Hum, 333

The Vanishing American, 334
Veronico Cruz, 335
Vietnam: In the Year of the Pig,
    336
Viva Zapata!, 337

The Wall, 339
The War at Home, 340
Wargames, 341
Watch on the Rhine, 342
Watermelon Man, 343
The Wave, 344
We of the Never Never, 345

We Will Never Go to the Woods
      Again, 346
The Weavers: Wasn't That a
      Time?, 347
Westfront 1918, 348
When the Wind Blows, 349
Where the Green Ants Dream,
      350
The White Rose, 352
Who Killed Vincent Chin?, 353
Wild Boys on the Road, 355

Windwalker, 356
Winter Kills, 357
Witness to the Holocaust, 358
A World Apart, 360
Year of Living Dangerously, 361
You Got to Move, 362
The Young Lions, 363

Z, 364
Zabriski Point, 366

APPENDIX II: LISTING OF FILMS BY RELEVANT ISSUES

ANTI-SEMITISM

Akropolis
Angry Harvest
The Assisi Underground
Au Revoir Les Enfants
The Blum Affair
The Boat is Full
Border Street
The Diary of Anne Frank
The Exiles
Forbidden: A True Story
Gentlemen's Agreement
The Great Dictator
Hotel Terminus
The Inheritors
Judgement at Nuremberg
Julia
The Last Seven Months of Anne
  Frank
Mr. Klein
Music Box
Nasty Girl
The Pedestrian
Ship of Fools
The Sorrow and the Pity
Witness to the Holocaust

ANTI-WAR
(see also, Vietnam, World
War II, Nuclear Weapons)

Abandoned Fields
All Quiet on the Western Front
Breaker Morant
Fires on the Plain

Gallipoli
Harp of Burma
Hiroshima Mon Amour
Johnny Got His Gun
MacArthur's Children
Paths of Glory
Running on Empty
Trial of the Catonsville Nine
24 Eyes
Westfront 1918

AMERICAN INDIANS

Broken Arrow
Buffalo Bill and the Indians
Cheyenne Autumn
Dances with Wolves
I Will Fight No More Forever
Indian Agent
Little Big Man
Raoni
Vanishing Americans
Windwalker

CAPITALISM

A Nous La Liberte
Animal Farm
Burn!
Class Action
The Coca-Cola Kid
Country
El Norte
Head Office
H-2 Worker

Hungry for Profit
Kamikaze '89
The Little Foxes
The Magic Christian
Metropolis
Milagro Beanfield War
Modern Times
Network
Roger and Me
Sugar Cane Alley
Tucker

FOR CHILDREN

Amazing Grace and Chuck
Animal Farm
Au Revoir Les Enfants
Cannibal Tours
Cheyenne Autumn
The Emerald Forest
Enemy Mine
The Great Wall
Harry and the Hendersons
Indian Agent
Master Harold and the Boys
MacArthur's Children
Milagro Beanfield War
Modern Times
My Brilliant Career
Never Cry Wolf
Running on Empty
Sparrows
Sugar Cane Alley
To Kill a Mockingbird
24 Eyes
When the Wind Blows
Where the Green Ants Dream

CIVIL RIGHTS

The Autobiography of Miss Jane
    Pittman
Betrayed
Black Like Me
Camila
Cry Freedom
Do the Right Thing
Gandhi
Guess Who's Coming to Dinner?
The Hollywood Shuffle
Home of the Brave
Imitation of Life
Intolerance
Judge Horton and the Scottsboro
    Boys
Jungle Fever
King: Montgomery to Memphis
The Learning Tree
The Liberation of L. B. Jones
The Long Walk Home
Malcolm X
Mississippi Burning
The Ox-Bow Incident
A Patch of Blue
Paul Robeson
The River Niger
Sayonara
To Be Young, Gifted and Black
To Kill a Mockingbird
Twelve Angry Men
Watermelon Man
Who Killed Vincent Chin?
You Got to Move

CULTURE/CLASH

Cannibal Tours
Come See the Paradise
Eat a Bowl of Tea

The Emerald Forest
Enemy Mine
Four Days of the Masai
Fringe Dwellers
The Gods Must Be Crazy
The Great Wall
Harry and the Hendersons
The Last Wave
MacArthur's Children
Mister Johnson
A Passage to India
Savages
Song of Freedom
Utu
We of the Never Never
Where the Green Ants Dream

DEATH PENALTY

Somebody Has to Shoot the Picture
The Thin Blue Line
The Wall

DOCUMENTARY

The Atomic Cafe
Berkeley in the 60's
Cannibal Tours
Coverup: Behind the Iran-Contra Affair
The Day After Trinity
Dear America: Letters Home From Vietnam
The Decision to Drop the Bomb
The Exiles
Four Days of the Masai
Good Fight
Harlan County, USA
Hearts and Minds

Hollywood on Trial
Hungry for Profit
H-2 Worker
Hotel Terminus
In the King of Prussia
King: Montgomery to Memphis
Malcolm X
Point of Order
Ranoi
Rate It X
Roger and Me
The Rosenberg-Sorbell Case Revisited
Sense of Loss
Sherman's March
The Sorrow and the Pity
Speaking Directly
Street Wise
The Thin Blue Line
Trial of the Catonsville Nine
28 Up
U2: Rattle and Hum
Vietnam: In the Year of the Pig
The Weavers—Wasn't That a Time?
Who Killed Vincent Chin?
Witness to the Holocaust
You Got to Move

DYSTOPIA

Alphaville
Fahrenheit 451
Kamikaze '89
Koyannisqatsi
1984
Powaqqatsi
Soylent Green
The Trial

ENVIRONMENT/ ANIMAL RIGHTS

The Animals Film
The Emerald Forest
Gorillas in the Mist
Harry and the Hendersons
Himatsuri
Never Cry Wolf
Project X
Umberto D

FEMINISM

Camila
Handmaid's Tale
My Brilliant Career
A Question of Silence
Street of Shame
We of the Never Never

INSPIRATION

Civilization
Diary of a Country Priest
Jesus of Montreal
Man Facing Southeast

IMPERIALISM

Air America
Above the Law
Alsino and the Condor
The Battle of Algiers
Chocolat
Gandhi
Hidden Agenda
Juarez
Latino

Missing
The Mission
The Official Story
A Passage to India
Salvador
A Sense of Loss
Storm Over Asia
The Ugly American
Under Fire
Utu

McCARTHYSIM/ ANTI-COMMUNISM

The Front
Guilty by Suspicion
Hollywood on Trial
Point of Order
The Rosenberg-Sorbell Case
    Revisited
Salt of the Earth

MUSIC

U2: Rattle and Hum
The Weavers: Wasn't That a
    Time?

1960's

Berkeley in the 60's
Medium Cool
Nashville
The War at Home
Zabriski Point

NUCLEAR WEAPONS/ENERGY

Amazing Grace and Chuck
The Atomic Cafe
China Syndrome
The Day After
The Day After Trinity
The Decision to Drop the Bomb
Dr. Stangelove
Fail Safe
In the King of Prussia
The Manhattan Project
The Mouse That Roared
On the Beach
The Sacrifice
Silkwood
Testament
Threads
Wargames
When the Wind Blows

POLITICS

Advise and Consent
All the King's Men
All the President's Men
The Best Man
Coverup: Behind the Iran-Contra
     Affair
The Great McGinty
Hidden Agenda
Mr. Hoover and I
Mr. Smith Goes to Washington
North by Northwest
Secret Honor: A Political Myth
Seven Days in May
Tanner '88

POVERTY

The Bicycle
Bye Bye Brazil
The Citadel
The Crowd
Dead End
Distant Thunder
Do-Des'-Ka-Den
Grapes of Wrath
Greed
The Harder They Come
Heroes for Sale
The Horse
How Green Was My Valley
Hungry for Profit
Meet John Doe
Metropolis
Our Daily Bread
Red Beard
Sparrows
Street of Shame
Streetwise
Sugar Cane Alley
The Tree of Wooden Clogs
Umberto D
Veronico Cruz
Wild Boys on the Road

PSYCHOLOGICAL PROFILE

Forbidden Games
Greed
Hanussen
The Heart Is a Lonely Hunter
Kangaroo
The Little Foxes
Meet John Doe
Mephisto
Mr. Klein
No Regrets for Our Youth

Rain Man
The Road to 1984
The Sacrifice
Sherman's March
Speaking Directly
The Trial
28 Up

REVOLUTION/THEORY

Another Country
Arsenal
Breaking with Old Ideas
Chapayev
Daniel
The End of St. Petersburg
The Falcon and the Snowman
Good Fight
High Hopes
The Home and the World
Juarez
Kangaroo
Katherine
La Muerte del Che Guevara
Love and Anarchy
Mother
1900
No Regrets for Our Youth
October
Reds
The Road to 1984
Romero
The Rosenberg-Sorbell Case
   Revisited
Running on Empty
Sacco and Vanzetti
Slave of Love
State of Siege
Storm Over Asia
Swept Away
Underground

Viva Zapata!
The Weavers: Wasn't That a
   Time?
Year of Living Dangerously

SOUTH AFRICA/AFRICA

Black and White in Color
Chocolat
Country Lovers, City Lovers
Cry Freedom
Dingaka
A Dry White Season
The Gods Must Be Crazy
Gorillas in the Mist
Mandela
Mapantsula
Master Harold and the Boys
Mister Johnson
A World Apart

UNION ORGANIZATION

Animal Farm
Black Fury
Bound for Glory
Harlan County, USA
How Green Was My Valley
Kameradschaft
Matewan
Mother
Norma Rae
Salt of the Earth
Strike
The Wave
You Got to Move

UTOPIA

The Lost Horizon

VIETNAM

Air America
Apocalypse Now
Born on the Fourth of July
Dear America: Letters Home
    From Vietnam
84 Charlie Mopic
Full Metal Jacket
Hearts and Minds
In Country
Jackknife
Kent State
The Killing Fields
Platoon
Speaking Directly
Swimming to Cambodia
Vietnam: In the Year of the Pig

WORLD WAR II

Angry Harvest
Assisi Underground

Au Revoir Les Enfants
The Boat is Full
Border Street
The Conformist
Forbidden: A True Story
Forbidden Games
Gallipoli
Generations
The Great Dictator
Hanussen
Hiroshima Mon Amour
Hotel Terminus
Julia
Judgement at Nuremberg
Kanal
Mephisto
Mr. Klein
The North Star
Paisan
Rome Open City
Soldiers of Orange
The Sorrow and the Pity
Tin Drum
Watch on the Rhine
We Will Never Go to the Woods
    Again
Witness to the Holocaust
The White Rose
The Young Lions

APPENDIX III: LISTING OF FILMS BY DIRECTOR

Alaux, Myriam: *The Animals Film*
Alexander, Barry: *The War at Home*
Altman, Robert: *Buffalo Bill and the Indians, Nashville, Secret Honor, Tanner '88*
Annaud, Jean-Jacques: *Black and White in Color*
Antonio, Emile De: *In the King of Prussia, Millhouse: A White Comedy, Mr. Hoover and I, Point of Order, Vietnam: In the Year of the Pig*
Antonioni, Michelangelo: *Zabriski Point*
Apted, Michael: *Class Action, Gorillas in the Mist, 28 Up*
Arcand, Denys: *Jesus of Montreal*
Armstrong, Gillian: *My Brilliant Career*
Arnold, Jack: *The Mouse that Roared*
Ashby, Hal: *Bound for Glory*
Attenborough, Richard: *Cry Freedom, Gandhi*
Auzins, Igor: *We of the Never Never*

Ballard, Carroll: *Never Cry Wolf*
Bannert, Walter: *The Inheritors*
Barker, Reginald: *Civilization*
Beatty, Warren: *Reds*
Beaudine, William: *Sparrows*
Bedham, John: *Wargames*
Bell, Martin: *Streetwise*
Bemberg, Maria Luisa: *Camila*
Beresford, Bruce: *Breaker Morant, Fringe Dwellers, Mister Johnson*
Bertolucci, Bernardo: *The Conformist, 1900*
Biberman, Herbert: *Salt of the Earth*
Black, Stephanie: *H-2 Worker*
Bogart, Paul: *The Citadel*
Boorman, John: *The Emerald Forest*
Bresson, Robert: *The Diary of a Country Priest*
Brickman, Marshall: *The Manhattan Project*
Bridges, James: *The China Syndrome*
Brown, Jim: *The Weavers: Wasn't That a Time?*
Buckner, Noel: *Good Fight*

Burstall, Tim: *Kangaroo*
Bunuel, Luis: *Los Olividados*

Capra, Frank: *The Lost Horizon, Meet John Doe, Mr. Smith Goes to Washington*
Chaplin, Charlie: *The Great Dictator, Modern Times*
Choy, Christine: *Who Killed Vincent Chin?*
Ciannelli, Lewis E.: *La Muerte Del Che Guevara*
Clair, Rene: *A Nous La Liberte*
Clement, Rene: *Forbidden Games*
Cook, Fielder: *Judge Horton and the Scottsboro Boys*
Coppola, Francis Ford: *Apocalypse Now, Tucker*
Costa-Gavras: *Betrayed, Missing, Music Box, State of Siege, Z*
Costner, Kevin: *Dances with Wolves*
Couturie, Bill: *Dear America: Letters Home from Vietnam*
Curtiz, Michael: *Black Fury*

Davis, Andrew: *Above the Law*
Davis, Delmer: *Broken Arrow*
Davis, Peter: *Hearts and Minds*
Davidson, Gordon: *The Trial of the Catonsville Nine*
Dear, William: *Harry and the Hendersons*
Demme, Johnathan: *Swimming to Cambodia*
Denis, Claire: *Chocolat*
Diegues, Carlos: *Bye Bye Brazil*
Dieterle, William: *Juarez*
Dmytryk, Edward: *Young Lions*
Dore, Mary: *Good Fight*
Dovzhenko, Alexander: *Arsenal*
Duigan, John: *Romero*
Dumoulin, George: *We Will Never Go to the Woods Again*
Duncan, Patrick: *84 Charlie Mopic*
Dutileux, Jean Pierre: *Ranoi*

Eisenstein, Sergei: *October, Strike*
Else, Jon: *The Day After Trinity*
Engel, Erich: *The Blum Affair*
Englund, George: *The Ugly American*

Feijoo, Beda Docampo: *Under the World*
Finkleman, Ken: *Head Office*
Fleischer, Richard: *Soylent Green*

Ford, Aleksander: *Border Street*
Ford, John: *Cheyenne Autumn, The Grapes of Wrath, How Green Was My Valley*
Frankenheimer, John: *Seven Days in May*
Freed, Fred: *The Decision to Drop the Bomb*

Giovanitti, Len: *The Decision to Drop the Bomb*
Goddard, Jean-Luc: *Alphaville*
Goldstone, James: *Kent State*
Gorris, Marleen: *A Question of Silence*
Green, Guy: *Patch of Blue*
Gremm, Wolf: *Kamikaze '89*
Griffith, D. W.: *Intolerance*
Guney, Yilmaz: *The Wall*

Halas, John, *Animal Farm*
Heffron, Richard: *I Will Fight No More Forever*
Helpern, David Jr.: *Hollywood on Trial*
Henzell, Perry: *The Harder They Come*
Herzog, Werner: *Where the Green Ants Dream*
Hines, Barry: *Threads*
Hitchcock, Alfred: *North by Northwest*
Holland, Agnieszka: *Angry Harvest*
Hua, Li Wen: *Breaking With Old Ideas*

Ichikawa, Kon: *Fires on the Plain, Harp of Burma*
Imhoff, Marcus: *The Boat is Full*
Ivory, James: *Savages*

Jewison, Norman: *In Country*
Joanou, Phil: *U2: Rattle and Hum*
Joffe, Roland: *The Killing Fields, The Mission*
Jones, David: *Jackknife*
Jost, Jon: *Speaking Directly*

Kagan, Jeremy Paul: *Katherine*
Kanievska, Marek: *Another Country*
Kaplan, Johnathan: *Project X*
Kaplan, Richard: *The Exiles*
Kazan, Elia: *Gentlemen's Agreement, Viva Zapata!*
Kinoshita, Keinsuke: *24 Eyes*
Kitchell, Mark: *Berkeley in the 60's*

Koenigsberg, Paula de: *Rate it X*
Kopple, Barbara: *Harlan County, USA*
Korty, John: *The Autobiography of Miss Jane Pittman*
Kramer, Stanley: *Guess Who's Coming to Dinner?, Judgement at Nuremberg, On the Beach, Ship of Fools*
Kubrick, Stanley: *Dr. Strangelove, Full Metal Jacket, Paths of Glory*
Kurosawa, Akira: *Do-Des'-Ka-Den, No Regrets for Our Youth, Red Beard*

Landau, Ely: *King: Montgomery to Memphis*
Lang, Fritz: *Metropolis*
Lean, David: *A Passage to India*
Lee, Spike: *Do the Right Thing, Jungle Fever*
Leigh, Mike: *High Hopes*
Lerner, Carl: *Black Like Me*
Levinson, Barry: *Rain Man*
Lilienthal, Peter: *The Uprising*
Lindsay-Hogg, Michael: *Master Harold and the Boys*
Lindwer, Willy: *The Last Seven Months of Anne Frank*
Littin, Miguel: *Alsino and the Condor*
Littman, Lynne: *Testament*
Loach, Ken: *Hidden Agenda*
Loader, Jayne: *The Atomic Cafe*
Logan, Joshua: *Sayonara*
Losey, Joseph: *Mr. Klein*
Lumet, Sidney: *Daniel, Fail Safe, Network, Running on Empty, Twelve Angry Men.*
Luyat, Jean-Claude: *Four Days of the Masai*

MacTaggart, James: *Akropolis*
Makavejev, Dusan: *The Coca-Cola Kid*
McElwee, Ross: *Sherman's March*
McGrath, Joseph: *The Magic Christian*
Menges, Chris: *A World Apart*
Merrill, Keith: *Windwalker*
Meyer, Nicholas: *The Day After*
Mikhalkov, Nikita: *Slave of Love*
Milestone, Lewis: *All Quiet on the Western Front, The North Star*
Miller, David: *Executive Action*
Miller, Roger Ellis: *The Heart is a Lonely Hunter*
Mizoguchi, Kenji: *Street of Shame*

Montaldo, Giuliano: *Sacco and Vanzetti*
Moore, Michael: *Roger and Me*
Morris, Errol: *The Thin Blue Line*
Moorman, Alan: *The Rosenberg-Sorbell Case Revisited*
Mulligan, Robert: *To Kill a Mockingbird*
Murakami, Jimmy T.: *When the Wind Blows*
Murphy, Geoff: *Utu*

Nava, Gregory: *El Norte*
Newell, Mike: *Amazing Grace and Chuck*
Nichols, Mike: *Silkwood*

Olmi, Ermanno: *Tree of the Wooden Clogs*
Ophuls, Marcel: *Hotel Terminus, A Sense of Loss, The Sorrow and the Pity*
O'Rourke, Dennis: *Cannibal Tours*
Ozgenturk, Ali: *The Horse*

Pabst, G. W.: *Kameradschaft, Westfront 1918*
Page, Anthony: *Forbidden—A True Story*
Pakula, Alan: *All the President's Men, The Parallax View*
Palcy, Euzhan: *A Dry White Season, Sugar Cane Alley*
Parker, Alan: *Come See the Paradise, Mississippi Burning*
Parks, Gordon: *The Learning Tree*
Pearce, Richard: *Country, The Long Walk Home*
Peebles, Melvin Van: *Watermelon Man*
Penn, Arthur: *Little Big Man*
Pereira, Miguel: *Veronico Cruz*
Peterson, Wolfgang: *Enemy Mine*
Phenix, Lucy Massie: *You Got to Move*
Peirson, Frank: *Somebody Has to Shoot the Picture*
Pontecorvo, Gillo: *The Battle of Algiers, Burn!*
Preminger, Otto: *Advise and Consent*
Pudovkin, Vsevolod: *The End of St. Petersburg, Mother, Storm Over Asia*
Puenzo, Luis: *The Official Story*

Radford, Michael: *1984*
Rafferty, Kevin: *The Atomic Cafe*
Rafferty, Pierce: *The Atomic Cafe*
Ramati, Alexander: *The Assissi Underground*
Ray, Satyajit: *Distant Thunder, The Home and the World*

Redford, Robert: *Milagro Beanfield War*
Reggio, Godfrey: *Koyaanisqatsi, Powaqqatsi*
Rensberg, Frank van: *Country Lovers, City Lovers*
Resnais, Alain: *Hiroshima Mon Amour*
Richards, Lloyd: *Paul Robeson*
Richert, William: *Winter Kills*
Richter, Robert: *Hungry for Profit*
Ritt, Martin: *The Front, Norma Rae*
Robson, Mark: *Home of the Brave*
Rosselini, Roberto: *Paisan, Rome Open City*
Rossen, Robert: *All the King's Men*

Saville, Philip: *Mandela*
Sayles, John: *Matewan*
Schaffner, Frank: *The Best Man*
Schell, Maximillian: *The Pedestrian*
Schlesinger, John: *The Falcon and the Snowman*
Schlondorff, Volker: *Handmaid's Tale, Tin Drum*
Schmitz, Michael: *Mapantsula*
Schoenfeld, Victor: *The Animals Film*
Schultz, Michael: *To Be Young, Gifted and Black*
Selander, Lesley: *Indian Agent*
Selver, Veronica: *You Got to Move*
Sen, Nguyen Hong: *Abandoned Fields*
Shah, Krishna: *The River Niger*
Shinoda, Masahiro: *MacArthur's Children*
Shumlin, Herman: *Watch on the Rhine*
Sica, Vittorio de: *The Bicycle Thief, Umberto D*
Silber, Glenn: *The War at Home*
Sills, Sam: *Good Fight*
Simon, Barney: *Country Lovers, City Lovers*
Sirk, Douglas: *Imitation of Life*
Spottiswoode, Roger: *Air America, Under Fire*
Stagnaro, Juan B.: *Under the World*
Stevens, George: *The Diary of Anne Frank*
Stone, Oliver: *Born on the Fourth of July, Platoon, Salvador*
Strand, Paul: *The Wave*
Stroheim, Erich Von: *Greed*
Sturges, Preston: *The Great McGinty*
Subiela, Eliseo: *Man Facing Southeast*
Szabo, Istvan: *Hanussen, Mephisto*

Tarkovsky, Andrei: *The Sacrifice*
Townsend, Robert: *The Hollywood Shuffle*
Trent, Barbara: *Coverup: Behind the Iran-Contra Affair*
Truffaut, Francois: *Farenheit 451*
Trumbo, Dalton: *Johnny Got His Gun*

Uys, Jamie: *The Gods Must Be Crazy*, *Dingaka*

Vassiliev, Georgy: *Chapayev*
Vassiliev, Sergei: *Chapayev*
Verhoeven, Michael: *Nasty Girl*, *The White Rose*
Verhoeven, Paul: *Soldiers of Orange*
Vidor, King: *The Crowd*, *Our Daily Bread*

Wajda, Andrzej: *A Generation*, *Kanal*
Wang, Peter: *The Great Wall*
Wang, Wayne: *Eat a Bowl of Tea*
Weir, Peter: *Gallipoli*, *The Last Wave*, *Year of Living Dangerously*
Wellman, William: *Heroes for Sale*, *The Ox-bow Incident*, *Wild Boys on the Road*
Welles, Orson: *The Trial*
Wells, Elder: *Song of Freedom*
Wertmuller, Lina: *Love and Anarchy*, *Swept Away*
West, Raymond B.: *Civilization*
Wexler, Haskell: *Latino*, *Medium Cool*
Wheatly, David: *The Road to 1984*
Winer, Lucy: *Rate it X*
Winkler, Irwin: *Guilty by Suspicion*
Wyler, William: *Dead End*, *The Liberation of L. B. Jones*, *The Little Foxes*

Yanagimachi, Mitsuo: *Himatsuri*

Zinnemann, Fred: *Julia*

SOURCE INDEX

Most of the films in this book are available on video and can be found at video stores—the bigger the store, the better the selection. Anyone living in a major city will have ready access to 90 percent of the titles. *The Wave, Wild Boys on the Road,* and *Heroes for Sale* are the only films I viewed on reeled footage that might not be available on video.

If you cannot find a particular title, check with a local independent theater. Public library collections can also be surprisingly eclectic, in part due to the generosity of the John D. and Catherine T. MacArthur Foundation, which has donated collections of socially relevant films to hundreds of public libraries in the United States.

I did a lot of my research at university libraries, which are extremely ambitious collectors of films on video and which have various lending policies for on-sight viewing, usually at no charge. (You don't necessarily have to be affiliated with the school.)

Due to the velocity of electronic generations and the appetites of the video age, I expect that all the films included in this book will be accessible to the general public in wide, although possibly specialized, release within the next ten or fifteen years.

In the meantime, the following is a list of very reliable sources, each with their own unique collection of films on video:

Facets Video
1517 West Fullerton Ave.
Chicago, IL 60614

Facets has almost everything—at affordable rates.

Animal Rights Resource Library
2512-B Plateau Rd.
Charlottesville, VA 22903

Collects films on all themes related to animal rights. Available for postage fees only.

Richter Productions
330 West 42nd St.
New York, NY 10036

Produces extremely topical, issue-oriented features rented at organization rates.

The Video Project
5322 College Ave., Suite 101
Oakland, CA 94618

Distributes film features, sub-features, and shorts on social, political, and environmental themes. Organization rates. Annual festival.

Image Film/Video Center
75 Bennett St., NW, Suite M-1
Atlanta, GA 30309

Hosts annual film festivals, rents equipment, promotes independent filmmakers, conducts seminars and workshops.

Kit Parker Films
1245 Tenth St.
Monterey, CA 93940

Offers classics—many well worth the trouble. For rental or purchase.

East West Classics
1529 Acton St.
Berkeley, CA 94702

Offers foreign language films concentrating on Japan. Rental only.

UCLA Film and Television Archive
1438 Melnitz Hall
UCLA Campus
Los Angeles, CA 90024

Offers an enormous collection of all kinds of movies, especially early Hollywood and television productions. On-sight viewing.

National Archives and Records Administration
Motion Picture, Sound, and Video Branch
7th and Pennsylvania Ave., NW
Room 2-W
Washington, D.C. 20408

On-sight viewing for researchers and serious scholars of film media.

National Center for Jewish Film
Brandeis University
Lown Building, Room 102
Waltham, MA 02254

Offers a wide variety of films on Jewish culture, World War II, and anti-Semitism. Collection open to researchers only.

First Run/Icarus Films, Inc.
200 Park Ave. South, Suite 1319
New York, NY 10003

Interesting collection of political and socially relevant films. For rental or purchase.

Phoenix Film and Video
470 Park Ave. South
New York, NY 10016

Offers a wide variety of social-cause films. For rental or purchase.

Wilmington College Peace Research Center
Hiroshima-Nagasaki Memorial Collection
Pyle Center, Box 1183
Wilmington, OH 45177

Collection of hard to find films on atomic bomb culture, World War II, bomb history and development, and Japan. Public rentals.

DEC Films and Video
394 Euclid Ave.
Toronto, Ont., Canada M6G 259

Offers films with political orientation, environmental awareness, and human rights themes. Open to Canadian researchers only.

Quest Productions
2600 10th Street
Berkeley, CA 94710

Films on war, poverty, and cultural inequity. Open to researchers. Fee.